For my wife and our children, grandchildren,
and future generations…

... Ending a conflict is not so simple, not just calling it off and coming home. Because the price for that kind of peace could be a thousand years of darkness for generation's Viet Nam borned.
RONALD REAGAN
THE 40TH PRESIDENT OF THE UNITED STATES

BEYOND THE FEAR OF DEATH

DY DINH LE

An Inspirational Memoir

Introduction by the Executed Soldier's Son:
CHRISTOPHER LE

PLATGEVITY
Bridging Asian - American Cultures & Sciences

Publication Section
PLATGEVITY, LLC
PO BOX 518
Harleysville, PA 19438
Copyright © 2023 by Dy Dinh Le
All rights reserved. No parts of this publication may be reproduced or used by any means (e.g., electronic, photocopying, mechanical) without any prior written permission from the author or copyright owner, except for book reviews and brief quotations.
For copyright inquiries, please contact Platgevity at:
beyondthefearofdeath.copyright@platgevity.com
Latest Edition: December 2023 (Print and eBook global distribution)
Library of Congress Control Number: 2023906018
ISBN: 979-8-9877347-3-5 (Paperback/softcover)
ISBN: 979-8-9877347-4-2 (Hardcover with the dust jacket)
ISBN: 979-8-9877347-5-9 (eBook)
Book Cover & Interior Design: Platgevity and LXT Media
For direct order, please contact author's website at:
https://dydinhle.com
For special discounts for bulk purchases, please contact Platgevity at:
beyondthefearofdeath.specialdiscounts@platgevity.com
Photo Credits: Google map from Imagery@2023 TerraMetrics, Map data @2023 Google (page xxix); Author's official pictures (pages 379, 380, 381, 384, 385, 387, 390, back cover) from the U.S. Army; Galang Barracks 9 (page 301), Galang Resettlement Processing Center (page 320), and Galang Refugee Camp Office (page 337) from Gaylord Barr; and the U.S. Capitol (back cover background) from Louis Velazquez/Unsplash.

Disclaimer

Beyond the Fear of Death is neither a history book nor a military memoir; it doesn't provide a comprehensive account of the Vietnam War. The author used certain political and wartime events to transcribe his life's journey and thoughts chronologically. The book is based upon actual events, with dialogues created from memory and changes to many names, locations, and identifying features to protect the privacy of those depicted.

This book is written in memory of the brave freedom fighters, including my older brother and unwavering uncle-in-law, whom the communist victors executed, throwing his body into the wilderness of the Hoàng Liên Sơn mountains.

And, especially for my younger brother, Dũng, who mended my tattered heart and provided me with living evidence and justification for the righteousness of my actions and steadfast determination to materialize Mother's wish.

I completed the first manuscript, *Beyond the Fear of Death*, in the spring of 2020, when humanity seemed to perish in the hands of Death at the height of the COVID-19 pandemic.

Let us begin by committing ourselves to the truth to see it like it is, and tell it like it is, to find the truth, to speak the truth, and to live the truth.
RICHARD M. NIXON
THE 37TH PRESIDENT OF THE UNITED STATES

CONTENTS

FROM THE EXECUTED SOLDIER'S SON xiii
AUTHOR'S ACKNOWLEDGEMENT xxvii
PREFACE: ONCE UPON A TIME xxxii
HELL ON EARTH 1
    Escape from the "Land Reform" Campaign 7
    Tết Offensive 11
    A Dark Negotiation 24
THE LAST WORDS 37
    The First "Black Sheep" 40
A FATEFUL TRIBULATION 50
    Following the Freedom Fighters 57
    Abandoning Nha Trang 61
    The Fall of Sài Gòn 81
THE RED SOCIETY 85
    "Peace" from the Paris Accords 98
    A Surprise Raid 106
BOILING HOT WATERWAY 129
    Escape Path 130
    Returning to My Hometown 143
    The Boat Owner and Teacher 146
THE LASTING TRUTH 151
    The Daring Plan 158
    Loose Ends That Changed Life's Journey 164
    Crossing the Mekong River with Gold 173
    Black Hands! 189

A Lasting Decision—Once Upon a Time 191
A Dark Time 204
Heart-Wrenching Departure 205
Angel or Messenger of Death 220
Farewell to the Motherland 232
THE ABYSS 246
A Resort and Tow Rope 250
Saved by the Mushy Ocean Floor 255
AN UNKNOWN ISLAND 262
Inhabitants 265
First Contact 270
GOD'S WILL 276
My Ill-Fated Student 285
The 81st Day After Separation 288
A FATEFUL DISEASE 300
The Disease That Changed the Future 307
Beautiful Souls and Hearts 309
THE PROMISED LAND 326
U.S. Joint Voluntary Agency in Singapore 328
An Unforgettable Reverend 332
THE FAREWELL 335
REBUILDING OUR FAMILY 343
THE DREAM WORLD 355
PUBLISHER'S WORDS 367
MY LIFE'S ANGELS 391
THE AUTHOR: DY DINH LE 397
THE EXECUTED SOLDIER'S SON: CHRISTOPHER LE 401
REFERENCES 403
INDEX 410

FROM THE EXECUTED SOLDIER'S SON

I still remember. After we lost South Vietnam, he rode a light blue bicycle, patiently traveling to various places to teach English. Once radiant with life energy, the man had a promising future as a military pilot for the Republic of Vietnam[a], but I watched it disappear before my eyes.

He had been in the U.S. for flight training, returning to Sài Gòn, the Capital of Free Vietnam, after graduation in December 1974—unfearful of any real danger to his life.

He was tall and strong, with the athletic physique of a bodybuilder, and full of determination. After the country had fallen, the soul of the man seemed all but gone; his will to live vanished as well. He aimlessly wandered amid the stream of life to evade the tongs of the communist security agents closing in on him, ignoring the need to nourish his body and mind. He is my older cousin, Lê

---

[a] "Republic of Vietnam": Former South Vietnam, non-communist country.

Đình Dỹ (Dy Dinh Le), author of *Beyond the Fear of Death*—and son of my blood uncle whom I used to call "Bác Cả."[b]

The author's nickname, which he is called at home, "Việt Hùng," is deeply meaningful. Every Vietnamese citizen, truly in their heart, is proud of the small but heroic motherland; "Việt Hùng" means "heroic Vietnam" in Vietnamese. Since the Hùng Vương dynasty, history has emboldened the sentiment of an "unwavering and heroic Vietnam."

According to Bác Cả, the author's name, "Lê Đình Dỹ," was given by his grandfather from my mother's side—also grandfather on his father's side. According to the Hán or scholar's scripts, similar to Chinese ideographs, "Dỹ" is from "dĩ lễ đãi chi," which means "use righteous principles to treat people," and "dĩ thiểu thắng đa," which means "use a few to win the majority." So, when he was born, his grandfather named him "Dỹ," perhaps hoping he would have such traits.

During the Việt Minh[c] period, North Vietnam's people experienced a variety of endless suffering and faced many adversities. But no matter how difficult the circumstances are, we must overcome and conquer. One must not mourn their life's challenges and surrender to the dark fate. Pine trees planted in harsh rocky conditions are always stronger than those grown in regions full of rich soil. Being afraid to confront obstacles to find resolutions but willing to surrender to Death only makes matters worse and resolves nothing. Surrendering is voluntarily inserting our hands into the iron shackles; it represents weakness and powerlessness. By not surrendering to the dark fate, one invites the opportunity to open the door to discover the light at the end of the tunnel.

So, when my cousin was born, he received the name "Dỹ." And indeed, strangely, his life has been attached to many adversities, leading him to many dark dreams. He had become that pine tree

---

[b] "Bác Cả": Used by people from the north to refer to an elder uncle.

[c] "Việt Minh": National independence coalition formed by Hồ Chí Minh.

grown in harsh conditions on the barren, rocky land where wild wolves still wander with Death, carrying a scythe on his shoulder.

My cousin's second name used at home is "Lê Việt Hùng." My elder uncle, Bác Cả, told me the following story.

When the author was still inside his mother's womb, Việt Minh labeled and accused Bác Cả as an "evil landlord." Subsequently, they confiscated his land and put him in jail where he awaited a trial with potentially deadly consequences. The method of indictment systematically used by the leaders of North Vietnam during that time, together with the cruelty of the executioners who mostly belonged to the social class of poor peasants, led to many fatal mistakes. As a result, they killed many country-loving landlords who had significantly helped Việt Minh during their rise against the French colonization. These cruel indictments eventually created serious tensions in the north, substantially reducing the support of the northern people.

My elder uncle was a victim of such stupid and savage leaders! When he was in jail, my elder aunt, the author's mother, whom I called "Mợ," was grief-stricken and extremely worried. Fortunately, my uncle didn't remain long in jail, successfully escaping and hiding in Vĩnh Yên, a small village in the north where the author was subsequently born. Upon hearing the news, my cousin's mother gave him a second name, "Việt Hùng," in remembrance of my elder uncle's heroic escape from prison during that time. So, I called my elder cousin "Anh Hùng."

When I began writing about Anh[d] Hùng, the memory of past years vividly returned. On the evening of April 29, 1975, my parents and six brothers and sisters, together with three of my elder uncle's children, including Anh Hùng, went to the U.S. Embassy to flee Vietnam. I recall hearing explosions and blasts from bombs and artillery shells in many places in Sài Gòn that were so close that they shook nearby buildings.

---

[d] "Anh" or "Brother": Used to call a male or older blood brother, cousin, etc.

At the U.S. Embassy, it was absolute chaos! People were pushing each other to move forward for a chance at escape. By the early morning, when the last helicopter left from the top of the building, we were not on it. Instead, we had to go home to find a different escape route. But, by then, it was too late! No paths remained to run away from the communist tribulation.

On the fateful morning of April 30, 1975, the streets of Sài Gòn appeared to be choking on their last breaths with sad partitions. Tears intermingled with screaming and crying amidst the disorderly scenes on the streets. People ran in different directions as if running for their lives. The many tearful separations and intense sadness of those days remained, cemented deep in the hearts of the people of Sài Gòn and boldly imprinted in their memories with the dense rows of hibiscus scattered here and there. All that existed before disappeared as raindrops broke free of the clouds, mixing with salty tears flowing from the edges of crying eyes.

How could one forget the day when the rumbling feet of the "revolutionary troops" marched down the poetic, dreamlike streets of Sài Gòn? It was finished, gone! I was still very young, at only 14 years of age. But the distinct memories of that turbulence remained, planting fears that took hold in my inner soul, born in the early days, and strengthened as days, months, and years passed.

Since that black day, Father, my elder uncle, Anh Hùng, and millions of other Vietnamese people no longer experienced safe, peaceful sleep. Instead, Father, my uncle, and hundreds of thousands of others—induced by the victors—were sent to what we later recognize as communist concentration camps.

Anh Hùng—who intentionally claimed to be a former air force mechanic—was only forced to attend a "three-day re-education" program locally. After that, night after night, he quietly sat at home, absorbing the vast openness of the Earth and sky, feeling growing desperation and suffering. The ups and downs he had experienced throughout the years, already come and gone, still ate at his inner soul, filling it with unhappiness and inducing him to embrace a miserable fate. An elite pilot—just returned home from the U.S. with an idealistic, noble way of life and a pledge to protect his motherland and "go where no one can find the fallen body"—was forced to drop his weapon and fold up his wings to allow the turbulences and storms to come without a fight. It happened unexpectedly and without warning.

When Anh Hùng heard of the "SURRENDER" order, out of extreme frustration and desperation, he tried to commit suicide by slamming his head repeatedly against the brick wall in the bathroom. He didn't want to suffer through what he knew was to come, particularly the horrific retribution that would undoubtedly befall his family and the miserable people of Vietnam. Anh Hùng wanted to die with Sài Gòn, the remaining piece of our motherland, but life had other plans, and instead, he lived. He survived after his family pulled him from the grasp of Death's blood-sticky hands during the last hours and minutes of Sài Gòn, as it, too, struggled to take in choking breaths. So, it was cemented in fate. He must live to find a righteous path to help others and serve a greater purpose. He must live to become a phenomenon, a symbol of the pine tree for the Vietnamese people still living in the region of the barren, rocky land, a world full of dark dreams.

So, he survived. And day after day, he rode his old bicycle to different places to teach "bộ đội"[e] physicians and pharmacists stationed at various communist military bases in Sài Gòn. And in the afternoons, he came to teach us English and visit our mother, the widow of the unwavering yellow soldier whom the victors executed in one of the communist gulags.

Every day that passed, when I saw his face—sometimes with a few reluctant smiles, slightly tinged with bitterness, and his eyes, deep and full of unresolved thoughts—I knew he was trying to conquer the disgraceful suffering within the region of the barren, rocky land. The time to create heroes had not yet come. Instead, there was

---

[e] "bộ đội": North Vietnam Army soldier.

only suffering. Phạm Ngũ Lão, a to-be-general from the Trần Dynasty in Vietnam, sat in the middle of the road knitting baskets. His mind was deeply preoccupied with tactical strategies, obscuring his eyes from seeing the incoming mandarin and his military escorts.

The soldiers clearing the road yelled at him to move, but Phạm remained sitting, knitting baskets. It wasn't until one escort pierced his thigh with a sharp spear that he acknowledged their presence. Still, the pain didn't seem to affect the basket knitter. It was as if nothing out of the ordinary was happening. The excruciating mental suffering, which he had grown accustomed to, surpassed the physical pain from the piercing spear, and he felt little pain!

Four years after tasting an inhumane ideology, Anh Hùng suddenly abandoned Hồ Chí Minh City. He left his family, all of us, and even his wife and son behind in Sài Gòn, a city that had already been dead on the surface, without a word of farewell. It bewildered us for months. We were still too young to recognize the "tactical strategies" he had been hatching since the victors came into our beloved Sài Gòn—and since the day his family rescued him from the hands of Death in his parents' bathroom where he wanted to end his life.

One night, unexpectedly, Anh Hùng returned—still with deep, thoughtful eyes and reluctant smiles toned down with a slight but noticeable bitterness. However, upon his return, he exhibited a somewhat thin and deteriorated appearance. That night, he took us to a strange place under a cover of dim lights and silence. We followed him into the very late night on June 16, 1979. There, when we reached our destination, with deep, thoughtful eyes and two bony arms and hands, he freed us from the yoke of the communists—just like millions of Vietnamese fleeing during that time. As though fate had fixed our future, after having lost our country, everyone faced the same predicament and uncertainty.

In 1977, the communist victors executed my father in one of their gulags and coldly threw his bloody body into the wilderness of the Hoàng Liên Sơn mountainous area. In doing so, they deprived my family of everything we needed to survive. Mother worked day and night to feed her six young children, raising us as best she could amid her difficult and bitter life. Hardship overtook us, placing a heavy load of responsibilities on her shoulders that would enable us to survive in a society facing extreme poverty in what was a primitive civilization during that time. Our family life was in shambles, and food was scarce. After fighting to meet our needs daily, mother's mind and body had become increasingly tattered. My elder uncle's family faced a similar fate. The seemingly endless suffering consumed their minds and bodies, weakening them as time passed.

Recalling that period still clenches my heart and inner soul tightly to this day, giving rise to mental pain and sorrow mixed with the lost happiness of my adolescent past. Mother sacrificed her life—through sweat and tears—and spent everything she had to gain sufficient knowledge and education for her children. She wanted us to have careers or to learn a trade to survive rather than sharing her miserable back-breaking fate of carrying the heavy load of the struggles of daily life for all of us.

Since the fateful night of June 16, 1979, when I fled, abandoning my beloved country, I went into exile. In the darkness of late night, I went to a strange place near the end of S-shaped Vietnam. Then, together with my elder uncle's children, we climbed onto a boat of only 19 meters to free ourselves from the yoke of the communists. Nervousness, wariness, and terror blanketed our innocent and immature minds as we left behind a place that held everything we knew and loved.

It was around 1:00 a.m. when we boarded on June 17, 1979. Shortly after that, exhausted from the events, unconsciously, I fell asleep. By the time I awoke, the sun had risen, gradually lifting the muddy veil of darkness. I saw a thin, long, dark strip of land, and the boat navigator told me it was the land we had departed—my motherland. It was a portion of the only home I had ever known that we just had passed for the first and last time. So, by following the dark distant sky and land, me, my seven blood cousins, Anh Hùng, and his own family, including his wife and 3-year-old son, were taken out of Vietnam, heading to the high seas. Bác Cả, Anh Hùng's father, after his release from the communist gulag because of old age and sickness, had fled Vietnam a few weeks earlier. We had received no news about whether he had made it alive.

Painfully, we had to leave behind many loved ones, including Anh Hùng's mother and two sisters, our elder aunt, and my mother and five remaining brothers and sisters. After we had left, all they could do was struggle with the excruciating mental pain of missing their loved ones, quietly withdrawing within their inner cells, particularly during afternoons of heavy rains, and dreaming that one day they might reunite with us. All those remaining pieces of memory, like the dark dreams, were just dreams from our lives. The weight of such dreams and memories is heavy—with no way to lighten the load and no ocean deep enough to hide the many tears shed by the Vietnamese people. It couldn't possibly be deep enough!

While the boat moved through the depths, parting waves and heading into a vast sky and salty high seas, I glanced around to look for my loved ones but, shockingly, could not see Anh Hùng. His next younger brother, Anh Dũng, was missing as well. Upon the realization, I could only sit and take in the unbearable piercing feeling in my inner soul! On the boat, I found my elder cousin sitting with his wife, children, and in-laws. I also saw the other five cousins of mine. Sadly, I caught an image of Chị[f] Mai holding her 3-year-old son on her lap, sitting alone in a dark corner of the boat's lower cabin, without Anh Hùng!

I was in shock. Where were Anh Hùng and Dũng? Why would my beloved cousins disappear without a trace when Anh Hùng himself had masterminded our escape? Why did Anh Hùng leave us back in the paranoiac Hồ Chí Minh City one night—without a word of farewell—only to return to take us to the place of our departure and then disappear again last night without a word? I felt an excruciating cramping pain lingering nonstop in my inner soul, but it was

---

[f] "Chị" or "Sister": Used to call a female or older blood sister, cousin, etc.

no match for the terrifying and profound sadness tearing Chị Mai's heart into pieces. She held her innocent, fatherless infant in her arms. Her still eyes penetrated deeply into the darkness from the corner of the boat's lower cabin, as though desperately trying to envision her husband's image. It must have been an unbearable grief.

Yet, she said nothing, probably to hide her internal frustration—which I now know—about why Anh Hùng abandoned his original plan to get on board together with his wife, son, and other loved ones that night. In her soulless eyes, she must have had so many unanswered questions. She was probably wondering how her husband could escape from the hell on earth in the country she had just left behind. Whether she and her son might live or die and how. Was there anything to eat or drink, clothes to wear, and who would protect mother and son during the long journey across the vast high seas? Thousands of questions dissolved, unanswered, into the emptiness of the dark, mystic ocean waves.

There was neither a crystal ball to reveal the woman's fate nor a clear escape route for a mother dashing into the high seas—taunted by the possibility of death—with her son but without Anh Hùng, her husband!

Each one of us present on that boat truly felt, shared, and shouldered some of the piercing pain and sorrow from the sister-in-law who had no husband or father to her child during the extremely hard and meandering journey. Nobody knew where the stormy winds and rising and falling waves of the vast open seas would take us—and that was frightening.

The rich Chinese boat owner was also shockingly surprised to learn that "Teacher Dỹ"—who gave English lessons to his children while hiding in Bạc Liêu trying to find a way for all of us to escape—was not on his boat. According to their plan, Anh Hùng was to act as the interpreter and spokesperson for the fleeing boat. That day, our boat ran into a large, unidentified vessel. Since he could not find Anh Hùng to communicate with the foreigners, the unnamed vessel had sailed away without saving us.

The Chinese boat owner, his face red with anger, jumped up and down, furiously asking why "teacher Dỹ" stayed behind and pondering how he didn't even know about it!

One day, miraculously, we found an island and landed ashore! After two months of traveling from place to place—including several days floating on the salty high seas and wandering in malaria-infested jungles of isolated islands such as Balai and Sedanau of Indonesia—the yellow Vietnamese refugees fleeing the communist tribulation looked like the local villagers with dark skin. Chị Mai was still weeping tears to match the soaking rains! She must have been suffering with many lingering questions about why her husband disappeared that night. Or she might have known but didn't want to tell. I, too, was still trying to absorb an indescribable sorrow, thinking I might never again see the deep, thoughtful eyes and bitter smile of a yellow pilot who folded his wings but did not surrender.

It wasn't until near the end of September 1979, with the help and arrangement of the local police, we reached the Galang Vietnamese Refugee camp, where the sky was full of miracles. Indeed! After every heavy rain and dark sky, there would come sunshine!

Anh Hùng and Dũng, who had disappeared that night, suddenly reappeared as if they had merely stepped out to another dimension temporarily, returning years later with no scientific basis or rationale. Sometimes we wondered if it was all an illusion, and they weren't there.

After everything, who could still disbelieve miracles and blessings? Who could deny the existence of the hands of angels, although invisible, in the region of the barren, rocky land, an atheist country? We were shocked but pleasantly surprised and felt an overwhelmingly extraordinary jubilance, something that had been missing for so many years, upon seeing both Anh Hùng and Dũng unexpectedly on that peaceful Galang island!

During that tragic night of broken hearts, when he rushed all of us, including his wife and son, onto the fleeing boat, he thought he might not see his loved ones again. While we were not even aware of it, quietly, he bit his tongue and stayed behind! I thought we would have been completely apart—perhaps for several thousand years! But, during those dark nights, while we were diving into the angry waves of the South China Sea, the invisible protective hands of angels hovering above the dead soul opened a narrow trail under sacred rays of light, shining a path for him to follow.

Finally, through an extraordinary miracle, he took Anh Dũng and his elder brother's remaining in-laws with him to sail into the darkness, beginning his own dangerous journey in search of the loved ones he had pushed out into the ocean two days earlier. Fate and angel hands—fighting against Death's scythe that overshadowed his path—quickly delivered Anh Hùng and Dũng to the Galang Vietnamese Refugee camp, where they would pick us up at the harbor on that miraculous day.

Indeed, he had done the unimaginable, hiding his broken heart to rush us, including his wife and son, onto a boat to run away from the communists. Anh Hùng stayed behind at the last moment to protect his loved ones, hopefully leading to their peaceful departure and unbroken kinships. And then, still with his iron heart, eyes full of tears and arms wide open, he came out to the Galang harbor to welcome us to a strange country full of love, acceptance, and humanity.

I now believe. There is no doubt in my mind that angel hands, invisible, had guided us through the dark years. We cried as we had never cried before when our eyes fell upon Anh Hùng and Dũng again. The most beautiful moment, however, was seeing Chị Mai's tears falling, full of love, longing, and hope—which no words could describe—when reuniting with her husband. Still, the most magnificent scene was seeing Huy safe within the warm protective embrace of his father, who was once thought lost.

The refugee camp on Galang island was a part of the Riau archipelago, near Singapore, which the United Nations Higher Commissioner for Refugees had established. They equipped the camp with the facilities, including a management office and the Indonesian Red Cross. Refugees received some supplies for their daily lives, and we felt safe and stable as we waited for the day we would resettle in another country.

Four months later, in January 1980, my cousins and I departed the Galang Vietnamese Refugee Camp for resettlement. Unfortunately, Canada kept Anh Hùng and his family behind because of a suspected tuberculosis diagnosis.

By then, we received the good news that my elder uncle, Anh Hùng's father, had successfully fled Vietnam before we left and was unharmed, living in the United States.

About 12 years later, my loved ones, including my mother and five siblings, and Anh Hùng's mother and his younger sister, finally reunited with us. Shortly after that, my elder aunt also migrated to the U.S. and lives with us all. Our pain and suffering had to pass for life to move forward. It was indeed a blessing for all of us to be together again.

After the past 40 years of struggling to find patience, endurance, and determination to learn and nourish our dreams, most of my elder uncle's children have achieved high societal positions. They are living in the U.S., peacefully and happily, far away from the dark world of years past. During that time, the former pilot has become a workaholic, focusing day and night on scientific research. In his own words, he longed to "forget the patches of the painful dark sky" and do something to "hopefully save people and help society."

In 2015, ABC WMAR-2 News[g] showed an interview with a Vietnamese-American scientist who had conceptualized and invented a method for civil and military aircraft to self-repair when damaged. The invention enabled the repair of flying aircraft in real-time, potentially saving flight crews, military troops, or air travelers when transported in midair.

There, he sat, in front of the moving camera lenses, still with his deep, thoughtful eyes, speaking calmly and softly voice in his foster country's language, exhibiting reluctant half-smiles—which

---

[g] https://www.youtube.com/watch?v=DHuw35ZkWNE&feature=emb_logo

seemed an attempt to hide the dark dreams and the remnants of damage from the life and journey he had passed in the region of the barren, rocky land, a terrifying world from years past.

As for me, I currently work for the U.S. government, providing social services, but I find additional blessings and happiness through music. I took my first step into composing music when I wrote the first sheet of lyrics to *Isn't That Really Sad?*[h] 41 years ago. These lyrics were born when I was drifting into exile, carrying the mark of refugees at the Galang Vietnamese Refugee Camp as a warning for the fate a life could have. Many songs I have subsequently composed are traveling with Vietnamese music performance shows, including "Thúy Nga Paris by Night," and, fortunately, welcomed warmly by the Vietnamese communities inside the U.S. and abroad.

I seriously think; life brings with it many sorrows. We sometimes worry about nonsense, fostering a baseless, latent sadness—without an escape route. Inevitably, living means facing potential struggles, but one needs to conquer them to pass through to the next stage of their life. Living also means seeking the beauty of the inner heart and soul—and the love and fate experienced during life. Each sorrow has beauty in its form. Recognizing its special glory and features and sharing them with strangers can help people live a more beautiful life. Hiding behind the tears are smiles, and at the end of complete and total sadness comes pure happiness.

Love allows the birth of music lyrics. Sorrow and happiness create a fetus, which embraces thoughts full of ups and downs, suffering, and joy of humans. Without ill fate or laughs, a piece of music notes would not have meant to be born.

Like the dark dreams of the past 40 years that Anh Hùng recorded, transcribing the suffering millions of Vietnamese people had also experienced. Those dreams never faded away in his subconsciousness. He wrote to freeze the moments of overwhelming feelings endured during human life and viewed them through two

---

[h] "Isn't That Really Sad?": https://www.youtube.com/watch?v=dmFucPCg06Y

different lenses—sadness and happiness. After all those years, Anh Hùng recognized in his heart that he was fighting against the dark forces when he was suffering injustices. We should know that we can still discover happiness where there appears to be none and where it is struggling to grow. Perpetual happiness is the emotional state life has tamed through extreme and unbearable suffering. Instead of looking at life through rose-colored glasses, waiting for offerings and rewards, we must be ready to absorb the muddy dirt, like a "clod of clay" molded into an "ugly shape," as he wrote, which may be thrown upon us to paint an outcast and spiteful impression. That way, as a result, we will not feel disappointed.

Remember, "Those who do not know how to smile when facing adversities will never know how to open dream doors." The half-smile of the yellow freedom fighter—still covered with a veil of lingering bitterness from experiencing hell on earth in years past and perpetually imprinted with the military marching lyrics: "Go where no one can find the fallen body"—has opened, for his loved ones and the next generations of grandchildren and great-grandchildren, a vast bright sky full of long-lasting freedom for them to take. In doing so, Anh Hùng discovered the happiness he sought in this life while enabling him to fight against the dark forces along his path.

As far as the name of "Dỹ" goes, sometimes one's life only fills itself with dark dreams; that may be the pre-destined life of those who bear that fateful name. However, we must rise out of the darkness and keep whatever goodness we discover along our path. We must appreciate the sadness of the past, and because of it, we will become much more mature.

CHRISTOPHER LE
Orange County, California, June 30, 2020

AUTHOR'S ACKNOWLEDGEMENT

I am truly indebted to Nguyễn Thành Nhân, a sworn younger and kind brother from Vietnam, who has translated the entire English manuscript of *Beyond the Fear of Death* into *Vờn Bóng Tử Thần*, a Vietnamese version. The translated manuscript becomes a precious and beautiful gift for the genuine brotherhood that has just come into our lives.

Even though Nhân has forever departed this world—right after completing the translation of *Beyond the Fear of Death*—his beautiful resonance will live permanently without fading, particularly in the heart of this sworn older brother from a faraway land. May you rest in peace in the rising sky of the firmament of Heaven.

Writing and telling a story about the journey my family has experienced to seek freedom was not a simple task. Without consistent encouragement from friends, I would not have completed this memoir. I thank Professor Fu-Kuo Chang, Irene Li, and their family for their precious friendship, love, and wholehearted support over the years. Your thoughts and connections about who I am and how I feel have touched my heart warmly and profoundly.

Especially, I thank my wife, who also encouraged me to write. She carried an extraordinarily painful feeling during the dangerous journey, having thought I was lost. Yet, still, she wanted me to revisit the ordeal with my pen after I had resisted it for almost four decades. I knew that to write it, I had to go back in time, tracing every step, recalling every death and painful feeling, walking through and reliving the moments that would cause even an iron-strong man to flinch.

While writing, the instances when I was struggling with Death and, particularly, in my inner soul, I felt the desperate cries of that 10-year-old boy return. The groaning in the darkness frequently forced me to wake up, overpowered by the shock of the dark dreams of the past—bringing back the most painful memories of loved ones who had passed or been killed. And now that the memoir is born, I have walked through my life journey twice, reigniting my memory with the separations and breaking hearts. As predicted, even though I survived the ordeal and reunited with my loved ones, this memoir floods my inner soul with more sorrow than happiness. The truth of my life story—and that of those I most cherish—has now awakened, no longer hidden in my inner soul's depths.

I am deeply gratified and moved by the timeless thoughts so elegantly transcribed by Christopher Le, my beloved cousin, in this book's introduction, "From the Executed Soldier's Son." As a victim of the Vietnam War, he is one of the loved ones who shared the treacherous journey on the high seas and endured hardship on the Indonesian islands with my wife and 3-year-old son. Thank you—for your unswayed, forever love for my family.

DY DINH LE
Pennsylvania, Winter 2022

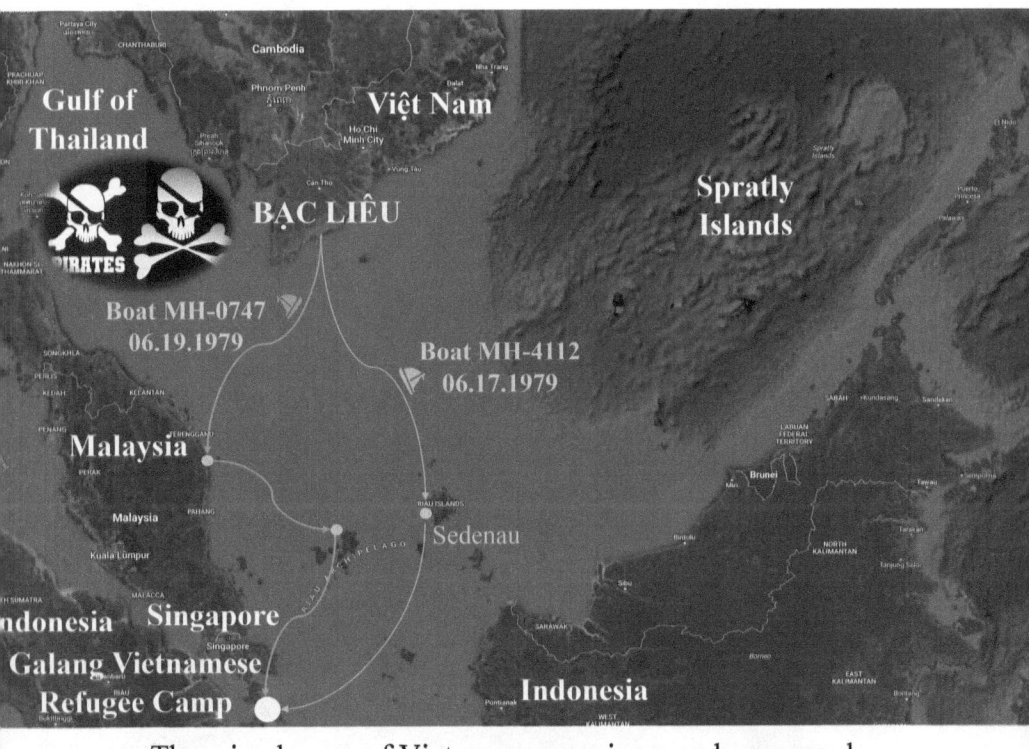

The miracle area of Vietnamese survivors and graveyard
of 200-400 thousand victims who tried to flee
Vietnam by boat after April 30, 1975.
(Imagery @2023 TerraMetrics, Map data @2023 Google)

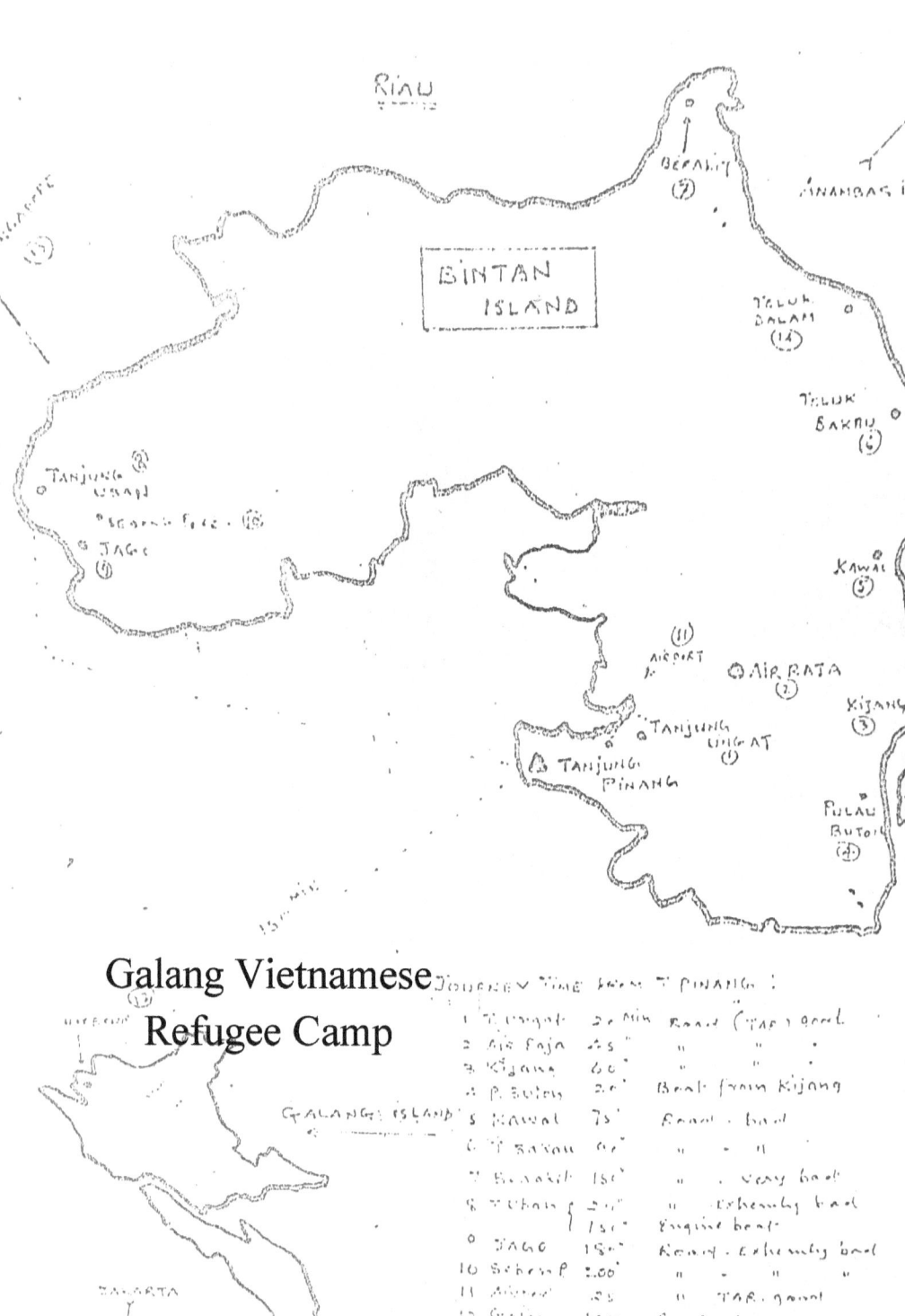

In an event related to war, when repeated, there are millions of people who are happy as well as sad.
VÕ VĂN KIỆT
THE 4TH PRIME MINISTER OF THE SOCIALIST REPUBLIC OF VIETNAM

PREFACE: ONCE UPON A TIME IN THE LAND OF DEATH

Why did approximately 800,000 Vietnamese people, including my family, from the north abandon our land and rush to the south of Vietnam in 1954?

Why did so many innocent people run toward the soldiers of the Republic of Vietnam when Huế City and Quảng Trị Province were "liberated" by North Vietnam in 1968 and 1972?

Why, after the "LIBERATION… the Glorious Victory of Spring 1975… the Great Transformation of People," did approximately a million Vietnamese people abandon the "Socialist Republic of Vietnam" and flee from the "LIBERATORS" who claimed they had established "Independence-Freedom-Happiness?"

Why did so many people escape the newly established socialist country—despite the potential loss of loved ones and the risk of being raped or killed on the high seas or in jungles while on the run?

…

… And…

Why did I push you out into the ocean?
Why... Why... Why...?
Oh my gosh! It was so dark!
Oh my gosh! It was so deep!
I wanted to be with you but couldn't.
I must stay, and staying I was for you.
Why did I cut you lose into the deadness?
I wanted you to be free, and free you were from me.
How did I hold my tears, my heart from breaking into pieces?
I wanted to die to feel no pain!

Why did I have to leave, instead of stay?
Why... Why... Why...?
Oh my gosh! It was hell on earth!
Oh my gosh! My land was dying!
I wanted to be with you but couldn't.
I must leave, and leaving I was.
Why did I leave, abandon you, my home behind?
I wanted to be free, and free I would from darkness.
How did I hold my tears, my heart from breaking into pieces?
I wanted to die to feel no pain!

Why couldn't I die, why couldn't I vanish?
Why... Why... Why...?
Oh my gosh! It was so dark!
Oh my gosh! It was so cold!
I wanted to be with you but couldn't.
I was lost, and lost I was in another world.
Why didn't I keep drifting, drowning into the veil of waving light?
I wanted to be free, and free I wanted from pain.
How did I hold my breath, my heart from breaking into pieces?
I wanted to die to feel no pain!

Why did you have to leave, instead of stay?
Why... Why... Why...?
Oh my gosh! You were so lonely!
Oh my gosh! Crows were coming!
I wanted to be with you but couldn't.
I must fight, and fought but failed.
Why did you leave, abandon me, a lonely soul to darkness?
I wanted to be free, and free I wanted from abomination.
How did I hold my tears, my heart from breaking into pieces?
I wanted to die to feel no pain!

Why do I still live, instead of you?

HELL

ON EARTH

It was a fateful tribulation—quickly spreading in the corner of the Southeast Asia region—and a long-lasting effect of the collapse of a tiny country recognized by the free world. The repercussions were so grave that the Vietnamese could not stand up freely for the next several decades.

The mental wounds and internal misery hurt so much that they, particularly the people of South Vietnam, would unreservedly agonize for eternity, wherever they might go in the future.

It was Black Wednesday, April 30, 1975, a date permanently imprinted in my mind. I could never forget it, at least during my remaining life's journey—a formidable path into exile with a deadly fate awaiting a particular group of yellow people. That was the day when army soldiers, called bộ đội from North Vietnam above the 17th parallel, finally flooded Sài Gòn (Saigon) with T-54 tanks, AK-47 automatic rifles, B-40 bazookas, and assorted weapons made by the Communist Bloc[1]. Some wore dark green army uniforms, made in the north, with dark green hats and unique black rubber flip-flops called "Bình Trị Thiên" sandals. Their skin looked pale. Some looked very young! They might have been younger than 18 years of age. But their faces showed more seasoned hatred than I had ever seen on anybody.

They looked deadly! Most of those soldiers belonged to the regular army units of the People's Army of Vietnam (PAVN)[2] that came from the north. They had been advancing through deep jungles for days and months before finally raging into Sài Gòn. They stormed into the heart of the Republic of Vietnam (RVN)[3], the second half of the small S-curve figure bordering the Pacific Ocean below the Demilitarized Zone at the 17th parallel[4], without many significant resistances or large-scale battles.

Some other fighters wore dusty black pajamas and dark green garment hats with chin strings that curled around the ears and notched below the jaw to keep the hat in place. Those were guerrillas, Việt Cộng[5] (VC), who belonged to the National Liberation Front (NLF)[6] formed by North Vietnam in 1960. NLF then merged into the new Provisional Revolutionary Government (PRG)[7] of the Republic of South Vietnam, also established by the North Vietnam communist government in 1969. Only the international Communist Bloc, not the free world, recognized and acknowledged PRG. Those guerrillas came from the countryside and jungles below the Demilitarized Zone.

Arrogantly running around the streets were also those from the so-called "April-30 Group," wearing plain clothes—the same apparel normally worn by the South Vietnamese people. They were regional underground southerners who supported North Vietnam or took advantage of the chaotic interim situation to switch to the other side, unabashedly flattering the victors to survive. VC and PAVN soldiers were all around the city—wicked in their eyes because it appeared so easy to walk into Sài Gòn—crisscrossing through noisy streets. Some drove dusty military jeeps made in America and abandoned by the RVN soldiers during the last days of Sài Gòn.

The bright yellow flags with three horizontal red stripes spaced evenly at the center[8], representing South Vietnam, quickly disappeared. The VC flags[9], red and blue with a big yellow star in the middle, representing NLF, engulfed Sài Gòn.

It was one of my darkest and longest periods—a doomsday during which the only piece of free Vietnam finally fell into the communist's iron pincers. On the last day of Black April, the Republic of Vietnam—a nontotalitarian country, which many North Vietnamese people, secretly in the darkness of the communist reign, looked up to as a predecessor to true liberation someday[10]—completely disappeared from the world map. With it, that hidden dream had also vanished!

Motionless and speechless, I stood a few feet away from the front balcony of my parent's house, looking down to witness the last breaths of Sài Gòn. It was early in the afternoon and a partly overcast day with the sun hiding behind thick layers of dark gray clouds. A few shimmering, widely scattered rays pierced through the clouds like transparent arrows flying at the speed of light. It was extremely warm, and the humidity was unbearable. "Is it the weather or my heart that is burning inside?" My chest tightened, and I tried to take a deep breath. Rage and anger were crawling into a dark space in my desperate mind. Occasionally, the sound of gunshots and explosions echoed from a distance. People looked suspicious and panicked; they seemed confused since nobody knew what might happen next.

It was April 30, 1975—the fateful day when South Vietnam, the last major strategic frontier to protect freedom, completely fell into the red hands. That was the day when VC publicly tore apart the Paris Peace Accords[11]. The invasion that Lê Đức Thọ, one of the North Vietnam diplomats during the 1970s, had wished for had finally arrived. And the Paris Peace Accords, which the world praised, turned out to be a fairy tale for the Nobel Foundation. Lê likely knew this, hence refusing the Nobel Peace Prize. He was probably well aware that North Vietnam would continue its bloodshed and eventually seize South Vietnam. At least he was honest. Amazingly, while Lê refused the Nobel Peace Prize, Dr. Henry Kissinger was "unabashedly delighted" when President Nixon recognized Kissinger's "art of negotiation," as reported by *TIME Magazine*[12].

North Vietnam fought for more than just the Marxist ideology. They also aimed to achieve the goal of "One Vietnam." South Vietnam simply fought against the expansion of the Marxist ideology, with no workable plan to reunite the country. The south should also have committed to fighting for their own "One Vietnam" goal, liberating North Vietnam and bringing the true meaning of freedom to the Vietnamese who had been tortuously living in the communist forceps in the north, waiting for the freedom fighters to break the pincers and yoke of a totalitarian regime.

Once upon a time, South Vietnam appeared to do just that during the early years of the Vietnam War. Unfortunately, the drive to achieve this eventually faded. We remained stagnant below the Demilitarized Zone, trying to protect our freedom, ignorant of the Vietnamese people's desire for "One Vietnam." From the moment the south established RVN until the day it collapsed, South Vietnamese military forces were mostly on the defense, rarely on the offense. When conducting offensive operations, South Vietnam focused on retaliating against North Vietnam or recapturing lost territories with no plausible grand plans for Vietnam reunification. Fighting such a reactive war was naïve! With the north's intent to invade the south at all costs, the Vietnam War destroyed 58,220 American lives[13] and caused over three million deaths[14] of the Vietnamese people and soldiers on both sides. The aggressiveness of the north, ineffective campaigns by the south against the communists, and mounting human casualties all helped intensify the impatience of the American people toward the bloody Vietnam War. As a result, the war had to end, putting the aggressors on the path to victory.

Unfair as it might seem, and it was, South Vietnamese soldiers distressingly followed through with the Paris Peace Accords under extreme duress from Washington. Since Black April, the impact of that fatal agreement has continued to send hundreds of thousands of innocent men, women, children, and unborn human beings into the abyss of the South China Sea to die[15]. The Paris Peace Accords' deadly effect would also result in the execution of over 100,000 South Vietnamese soldiers[16] for trying to defend their country from North Vietnam's heinous red hands or subject them to death from sickness or torture while imprisoned in the communist gulags disguised as "re-education" camps[17].

The U.S. spread the freedom ideology throughout the world. But the South Vietnamese people didn't fully understand what it meant until after Black April in 1975. For many years during the war, the U.S. and North Vietnam had misjudged the mindset of the true freedom-loving people. As a result, only after the deadly exodus to the South China Sea began a few years after Sài Gòn had fallen into the communist hands did Americans and arrogantly exaggerating victors suddenly realize the shocking reality. Only then did they see the firm determination of South Vietnamese citizens, who fully understood the meaning of freedom and were ready to die on the high seas or in the jungles to seek new land.

Humanity, someday, must tally the death tolls and should not ignore the human-killing aspects triggered by the signed Paris Peace Accords, credited to both Lê Đức Thọ and Henry Kissinger's effort and subsequently praised by the Nobel Peace Prize selection committee. As soon as Washington and Hà Nội (Hanoi) signed the peace treaty, people in Sài Gòn knew it would not last long. They believed it was just a matter of time before North Vietnam would inevitably violate the agreement and send regular troops to capture Sài Gòn and the surrounding cities. As feared, they eventually did. The fall of Sài Gòn did not occur because of the South Vietnamese people's fading will to stand against the communist aggression; it was because two systems were politically governing the country—one run by the constrained South Vietnamese government and the other by the U.S., heavily affected by a powerful group of self-serving American politicians, filthy-rich capitalists, and fake news organizations.

Sài Gòn and Washington were partners with a similar ideology and, initially, a compatible goal—foiling the communist domino effect. Unfortunately, they executed it poorly without an absolute desire or solid winning strategy. Ultimately, many feel that Vietnam was just a testing ground for U.S. technological advancement and a marketplace for Washington's economic expansion.

Freedom, orchestrated to comfort the South Vietnamese people's agonizing minds, was just a dangling carrot for them to chase. American and allied soldiers fell into the same trap that crippled their original mission goals.

On the last day of Black April, the yellow freedom fighters, abandoned by their partner, were forced to put down their clumsy weapons because they could not fight effectively against the entire North Vietnam troops. Bộ đội had already flooded the South as a broken dam, with modernized killing machines supplied by their loyal partners, including Red China and the Soviet Union from the International Communist Bloc. Hà Nội had brainwashed North Vietnamese soldiers' minds with illusions to justify their heinous acts. They wanted to "liberate" innocent people below the 17th parallel who were being "tortured" under the "yoke" of the "evil American" and "puppet" South Vietnamese government.

We were all just soldiers who remained closemouthed, biting our tongues bitterly. We followed the last order, "SURRENDER," and dropped our weapons to avoid further bloodshed. The dark day I feared as a 10-year-old boy had arrived. It came much sooner than I expected and was less violent than I had imagined, but it was more heartbreaking than anything I had ever experienced.

South Vietnam collapsed quickly because Sài Gòn didn't give us orders to fight to the very end to protect our land during those last few months. We fell flat on our faces because they asked us to abandon our provinces, one after another. While we fell, our American partner and allies, who could have easily crushed North Vietnam militarily, stood on the sidelines, watching Sài Gòn gasp for its last breath. South Vietnamese soldiers laid down their weapons and retreated involuntarily. We had to follow orders. Supplies and reinforcements didn't come because Sài Gòn tried to bluff its partner, who had already experienced a change of heart. We knew the U.S. had already lost the will to fight and protect freedom. It was an extremely sad and disappointing moment for those who had held firm grips on their weapons for over two decades to stop the flow of the fierce red forces. Millions of South Vietnamese soldiers—not counting an addition of 58,220 American lives—died in the war our partner didn't have any desire to win.

The fate of South Vietnamese people seemed doomed from the beginning of the Paris Peace Accords. It took only two years and three months for VC to void the agreement entirely and reach their red hands into Sài Gòn. That day, April 30, 1975, PAVN soldiers ecstatically rambled into Sài Gòn with arrogant triumph.

Where would the South Vietnamese people, particularly those who knew the VC's atrocities very well, go from here except the South China Sea? Contrary to the Vietnamese legend and fate of "50 Children of King Lạc Long Quân"[18]—migrating to the East Sea to build and establish a strong, peaceful, and prosperous country for the Vietnamese people—a few years later, humanity would witness the horrific and deadly journeys of the "children of the dragon and grandchildren of the fairy" when they abandoned their land and plunged into the South China Sea to avoid the Vietnam communists.

In 1954, our family fled from the north and migrated to the south to avoid execution during the "land reform" campaign[19] established in the 1950s by Việt Minh[20]. Father barely escaped the deadly Special People's Court created by the communists.

Escape from the "Land Reform" Campaign

FATHER WAS BORN into a wealthy family. His parents had about 140 acres of rice fields and coffee plantations in Vĩnh Yên in northern Vietnam. It was my birthplace. During the famine in the north that killed millions of Vietnamese people[21], my grandparents used to distribute free rice and other food to starving people.

Unfortunately, Grandmother passed away when Father was around the age of 13. Subsequently, Grandfather also died, leaving behind a 17-year-old son, my father, and two younger daughters, my aunts, from his second marriage. With the family's established traditional moral values, despite being from a rich family with no parents around, my father and aunts grew up to become good people. From a young age, Father suddenly had to manage the entire operation and sustain the family's plantation business, besides taking care of two younger sisters. He taught himself to ride horses, use rifles to protect his land and family, and master agricultural and irrigation techniques to sustain the rice field and plantation operations.

In 1953, Việt Minh labeled Father as an "evil landlord," confiscating my family's land and jailing him to await trial. In the early 1940s, Việt Minh was originally a military coalition comprised communist cadres and nationalists assembled to fight against French colonists and restore independence for Vietnam. After the well-known battle of Điện Biên Phủ[22], the French government conceded the defeat, signed the 1954 Geneva Accords[23], and withdrew from Vietnam. Unfortunately, the peace accords also divided Vietnam into the north, controlled by the communist armed forces led by Hồ Chí Minh[24] and supported by the Communist Bloc, and the south, briefly governed by Emperor Bảo Đại[25], supported by France. After the battle of Điện Biên Phủ, Vietnam's communist and nationalist forces separated because of ideological differences. The north became the Democratic Republic of Vietnam, led by Hồ Chí Minh, who was committed to Marxist ideology[26]. The south, below the 17th parallel, became the Republic of Vietnam and elected Premier Ngô Đình Diệm[27] as its first President.

The "land reform," created by the Việt Minh communists in the 1950s, originally seemed to be a non-violent redistribution of wealth among residents in the north—a characteristic of the socialist system. Unfortunately, it quickly turned into deadly violence. It led to personal vendettas when communist cadres and passionate followers of Marxism condemned wealthy landowners to death without clear rules and laws. Sometimes, it was just a vengeful act committed by poor people who once lived in the same villages as those condemned. Many "evil landlords," the title given by Việt Minh, were spat on and stoned by their own family members, former servants, neighbors, or local peasants, encouraged by the communist cadres to fabricate the condemned landlord's crimes fictitiously. Those innocent landowners couldn't defend themselves. They knelt in a large dirt area, awaiting the public announcement of their death sentences. My parents and aunts used to tell us stories of these times, during which hundreds of thousands of people in the north were openly executed[28] because of the "evil landlord" title.

There were many horror stories of executions, in which they buried landlords from the neck down and decapitated them using a rusty soil-cultivating blade. *We Want to Live*[29]—a famous black-and-white movie I watched during my teenage years—depicted those deadly events vividly.

So, one day, they labeled Father with the title "evil landlord," arrested and put him in jail, and confiscated all his land while he awaited trial before the Special People's Court. Deceptively and intentionally, the trial was prepared and set up with a death sentence, which was already the outcome in the minds of the communist cadres. Fortunately, while in prison, Father escaped and eventually ended up in the south. Once settled, in 1954, Father asked some close friends and relatives from his parents' side to help move our family from the north to the south.

According to the Geneva Accords, South and North Vietnamese could migrate under the protection of "Operation Passage to Freedom."[30] It was a 300-day grace period facilitated by the French and U.S. Navy. After that, Hiền Lương Bridge[31] at the 17th parallel, like the infamous Berlin Wall[32] that divided East and West Germany, separated South and North Vietnam.

With the help of Father's close relatives and friends in the village, Mother, together with four small children, including me, and Father's younger half-sisters, began a long journey from Vĩnh Yên through Hà Nội, Hải Dương, and, finally, to Hải Phòng where we boarded one of the amphibious ships to flee the communists.

From Vĩnh Yên, we had to walk a long distance. Mother and my aunts told me that when passing an unknown crossroad, a servant, who carried me in her arms, got lost and inadvertently followed a different direction. After a panicked search, Mother and my aunts luckily found us wandering on a winding road nearby. If they had truly lost us, I would have remained in the north and probably become one of the bộ đội soldiers.

During the journey from our village to Hải Phòng, my family went through many checkpoints with the help of close friends. Sometimes, we had to hide from the communists who used threats and force to stop people from migrating to the south. We sneaked in and out from certain sections to pass key areas controlled by the communist cadres.

While under duress not to leave, about 800,000 or more Vietnamese people[30] still fled from the north to the south. It was the first exodus of the "children of the dragon and grandchildren of the fairy," who abandoned their land and birthplaces to escape the communists. One would think, in 1954, leaders from the north could have learned a valuable lesson and changed their flawed policy and ideology—adopted from Red China and the Soviet Union and brought to Vietnam to suppress the yellow Vietnamese people—to return freedom, democracy, and true peace to Vietnam. The sugar-coated, polished communism manifesto, indoctrinated from those foreign countries, had fiercely intrigued the leaders of North Vietnam to follow the same bloody path, cruelly pushing their citizens against the dead end. And the peace-loving Vietnamese people had only one option—abandon their ancestor's birth and burial places to go south and seek protection from the hands of the newly established Republic of Vietnam.

During the first few years in the south, we lived in a few locations like Pleiku and Ban Mê Thuột, well-known cities in the Central Highlands of South Vietnam, and, subsequently, Sài Gòn. We also lived in Vũng Tàu, a coastal town located southeast of Sài Gòn. By that time, Father had joined the South Vietnamese Army and became an officer from the Republic of Vietnam, first under President Ngô Đình Diệm and, later, under President Nguyễn Văn Thiệu[33].

Because of Việt Minh's "land reform" campaign, our family became poor and struggled to make ends meet. Raising many children while only Father could earn income didn't go well in a big city like Sài Gòn. Thankfully, our parents could borrow some money from the lady who owned the coffee shop at the end of our street to open a small convenience store. We sold rice, condensed milk cans, candies and ice cream, and other miscellaneous products to people who lived nearby.

VC's red hands didn't satisfactorily stop there in the north and at the 17th parallel. Obviously, they learned nothing from the first exodus of the "children of the dragon and grandchildren of the fairy" in 1954. But the people from the north, who had already run away from the communists or remained pinned between the hot red pincers, would never forget about the extremely bloody "land reform" of the 1950s. In 1968, Hà Nội's bloody, greedy hands desperately tried to reach into Sài Gòn and other key strategic provinces and cities in the south, including Huế, and, without the need to conceal, eventually exposed the dark souls of the communists. To this day, I still have not forgotten the VC's black shadows wildly roaring on the streets of Sài Gòn. They have established permanent residency in my dark dreams since North Vietnam's spring invasion during the Lunar New Year or Tết (Tet) in 1968. By that time, our parents had already had 11 children. I had just reached the age of 14.

Tết Offensive

AT THE AGE of about ten, four years prior to the Tết Offensive[34], I experienced an abnormal sleep-crying phenomenon full of nightmares. Once I started crying in the middle of the night, it was impossible for anyone to stop me. My aunts used to hold and comfort me. It didn't work! When the sleep crying started, it didn't stop after just a few seconds; it lasted several minutes and sometimes went on for what felt like forever. People called it by many names, including mental illness. In my fragile mind, as a boy, it was a menace. Nowadays, some might call it a "psychic warning." They were very dark dreams, and I told no one, not even my parents or close friends, about what I saw in them.

In the fragile mind of the 10-year-old boy, I believed what I saw to be reality—darkness would come, and Death might destroy the future of my loved ones. During the nightmares, which frequently occurred in the 1960s, there was a warning of a funeral on a somber winter day. It repeatedly came into the mind of that frightened 10-year-old boy. Over the next few years, believing in the ill omen, I would always try to protect one of my younger siblings, Dũng, whom I somehow thought might be the ill-fated one, the "black sheep" in the family. Somehow, even from a very early age, I had always feared the omen from the dark dreams might be in connection with him. It was a psychic sense I didn't fully comprehend, but it remained in my mind for a very long time.

One evening during my childhood, a large fire broke out in our neighborhood. It was burning about a block away from the back of our house, so we all ran out and away from our house and stood, watching the fire, at the intersection near the Children's Hospital.

While standing there with some of my siblings and parents, I kept shouting nervously that somebody must go inside our house to save Dũng. Even though my parents repeatedly assured me he was already out of the house, I kept yelling and crying about the delusional fear he was still inside the house until my parents angrily shut me up. That night reminded me so much of the omen from the dark dreams, which continued to haunt me for years, beyond anyone's understanding, and to the point at which my family worried about the stability of my mind. Those dark dreams became darker a few years later with the help of the communist leaders from the north!

In January 1968, shortly before my 14th birthday and during Lunar New Year or Tết, NLF forces launched an invasion called Tết

Offensive to show the world they could invade or take over South Vietnam by force. It was the first time battles erupted in cities like Sài Gòn—the Pearl of the Far East[35]—in the south, and Huế, a historical city in Central Vietnam.

It was the first time I saw the communists' black shadows. For several weeks, Sài Gòn was a bloody battleground. Bodies from both sides were littered everywhere—at street corners, alleys, and battle-damaged houses. They abandoned corpses there for days. The decaying bodies were feeding scores of dark green flies and healthy creamy maggots crawling along the contours of the deteriorating, unrecognizable human faces.

Even before the start of the offensive during Lunar New Year's Eve, VC shadows had already moved along the highways and country roads in the middle of the night and were all over inside the slum areas and dark alleys. They traveled in small groups and didn't have tanks. But the international Communist Bloc had equipped them with other firepower for killing and achieving their goals.

Their leaders and the stubborn members of the Communist Party of Vietnam filled their minds—once full of peace-loving sentiment—with spewing thoughts of rage and revenge.

Their arms were firm. With blood boiling inside their hearts, they aimed guns at their countrymen and women from the RVN armed forces, shot at unarmed civilians on the street, and killed innocent people in their homes. With enraged hearts, PAVN and NLF soldiers turned the blessed night into a curse of darkness.

That evening was no longer the peaceful Lunar New Year's Eve we used to celebrate, with explosions and smoke from firecrackers now mixed with the erupting rage of the black shadows. It tattered Sài Gòn with groans of dying, bloody bodies splayed across deserted streets. The night held the familiar smell of firecrackers, now intermingled with blasts of gunpowder and firearms, sending people into hell on earth. Viciously, the black shadows emerged through the veil of milky firecracker smoke, seeking to cause harm! For the next few weeks, people in my neighborhood deserted the streets. We closed the sliding iron panels of our house's main door tightly and stayed indoors as though we were trying to shield ourselves from the plague. My siblings and I crouched down under the wooden bed and table as if they would protect us from the black shadows. We hid under the cement stairs when we heard an explosion or a gunshot.

During the day, everybody moved around quietly, trying to cook and eat without making even the smallest noises. We ate canned food sparingly because we were afraid it might run out before the invasion was over.

One day, a bullet strayed into our home, making a small hole in one of the living room walls. That petrified me, sending a shiver down my thin spine. Those were the days when I heard the song of Death constantly humming in my ears, skillfully playing with my childhood mind and paranormally dancing in my dark dreams.

During the day, it didn't seem as deadly because the black shadows didn't want to be visible on the streets. They were hiding inside the temple nearby. We lay under the bed at night, flat on the floor and far away from the iron door's sliding panels, which could fold together when pushed wide open from the middle. While hiding under the bed, we listened to the strange sounds and rushing footsteps on the streets.

During the night, the black shadows freely walked around our neighborhood searching for anti-Marxist and anti-revolutionary collaborators, those who served the South Vietnamese government or those whose names appeared on the "blacklist" compiled by their regional underground VC for execution.

One particularly scary morning, we learned that the black shadows had executed one of our neighbors who owned a lumber warehouse located only a few houses away from our home the previous night. I knew him well since I used to play with his son.

Mother knew the terror of being on the VC's execution "blacklist." Eventually, I learned too! During the Tết Offensive, the song of Death became the music of my childhood, which gradually put me to sleep when I became so scared and exhausted.

The war dragged on for several weeks in Sài Gòn and other regions in the south. The northeast monsoon season came, sometimes bringing enough cool air to cut through the mugginess. During those times, we hid in the corner of our house, listening to the whistling sound of the VC's mortars randomly flying. We prayed and hoped they would not land on us—only to find out later the blast had killed others somewhere else in Sài Gòn.

During the Tết Offensive, when the fighting escalated in our neighborhood, we moved and temporarily stayed on the streets in different areas not yet touched by the VC's deadly intrusion. We stayed there for several days in the rain, in the dark, and on the sidewalks. I got used to the high-pitched whistling sound of the flying mortars and their loud explosions, echoing through chilling nights as a sounding board when they hit the ground. I sensed the smell of gunpowder and familiarized myself with the sound of blasts in the dark. After several days on the streets, in and out near the war zones, we could finally move into the house of Father's younger sister. She married an army officer, Uncle Long; he served in the Vietnamese Army Rangers, trained by the American Special Forces and one of the most effective forces of South Vietnam during the war. During that time, my aunt's family lived in the military housing inside the Capital City Special Command, about a 20-minute drive from our house. We stayed with her family for a few weeks under the South Vietnamese soldiers' protection on base.

Fortunately, after about two long months, South Vietnam defeated the communist forces, and the 1968 invasion from North Vietnam ended. The black shadows quickly retreated from dark alleys, temples, and other occupied towns. It was time to clean up and identify the rotten bodies on the streets. Father returned home unharmed. We were lucky the black shadows didn't come to our house and knock on the door during their occupation. The clanging and rattling sounds from the iron door under intruding, pounding hands permanently seared those horrific scenes into my childhood memory. I will never forget those musical notes of Death!

Tragically, the time to rebuild also became a time to uncover atrocities the black shadows left behind. In Huế, one of the oldest historical cities in Central Vietnam, VC buried thousands of innocent people alive during the Tết Offensive—shortly before the North Vietnamese soldiers withdrew into their hiding cells in the jungles. Those discovered bodies were not South Vietnamese soldiers. They were powerless, unarmed civilians who could not fight! They were innocent human beings, including young and elderly men and women shackled together by long, bloody ropes. There were mass graves containing many victims of executions! Their loved ones were eventually called to identify them, with hands tied behind their backs and faces covered with dirt, showing the intolerable horror they were about to endure. The eyes of some victims remained open as though they were trying to see into the evil souls of those who buried them before the heavy mass of soil fell upon them. Others were trying to see beyond the edge of their mass grave, looking for even just a sliver of the vast blue sky they once saw.

It was one of the darkest and saddest moments in Vietnam's history! Those deadly images from the Tết Offensive atrocities in Huế haunted me during childhood and adolescence and continued to follow me as I journeyed into the future. Time might be a cure for everything to some extent. I know people seem to believe that, but not for this extreme deficiency and reprehensible flaw in humanity.

It took the people of Huế months to complete their search for the unmarked burial sites. Month after month, they hoped not to discover their missing relatives in one of those mass graves. Sadly, most of the time, they found them. It didn't take them long to identify their loved ones. The North Vietnamese soldiers, while on the run and in the act of desperate revenge or for other unknown reasons, didn't take the time to strip all unique personal identities from them. Finally, Huế people found their missing relatives, hands tied behind their backs, eyes opened in terror, and mouths filled with mud!

Fortunately, or so they thought, many Huế people could not find their loved ones in those mass graves, but they faced a different cruel reality. A daughter of the Deputy Mayor of Huế recalled[36] VC took her aging father, who had about a year before retiring from his job in 1969, away during the early days of the north's invasion of Huế. They ordered him to take enough clothes for about ten days to attend the "re-education" program.

While searching for him, together with other Huế people who also had missing relatives, the mayor's daughter had seen many mass graves full of writhing bodies with her own eyes. They were in the curving positions as figures of unborn children, still in the womb but with hands tied in the back and smashed-open heads. Fortunately, she could not find her father in those mass graves. Unfortunately, she would never see her father again!

Near the end of 1969, Don Oberdorfer, a professor from Johns Hopkins University, together with Paul Vogle, who was teaching English at Huế University, spent several days traveling around the city to meet and interview witnesses[36].

They got an earful of bloody stories! A few days after the invasion, while under the North Vietnamese soldiers' control, VC executed about 400 people, including juveniles, around 15 years of age[36], who were hiding in the Phủ Cam Cathedral.

After they retreated into the jungles, Huế people eventually discovered a mass grave full of those innocent young people's bodies in the Khe Đá Mài area. According to one of the VC commanders who was in Huế during the invasion and was interviewed by Oberdorfer many years later, the people of Phủ Cam, "who were Catholics, were our special enemy… the enemy of the Vietnam Communist Party."[37]

After the interviews with witnesses, Oberdorfer categorized victims who were on the communist cadres' "blacklist" and killed by North Vietnam into two groups: those who worked for the "U.S. and South Vietnam's puppet government" and those who were reactionary with a "bad attitude" toward "revolution."[38]

When I watched those terrors on black-and-white television, they magnified my sorrow and amplified the song of Death. The lingering music notes of the Exodus soundtrack danced on the partially rotten bodies of those uncovered. Sometimes, the music was as slow as the lethargic motions of those about to breathe in their last bit of fresh air. In other pitch segments, the music seemed to surge while the black shadows threw the dark soils upon those victims before they retreated to their hiding cells. During the nights when I watched those horrible images, I looked upon the dark world in which I lived with an overwhelming sense of dread. Decades later, I could still clearly depict the unbearable, painful faces of those who had lost their loved ones in mass graves. And I could deeply feel their excruciating pains in my juvenile heart that gradually became tattered as the war continued.

It was a dark time in Vietnam's history—when our countrymen and women killed each other in the most inhuman ways possible! The world human beings have created is far from perfect, as is our generation!

At 14, I didn't really understand why VC had to kill those innocent people.

"Why did they kill those people, Mợ?" I asked Mợ[i], my mother.

"Because they are monsters!" Mợ replied.

"Monster!"

Many self-serving news organizations or networks in western countries had different perspectives during that time, partly because of North Vietnam's extremely deceptive propaganda. Hà Nội cleverly took advantage of the West's cloudy and biased magnifying glass and transformed it into the anti-war sentiment taking shape in the U.S. Instead of opening their mind and eyes to see the truth and reality of the situation, news networks veiled their eyes to twist their mind and ignore North Vietnam's blatant invasion and the atrocities committed. To make matters worse, those networks frequently buried the truth and used their communication power to distort, exaggerate, or unfairly judge many killings—mistakenly or

---

[i] "Mợ" or "Mother": A term used by many children in the north.

intentionally acted upon by some extreme individuals from the U.S. and RVN—intending to create an ugly image of the American and South Vietnamese "monster" and "murderer."

For those self-serving news networks, the true atrocity—when VC buried several thousand innocent civilian people, including many juveniles[39] alive, in Huế City during North Vietnam's invasion—appeared to have no impact on their judgment. There was no global condemnation or shocked or appalled feelings toward VC and their leaders from the north. But when a general from the South Vietnam Police Force, standing right in the middle of the Sài Gòn battle during North Vietnam's invasion in 1968, directly shot a blood-thirsty assassin, they circulated the image of his action to the entire world to achieve condemnation.

The press didn't want to know the killed VC, disguised in plain clothes, was a cold-blood murderer who had executed many innocent people in Sài Gòn. That morning, he stealthily blended in with the locals and killed an entire family, including a wife, six young children, and the 80-year-old mother[40] of a police officer. But that didn't matter at all to the self-serving news organizations! The only thing that mattered to them was the eye-catching, gruesome picture of a shooting general. Under the eyes of many dishonest and lying journalists, they instantly depicted the general as a typical South Vietnamese "murderer" or "monster."

They did not tell the entire world the story of the police officer's young and old loved ones' pain and suffering. Instead, they unjustly painted a cold-blood murderer—a VC disguised in plain clothes while fierce battles and fighting took place in Sài Gòn—as one of the "good guys." Those news networks and journalists were smart enough to judge whether the South Vietnamese general had acted according to the 1985 Geneva Convention laws. Even when looking at the picture of the general with his gun pointed at the VC's temple, captured by Admas and circulated throughout the entire world, one could see the underground VC, wearing a civilian shirt and shorts, was not a legitimate soldier captured during the war and, therefore, that the Geneva Convention laws did not apply; he was a "francs-tireurs," or an "illegal soldier,"[41] and a murderer taking orders from Hà Nội to kill innocent people in Sài Gòn.

During the first major invasion from the north in 1968, while the American and South Vietnamese military forces were fiercely fighting to recapture town after town, destroying North Vietnam's regular units and VC, many biased news networks in the West, particularly in the U.S., continued to influence the hearts and minds of the American public systematically, psychologically inducing them to protest against the fight for freedom in Vietnam.

At the end of the Tết Offensive, the year of the monkey, many news television networks and newspapers in the U.S. overwhelmingly related one-sided stories of the Vietnam War, sympathizing with the communist motive of invading the Republic of Vietnam. Even after the south had defeated the north's blatant invasion, the U.S. news networks discouraged the will of the Vietnamese people with negative comments that South Vietnam and, particularly, the U.S. would not win the war.[42]

This kind of brainwashing gradually produced many people who were unabashedly "enjoying the national feast but worshiping the communist ghosts," both in Vietnam and the U.S. In July 1972, a famous American actress visited Hà Nội. She straddled the VC's anti-aircraft gun—which had killed and was being used to kill American airmen—while praising and applauding North Vietnam's bloody policies[43].

The Mỹ Lai massacre in March 1968—a devastating episode and nightmare that killed over 500 innocent people[44] based on the order of an extreme and unstable-minded U.S. Army officer—was the atrocity that helped many news organizations and anti-war movements place South Vietnam on a silver plate for North Vietnam to take. And those self-serving and biased groups deliberately ignored the differences between the bloodthirsty policy from the north and the isolated killings from the unstable and extreme minds of a few U.S. soldiers during the Vietnam War.

HELL ON EARTH | 21

After the first major invasion, North Vietnam hastily hid and flatly distorted the atrocity of several thousand people in Huế during the Tết Offensive and continued the bloodthirsty policy and invasion of South Vietnam. In contrast, after the Mỹ Lai massacre, the U.S. government brought those extremely crooked soldiers who gave the order or pulled the trigger to kill innocent Vietnamese people from that doomed village to court to face trials[45]. Washington wanted to make sure those crazy cowboys would never hold a gun to kill again.

Even in the immature, innocent, juvenile mind of a 14-year-old boy—who would hide horribly under the wooden bed frame every time he heard the footsteps of the VC shadows passing by his house in the middle of the night in Sài Gòn during the Tết Offensive—he could recognize the bloodthirsty minds of the communists. He didn't need a college degree in journalism like those news anchors worldwide, particularly in the U.S., held to realize it was wrong.

General Võ Nguyên Giáp[46], for many years, was the director and mastermind of North Vietnam's military strategies, which had brought much destruction to both the south and north. He was also responsible for many recruited southerners whom he turned into the underground VC and systematically embedded below the 17th parallel, waiting to kill and be killed.

In his mind, Giáp realized Hà Nội's regular forces and guerrillas, during that time, were minuscule compared to the South Vietnamese military forces, which were strong and supported by the U.S. and the free world. Giáp knew the south would crush his forces; he would lose militarily. But inspired by the Marxism doctrine—to use whatever means, however cruel it might be, to achieve the final goal—Giáp was ready and willing to sacrifice untold numbers of soldiers[47], fully brainwashed, to give the world the bloodiest pictures of the Vietnam War. Giáp's military strategies were so heinous that they chained soldiers to their heavy machine guns during the early years to prevent them from running away. They had to fight to the end and could not desert. Those bộ đội soldiers, many still juvenile, had only one option: to pull the trigger until they ran out of ammunition, got burned by fire, or were killed by the freedom fighters from the south.

Even the soldiers who drove tanks had the same fate! During the An Lộc battle, the U.S. and RVN soldiers discovered the dead body of a North Vietnam tank commander with his leg near the ankle chained with "quarter-inch-thick chain links" to a solid, internal structure on his tank[48].

In 1968, North Vietnam received a devastating punch, which Giáp could have reasonably predicted, from the counterattacks conducted by South Vietnam and U.S. forces to expel their invasion during the Tết Offensive.

The bloody intrusion almost destroyed Giáp's military forces and infrastructures. They were not strong enough or well-supplied for conventional battlegrounds and were only good at fighting guerrilla warfare and hiding in the jungles instead of fighting in the cities. The defeated invasion of North Vietnam in 1968 exposed their dark mind, propagandized strategies, and blatant lies to their own soldiers who were sent to the south to fight that the people of South Vietnam would rise to expel and destroy the "evil Americans and puppet South Vietnamese Government."

Swallowing the poignant defeat but with flexible two-tongs, Hồ Chí Minh and Võ Nguyên Giáp continued to lie and brainwash people from the north, behind the communist iron curtain, insulting the understanding and morale of their military forces, which the south had violently expelled during the Tết Offensive.

Hồ wrote to the North Vietnamese people[49]: *In the first few days of spring, our military forces and people from the south fought very well with good coordination and steady advancement, fought everywhere, and won big everywhere. As thunder from the sky, we struck and punched the American aggressors and their followers. We confused and embarrassed them, and the puppet government and forces were disintegrating into pieces. The people of the entire country were very excited and proud, and our friends and supporters around five continents are excited!*

In reality, the south had crushed Hà Nội's delusional plan to swallow South Vietnam by whatever means necessary and impart their dream, the expansion of Marxism and communism doctrine, onto the entire country.

In 1968, Giáp lost over 40,000[50] North Vietnamese soldiers. Hồ, Giáp, and the Vietnam Communist Party knew there were two ways for the Vietnamese people to eat noodle soup: one way was to pick the noodles up using chopsticks and voluntarily suck them in; the other to squeeze one's mouth to force it open and then jam into the hot noodles. Hồ used both tricks: lying to the people of North Vietnam, so they would happily close their eyes and voluntarily suck in the noodles of Marxism, then using deadly tactics to force others to eat cold, stale noodles imported from the Communist Bloc, which was on a self-destructive path because of the immoral and soulless "the end-justifies-the-means" methods they employed. After the Tết Offensive in 1968, North Vietnam must have conceded in their soulless minds that they were not capable of invading South Vietnam by force during that time.

But Hà Nội also realized they could use many self-serving, fake news networks to wear out the American people's patience, foil Washington's strategic plans, and speed up the anti-war movement. Unfortunately, Hà Nội could eventually squeeze the throat of international communication networks and, literarily, only allow them to spread their blatant but formidable propaganda about the "suffering" of the Vietnamese people under the "U.S. expansion and invasion" and a "puppet government" in Sài Gòn.

North Vietnam sat back and waited longingly for the bloody seas of the Vietnam War, so they could use them to boil the sentiment for the anti-war movement in the U.S. and South Vietnam.

After learning a hard lesson through the defeated Tết Offensive, they didn't stop following the communist direction and were even more aggressive and violent. Hà Nội was waiting for Giáp to hatch and direct new bloody chess games to bring dark skies to strategic military regions below the 17th parallel. They wanted to continue to color the lives of the South Vietnamese people with a deadly shade of red from foreigners.

A Dark Negotiation

AFTER THE U.S. and South Vietnam defeated North Vietnam's first major invasion in 1968, war activities moved toward the north and Hồ Chí Minh Trail (Ho Chi Minh Trail) between Lao and Vietnam. Even though they had suffered heavy casualties, North Vietnam still unabashedly claimed victories.

For many years, those black shadows hid in the regional war zones and secret cells inside the jungles along the deadly territorial borders full of malaria and other diseases, trying to build up and regain the strength of the defeated and almost-disintegrated groups of bộ đội and VC.

For the first time, it forced the leaders of North Vietnam to learn a costly lesson—they could not invade and permanently occupy South Vietnam by force alone. The defeated Tết Offensive in 1968 was a powerful and long-lasting punch, making the heads of Hà Nội's leaders spin.

No matter whether Hồ died because of the heart attack[51] in 1969, the reflection of the defeated Giáp in 1968 and images of disintegrated bộ đội remnants hiding in the jungles were more than enough to deprive the remaining breaths of a delusional mind and bitter heart. He only wanted to serve the foreign party and was not reluctant to free the Vietnamese people—who were living in the south and north and didn't want to eat the cold, stale Marxism noodle soup—from the world they were in, for good!

In the following four years, willing to let people in the north get poorer and hungrier but unable to stand the disintegrated bộ đội and VC remnants hiding in the jungles along the Laotian borders, North Vietnam begged the Communist Bloc, especially the Soviet Union and Communist China, for more weapons and military supplies. They wanted to regain the deadly strength almost destroyed during the Tết Offensive in 1968. Flows of weapons and ammunitions[52] from the international Communist Bloc, disguised under the peace-loving propaganda, again, were abundantly coming into the north.

Unable to sit patiently in peace after a powerful slap on the cheek in 1968, Giáp prepared for what we then knew as the "Red Fiery Summer" of 1972 as retaliation. The north started implementing an "attack-while-negotiating" diplomatic strategy during the peace negotiation meetings taking place in Paris, France. In fact, because of the defeated Tết Offensive in 1968, Hà Nội also strategically programmed the second invasion in 1972 to destroy the patience of Washington and the American people, forcing the U.S. to withdraw their troops from South Vietnam completely.

During that time, the U.S. policy for Southeast Asia, particularly Vietnam, had changed direction. It was mainly because of the agony and vehement opposition from the American people, including those whose loved ones had shed their blood and lives trying to protect a tiny country that was not their homeland.

President Richard Nixon and the U.S. National Security Advisor Henry Kissinger[53] wanted an upper hand in the cold war between the Soviet Union and the U.S. As a result, Washington reached out and shook China's red hands[54] in a strategic move to weaken the relationships among the Communist Bloc countries, especially the Soviet Union. But it was also an attempt by the U.S. to side with North Vietnam's big elderly brother, keeping a tight leash on the escaping animal, which was uncontrollably roaming the Laotian jungles, waiting to break loose, kill innocent people, and eat South Vietnam alive.

Nixon wanted Hà Nội to come to the negotiation table honestly, without arrogance, to discuss a true peace for Vietnam—one that would enable U.S. troops to withdraw with their dignity intact. Simultaneously, Nixon also hoped the handshake between Washington and Beijing[j] could reduce the flow of weapons and ammunition being used to invade South Vietnam.

---

[j] Capital of People's Republic of China.

At first, the change in the U.S. policy for the Vietnam War in Southeast Asia seemed like a well-thought-out chess move. But when Nixon allowed Kissinger, who was thought to be well-experienced in foreign diplomacy and negotiation, to conduct secret meetings[55] with Beijing and Hà Nội, the U.S. strategic chess maneuver gradually backfired on them and became a political disaster. Intentionally, Hà Nội tricked Kissinger, inducing him into harmonious relations.

The desperate wish, longing for a complete military withdrawal in honor, had turned the U.S. into an amateur player incapable of showing a cold, inscrutable face—a poker face! Seeing this fatal weakness from the enemy—from the first day Kissinger met with Xuân Thủy[k] lasting throughout several other dark secret meetings with Lê Đức Thọ[l] in Paris—Hà Nội knew they were winning. When they signed the Paris Peace Accords, Sài Gòn would be like a dying fish struggling on the cutting board, gasping for air.

With a desperate and failing hope that he could save the dignity and honor of a superpower, Kissinger would become the U.S. diplomat on his path to undercut a tiny country, which, for several years, had been Washington's fiercest ally in the fight for freedom and against the expansion of communism in Southeast Asia.

By that time, in the early 1970s, at least from the observations of many South Vietnamese people, Kissinger had already made a disturbing concession: willing to agree to Hà Nội's demands for a complete withdrawal of the U.S. troops from the south six months after having signed the peace agreement.

The accords would also force Thiệu, the President of South Vietnam, to resign before the general election for a new leader to govern the south.[56] The U.S. negotiation and chess game, masterminded by Kissinger, appeared incoherent from the beginning. And Nixon's U.S. foreign policy eventually failed to stop the spread of

---

[k] Hà Nội's negotiator.
[l] North Vietnam's diplomat.

communism throughout Southeast Asia. Beijing couldn't stop or control the fierce animal waiting to splash in the bloodbath of innocent Vietnamese.

Over 200,000 North Vietnamese regular units[57], well equipped with modernized weapons from the Communist Bloc, roared out from dark hiding cells in the jungles and marched down from the north, inserting into areas below the 17th parallel. They channeled blood flows into all four strategic military regions of South Vietnam and created a "Red Fiery Summer," the likes of which we had never seen during the Vietnam War until 1972.

Neither was Kissinger able to stop the flow of weapons and ammunition from falling into the bloodthirsty hands. During that time and the years that followed, Beijing contributed about 70-86 percent of the entire weaponry arsenals given to North Vietnam by the Communist Bloc.[58]

As a Vietnamese proverb states, when "walking during the night, you will someday run into ghosts." Kissinger must have finally experienced the heebie-jeebies seeing the Hà Nội ghost. Those vulnerable diplomatic negotiation skills, under the image of a "paper tiger,"[59] used by Red China to mock the U.S., transformed Sài Gòn into an incomprehensively unhappy ally. They both quickly became distrusting partners!

Subsequently, the U.S. government sped up the military Vietnamization program to prepare for a complete withdrawal of their troops, hoping to save some remaining dignity and honor not already lost to the Vietnam War. The U.S. race against time to withdraw all muddy military boots from rice paddy fields and strategic regions in the south—while trying to hold their heads up high and save face from losing the war—seemed desperate. U.S. foreign policy, once again, had hiccupped! Acknowledging the pattern, Nixon said, "Instead of teaching someone else to do a job, we like to do it ourselves. And this trait has been carried over into our foreign policy."[60]

When the secret negotiation games were not going the way they wanted, Hà Nội returned to the bloody path of war to create and facilitate the release of false, one-sided war stories into the ears and mouths of U.S. news networks to induce the anti-war groups and protesters into extremities—fighting against any remaining ideas of support or fair solutions from Washington regarding the Vietnam War, which became visibly bloodier quickly.

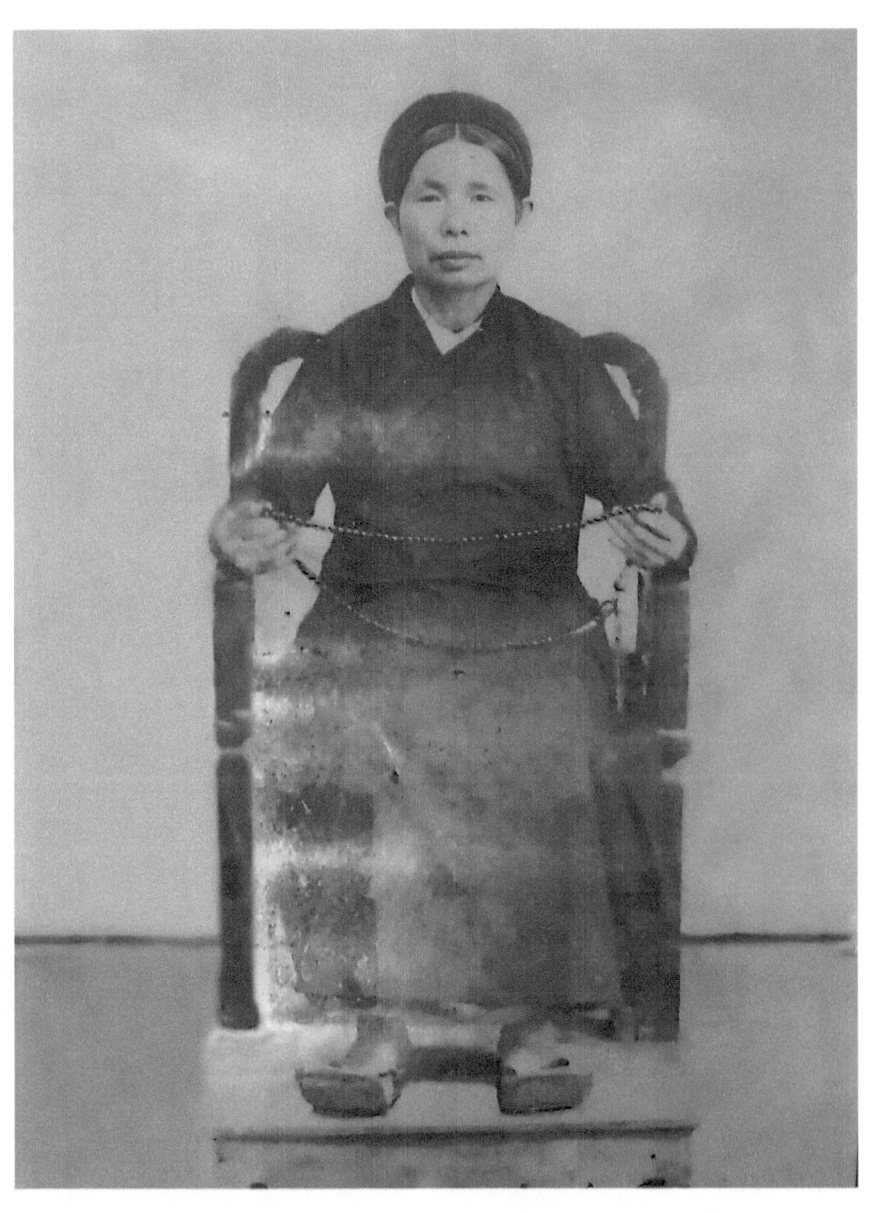

**My maternal great-grandmother.
(Pre-1954 Vĩnh Yên, North Vietnam)**

My maternal grandparents.
(Pre-1954. Vĩnh Yên, North Vietnam)

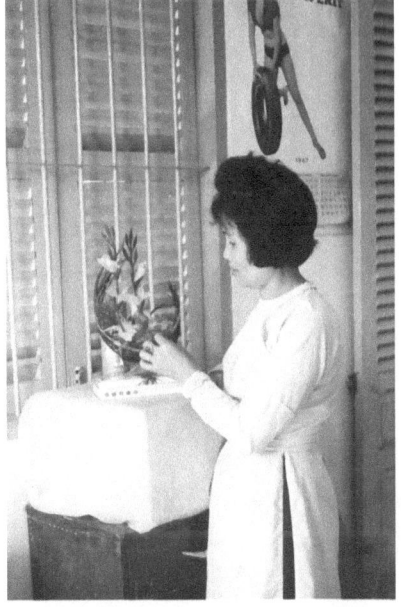

Parents in Sài Gòn, South Vietnam.

From left: My elder brother, Brother Giới, Sister Minh, and me (born in the north).

First row: Four children born in the north. I was the youngest one at that time. Second row from left: Aunt Mi, Cậu, Mợ, and Aunt Môn in the traditional Vietnamese Áo Dài clothing and Khăn Đống headdress.

Picture below: From left, Father's younger sisters, my elder brother, Father, Brother Giới (standing), Mother, me, and other siblings.

Father in the U.S. for military training under President Diệm's regime.

At Tao Đàn Garden. First row from left: My elder brother, Brother Giới, Sister Minh, me, and younger siblings. Second row: Cậu and Mợ carying my younger brother.

Parents at Tao Đàn Garden.

Mother with children born in the south after we fled from the north. Going clockwise: Mợ (behind, in the middle), Dung, Tuân, Khôi, Hạnh (my youngest brother), Vinh, Nga (my youngest sister), and Dũng.

With my younger siblings in Vũng Tàu. Dũng was poking his cheek.

Parents at Tao Đàn Garden.

At Lăng Ông Temple with Mợ and my younger brothers. (1970, Sài Gòn, South Vietnam)

THE LAST WORDS

On April 29, 1975, sometime around noon, Sài Gòn—the Pearl of the Far East—would cease to exist in less than 24 hours. Her American partner quickly launched a massive airlift to save the remaining Americans and Vietnamese collaborators who had ties with the U.S.

The black shadows, who had been part of my nightmares, were about to return. But this time, they would come back as victors, with defined shapes and an even stronger presence rather than hidden shadows of the past who were struggling to regroup because of the defeated Tết Offensive.

All this was because of the fatal Paris Peace Accords and the bitterly crumbling relationship between Sài Gòn and Washington.

In the meantime, the people of Sài Gòn were left shocked, helplessly observing the inevitable transition and their unfolding fate. They were about to surrender both their souls and bodies differently. Soon, the communists would witness several high-ranking South

Vietnamese military officers and soldiers commit suicide or fight to the death rather than fall into the red hands of North Vietnamese soldiers. They refused to surrender or flee, taking those pitying hands of their rapidly exiting partner—the U.S.

In the next few days and months, when the communist victors arrogantly pushed the nozzle of their AK-47 against the temple of a to-be-executed colonel from South Vietnam, they would hear unyielding words as strong as steel: *Nobody has the right to judge me. History will judge you as the red invader or me as the "puppet soldier." I fought for the freedom of my people. I have served my country, and I am not guilty. If you want to kill me, kill me. Do not blindfold me.*[61]

Soon, the world would see not only the flashing images of the U.S. Marines helicopters hastily taking off from or landing on the U.S. Embassy's rooftop but also the desperate facial expressions of the Vietnamese people who were about to storm into the compound, hopefully, to escape from the communist plague. Once in the courtyard, they would finally discover many self-serving U.S. politicians had already abandoned them—for good!

On April 29, 1975, sometime around noon, I stood behind the door leading to the front balcony on the second floor of my parents' house, still wearing the gray military flight suit that I hadn't washed for a few days.

I had just come home. I couldn't stand staying downstairs, hearing my siblings talking about having waited for my helicopter because I was hiding somewhere cowardly. It caused a violent hurt in my inner soul, and my heart felt like it bled from the pain. I didn't have a strong enough stomach to look at their innocent faces anymore. Inside my ragged mind, I had no remaining sense of hope.

I became confused, lost, and mentally disoriented because Sài Gòn caved in so quickly. The collapse of South Vietnam deeply and irreparably upset many other Vietnamese people and me. I was trying to convince myself that it was not happening. But the commotion on the street below the loosely closed wooden door on the second floor of my parents' house told me the painful reality I was forced to come to terms with.

I crept away from the door where, for an hour, I peeked at the events below as they transpired, transparent down below, while my mind drifted back to the nightmares of the Tết Offensive. Then I sat down on the wooden flatbed where I had slept and cried several times throughout my early childhood.

It was too much for me to comprehend! The one-piece flight suit became clumsy, tight, and wet. The sweat ran all over my body, leaving hot traces on my irritated skin. I didn't even notice when my air force dark blue folding hat dropped onto the squeaky wooden floor below.

The dog tags, chained around my neck and suspended in front of my chest, stopped chattering as they used to when I played with them while waiting for the preflight briefing. I sat there, elbows on my knees and hands on my face, searching for the answers to the questions I had never allowed myself to ponder.

"Why am I still here? What am I going to do now? Am I now a prisoner of war? Are Huey pilots the ones VC will execute first out of revenge? What will they do to me? Should I go into hiding in the countryside? Should I go to the harbor to find a way to the U.S. Seventh Fleet?"

I kept asking myself the same things again and again.

"What happened to my father?"

I suddenly cut off the flow of my thoughts with that one stinging question because the last question reminded me that my father, an army captain from South Vietnam, was still out there somewhere.

"Where is he now?"

"Did they capture him?"

My eyes felt irritated. I sensed the tension in my temples. I feared the worst. The omen from the dark dreams might strike my loved ones again, and I couldn't do anything about it.

That was the second time in my life I felt completely useless. It was the second time in my life I believed I would lose any prospects of a future that seemed to exist only in another distant dimension—virtual, hard to reach, and full of mental agony.

The First "Black Sheep"

AFTER SOUTH VIETNAM had defeated North Vietnam's first invasion in 1968, our lives slowly returned to normal. But Sài Gòn's relationship with Hà Nội progressively deteriorated.

In the south, the military draft was coming to those aged 18 or older who were not in college. My older brother, Anh Giới, could have finished high school, gone to college, and eventually become a teacher, as my elder brother was pursuing during that time. But, in 1970, he dropped out of his last year of high school to join the South Vietnamese Army to protect our country.

After military training, my older brother left for the Central Highlands, leaving us behind in Sài Gòn. We were a family of 11 siblings. He was the second older brother. I was the fourth child after my older sister.

When Anh Giới returned to Sài Gòn on his military leave, he used to take me out to one of the cafés in a quiet section downtown, where we sat and talked as friends, mostly about our family.

As he talked—and he talked little—I sensed the sorrow in his eyes. I could only imagine the mental agony of his inner soul and felt the suffering in his words. I knew he was struggling to suppress the emotional pain he carried in his heart for being away from his loved ones.

"Hùng, take care of the young siblings for me!" my older brother said during one of our café meetings. "Cậu Mợ"[m] may not have much time to care for each of you. I will not be around you guys that much, you know."

"Hùng" was my second name used at home. Through his voice, I could somehow feel the mental agony he was struggling with.

"I know!" I nodded and almost cried.

---

[m] "Cậu Mợ": Terms sometimes used in the north for father and mother.

"Don't make Cậu mad, remember that!" he said, and I knew what he meant, as though I could read his mind. He and Father didn't get along well.

After my older brother had left, I started sleeping on the open patio above the second floor of my parents' house. The area was just a third floor without a roof and had an unfinished cement floor with a rough surface surrounded by brick walls that extended just a little above my belt. It was there where I often flew my kite high in the blue sky in the afternoons. It was the place where I used to hide when I had acute headaches and wanted to be away from the crowds. From there, I could see far away and even spot other towns in the distance. I could recognize the foosball tables at the small store across the street, a few houses away, where I had become a fierce contender in my neighborhood for several years.

Sometimes, Sài Gòn was very windy!

One night, the wind was strong, and its hissing sound was coldly bitter. It was cooler than normal. That night, my sleep was also rougher than any other. I knew my older brother had been wounded and was being treated in a military hospital in Qui Nhơn Province. He was fighting for his life.

It was past midnight. Sài Gòn was asleep. I still vividly recall the crying voice that delivered bad news from where my older brother was stationed. Through the dark, I saw a dark figure screaming while protruding from the opening where the cement stairs went from the second floor to the top.

"Dear Hùng... Dear Hùng... Oh, Heaven... Oh, Buddha! Brother Giới is dead... Brother Giới is dead!"

The devastatingly painful news—piercing my heart like a lightning bolt had struck it from the dark sky—immediately took me out of any lingering sleep.

"WHO SAID HE WAS DEAD? WHO? WHO? WHO?"

Snapping back at my aunt's dark silhouette, I abruptly sat up, throwing the blanket to the side. I didn't recall whether my aunt said anything after that beyond groaning my brother's name all the way to my parents' bedroom on the first floor. There, I spent the rest of the night crying with my siblings and elder aunt.

Mother later told me about Anh Giới's last few days. After they had transported him to the hospital, where they performed an operation to remove a piece of the mortar from his abdomen and later treated him for a leaking and infected intestine, he asked her whether I could come to be by his side. I believe he sensed his deadly fate and wanted to see me one last time. My parents arrived at his deathbed in time, but immediately died in their own hearts. They saw their beloved son abruptly gasping for air. It was his last breath on Earth. I wasn't there! And the omen from the 10-year-old boy's dark dreams seemed to become a reality.

A few days later, my brother's air-sealed coffin, covered with the yellow flag with three red stripes, arrived home from Quy Nhơn. I sat in my parents' bedroom, quietly looking through the interior window to the front room where they placed his flag-draped casket—until someone discovered me and realized I had already gone into shock.

My body and face were frozen like a rock slab and showed no emotion, my eyes open but unmoving. I couldn't absorb the emotional pain, hide my mental agony, and push it into a dark corner of my bleeding heart since it was already full of piercing anger.

I hated the world I was in so much and wondered what it was like to be in the strange place that comes after death. "Will I see my brother on that side?"

I let myself go because I could no longer contain the mental pain and excruciating suffering. While growing up, I was expecting something that I could easily comprehend. Instead, it bombarded me with life's cruel reality and deadly face. "Will he be the only one, or is this just the beginning?" I was so scared of the omen from the dark dreams that I didn't know what to do. As the mental pain grew and my fear expanded exponentially, it got to a point where it completely blocked my vision, numbing all my feelings and senses. I gave up entirely. I fell into the hands of Death.

First row from left: Brother Giới with younger siblings. I was in front of the elder brother. Second row from left: Elder brother, Mother, Father, Aunt Mi, and Aunt Môn.

First row: My sister and me. Second row from left: My elder brother, Father, and Brother Giới.

Our family's first contribution to the fight for freedom.
(1971, Sài Gòn, South Vietnam)

Brother Giới.

The first "black sheep."
(1971, Sài Gòn,
South Vietnam)

I sat in my parents' bedroom, quietly looking through the interior window to the front room where they placed his flag-draped casket —until someone discovered me and realized I had already gone into shock.

From left: Dũng, me, my elder brother, Sister Minh, and other siblings standing next to our brother's flag-draped casket.

Brother Giới's military funeral. (1971, South Vietnam)

From right: Father, my elder brother, me, the cousin who died during his escape by boat after 1975, Aunt Môn, Sister Minh, Aunt Mi (covering her face), and Mother (sitting on the ground next to her son's coffin).

Visiting her son's newly built tomb.

The only sound I heard was the music of Death triumphantly rumbling in my ears. For the first time, I was glad I ignored it while tiny pixels of darkness quickly spread into the field of vision from my frozen, tearful eyes. And the bony hands of Death quickly cut off all the remaining senses of my soulless body.

My older sister subsequently took me to the hospital emergency room during my older brother's funeral. Physicians wanted to close my open but frozen eyes and put me to sleep for a few hours. I lay in the hospital bed covered with a white sheet, but my lost soul was wandering somewhere in a familiar place—cold and dark.

I didn't want to wake up because there was no remaining energy to live. It was too painful for me to go on and endure the cruelty of life and the shocking reality of death.

My mind sank to the bottom of the darkness! I cried, cried, and cried until my eyes became dry, irritated, and showed no emotion of a living body. The mental agony was so real, and the cut was so deep in my heart. The suffering was intolerably massive for a young man who had reached his limit on emotional endurance.

I knew I would carry the painful loss for eternity wherever I would pass through in my life—if there would even be any life left. The psychic feeling and dark dreams had redeemed its prescience. I thought I was wrong. It wasn't my younger brother, Dũng—whom I had been trying to protect for fear of this dark fate—but the older one that Death swiftly swung the bloody scythe at, removing him from my world.

A FATEFUL TRIBULATION

The "Red Fiery Summer"[62] of 1972 began when I was still burning the midnight oil to take the high school Baccalaureate Part-I examination. After witnessing and learning more about the cruelty of the Vietnam communists through their invasion during the Tết Offensive in the monkey year, I was distraught.

The leaders of Hà Nội were stubborn and hysterical. Over the next few months, they were planning to annihilate the existence of hundreds of thousands of young soldiers from North and South Vietnam to bring the faithless communism doctrine into the remaining land of S-shaped Vietnam.

During that summer, the south would be horribly and excruciatingly devastated by extreme cruelty, burning the peaceful souls and hearts of innocent, simple, and hard-working people from the central and south regions below the 17th parallel.

So, as planned, after Hà Nội had brainwashed the North Vietnamese soldiers behind the red iron curtain for many years, about

200,000 of them[57] with raging hearts, were anxiously awaiting the opportunity to "liberate" the southern people. They fiercely and unapologetically attacked three strategic military regions below the 17th parallel.

Completely in contrast to what was being indoctrinated, South Vietnamese citizens were happy with their land and free to cultivate and conduct business. Sài Gòn, the capital of the Republic of Vietnam, which, if not seen as the Pearl of the Far East by the entire world, was at least a considerably growing economic stronghold in the south during that time. From the late 1950s to the early 1960s, the peaceful atmosphere and prosperous economic environment under President Ngô Đình Diệm's regime represented the golden time and period of South Vietnam.

The cost of living and inflation were low. A few piasters, "đồng,"[n] could afford people in Sài Gòn a big bowl of delicious beef noddle soup or "Phở," satisfactorily filling up one's hungry stomach. A few coins or "xu"[o] would give people in Sài Gòn loaves of hot, crunchy bread fresh out of the oven!

During the first few years under the Diệm presidency, the Gross Domestic Product of South Vietnam increased quickly and was twice that of North Vietnam's economy[63]. Southern people—many among the 800,000 people[30] who ran away from the communists in the north in 1954—were happily and prosperously living in a stable and free society.

After the coup d'état—with the U.S. government and CIA support implicitly confirmed by the Pentagon many years later[64]—which turned out to be bloody, plus the frequent attacks by North Vietnam, South Vietnam's economy was still intact, unaffected by the war, and still much better than the economy in the north.

Many people in the south were happy and prosperous, completely contrary to what Hà Nội had brainwashed their fellow

---

[n] "đồng": Currency of South Vietnam.
[o] "xu": Currency of South Vietnam. One "đồng" was subdivided into 100 xu.

citizens behind the red iron curtain—inciting an illusion and enough ill will to drive the "liberation" of the South Vietnamese people from the "foreign aggressor," "U.S. Empire," and "puppet government." So, after four years of hiding and building up the troops in the jungles and along the Hồ Chí Minh Trail as they prepared to hatch cruel tactics and military strategies, the rage of the communists once again was about to rise. They wanted to force southerners to swallow a foreign doctrine in which killing people was a means to achieve their "revolution" goals.

In the summer of 1972, Hà Nội brought to the south, below the 17th parallel, the burning heat of battle fires from Quảng Trị's "Horrible Highway,"[65] to the Kontum highlands and An Lộc plateaus. The military forces of North Vietnam, including 14 divisions and 26 battalions, together with modernized artillery and weapons, mostly supplied by the Soviet Union and China[66], advanced into the south.

They disguised the invasion intent and goal as a patriotic revolution to "liberate" the southern Vietnamese from the "U.S. aggressor." Their actual goal was to abolish the Geneva Agreements that had split Vietnam into two countries but successfully saved 800,000 North Vietnamese from the wrath of faithless communists.

By then, the people of South Vietnam were well aware of the ill intent of Hà Nội. The horrifying feeling of dread flooded their minds, particularly those who had been running as fast as they could in 1954. They had once abandoned their birth and family burial places to seek a haven from the south and knew what would happen if the communists came. Where would they go if red forces continued their uncontrolled rise to power and prominence?

Quảng Trị was one of the strategic provinces in the Central region, near the narrowest waist of the Vietnam S-shape, about 30 km below the Hiền Lương bridge at Bến Hải River and 86 km north of Huế. The demilitarized zone lay parallel, a few kilometers from the bank toward the north and south, along both sides of the Bến Hải River. Land in Quảng Trị features many hilly areas and jungles, including the mysterious Annamese (Trường Sơn) mountains, located west of the city, running parallel to National Highway 1. The highway ran along shorelines, stretching extensively through Huế, Đà Nẵng, Quy Nhơn, and Cam Ranh before entering Sài Gòn and the heavily populated western provinces.

On the last day of March 1972, North Vietnamese soldiers filled the skies over Strategic Tactical Region I, where the freedom fighters of the 3rd Division of South Vietnamese Army Infantry were stationed, with 122- and 130-millimeter long-range artillery shells, scorching the motherland, staining it with the blood of innocent people and South Vietnamese soldiers who had a different ideology and simply wanted to defend their land from aggression.

After the rumbling, sky-breaking explosions from the rain of artillery faded, seas of faithless red soldiers flooded into strategic, tactical key locations below the DMZ, south of the 17th parallel and west of Quảng Trị. They intended to annihilate critical military bases, including Fuller, Khe Gió, Sarge, and Holcomb.

Row upon row of iron tigers T-54, T-55, and PT-76 tanks roared and rumbled like stormy winds, crushing the writhing motherland as they penetrated the northern and the western fronts before crossing the Thạch Hãn River. All the way, they painted their path with the fresh blood of the children of South Vietnam.

The rage and hysterics that Hà Nội had incited, together with the powerful, modernized weapons of the Communist Bloc, especially their big brother China, were no longer under any constraints to "liberate" people from their prosperity and peace. They wanted to throw the south into hell, the sheer hell North Vietnam had created along their path into the region.

In the meantime, Washington was in a hurry to withdraw their troops; one of them was the U.S. 196th Battalion, idly waiting to be sent home[67].

During that time, almost no American ground forces took part in the fight. South Vietnamese freedom fighters directly engaged the enemy with limited U.S. air power support. Anti-war protesters and sympathizers, as predicted, ignored and didn't protest or call upon

North Vietnam to cease fire, stop killing innocent people, or abandon their bloody invasion into a country that the entire world had legitimately recognized under the Geneva Agreements.

Of course, the Communist Bloc, including the Soviet Union and China, must have been waiting for the victory by force during the "Red Fiery Summer" of 1972 while South Vietnam's allies—who had already reduced their military strength and support—likely assumed that would be the last summer of Sài Gòn.

Within a few days, dead bodies from both sides, north and south, fell upon each other in layers, filling up the battlegrounds. The entire region's strategic bases, north and west of Quảng Trị and the surrounding area, became muddy with blood from the yellow children, who gave their lives to protect freedom and the motherland, mixed with dead bodies from the sea of bộ đội soldiers of North Vietnam who jumped in with the vigor of suicidal fireflies.

My friends served in Platoon 2, which merged into the 56th and 57th Platoon of the 3rd Division of South Vietnam. After a few bloody weeks, they had pushed back many fierce mass attacks. But with the iron wish from Giáp to burn and kill as many as possible to achieve the military goal, the freedom fighters from Strategic Tactical Region I, while they bravely fought in hell on earth, gradually added to the body count, torn apart by the bloodthirsty roaring wolves that Giáp had harbored for years in the jungles.

The mass-attack tactics and willingness to sacrifice three or even six bộ đội or North Vietnamese soldiers to kill one South Vietnamese freedom fighter[68] in the second invasion were brutal. It ripped apart countless families in both countries, leaving the survivors to live in hell with the excruciating suffering generated by the false promise of a delusional paradise created by Hà Nội.

During the last days of April 1972, South Vietnamese troops lost the ability to protect Quảng Trị forever.

With already fading strength, they faced critical supply issues and gradually ran out of ammunition. There were few supply flights made by helicopters from the south because of thick layers of SA-7 anti-aircraft heat-seeking missiles, creating an unbearable heat that burned for days and nights high above in the Quảng Trị sky.

Finally, South Vietnam abandoned Quảng Trị, withdrawing their troops along National Highway 1 while waves of North Vietnamese soldiers and their tanks fiercely crossed the Thạch Hãn River as if through a broken dam.

During the "Red Fiery Summer" of 1972, I was burning the midnight oil, trying to keep the dancing words and mathematical equations clear in my agonizing and fuming mind.

While I was sitting at home, comfortable and safe, preparing for the high school Baccalaureate Part-I examination, the South Vietnamese freedom fighters were wrestling with Death on the "Horrible Highway," intermingling their blood with that of the dead bodies of innocent people running away from the "liberation" at the hands of Bộ đội.

If Hà Nội tried to hide the atrocity of killing several thousand Huế people[36] like a cat hides its waste, many U.S. news networks and anti-war groups must have closed their eyes, hidden the truth of the "Red Fiery Summer" and distorted the reality of what happened during the evacuation of the 3rd Division of South Vietnam and people from Đông Hà and Quảng Trị along National Highway 1.

The "Horrible Highway," southeast of Quảng Trị and along the Hải Lăng to Bến Đá areas, lay in the middle of a desert-like region featuring beautiful white sands.

In the burning heat of the summer, flows of people from Đông Hà and Quảng Trị made their way throughout the region as they ran away from the North Vietnamese troops, closely following the South Vietnamese freedom fighters retreating toward safer locations where still under the control of the RVN soldiers.

National Highway 1—which my friends from the 3rd Division had walked while withdrawing from key lost strategic, tactical areas—became a killing path for the North Vietnamese soldiers. There, they were free to launch as many mortar and artillery shells as possible on the retreating troops and innocents following the

RVN soldiers. South Vietnamese freedom fighters, when retreating, often carried children and held the hands of elderly men and women—still carrying weapons on their shoulders to protect the central region's people as they escaped the influx of bộ đội soldiers. The heavy waves of mortar and artillery shells didn't discriminate, targeting the old, young, children, pregnant women, and disabled equally. The highway was littered with the dead bodies of freedom fighters from the south and the charred black bodies and disfigured innocent people—often with smashed heads, missing legs and hands, or fully soaked with blood.

Many bodies sandwiched between the remains of military vehicles and other means of transportation people from Đông Hà and Quảng Trị had been using. Those innocents were merely attempting to escape the horrible rage and revenge incited by Hà Nội after their defeated invasion in the Monkey New Year of 1968. Regardless of whether they had received direct orders, Giáp's Bộ đội soldiers committed an unforgivable—and unforgettable—atrocity in killing thousands of innocents in their motherland in cold blood.

The yellow freedom fighters shed their blood and sacrificed their lives to protect unarmed people along National Highway 1. Eventually, the South Vietnamese freedom fighters successfully launched a fierce offensive to recapture Quảng Trị.

Some of my soldier friends were wounded but came back alive, forced to live out their remaining lives facing horrible nightmares that reflected the blood-thirsty rage and hatred of their half-brothers and sisters who came from the north.

Hearing what was happening, I could not sit and wait any longer while my heart burned with anger and sadness over the blood spilled and fires set across my motherland by North Vietnam. I could no longer ignore the innocent lives lost.

Near the end of the "Red Fiery Summer," I volunteered to join the Republic of Vietnam Air Force immediately after passing the High School Baccalaureate Part-I examination. My journey to fight against the dark forces then began head-on.

Following the Freedom Fighters

AFTER FINISHING BASIC military training, in the summer of 1972, and passing the English language program with the required proficiency, in November 1973, South Vietnam selected several other air cadets and me to travel to Lackland Air Force Base and Fort Rucker Aviation Training Center in the U.S. for flight training.

In 1974, the U.S. Congress and President appeared to have lost sight of their strategic goal, whatever it might have been, in Southeast Asia because of the overwhelming anti-war movement taking over the nation. It resulted in substantial cuts to U.S. military aid for South Vietnam.

For the time being, the Communist Bloc was still pouring weapons into the north to support Hà Nội's southern invasion plan. Washington, at least in secrecy, no longer believed there could be any positive resolution for Sài Gòn. The newspapers and U.S. news networks were crystal clear on the fact that the certain demise of South Vietnam was forthcoming.

The immediate impact of the budget cuts was the cancellation of the U.S. flight training program established for the Republic of Vietnam Air Force. We heard many rumors and were waiting to find out what classes they might cancel and who would be the unlucky air cadets to be sent back to Tân Sơn Nhứt Air Base.

Then one day, as predicted, a spokesperson for the Fort Rucker Aviation Training Center announced the cancellation list. They abolished all classes for the South Vietnamese air cadets who had begun the flight training program just after mine. They asked those from those unlucky groups to prepare to go home.

Eventually, in the fall of 1974, many South Vietnamese air cadets returned home without completing their training.

I felt depressed and somber for those comrades in arms who had to turn and head home without that prized military flight certificate and sterling silver navigator wing. Some only had a few hours remaining to meet the flight training program requirements for graduation. Miraculously, my flight training class was not on the list, and they ordered us to stay to complete the flight training as originally planned. We might be the last South Vietnamese air cadets from Fort Rucker to fly home after the graduation ceremony in December 1974.

The U.S. budget cuts were detrimental to the survival of the Republic of Vietnam. It officially canceled the flight training programs with the original strategic goal of training a select group of South Vietnamese youths as an elite force of military pilots tapped to protect their own country instead of depending on U.S. airmen. The Nixon Vietnamization policy and program[69], which aimed to hand over military capability to South Vietnam to pave the way for the American military withdrawal, finally came to an abrupt end.

In the meantime, the reduction of U.S. military strength continued to accelerate[70] while critical aid decelerated. U.S. troops were departing as quickly as they had arrived in Vietnam at the beginning of the Vietnam War.

We became confused and worried about our unknown future and what would happen to us upon returning to Vietnam.

In the late fall of 1974, each time we took off and roared our birds through the open sky, learning day-and-night tactical flight maneuvers to plunge into irregular pinnacles, our blood boiled. We were angry, thinking about the dark fate of our country, which became more certain as days and months passed. In the last few days of November 1974, while still in the U.S., we, the children of South Vietnam from Fort Rucker, could feel the demise of our motherland in our hearts. After graduation, one of us had given up, deciding not to return home and illegally traveling to Canada a few days before the scheduled departure for Tân Sơn Nhứt.

For me, the increasing worry I felt when thinking about the demise of South Vietnam was not enough to abolish my dream of becoming a military pilot for the Republic of Vietnam. So, I swallowed the pain, gradually eating at my soul every day, and worked to complete the remaining flights during the early winter days in Alabama. With all my heart, I wanted to accomplish the training program I had agreed to complete. My beloved motherland had placed her full trust in me fully, believing in my commitment to the pledge to serve the country. I would "go where no one can find the fallen body"[71] to fulfill my duty.

During the last flight at Fort Rucker, while walking around the iron bird to conduct the pre-flight visual inspection, I suddenly saw a dark brown butterfly sitting on the edge of the cargo door behind the cockpit. In Vietnam, many people were superstitious and believed that sometimes the soul of a deceased loved one could transmigrate into the body of a butterfly and return to this world to warn relatives that something bad might happen.

At that moment, I was curious. My eyes were glued to the butterfly, which remained perfectly still, as if waiting for something. I wondered how it had made its way here to the flight line. I had never seen a butterfly fluttering near the runway while conducting flights over the last several months. The aircraft's engine noise, breaking the sky's quietness, and the strong downwash and outwash generated from the rotor blades were strong enough to scare any butterfly that might wander around the iron bird. Yet, during the last day of my flight training, why did the butterfly come here to sit quietly on the iron bird I was about to dive into the somber, gray late fall sky?

It was the last flight we had to complete that week. They had scheduled the graduation ceremony for the Orange Hat Class 74-42. Major General William J. Maddox, Jr., the Commanding Officer of Fort Rucker, would soon present the flight diplomas and pin sterling silver navigator wings on our dark Navy-blue uniforms. We had received a military order to return to Vietnam after graduation, with no delays.

I seriously focused my perplexed eyes on the quiet butterfly, thinking it could be my older brother killed in action in 1971. He was waiting to tell me something. I sat down on the edge of the cargo floor of the iron bird, where we would have an automatic machine-gun M-60 mounted during actual combat missions, with a confused expression and jumbled thoughts.

"What do you want to tell me, Anh Giới?" I whispered, my eyes looking downward. "You don't want me to fly today, do you?"

I talked to the butterfly as though I was speaking with my older brother in a small café years ago, forgetting I should be in the cockpit preparing for the last flight. The butterfly still didn't move. My mind became nervous, thinking about the potential that the butterfly was a bad omen.

"Hey! Dỹ! Let's get going!" the co-pilot urged me to enter the cockpit after completing the iron bird's visual inspection.

"... Alright!" I reluctantly replied, gently touching the butterfly to make it fly away safely before we took off. My eyes followed its dark brown wings, buoyantly floating with the wind. I intentionally waited until it had completely flown away—far beyond the effects of the iron bird's rotor blades on the air around the helicopter—before climbing into the cockpit.

That day, our flight was the most peaceful and uneventful I had conducted since arriving in the U.S. for training. My co-pilot was also a Vietnamese air cadet from South Vietnam. We quietly flew into a wide-open sky, saying nothing much except communicating to the military field's air traffic controller to get permission to take off and to inform them of our flight path. We were deep in our own thoughts. I imagine the co-pilot was visualizing his return-home day, wearing the heroic dark Navy-blue uniform with a sterling silver navigator wing.

I was still thinking about the butterfly and struggling with the agony of missing my brother, which caused a strange, superstitious feeling in my mind. Finally, we completed the last flight successfully without running into any complications. I assured myself that my delusions of the bad omen and the accompanying feelings were truly silly and absurd! We landed softly on the airfield runway, maneuvered the iron bird into its original parking spot, shut down the engine, waited for the rotor blades to stop, and climbed down from the cockpit. I curiously look around, wondering where the butterfly might have gone.

"Thank you, Anh Giới!" I whispered to the imaginary soul of my brother, who had given up his life for our motherland. "I have done all I can. Thank you for accompanying me on this last flight." At that moment, I reinforced my decision. I would return to Vietnam to fight, no matter what, together with my comrades in arms. I pledged to protect the south from the communists at all costs. Relentlessly, those atheists, wanting to raise red flags with yellow stars and the "hammer and sickle" symbol, continued to sacrifice the Vietnamese people. They wanted us to worship and display pictures of Mao Tse Tung, Lenin, and Stalin on our peaceful, beloved streets of Vietnam after a 4,000-year history of our ancestors dying to protect it against obliteration by foreigners.

In December 1974, I returned to Vietnam, stationed at the air force headquarters inside the Tân Sơn Nhứt airport before flying to Nha Trang Air Force Training Center. One day, while in Sài Gòn, I told Mother about the butterfly I had run into on the runway during that last flight. "That was your brother!" Mother said. "He came to protect you!" Then she sobbed, which almost made me cry. "He wanted you to come home!" Then, Mother cried again and wept whenever somebody or I mentioned her son's name, Anh Giới.

Knowing she was deeply worried about the escalating war, I had never told her or anyone in my family about my near-death experience flying with Long, another Vietnamese co-pilot I had also flown with at Fort Rucker. Our aircraft had quickly plunged to the ground, violently tracing skid marks on the runway during the autorotation landing because of the engine's faulty instrumentation readings. Luckily, we got out of the aircraft unharmed.

Abandoning Nha Trang

IN JANUARY 1975, together with my comrades in arms from the U.S. flight training class, I left Sài Gòn on a military transport aircraft, a C-130 Hercules, to fly to Nha Trang Air Force Training Center. Our arrival in Nha Trang was significantly less stressful than when we came for basic military training.

The protocol was different this time, as we had become the South Vietnam Air Force pilots who had just returned from the U.S. A sterling silver navigator wing, about the length of the index finger, firmly pinned on our dark Navy-blue military uniforms by Major General William J. Maddox, Jr., was an invaluable piece of metal to be admired by the many other air cadets who didn't get selected for the flight training in the U.S. We were ready to fight! Our duty was to protect the motherland at all costs. All we were waiting for was a well-armed helicopter, a military order, and precise tactical coordinates. That's all we were waiting for. We impatiently wished for a chance to die for our country.

Near the end of February 1975, North Vietnam, for the third time, systematically continued to launch its aggressive campaign into the strategic, high-value regions of South Vietnam. Hà Nội knew they had extirpated the will of the U.S. to protect freedom in Southeast Asia.

In March, President Thiệu ordered the South Vietnamese forces to abandon some provinces in the Central Highlands. The communist troops subsequently occupied Kontum, Pleiku, and then Ban Mê Thuột, all of which were deemed to have critically strategic military value.

Quảng Trị, the province taken by the north during the "Red Fiery Summer" of 1972 and eventually successfully retaken by the south, was also under siege by North Vietnamese soldiers in March 1975. Ban Mê Thuột was a strategic location north of Nha Trang, a four-hour drive by ground and less than two hours by air.

During that time, we saw refugees fleeing from bộ đội soldiers while following the South Vietnamese troops retreating to Nha Trang in badly damaged convoys. Nha Trang became a focal point for troops withdrawing from the Central Highlands regions of South Vietnam and a haven for refugees.

We felt the pressure of our demise! Some of us, who just came back from the U.S., asked our first-line commander to convey our willingness to engage to the Air Base Commander. However, I heard a rumor that he did not want us to engage for fear of inexperience and wasting "expensive young pilot resources, which our country had made significant efforts and spent a substantial amount of funding to train." As a result, we kept waiting while streams of refugees and South Vietnamese soldiers continued to surge into Nha Trang.

In late March, the city was in utter chaos, full of exhausted soldiers retreating from the abandoned regions of the Central Highlands. A few of them lost control and became reckless, feeling betrayed and broken. Some had gone rogue during their retreat from the territories South Vietnam had abandoned for VC to take control.

One day, we, a small group of inexperienced junior pilots, armed ourselves with whatever weapons we could get our hands on to defend our base from the North Vietnamese troops' imminent attacks. We also needed weapons to protect ourselves out of fear of ongoing riots. Our barracks were not too far from the perimeter of the base. I found an M-16 assault rifle equipped with a muzzle grenade launcher and some ammunition.

Around noon, there was a loud explosion somewhere behind our barracks. While trying to pinpoint the exact direction of the explosion, we ran into a group of South Vietnamese soldiers passing by our barracks on foot. A few of them were officers of the South Vietnam Air Force. It was then that they informed us of the evacuation already underway.

We finally accepted that we had to abandon Nha Trang and knew the runway might no longer be an option for evacuation. In the late afternoon, some of us re-grouped in our barracks to discuss the options to leave the base. We explored the possibility of taking some of the remaining choppers and flying southward. We might land in Cam Ranh, a major naval port of South Vietnam where the U.S. Naval Forces used to station. Cam Ranh province remained untouched by the North Vietnamese troops then, and the flight time was short, depending on how fast we wanted to maneuver. Certainly, we could do it—if we have access to our choppers. Unfortunately, we were told that most of the aircraft from the base had already left to seek safety elsewhere. So, our small group of newly commissioned pilots who had just returned from the U.S. a few months ago didn't even know about it.

There was no time to feel bitterness or place blame, as any paths for leaving were quickly narrowing.

It took us about an hour to assess our situation and determine the best way out of Nha Trang. Some of us had small radios and tried to tune in for the latest news from the Voice of America (VOA) station[72]. That day, according to VOA, the Nha Trang military defense had already broken down, and the city was under the control of the North Vietnamese troops. This news confused us.

As the sun slowly set to the west, a military jeep with an open roof suddenly came to a screeching stop in front of our barracks. Many members of our group rushed out and jumped on it. Unfortunately, by the time I got outside, it was full and jerked forward at high speed, throwing other soldiers clinging to the sides out of balance. I didn't know where the jeep was going, but my common sense told me it was heading for the runway.

"STOP, STOP, STOP!" I yelled in vain, lifting the M-16 assault rifle to shoulder level amid the blowing dust the jeep left behind.

Through the dust, I aimed the barrel of the gun at the jeep full of my friends and other soldiers. My index finger was about to touch the cold trigger when my eyes briefly drew an imaginary straight line through the M-16 front sight post, coincidently connecting with a familiar face in the back of the runaway jeep. In a split second, through the sight post, a terrified facial expression filled the tiny hole, causing an intense horror to rise within me. Instantly, my mind flashed back to a blurry image of my face, wide-open eyes full of tears, staring at my brother's coffin that had his senseless body. Pressure filled my nostrils as my hands were shaking with strong resistance against pulling the trigger. I quickly lowered my left arm, carelessly dropping the M-16 rifle nose down toward the ground. I stood there shocked while the jeep hastily sped away, dragging soldiers along, clinging to its sides.

QUI CHẾ XUẤT TRẠI

NGÀY THƯỜNG : 16 giờ 00 đến 21 giờ
CHIỀU THỨ BẢY : 12 giờ 30 đến 21 giờ
CHÚA NHẬT và NGÀY LỄ : 07 giờ 30 đến 21 giờ

CƯỚC CHÚ :

• KS chỉ được phép xuất trại trong phạm vi Biệt Khu Thủ Đô.
• Giấy phép này CHỈ ĐƯỢC CẤP PHÁT cho KS khi có lệnh xuất trại của Chỉ Huy Trưởng/TTHLKQ hoặc Bộ Chỉ Huy/Liên Đoàn Khóa Sinh.
• KS phải hoàn trả giấy phép này khi rời quân trường.
• Ai lượm được thẻ này, xin chuyển đến KBC 4721/LĐKS.

PHÉP XUẤT TRẠI

TRUNG-TÂM HUẤN-LUYỆN KHÔNG-QUÂN
LIÊN-ĐOÀN KHÓA-SINH

Số 090/KS

CHỈ-HUY-TRƯỞNG TRUNG-TÂM HUẤN-LUYỆN KHÔNG-QUÂN CHO PHÉP :
Khóa sinh LÊ-ĐÌNH-DY   Cấp bậc SSQ
Số quân ████████   Khóa 67 DCSQ
ĐƯỢC PHÉP XUẤT TRẠI THEO QUI CHẾ GHI Ở MẶT SAU.
Chuẩn-Tướng   KBC 4721

Military badge issued after returning from the U.S. (Spring 1975, Nha Trang, South Vietnam)

Picture taken during basic military training at Nha Trang Air Force Training Center. (Summer 1972, Nha Trang, South Vietnam)

With Father at Tao Đàn Garden.

With Mother before going to the U.S. for flight Training. (1973, Tao Đàn Garden, Sài Gòn, South Vietnam)

At Tao Đàn Garden with Aunt Môn and sisters.

With my elder brother and sisters.

With Dũng (my next younger brother) at Tân Sơn Nhất Airport.

With my loved ones and friends (on my left) before departure for the U.S. (1973, Tân Sơn Nhất Airport, South Vietnam)

Mợ at the airport check-in area.

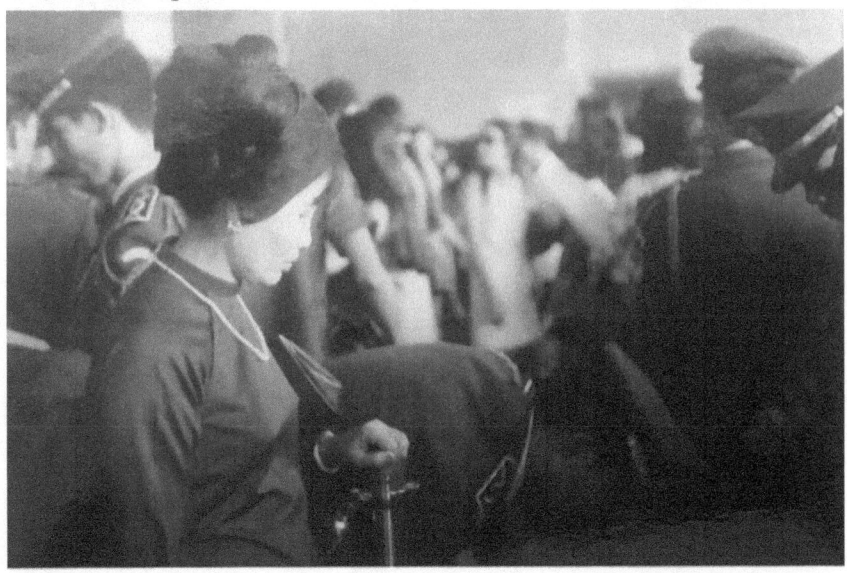

Reception at Lackland Air Force Base. (12/1973, San Antonio, Texas, U.S.)

In the U.S. for flight training. (1973-1974)

In transit to Fort Rucker, Alabama.

Visiting Alamo with international classmates.

**In transit from Lackland Air Force Base to Fort Rucker.
(03/1974, New Orleans, Louisiana)**

South Vietnamese air cadets. I was in the second position from left.

At Fort Rucker.

First row from left: Cường (4th) and me (6th). Flight instructors standing behind.

**South Vietnamese Flight Training Gray Hat Group.
(1974, Fort Rucker, Alabama)**

Refueling.

In my room (Fort Rucker Bachelor Officer Quarters).

**Flight training.
(1974, Fort Rucker, Alabama)**

Flying in formation.

**Ready to go to the airfield.
(1974, Fort Rucker, Alabama)**

With Major General William J. Maddox, Jr.
(12/17/1974, Fort Rucker, Alabama)

With the aviator badge pinned on my uniform and flight diploma held in my hand, I was ready to fight for my country. (12/17/1974, Fort Rucker, Alabama)

**After graduation, a few days before flying home.
(12/17/1974, Fort Rucker, Alabama)**

I couldn't pull the trigger because I thought they might have siblings waiting for them to come home. I had already gone through unbearable grief, continuously mourning my beloved brother, not to mention witnessing countless deaths on television, on the streets, and in my dreams. Death haunted most of my childhood memory. I could not take away the lives of my comrades in arms. I didn't want to see the bloodshed!

In that moment of uncertainty, I became lost. I felt an overwhelming sense of resignation and emptiness as I quietly stood there. Nothing mattered anymore. My head felt like it contained a big, heavy rock. I wasn't sure what to do next, but I knew the black shadows would soon come. We hadn't even engaged with VC, yet we had almost killed each other already.

Finally, I let the M-16 rifle go entirely, dropping it on the ground. Darkness eventually covered the entire area, and I started looking around under the light from the barracks and streets. The whole place looked like a ghost town. People are all gone, I thought. Weapons and junk littered the streets like a disaster area—I guess it was one, really. Unsure of where to go or what to do, I walked in the direction I thought would lead me to the runway. Occasionally, I heard an explosion in the distance and continuous traces of bullets piercing through the dark sky. Nothing scared me anymore. Either I would die, or I wouldn't. So, I kept walking, carrying the weight of my exhausted, soulless body.

While dragging my feet on the deserted road that night, another military truck went by, saw me, and picked me up. I squeezed my body among the other strange soldiers. Eventually, we reached a dark area not too far from the runway. A fairly large number of South Vietnamese soldiers occupied the location, waiting and hoping for flights to arrive from Tân Sơn Nhứt so they could evacuate them back to Sài Gòn. Those soldiers had been there for several hours and had heard that the evacuation had stopped—but they were still hoping for a miracle. My classmates were among the soldiers waiting on that quiet runway in the dark.

It was the very spot the evacuation plan had taken place over a day ago, as my classmates and I were still naively waiting at the base for orders to take our helicopters to the sky and fight. Sitting on the ground with a confused mind and tattered body, I felt humiliated, worthless, and in deep mental anguish. I didn't know what to hope for, and my mind went completely blank, merging into the darkness.

Around midnight, we could hear a distant flying aircraft. We nervously glued our eyes to the open sky, trying to make out the shape of a friendly plane. Finally, a dark gray C-130 Hercules military transport aircraft came into view.

After the plane made its final approach and touched down on the ground, we all ran toward the grassy side of the runway near the end, where the plan would stop. It might be the last evacuation of South Vietnamese military personnel and soldiers out of Nha Trang.

The C-130 planes used during the Vietnam War normally had a capacity of 100 people or fewer. That night, there were a few hundred cramped people on board. Completely exhausted, I tightly squeezed my body among the other soldiers while the aircraft took off. I finally left Nha Trang for the last time. We abandoned the city. Another piece of my country, which I had pledged to protect, was falling easily into the red hands of North Vietnam with no considerable resistance. They trained me to fight, not to run. I had pledged to die for my homeland; then, I was trying to save my own life. But what else was I supposed to do? The political gamble of an extravagant bet by the South Vietnam President and his administration to test the prudence of the U.S. had completely backfired—and the situation was beyond recovery.

We were merely the begrudged soldiers whom our leaders distressingly ordered to abandon our land and retreat. Sài Gòn had no known solid strategic military plans to reclaim the lost territories in the future.

That early morning—only a few weeks before South Vietnam would completely collapse and fall into the red hands—we landed at Tân Sơn Nhứt Air Base in Sài Gòn.

The Fall of Sài Gòn

AROUND NOON ON April 29, 1975, Sài Gòn, once called the Pearl of the Far East, had less than 24 hours before ceasing to exist while her powerful partner, Washington, rapidly launched a massive airlift to save the remaining Americans and Vietnamese collaborators who had ties with the U.S.

By then, the false hope that U.S. military interference would expel the communist forces had completely evaporated—it was gone! Apparently, the allies that had preached the value of freedom no longer considered South Vietnam a critical strategic front to stop the communism "domino" effect[73] in Southeast Asia.

Certainly, no war protesters were calling for North Vietnam to stop their flagrant invasion of South Vietnam—a legitimate country fully recognized by the free world. And unfortunately, there was no way the bravery and desire of the South Vietnamese soldiers to fight to the end could withstand such a fierce invasion strongly supported by a solid coalition of weaponry and aid from the loyal Communist Bloc. I had sensed the demise for months but still held onto faint hopes for a political change; that feeling disappeared completely. I was no longer in denial. Our allies had coldly abandoned South Vietnam despite the potential it opened up for slaughter and mayhem left in the hands of the communists. The black shadows, who had been a part of my dark dreams, were about to return, but this time, as victors with defined shapes and louder voices.

That day, I came home in the early morning—after staying the night near Tân Sơn Nhứt Air Base—still wearing my wrinkled air force flight suit, which I hadn't washed for days. I rushed inside my home after Mother quickly opened the door for me. The store was closed that day, and she was extremely worried. After I stepped inside the house, Mother closed the door behind me and told me to take the military flight suit off. Unintentionally, I didn't pay attention to what she had said. My ears were half-deaf!

While most of my loved ones were safe inside the house, Father was still not home. My elder brother and younger siblings told me they had been waiting for my helicopter. They stood in the open area on the flat roof of our house and, with the emergency signaling mirror I gave them a few days ago, kept flashing it every time a helicopter flew by. But none of the choppers landed!

They saw quite a few military helicopters flying by. One carried many people, including some dangling in midair, clinging to the helicopter skids. To my family's horror, that helicopter eventually crashed a few blocks away. They were terrified, but they kept waiting for me to appear. Then, when I finally showed up, I walked inside the house and completely dissolved my loved ones' hopes of leaving Vietnam that day.

It was downright excruciating to listen to them talk. That was the end of everything. I felt I had failed miserably and was merely a coward who had disappointed them. I had just killed their one dream and hope; with that, my remaining desire to survive ceased to exist. I didn't know what to say, so I sat there expressionless, as if already dead, gazing down in search of something to purge my unbearable mental anguish. My mother and aunt quietly sat in my parents' bedroom, far from the main door. They looked frightened. They had seen what the communist factions did to the landlords and other people in the north in the 1950s.

Mother speculated on the cruelty and atrocities that were likely to come to the people of South Vietnam, including our family. I couldn't stand to hear anything further.

Suddenly, I stood up and went to the stairs that led to the second floor. Then I went to the poor-looking wooden door leading to an open balcony above the storefront of my parents' house in Sài Gòn. I stood there behind the door, motionless and speechless. The door was slightly ajar, letting in the sounds of the noisy street down below. The commotion and chaos overwhelmingly filled my eyes and ears. People were hastily walking toward their homes. Some seemed to run with no obvious purpose. My delusional mind successfully transformed the dynamic commotion from the street into a long, dark tunnel, just waiting for me to enter. There was no future anymore, my mind concluded. And the song of Death hummed through my eardrums.

I sweat profusely in my flight suit and felt a pang of nausea. I turned away from the door and sat on the wooden flatbed for a while. My head pounded hard while my body shook and trembled with horrendous waves of emotion. Then I lifted my exhausted body up and walked toward my unfortunate brother's altar. I stood before the dark brown Formica-laminated cabinet for a few minutes, saying nothing of great importance. However, I finally found the courage to ask him for forgiveness. "Forgive me, Anh Giới," I uttered quietly, raising my head to look at his portrait momentarily with my soulless eyes. Then I crossed the living room to go downstairs. At the bottom of the stairs, I turned left, dashed through the kitchen, and entered the dark shower room. There, I started screaming violently while brutally whacking my head against the dark brick wall.

I don't remember how long I kept banging my head and exploding mentally, but the unbearable anger poured out—uncontrollably. Suddenly, I felt someone yanking me away from the wall and pulling me out of the shower room by force.

My head and heart were wilting under the weight of excruciating pain, as though they were being crushed. My ears were half-deaf but still filled with the frightened, crying voices of my mother and elder aunt as they came running through the kitchen area.

I tried to resist the pulls by grabbing the edge of the shower door, all the while hearing the voice of my elder brother repeatedly asking me to stop while forcefully dragging me out of the dark shower room. I was there—in a dark tunnel! Submissively, I had completely abandoned my desire to live and was ready to hold Death's hands willingly.

"Why can't I just go with him?"

My mind floated crazily, as if out of my body, amid the dreadful crying and yelling of my loved ones. Mother gripped my other arm, pulling and shaking it while crying, just as she had wept for my ill-fated older brother. I saw nothing clearly because tears filled my eyes, which became slivers of cold emptiness. I felt so exhausted! Finally, I let my hands go free, allowing my soulless body to drop, and darkness overtook my empty eyes and broken mind.

I didn't know how long I remained passed out. Later, I awoke and found myself lying on my parents' bed—the same place where, in 1971, I sat motionless, blindly staring at my brother's coffin resting on two wooden sawhorses behind the main door of my home. That afternoon, April 29, 1975, I stared blankly at the old ceiling while someone smoothed out the bruises and bloody scratches on my head with a wet cloth.

Warm tears were quietly rolling down my cheeks. Eventually, the world disappeared again. I was exhausted and eventually fell asleep, still broken beyond recognition in body and mind.

That night, my uncle-in-law and younger aunt took their six small children to the U.S. Embassy, hoping to leave Vietnam in the last hours before the fall of Sài Gòn. Seeing my crumbling heart and soul and realizing it was too dangerous for me to stay, Mother urged me to follow my aunt's family. I quietly listened and did as she said.

Without saying much with goodbyes, I took the red Suzuki motorcycle that Dad and Mother bought for my elder brother and rode it with two of my younger brothers, including Dũng, sitting behind. Upon arrival, we waited all night outside the iron fence until the morning when the last U.S. Marine helicopter took off from the top of the U.S. Embassy in Sài Gòn—never to return.

Disappointed, we went home together, abandoning all hope of leaving Vietnam during the final collapse of Sài Gòn. To make matters worse, amid the chaos, I could not locate my elder brother's red Suzuki motorcycle and completely lost it that day.

THE RED SOCIETY

On April 30, 1975, while Sài Gòn was inhaling and exhaling its last gasps, I went into the kitchen and hid my U.S. flight diploma in the main hollow baluster, which connected the rail firmly at the end of the stairs going up to the living room on the second floor. Then I went to the wooden door leading to the open balcony and stood behind it, watching the street through the gap. With ease, the North Vietnamese soldiers finally flooded into Sài Gòn with T-54 tanks, AK-47 automatic rifles, B-40 bazookas, and a variety of other killing weapons provided by the Communist Bloc.

Our convenience store was closed that day and during the next few days. Then, one day, Mother opened the store for business. She said the store could not be closed forever. We also needed to get out of the house to buy food. Mother had already accepted the reality that if the communists wanted to kill us, they would—and it wouldn't be difficult. Our ongoing existence rested in their hands. And hiding inside the house would not help us survive.

Over the next few weeks, the people of Sài Gòn were slowly shifting back to their usual daily business and activities, but with extreme caution and lifeless eyes.

The victors renamed Sài Gòn as Hồ Chí Minh City (Ho Chi Minh City). Inescapably, I accepted the dark fate. Along with other Vietnamese soldiers from the south, I transformed my military life into a civilian one in the newly established socialist society, but it was difficult.

They scrutinized everything, including our ability to think and speak freely. At the very least, we knew we must say nothing bad about communism and communists if we wanted to live.

On May 14, 1975, Mai and I got married. She was my cousin's high school classmate whom I met a few days after I had come home from the U.S. We conducted our wedding ceremony with a few close relatives on both sides without lengthy traditional Vietnamese wedding fanfare or a reception. It lasted for about an hour. Then, my wife moved in and lived with me at my parents' house.

Shortly after our wedding, my elder brother married his next-door girlfriend. His wife's family owned and managed a bus company, transporting people to and from many destinations, particularly the western provinces of Vietnam during that time.

It would not take long for the newly established socialist government to round up South Vietnam's soldiers and officers to face war repercussions. They called the former freedom fighters "puppet soldiers" and told us to register immediately at the district security offices. We were told that non-commissioned officers and administrative personnel from South Vietnam would undergo a "three-day reform study."[74]

Those people had to report to a designated location in the morning to be "re-educated" and then would return home the same day. The victors induced the commissioned officers and high-ranking administrative personnel into a different "reform study," directing them to bring belongings, food, and money—enough for a "short period" because it would only last about "ten days."[75]

So, my father, uncle-in-law, elder brother, Mai, and I registered for the "reform study." Prior to April 1975, my father was an Army captain at Quang Trung Training Center. Uncle Long was also a captain in the Army Rangers, who married Father's youngest half-sister. They had six children. Their oldest son was about 13, and the youngest was about three. My elder brother, just married, was a Red Soil Junior High School biology teacher and a second lieutenant in the Army Reserve.

During those early days of the Vietnam socialist regime, Father told us of his experience living with the communists in the 1950s before fleeing to the south in 1954. He insistently advised me not to report as a former military pilot.

"Don't say that!" Father raised his voice. He then gave Uncle Long, his brother-in-law, similar advice, urging him not to mention his past military counterintelligence activities.

Father thought my elder brother's situation seemed relatively safe since he was formerly a teacher and had never fought during the war. He joined the South Vietnamese Army Reserve to meet the requirements for teachers during the war. Mai was a student scholarship processor working in the Department of Education in Sài Gòn; she should be fine.

So, in May, my wife and I reported to the district security post in her neighborhood. She registered as administrative personnel, and I claimed I was an aircraft mechanic from South Vietnam. Then, in June, together with many other people, I attended a "three-day reform study" on the playground of a local high school nearby in Hồ Chí Minh City. But Mai had to ride a bicycle every day to Tự Do Street near the Department of Education for almost an entire month for the "three-day reform study."

During that time, my father, elder brother, and uncle-in-law registered as former commissioned officers. Unfortunately, the "reform study" for the military officers and high-ranking personnel from South Vietnam became much longer than we all expected or were told. As Father had suspected, the victors kept many of them in isolated hard labor camps throughout Vietnam for a very long time; few people who had reported returned home early. Eventually, we finally learned of many other false promises from the communists.

None of my loved ones who had reported to the socialist government came home in ten days. Except for my elder brother, no one returned home, even within a few months.

During the war, my elder brother's in-laws had connections with VC and underground communist cadres, I was told, through family relationships and also because of their transportation business operations.

Sometimes, they had to deal with the communist factions on certain routes, which VC controlled. So, when my elder brother was in the "re-education" camp, his wife's family capitalized on those relationships and successfully attained the early release of my brother. He eventually came home—but still not within ten days, a month, or the "short duration" promised by the government.

During the early months of the socialist regime, after we had married, my wife became pregnant. We were both happy but also shared concerns about our jobless situation and how we could raise our child. My wife was an administrative clerk in the former Department of Education, responsible for student scholarship applications and related educational programs. After the war, the victors permanently dismissed her. During that time, it was very difficult for personnel and officials from the former regime to get and hold a job within the "revolution government."

So, neither she nor I had a job. We both depended on our mothers to survive and raise our future child. My wife, who had never experienced a rough life before, suddenly faced extreme difficulties adjusting to poverty. Meanwhile, my mind lingered on the past—it was too difficult and uncertain to look ahead to the future.

I didn't know how to support my family financially and prepare to have a child. We were unprepared and clueless concerning re-establishing our life in the socialist society that had abruptly formed in the south.

My wife's grandmother.

Her father passed away in 1963.

Her mother.

My aunt-in-law, Aunt Bích, took great care of our son.

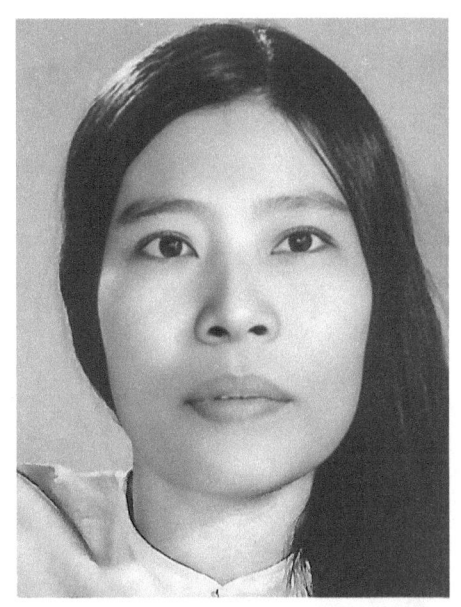

**My wife's family.
(Pre-1975, South Vietnam)**

Before North Vietnam took over the south, my wife's family was prosperous. After April 1975, they eventually became so poor that they saved every "sous" or penny they made to buy food for our son. So poor that they could only buy beef-noodle soup or Phở for him without meat because it was cheaper that way. While I was away from home and his grandma and mother worked during the day, my wife's aunt devoted her time to caring for our son.

Mother and daughter.

Mai.

Mai at the age of four.

**My small family.
(Pre- and post-1975, Vietnam)**

Me and my 3-year-old son.

One day, in response to the government's widespread economic plan and with many other city people, I volunteered to go to an area called the "new economic zone"[76] to clear acres of land for agricultural and housing development purposes.

It was located around 32 km west of Hồ Chí Minh City. There, hundreds of people, including me, worked very hard under the burning sun or heavy rain to dig long canals and ditches.

At lunchtime, there was not much food to eat. Similarly, they provided only a bowl or two of cooked rice in the evening with small pieces of dried salty fish to consume. At night, groups of ten to twenty people slept together on bare ground in one of the thatched houses scattered around the "new economic zone."

There was no electricity. Neither showers nor restrooms were available. We had to find somewhere nearby without many people around to release our waste when needed.

One day, they gave us some rations—rice, sugar, and salt—to bring home to feed our families. Our lifestyle had suddenly gone back several decades. Our well-being was in free fall. Darkness had already come, and all I could think about was the doomed future of my loved ones.

After all, mine had already sunk deep into the mud—disappeared! The omen hidden inside the 10-year-old boy's mind triumphantly resurfaced in the fallen pilot's ragged mind and tamed body. My "psychic powers" seemed focused solely on speculating on who and when Death might strike. And there I was, in the mud, deep in the new ditch under the burning sun, with absolutely no clue how to save myself, let alone my loved ones.

I wanted to be a "good citizen" as best as I morally could under the laws and rules of the socialist society and Vietnam communists. But the government's poor treatment of our people and my hard labor contribution to the new socialist society while my family was starving didn't sit well with me.

After working in muddy ditches for a few weeks, I quietly left the "new economic zone" and returned to my family. I stayed at my parents' house with my wife, who was carrying our first child. Living with my family also became increasingly difficult, as Mother had many mouths to feed, but few were working. We all depended on Mother's small convenience store, which produced little income to support the entire family, including my wife and me.

During that time, the food shortage in our family was disturbingly visible. Mother had to buy cheap "bo bo"—very tough grains, which farmers normally feed pigs or horses. She cooked them in large quantities for the entire family to eat instead of white rice. Rarely did we have a little piece of meat to eat.

My wife was uncomfortable with the situation and tried to get extra food from her mother to supplement our daily meals, nourishing her pregnant body's demands while living with me at my parents' house. Sadly, it backfired, and we received serious criticism from my family for those attempts.

My elder brother's family, fortunately, was financially alright. After he had come home from the "re-education" camp, he helped run the transportation business of his wife's family. Graciously, he occasionally gave Mother some money to soften the severity of our family's impoverishment.

My elder brother could also get me a job as a ticket seller for his in-laws' company. I accepted the job but only worked for about a week, then quit simply because I didn't like it. I hated the boring, repetitive nature of the job!

My mother and elder brother were very upset, but no matter how much they rightfully berated me for quitting, I never returned to work—even though I was dead broke.

Sometimes, my wife and I returned to her mother's house and stayed for a few days or longer. Her home was only a few kilometers away. One early morning, while I was at her home sitting and drinking tea in the living room, three district security cadres with AK-47 rifles suddenly appeared in front of the house. Without knocking, they pushed the half-closed door open and rushed into the living room, located just a few meters behind it. As soon as they were inside the house, they suspiciously looked around, finally zooming in on me—the only man in the house.

"Do you live here?" one guy asked while looking at me.

"No!" I stood up, sensing something bad was about to happen.

"Follow us!" he ordered, without even asking who I was.

Shockingly, Mai just stood there, unmoved! Her mother rushed out of the kitchen and tried to explain that I was her son-in-law. Ignoring her, they kept pushing me out of the front door using the AK-47 rifle nozzle. I walked out of the house, saying nothing. My mother-in-law followed them from behind, lightly grabbing the cadre's khaki shirt sleeves while begging them to let me go.

I followed the cadre in the bộ đội uniform while the other two guys walked behind, knowing they might shoot me if I acted up or resisted. I realized my time might be up, and I feared I might not see my wife and family again. Since the day they stormed into Sài Gòn, I accepted they could kill anyone, including me, with no mercy. The situation scared me, but I could hide my fear. So, I walked down the narrow alley leading to the district security office without stopping. But I knew why they had come.

There, in a room with other district security cadres, they searched my body and took out everything I had in my pockets, including my identification paper.

In the next hour, they interrogated me, repeatedly asking why I was in their district. My paper showed I lived at my parents' house in another area—a 20-minute walk!

They wanted to know why I didn't get a paper from the local district security office to allow me to visit or stay in another area of Hồ Chí Minh City.

The men questioned me about my past and what I did during the war, interrogating me as if they were trying to find any inconsistency in my statements that would give them a reason to kill me or send me to one of the "re-education" camps in the jungles.

Persistently, I gave them the same information about me, including that I had completed the "three-day reform study" and volunteered for hard labor. The only thing I left out was that previously, I was a military pilot from South Vietnam.

Eventually, they ran out of questions. I guess I didn't seem dangerous. A few weeks of digging new ditches under the burning sun at the "new economic zone" without eating much had made me look like one of them when they first intruded into Sài Gòn during the Tết Offensive or on April 30, 1975. I become thinner with a poor-looking appearance. I looked neither intelligent nor arrogant. Finally, one of them made a gesture to let me go.

"Go!" he said. "Next time, you must ask permission to come here and report to us whenever you stay at your wife's house. You understand that?"

"Yes, comrade!" I replied, trying to hide my anger and annoyance at the unreasonable instructions.

Why should I need their approval to go to my mother-in-law's house, which was only a few kilometers away from my home? I completely forgot they could have easily killed me.

The irritation and frustration, mixed with my lingering depression, gave me the strength to think they were stupid. But they surprised me. They didn't beat me up during the interrogation, so I considered it a rare lucky day for me!

Shortly after that, I walked home unharmed.

My wife and her family were grateful for the relatively easy release. When I told them the story, they got very nervous each time I called the district security cadres "stupid!"

After the incident, I never told my mother or anyone else in my family that it had happened. I didn't want to cause any more fear. I knew Mother and how she would feel about the situation. Even though the incident ended peacefully, I became deeply concerned. To avoid being scrutinized by the district security cadres again, my wife and I stayed at my parents' house longer and visited her family less frequently.

Then, one day in February 1976, my wife felt the movements in her belly grow more and more erratic. That morning, my wife gave birth to our first beautiful son. It was the first moments of pure joy and great happiness we had experienced since the start of Black April. I became a father at 22—too young, financially ruined, and without a job.

In the following months, my wife and I continued to stay at my parents' house. Mother wanted to teach my wife how to care for herself after delivery according to the traditional ways from the north and to help feed our son. But during the remaining months of 1976, it was a tremendous challenge for my wife and me to feed our newly born child and survive the deteriorating family situation.

Although I had significantly curtailed my habit of hanging out with friends, sometimes for days at a time without coming home, it didn't financially help us much. My mind often fondly recalled the past and that deep sense of pride that came with being an air force pilot from the Republic of Vietnam.

I still didn't like the ticket-selling job. Of course, as a result, I had no money to support my family, nor did Mai have a job!

We frequently had serious arguments, trying to figure out ways to survive under the socialist regime. We were also struggling to eliminate the economic burdens placed on both of our families because we had no income—not even enough to feed our son.

While we continuously fought against our internal discomfort, we alternately went back and forth between both houses. Stubbornly, I had never reported or asked for the district's approval to allow me to stay at my mother-in-law's house. I didn't really care if they dragged me to the district security office at gunpoint again for interrogation. I was becoming overwhelmed and constantly bombarded with too many life issues, including noticeable signs of increasing friction between me, my next younger sister, and the wife of my elder brother.

Being poor was a sin. At the very least, it discredited whatever genuine intent or spiritual wealth one might have and formed a basis for spreading gossip and increasing segregation of the family. I went from being a trusted national hero in our family to being ostracized in a short time. I became worthless—an outcast who saw personal destruction as the only likely outcome of my predicament.

"Peace" from the Paris Accords

ONE SOMBER MORNING, the omen from my darkest dreams returned with a vengeance when Death suddenly maneuvered his bloody scythe again.

That day, the district security office sent someone to my younger aunt's house and asked her to come to their station. When she arrived, they gave her the death certificate of her husband, whom the victors had previously sent to one of the "re-education" or concentration camps somewhere in the north.

They stated her husband "defiantly went against the revolution, didn't want to be re-educated, tried to escape the camp, was shot to death." According to the government-issued death certificate, the victors killed him on July 13, 1977—about two years after he had reported for the "ten-day reform study."

They dumped his body somewhere in the Hoàng Liên Sơn mountain area in the north where Hà Nội was openly waging their repercussions and bloody vendetta policy.

The entire sky must have collapsed and fallen upon my aunt in those moments. I could feel what she was going through because I had been there, lost in that same strange dimension—like a living death. Vividly, I recalled crying incessantly and wanting to die, and I knew she must feel the same. I felt as if I had lost a precious blessing in my life, and in its place, there was a frightening, depressing void in my broken heart and collapsing mind.

Certainly, she must have felt the same. The district security cadres didn't even have the courtesy to appear in person at my aunt's house to inform her of the news. She had to go to their office to get her husband's death certificate—without his body. There, in their comfortable, secure office, they heartlessly gave my aunt the chilling news by handing her a piece of paper imprinted with her husband's fake crime and date of death.

**Aunt Mi, Uncle Long, and us.
(1960s, South Vietnam)**

Aunt Mi and me.

Aunt Mi and Brother Dũng.

My aunt and uncle's wedding. (Sài Gòn, South Vietnam)

From left: Aunt Thủy, Aunt Mi, Aunt Yên, and Aunt Môn.

```
BỘ QUỐC PHÒNG                CỘNG HOÀ XÃ HỘI CHỦ NGHĨA VIỆT NAM
ĐOÀN                              Độc lập – Tự do–Hạnh phúc
Số:
                                Ngày      tháng      năm 1978

                           G I Ấ Y   B Á O   T Ử
         Kính gửi : UỶ BAN NHÂN DÂN
                              Thành phố  Hồ Chí Minh .
ĐOÀN      xin trân trọng báo để quý bạn rõ :
— Anh ....                                        tuổi .1939
— Là . Đại uý. ....      tình báo kỹ thuật , ( Nguy ) .
— Sinh quán tại .              Hà nội
— Trú :                                   TP Hồ chí Minh .
— Đi tập trung học tập cải tạo ngày .15.tháng . 6 . năm 1975
— Đã chết ngày .  .tháng .  . năm 1977.
— Vì Ngoan cố chống đối cách mạng, Không chịu cải tạo ta chốn trại bị bắn chết
— Địa điểm mai táng tại Đồi
                              Thứ .. Hoàng Liên Sơn .
— Đơn vị chịu trách đã tổ chức mai táng cho anh
                      theo đúng chính sách nhân đạo của Đảng
và Nhà nước Cách mạng , có bia ghi dấu mộ phần , có hồ sơ tử
vong và sơ đồ mộ địa điểm mai táng hiện lưu trữ tại đơn vị .

                            ĐỀ NGHỊ QUÝ BAN
— Báo cho thân nhân anh ....
— Là Vợ
— Hiện ở
                                                    biết.

                              (HU-TRƯỞNG ĐOÀN


Ghi chú: Giấy báo này có hai bản, một bản thông báo về Uỷ ban
         địa phương , một bản giao   gia đình thân nhân anh
                          để khi   thông báo được chép đi
thăm mộ chỉ thì dùng giấy này là  phương tiện giao dịch ./.
```

"Cause of Death: Defiantly went against the revolution, didn't want to be re-educated, tried to escape the camp, was shot to death." (Translated from the Notice of Death)

**The Notice of Death from the Socialist Republic of Vietnam.
(1977, Vietnam)**

... unwavering uncle-in-law, whom the communist victors executed, throwing his body into the wilderness of the Hoàng Liên Sơn mountains.

My younger aunt, a beautiful woman, became a widower at an early age. She never remarried, devoting her entire life to raising six small children.

"Peace and Happiness" after 1975.

Aunt Mi. (2016, Orange County, California)

Isn't That Really Sad?
(1979, Christopher Le)

I love you, Mom!
Lê Xuân Trường

They didn't even allow my aunt to have her husband's body back for a proper funeral. By the time we received the news, his killers had already thrown his body away, dumping it somewhere in the Hoàng Liên Sơn mountain area.

When my aunt came to our home to tell us, I cried tears from the deepest reaches of my heart while looking at her and thinking about their six young, innocent children. They had just lost a father at an age when they could barely realize the absolute cruelty of life and the world surrounding them.

I lost the use of my tongue—there were simply no words! Something painfully clenched my heart as I sat there with a deep mental agony fiercely spreading through my mind. Another death of a loved one caught me off guard, and a piece of my already-broken heart crumbled! I could not stop the flow of my turbulent anger boiling in my blood. I thought I would go insane.

I felt like Death had been waiting in silence, ready to pounce at the moment it was least expected, yanking one of us out of our miserable lives. The 10-year-old boy's omen from the psychic nightmares creepily crawled out from a subconscious place in my mind; I believed it was real.

That day, I left my house and wandered, with no purpose, through the streets under the gloomy shadow of the Sài Gòn ghost. I walked for hours, eventually sleeping under a big, old oak tree in the Big Lady Garden until the morning sun rose.

My uncle-in-law was a good and brave man. He served in the South Vietnam Ranger Corps several years before my older brother joined the army. When I got home from the U.S. flight training program at Fort Rucker in 1974, I bought him a beautiful Texan leather belt as a gift. He told me he liked it.

He and I got along very well, and I loved him just like my father. Whenever he was in town, after a long fight somewhere against the communist aggressors, he always visited and took us to "Phở Tầu Bay" or "Airplane Phở" restaurant. Together, we ate the delicious steaming Phở—the famous Vietnamese soup served with white rice noodles and thinly sliced pink pieces of beef mixed with basil leaves, green and white onion, and throat-burning spicy peppers.

My father was very strict with his children. My uncle-in-law was easygoing, funny, and simple.

He frequently played and joked with my younger siblings and me while visiting my family in Sài Gòn. It was an unbearable shock to learn they had killed him. And the victors had imprinted a scar in my heart that I would never forget. He was dead just like that, tossed somewhere in the wilderness of the Hoàng Liên Sơn mountain area, leaving a wife and six children behind. One of them was still a babbling toddler, trying to say bố[p] with his innocent lips during the dark days of his life without a father.

The death certificate from the "revolutionary government" stated that they shot and killed him. It was a pre-printed notice for former military officers and high-ranking personnel who had surrendered and gone to the disguised communist gulags. They had fallen into the "ten-day reform study" trap deceitfully devised by Hà Nội to satisfy the north's thirst for vengeance. Before or after they killed a prisoner, the government only needed to fill in a few lines of personal information and scribble a couple of short sentences accusing the victim of fake crimes.

Tragically, nobody knew how many former military officers the victors killed like that in the concentration camps throughout Vietnam under the communist regime.

But the world warned there might be hundreds of thousands of people whom the communists had executed or killed in the Soviet-style gulags[77]. Nobody, except the victors, knew how many death notices they had pre-printed for the families of those they lured into the disguised "ten-day reform study."

The Vietnamese communists were no strangers in the history of our land, particularly since 1954. Their bloody actions chilled people to the bone: the executions of "evil landlords" under the

---

[p] "Bố": Similar to "daddy" and used by some in the north.

"land reform" initiative in the north during the 1950s, the unmarked mass graves in Huế during North Vietnam's short occupation in the spring of 1968—"Tết of the Monkey"—and the "Red Fiery Summer" invasion in 1972 that forced innocent people from Quảng Trị onto the "Horrible Highway" and to their slaughter.

Then, after their successful invasion of the south, they killed or executed hundreds of thousands of yellow freedom fighters in Hà Nội's gulags, disguised as "re-education" camps, to please the vendetta-seeking souls of the victors.

The arrogant and exuberant victors of the socialist ideology, carrying the meaningless sugar-coated promises of "Independence-Freedom-Happiness," had coldly taken away many beloved fathers of the innocent children of South Vietnam. My younger aunt, a beautiful woman, became a widower at an early age. She never remarried, devoting her entire life to raising six small children.

The "reform study" and prosecution of unjustified or faked "war crimes," without legitimate trials and using force to punish South Vietnamese military officers and officials instead of reconciliation, were indelible mistakes.

The Vietnamese communists had lost an excellent opportunity to heal the old scars from the long, excruciating war, instead choosing to kill people over ideological differences.

The wound may never heal at all after it created so many dead souls and broken hearts amongst Vietnamese families who have lost spouses, parents, children, siblings, and friends—because of the cruel retaliation disguised as the "reform study" or "re-education program" in the "paradise" of the communists.

Two years later, one of the unyielding Vietnamese refugees and a fellow exile, the oldest son of my deceased uncle—an indomitable yellow freedom fighter killed in the communist concentration camp—was wandering alone in the Galang Refugee Camp at 14. Through the lyrics he composed, *Isn't That Really Sad?*, the boy still mourned deeply from a writhing, broken inner soul and a permanent, piercing pain in his chest.

The sadness of a broken heart, so deeply embedded in the flows of the musical notes, echoed within Vietnamese communities worldwide, causing endless tears from those in exile. They will never forget, even for a few brief moments, the deadly fates forced upon those when we lost our free Vietnam.

The South Vietnamese people still see evidence of the effects of North Vietnam's concentration camps, which imitated the work of the Soviet Union, their big brother. In the name of the delusional "paradise," the communists broke many families from both the north and south, causing endless tears and permanent scars in their hearts and souls.

This horrifically dark time will never cease to exist in Vietnam's history and has already deeply imprinted on the hearts and minds of hundreds of thousands of family members, children, and the next generations of families who had suffered senselessly over the effects of what the victors called "re-education."

Isn't that really sad?

We inherited a 4000-year-old civilization, which had no atrocities until the north indoctrinated communism and foreign ideology into the beloved, free country of the yellow people.

Wars are always deadly—but with communism, particularly in Vietnam, even the prospect of peace did not stop the communists from believing in deleterious means and killing to justify their cause.

A Surprise Raid

THEN ONE DAY, in 1978, Father finally came home from the "re-education" camp. Even though it was painful to witness his weakness and fragile physical appearance, we were all so happy to have him home safely.

He used to be a healthy man. Sadly, when Father came home, he looked more like an opium addict.

He was very thin and frail. His hair had turned mostly white. He had also grown a long white beard. The victors eventually let him go because he was so sick and unable to do any hard work or produce anything for them. He hadn't appeared to have committed any "high crimes" except that he was an ex-army officer who trained South Vietnamese soldiers to use communication equipment. It took several months for Father to recover from severe malnutrition.

Unfortunately, our daily meals with little meat didn't help him much at home—but his will and mind remained strong.

After Father recovered some strength, he bought a few repair tools for bicycles and set up a spot on one of the major streets intersecting the narrow alley where my wife's family lived during that time. His primary purpose was to avoid the communist cadres' eyes and show they had fully "reformed" him.

Every morning, he stayed there all day to repair flat tires or fix broken bicycles for a few bucks. Eventually, the district security cadres didn't seem to bother or care about him because he was simply a poor old man fixing bicycles on the street. He didn't look like someone who could pose any harm to the socialist society.

~

MY MOTHER HAD an older brother and other relatives still living in Vĩnh Yên in the north. One of her nephews was a military nurse from North Vietnam. After the fall of Sài Gòn, his unit went to Hồ Chí Minh City and was embedded inside a military hospital.

He often visited my mother while working there. I met him at my parents' house a few times. He knew I was in the U.S. for military training, which I told him. Once, he told me how much he liked my old air force uniform vest and offered to pay for it. His family still lived in the north, where it would freeze during the winter. My old dark Navy-blue officer vest was thick and still looked like new. It would be good for him to wear when visiting his family in the north during the winter, so I gave it to him for a few bucks.

One day, while at my parents' house, he told me the military hospital where he worked was looking for someone to teach English to bộ đội physicians. They wanted to improve their professional knowledge and skills by reading medical books written in English. He asked if I would be interested since he knew I had lived in the U.S. for over a year and spoke English.

Right away, I told him I was interested.

A few days later, my cousin asked me to come to the base to meet with someone, and I did.

A week later, I got the job. It was a part-time role teaching medical doctors how to read and write in English. The pay wasn't great, but it was better than nothing and would help pay for milk for my son. It also gave me a solid new identity, which might soften the image of my past military involvement in the former regime. They gave me a paper badge to enter the military base, which was off-limits to civilians and prohibited from the ex-military personnel of the "puppet government."

Three nights per week, I rode my old bicycle easily through the guarded gate of the military hospital with my badge, which was signed by the commanding officer of the base. The paper had an imprint of a red military emblem encircling a star and other military symbols printed inside. With that pass, I could go freely inside the base to teach English without security escorts or concerns regarding my presence at the hospital.

The physicians and nurses who worked on the base were kind. They treated me with respect. For several months, I gradually became their friend and trusted teacher. In the evenings, I spent about an hour on base teaching them how to write, read, and speak English. During the day, I often sat in the hospital library doing literature research and reading medical books to educate myself.

Many of the children of military personnel stationed there often came on base and played in the library. Sometimes, I sat down with them to tell stories and teach them a few English words. Most of the kids spoke Vietnamese with strong accents from the north. The head of the library, a young lady about my age, also became my friend. She welcomed me cheerfully whenever I came to play with the kids. People I met and talked to over the course of my days there didn't seem to care much about my past, whatever it might be. They never asked, and I told them nothing about my military background with the ex-regime.

One evening after a long English class, a soldier with an AK-47 rifle strap over his shoulder came into the classroom and asked me to follow him. He said the commanding officer wanted to see me in his office.

By that time, although I knew quite a few bộ đội soldiers and military officers on base, the request still worried me. It was late in the evening, and the subconsciousness of a fallen pilot suddenly opened a dark inner space full of concerns. For the last few months, I had never met the commanding officer. He was probably one of those fierce commanders who slept and moved with his soldiers along Hồ Chí Minh Trail to provide medical support to Hà Nội's regular army troops during the war. He might have experienced many close encounters with death and survived the worst hardships of war imaginable.

When he asked his guard to bring me to see him, I suspected it might not be about something good. And it rang a chilling alarm in my ever-vigilant mind. What does he want?

While walking with the guard to the commander's office, I quickly contemplated what I might have to say—particularly about my past in the former Republic of Vietnam Air Force. What does he want? I quietly asked myself, repeatedly, with a nervous feeling in my gut, fearing bad things might be coming.

After a short walk, we entered another building and arrived in front of an office. The guard lightly knocked on the door.

"Come in!" I heard a voice with a southern accent coming out of the room. The guard slowly opened the door and gestured for me to walk in. Once I was in the room, he quietly closed the door behind me and stood outside.

It was an office with a large old desk, a few wooden chairs, and bookshelves. My heart was beating a little faster than normal. The ceiling was low, making it more difficult for me to breathe. A man in uniform with an open collar stood up from the chair and walked toward me.

"Chào Thầy!"[q] he smiled warmly, extending his hand to shake mine. I respectfully shook his hand and greeted him back.

"Yes, Commander!"

"Sit down, please," he said in a friendly manner, pulling a chair to the front of his desk.

"Thank you, Commander." I sat down, cautiously trying to guess what I should expect from the situation.

The commanding officer was a colonel. He was a middle-aged man, probably twice my age, and stood about my height with salt-and-pepper hair. His face looked humble and honest, but he wore many telltale characteristics of one who had faced many hardships. He was not born in the north. His voice was friendly and warm with a southern accent. I believe the north recruited him to join the National Liberation Front—formed by North Vietnam during the early years of the Vietnam War in the 1950s.

The commander did most of the talking for the next 20 minutes, but the exchanges were cordial.

I only responded when needed. He asked a few things about my family, but it seemed he was merely trying to make conversation. Before granting me access to his base, he or somebody must have already asked my cousin, who worked there, to learn about me. Then he talked about his family.

With a son and daughter around 11 and 14, he was wondering if I could go to his house a few days per week to give paid English lessons to his children. Both he and his wife were working full-time. I guessed his wife might also have come from the south during the early years of the Vietnam War.

His offer astonished me! I slowly exhaled with an enormous sense of relief. A bộ đội colonel wanted me to come to his house to teach his children English without their parents present?

---

[q] "Chào Thầy!": "Greetings, Teacher!" or "Hello, Teacher!"

Didn't he know I was from the "puppet regime"—he had to be aware of that, right? I was trying to reason with myself to see if he was sincere.

"If you can't, that's fine," the colonel said in response to my hesitation to accept the offer immediately.

"No… no, I can teach your children. I can come," I quickly told him. "Where do you live?"

"Great! I will give you the address and show you how to get to our house," he said. He seemed happy with my response. Shortly after, I said goodbye to him and left the base feeling good about the encounter and prospective position.

Subsequently, over the next several months, two times a week during the day, I rode my old bicycle to the colonel's house to teach English to his children. His two-story townhouse was about 25 minutes away from my parents' house. His children were friendly but didn't know a single letter of the English alphabet. So, I taught them slowly from the beginning. Many times when I came, they were home without their parents.

One day, the colonel's wife came home early while I was teaching. She looked a little older than he was, probably because of her darker skin. We talked for a few minutes, and then she went upstairs. She also seemed nice and didn't appear concerned about my presence in her house with her children.

I gave private English language lessons to the colonel's children for almost an entire year. The children liked me and might have told their parents about our interactions. Eventually, the military hospital—probably under the colonel's orders—allowed me to buy essentials such as rice, milk, salt, meat, and other miscellaneous items at the military discount price. That year, I became quite busy teaching and trying to learn as many medical terminologies as possible in English.

One day, a physician gave me an old French-English-Vietnamese medical dictionary, which they had published in the north a few years back, as a personal gift. He signed his name on one of the front pages of the book. It truly surprised me. He was one of the bộ đội physicians who entered Sài Gòn during the early days of the intrusion. He was around 35 and had a kind-looking face. When he talked, he usually smiled with his warm eyes.

Like other people on the base, he treated me with great respect and sympathy. When we talked, we never discussed the past or any current political issues.

After I had taught English lessons for a few months, the base commander called me into his office again. He told me about one of the military pharmaceutical laboratories on the opposite side of Hồ Chí Minh City. They were also looking for an English teacher.

To make a long story short, he referred me to the commander of that laboratory. Subsequently, I also got that job.

While teaching at the military hospital and pharmaceutical laboratory, I found a little peace in the perceived haven. I felt more secure and less stressed by the lingering threats of the socialist state. Whenever I was on base teaching, I felt as though I was somewhere outside of Vietnam. They respected me as a teacher—a human being. Honestly, I will never forget the beautiful hearts and kind treatment I received from those physicians, nurses, and personnel I came to know at the military hospital where I worked as an English teacher. Unfortunately, it didn't last long enough to mend my broken heart and tattered mind.

Then the soaking rainy season returned. During that time, in 1978, I frequently became ill. I didn't know what it was, but I felt tired and sometimes experienced severe headaches and dizziness. I believed the frequent sickness was probably a result of the endless sorrow, mental anguish, and unhappiness of the whole situation.

The money I made from the English teaching jobs produced a very modest salary, barely enough to help my wife feed our son. It was not even sufficient for me to live a healthy life or help my parents to reduce the food shortage burden I had partially inflicted on my family. Living with my parents, I felt like a parasite clinging to a host body to live—and there was no one to blame but myself!

Feeling emotionally uncomfortable, several times when I got sick, I didn't want to stay at my parents' house for fear of an additional burden on them. When I was ill, I often stayed at my mother-in-law's house.

My parents didn't know I was frequently sick because I had never told them and rarely stayed home. One day, Cường, one of my friends from the Gray-Hat Class of 74-40 flight training at Fort Rucker, unexpectedly came to visit me at my parents' house. Mother told him to look for me at my wife's home.

Subsequently, he went there only to find me sick in bed. I could barely sit up to talk with him.

"Why didn't you stay home… did you take any medication?" he asked.

Reluctantly, I told him I didn't want to bother my parents and simply didn't want to take any medication. He sensed I didn't have money. Immediately, he took out some cash from his wallet and wanted me to buy medicines for my sickness. After that, we talked for about an hour. He encouraged me to be strong. He urged me to stand tall, continue to live, and hold hope tightly in my heart. Then he left. His words, in one of my life's darkest moments, awakened me and gave me a sense of purpose.

The next day, I went to the military hospital where I worked. It was not too far away from my wife's home. I wanted to ask my students about how I could get examined there. Since I hadn't come to teach for the past week, my students knew I was sick. I had no medical benefits because I was not a full-time employee.

Thankfully, one of my students, a physician, examined me. He then gave me intravenous therapy, injecting sterile saltwater into my body to provide hydration. He also prescribed an X-ray procedure for my lungs, which, a few days later, revealed nothing suspicious except for a small scar. I told him the scar he saw on the X-ray film had been there since high school.

In 1971, doctors treated me with prescribed penicillin injections to remedy that scar. They could not get rid of it, but neither did the scar grow. Besides, in 1972, I passed the South Vietnam Air Force's medical screening for the pilot program.

After my student had intravenously injected me with the sterile saltwater, I felt much better but didn't return to my parents' home. I went back and stayed at my mother-in-law's house to recover.

Her home was a small two-story wooden row house in a narrow alley. I slept on the cement floor with my wife and son in a room only a few meters away from a deteriorated wooden main door with several small rotten holes. We used that portion of the house as a family room and bedroom for my family.

The house's kitchen was in the back, separated from the family room by a wall with a doorway. In the kitchen and along the partition wall, there was a stairway going up to the second floor.

The kitchen also had an enclosed space for a shower and a restroom in the back. My wife's entire family normally slept on the second floor.

Dangerously, the house design didn't include a back door. The only way to leave the house was through the first floor's main entrance or the second floor's front balcony, a few meters above the ground—far enough to break one's legs if jumping down!

One night, several people suddenly came and violently banged on the rotten door. It was shortly before midnight, and we were all asleep. They were district security cadres!

I was off-guard, naively thinking my part-time job at the military hospital would save me from the complications of my past. I seemed content with my teaching status.

Few people from the ex-regime would have access to the communist military bases in Hồ Chí Minh City, especially to teach English to bộ đội medical doctors. I had a badge signed by the commanding officer of one of the fiercest guerrilla fighting groups in the world. I figured I was safe as long as I worked there and tried not to do anything stupid.

Unfortunately, that false sense of security would quickly evaporate with the appearance of the men who stormed into my mother-in-law's house that night. The continuous pounding forcefully rattled the wooden door frame, only locked by a padlock.

"OPEN THE DOOR… OPEN THE DOOR!"

The pounding reverberated down the entire narrow neighborhood block. It surely woke my entire family up. The loud thumping on the door penetrated the dark alley and probably yanked many unsuspecting people out of their beds. The poundings were so loud that they suddenly yanked our son out of his peaceful sleep. My wife was terrified, recalling the horror of seeing the AK-47 rifle nozzles pushing against my back at the previous house. She got up and held our son in her arms, trying to calm his crying while looking at me desperately. There was no escape path. The communists were right there in front of the house, eager to storm in, I imagined, with guns and bayonets in their hands.

My wife's mother and aunt rushed down the wooden stairs, which made annoying, loud, squeaky noises whenever someone stepped on them. We were still in the dark. My wife's mother turned on the light and quickly pushed me toward the kitchen. She softly told me to let her open the door. I stepped back as far as possible but remained in the front room, letting my mother-in-law unlock the padlock from the main door.

Three men with AK-47 assault rifles in their hands rushed into the room. Two wore civilian clothes, and one wore an oversized dark green uniform. They did a quick survey around the room, and then one paused while looking at me.

"Is that the one?" the one in uniform asked while gesturing toward me. Immediately, the man in civilian clothes looked at me with his provoking face and knocked his head.

"Yes, it's him, comrade!" he said.

For a few seconds, I felt a deep sense of regret. They caught me off-guard. How could I let this happen? Didn't I see that this moment might come? Hadn't I learned anything from the chilling nights during the Tết Offensive, peeping through the cracks in my parents' iron door and following the black shadows' footsteps? Didn't I remember what had happened to the father of one of my childhood friends who lived a few houses away? They executed him in cold blood at night while I was snooping through the door. The black shadows were coming for me this time. It was my turn!

What was I supposed to do? Rumbling thoughts about my fate and stupidity ran through my mind. The man in uniform intruded further into the room and pushed his AK-47 rifle nozzle against my ribs, just below my scarred lung, which was trying to get more air.

"GO!" he screamed at me nastily, repeatedly poking the rifle nozzle into my skinny ribs.

My wife's mother freaked out!

"WAIT! WAIT!" she said, almost yelling at them. "Comrade, he works for the government!"

She desperately tried to stall the men from pushing me out of the door.

"Can I get my pants?" I asked, making a slight gesture toward the dark brown pants hanging on the backrest of the wooden chair near the bed. I was only wearing thin shorts and a light grey striped pajama shirt, acceptable for staying inside but not outside the house.

"NO!" he angrily said, straining his eyes wider and yelling at me loudly.

"I need to get my ID paper!" I kept insisting.

"My wallet is in the pants pocket!"

"NO! GO!" he continued screaming, forcing me to walk out the door. One man quickly took my pants and followed us.

I tried to glimpse my wife and our son one last time before walking out. She cradled him slightly from side to side, trying to soothe his crying.

Even though the light was not bright enough from the milky white neon tube under the ceiling, I could still see that she was also quietly crying. Then they shoved me out of the house and into the dark night.

While dragging my feet in the dark empty alley, my mind devastatingly restored the images of the "Tết of the Monkey" black shadows. They had forcefully returned and were viciously circling me. For years, they had warned me, and I continued to blame myself. I'm ruining my life again, I thought, and this time it may have deadly consequences.

"GO FASTER... FASTER! GO... GO!"

The men pushed me through a dark, narrow alley leading to their district security office while yelling nastily behind me. Their dreadful voices resonated through the night, dominating the lonely, winding path that boasted no other signs of life. But I was sure some neighbors were peeping through their house windows or cracked doors and feeling pity for me.

In a few hours, they may wake up to hear a rumor of a dead man in their neighborhood—my mind continued to play on these thoughts in fear. There will not be any announcements. The victors may not even return the body to my family.

My aunt has never received the remains of her husband, my uncle-in-law. Her six children, including the toddler, didn't have the chance for the closure of seeing their father one last time. Instead, they dumped his body somewhere in the wilderness of the Hoàng Liên Sơn mountains and let earthworms consume it.

I am still one of the lucky ones. I have seen my brother's military coffin solemnly draped with the flag of South Vietnam. We buried him with military honors. We surrounded and embraced his soul when he came home to rest in eternity.

The district security office was not that far, but the walk seemed like a slow-motion video reel of the eternal agony felt by the victim before his death.

My brain was going numb, and my legs didn't want to go faster.

"GO!" One man pushed his AK-47 rifle nozzle against my back again while the one in uniform opened the main door. I reluctantly followed them, walking through the front office, where another man abruptly raised his head from the table near the partition wall, looking over with sleepy eyes. They pushed me into a spacious room in the back and pressed me down on a wooden chair behind the table, which was large but had nothing on it. A bright amber light shone from the old metal cone hanging from the ceiling above the table.

The civilian who took my pants pulled out my severely worn wallet and tossed it to the man in uniform. I had a few bucks and the paper badge from the hospital. He took out the pass and brought it closer to his face, trying to read small letters with squinting eyes. My badge was simply a folded paper about the size of my palm with some personal and military base information on the inner surface.

"What do you do at this base?" he asked, returning my paper to the other man.

"I work there, comrade," I responded.

"DOING WHAT? TALK!"

The man in civilian clothes suddenly stepped closer to the table while nastily snapping at me and raising his AK-47 as though he was about to smash my face with his rifle's dark brown butt.

Luckily, the man in uniform quickly pulled him back.

"Calm down," he softly whispered into the other man's ear. He reluctantly relaxed his AK-47 but said nothing back. Then they all went into the other room.

I wasn't sure why they left. If they wanted to kill me, I thought, they wouldn't shoot me because it would be so loud in the middle of the night. They didn't carry any bayonets. It was possible they were looking for one, so they could slice my throat. That's the most efficient way to kill people without wasting a bullet.

I was sweating heavily! Of course, I was nervous. But I wasn't sweating just because they tried to intimidate me. It was because the room was very humid and warm. The office had no air conditioner. There was no window in the back room. My blood pressure might have also gone up very high.

I was at the bottom of the newly established socialist society where people's lives, like mine, from the "puppet government," seemed easily expendable. I had nothing much to lose except my life, which was no doubt worthless, I thought. But I should not give up. I must be strong, as Cường reminded me a few days ago when I was on my sickbed. I wanted to live, but I wasn't sure how to survive the ordeal. It might be too late to fear death!

A few minutes later, two of those men returned. The one in uniform came out with a piece of white paper normally used by students and an old Bic pen in his hands.

He put them on the table in front of me. His voice suddenly seemed less nasty than when he snapped at me angrily, pushing his AK-47 rifle nozzle into my ribs. I thought he might try to act nice, so I would disclose information, whatever he might try to extract from me.

The provoking guy stood behind him with a grim face and his mouth shut. But he was still looking at me with his owl-like eyes. I didn't know why he looked so hateful!

"Write everything about you," he said. "Where you went to school; what you did after school and in the previous regime; what rank you had; and what you did after the liberation of the south."

He explained slowly while counting each thing he listed using his fingers.

"Don't leave out anything! Include all information about you!" he emphasized. "By the way, how did you get that job at that base?" he asked, bending forward a little with his hands on the table. He was a tall guy.

"My cousin referred me to the job. He is in the regular army unit assigned to that hospital," I said.

I particularly mentioned "regular army unit," which I thought might have a more positive effect and soften his suspicion of me at that moment. It worked! He seemed satisfied with my answer and walked away with the owl-like guy. Then they closed the door and left me alone in the room with little air to breathe.

The room was getting warmer. I tried to piece my past life together one by one. It was an ink pen, so I had to think twice before writing. I was thirsty, which irritated my throat—probably because I was trying to catch more air from the room. I had also not fully recovered from my sickness yet, and the headache's throbbing pain was a constant nuisance. Whenever my brain thought about writing something, my hand wanted to pull it back. Then Father's advice flashed back, "Don't tell them you are a former military pilot!" I have no choice, I thought, but to keep the same lie going!

In May 1975, when the "revolutionary government" ordered South Vietnam's officials, military officers, and soldiers to register for the "reform study," I had claimed I was an ex-military aircraft mechanic, not an air force pilot.

If I reversed and told them the truth this time, I guessed, they might execute or send me to one of the "re-education" camps throughout the jungles up north for lying. But if I kept the same story, I might have a chance. "Learn from the fate of my uncle-in-law!" I said to myself.

I don't recall exactly how long it took to detail my past activities. It must have been at least an hour. Carefully, I scribbled down whatever I could remember about what I did in the past, including my military service in the former regime. Consistently, I maintained I was an aircraft mechanic, trained in the U.S. By the time I had filled up two sides of the paper, I felt exhausted. Then, I tried to read it repeatedly, committing what I had written to memory while pretending I was still writing something.

It was very early in the morning, around 2:00 a.m. The men must have been sleeping. They didn't come in to check up on me. Similarly, like my mother-in-law's house, the district security office had no back door. So, they were not afraid I might try to escape. I took that opportunity to review and learn by heart what I had written on that piece of paper.

Eventually, the man in uniform opened the door and walked in. I tried to open my eyes but could only lift the eyelids partially. I handed him the paper full of my handwriting in ink and waited for him to read.

He quickly scanned through all of them, then left. A few minutes later, he returned and gave me a few more blank papers. He didn't return the one I wrote.

"I want you to write about all of your activities during the war again!" he said, straining his tenacious eyes.

"I did, comrade!" I pretended I didn't understand what he said.

"I want you to write again, everything… everything about you in more detail!" he said with his raised voice and firm jaw.

I quickly grabbed the blank papers and followed his stern order to ease his edginess.

It took me about another hour to write a three-page report. Luckily, since I had memorized what I wrote, I simply expanded upon the ideas to fill up blank pages. While learning how to fly at Fort Rucker, they also trained me in aircraft mechanics, including engines, electrical, and other mechanical systems. Providing more detail about me being a military aircraft technician didn't seem difficult. I intentionally exaggerated those activities and overwhelmed them with technical information about which they were clueless.

When they came into the room again, it was close to 5:00 a.m. All of them returned. I could hear footsteps and motorcycle engine noise from a distance through the front room when they opened the interior door to walk in. Luckily, they left the door open!

The government embedded the district security office within the crowded residential areas. People woke up early, normally to do their business somewhere in Hồ Chí Minh City or at the market nearby. The ghost of Sài Gòn, the Pearl of the Far East, had just risen from her death, giving me a lingering memory of the missing past. If I closed my eyes, which I did for a moment since I was so sleepy, and pretended the collapse of South Vietnam had never happened, I could feel and sense the Sài Gòn's fresh morning breath of drifting Jasmine and other fragrant scents in the air.

But the man in bộ đội uniform painfully brought me back to the cruel reality. Only then could I fully realize and feel the precious value of what I had already lost. Sài Gòn had already vanished, but her soul still lingered around her dead body. I missed her dearly! I felt I had nothing left to hold on to and nothing more to live for. The land I loved—and would still love wherever I might go—was full of sorrow and suffering, particularly for those who had truly put everything on the line and fought for South Vietnam. I had officially become an outcast and a suspected enemy of the state. I was a part of the decaying dead body of Sài Gòn that the communists wanted to dispose of efficiently.

Two civilian men carrying AK-47 rifles stood near the interior door as though they were about to escort me somewhere. The man in uniform approached the table where I sat. I slowly stood halfway and slightly bent forward to hand him the papers I wrote. He quickly grabbed them, pulled another chair near the table, and sat before me. He was probably a few years older than I, but he looked much older with his dark, wrinkled skin and slim body. His shirtsleeves were slightly above his elbows, as though he was ready to beat me up.

I felt exhausted and sick, and I was no longer thinking much about why they didn't just kill me during the night. I knew my life was in their hands. They were not afraid to make mistakes. I thought they would rather kill the wrong man than release a potential "war criminal," as VC used to taunt the American soldiers and us. They executed one of my neighbors during the Tết Offensive, and nobody ever knew why.

After the war, instead of promoting sincere kindness to those who dropped their weapons to unite the war-torn country, they continued to "liberate" people, including my uncle-in-law, who had six young children, all little kids. His wife had no job and very little money. She neither knew the truth about why they killed him nor received his body for a proper funeral. The reality she experienced contradicted the communist propaganda about the "liberation of the south." The victors loudly sang and persistently claimed the "glorious victory of spring" in 1975 and unabashedly declared it a "victory for peace and prosperity." They had already forgotten the bombing campaigns from Washington in the north during the war, which almost forced Hà Nội to surrender[78]. The devastating bombings could have flattened the north's entire military defense systems during their darkest and lowest time. And had it happened, the Vietnamese people could have been enjoying genuine peace, true freedom, and a future full of prosperity and happiness. Hundreds of thousands of former military officers from the south might still have their lives and be living with their families peacefully.

The communists had taken our land by force but had never truly received the welcoming hearts from the southern people—merely the false mass support of those who wanted to survive their deadly wrath. Even those who lived in the north felt bitter about the unexpectedly easy victory of Hà Nội in the spring of 1975[10].

When entering Sài Gòn and other cities below the 17th parallel, the prosperity in the south and the state of the free world, as seen in the remains of Sài Gòn, surprised them as it was completely contrary to the propaganda and brainwashing to which their leaders had subjected them.

Of course, I wanted to live to see my loved ones, and I still remembered what I had promised to my ill-fated brother. In asking me to protect the family, he had laid out a deeper purpose in the subconsciousness of a young boy whose dark dreams had already tattered his mind. Sitting in the district security office with a feeling of dread growing stronger by the moment, I finally understood the will to survive and the justification for living. I could feel the desire that motivated those who tried to escape from the Soviet Union's deadly prison camps.

Looking at the armed men in ready position at the interior door, I thought it might be too late. I should prepare for the beginning of the incarceration, moving from one concentration camp to the next, perhaps passing through where they executed Uncle Long, or the Soviet forced labor camp, "gulag," which Solzhenitsyn described in his novel *One Day in the Life of Ivan Denisovich*.[79] His novel famously depicted a typical day of a man the government accused of acting as a spy and was, therefore, captured and imprisoned in the Soviet gulag system.

It took the man in uniform a while to review the three-page report about me. I hoped he could read and understand most of it.

During the war, some bộ đội from the north could not write or read fluently at all.

If he couldn't understand what I wrote, he might just assume that I was one of the "war criminals" from the "puppet government."

The young men in civilian clothes, with looks of pure hatred on their faces, stood near the door without talking. They were patiently waiting with tight grips on their AK-47 rifles.

They likely assumed they would soon either be killing me or preparing the paperwork to send me to one of the concentration camps in the north. It probably pleased them, as it would make them look good during self-assessments of their accomplishments.

After the fall of Sài Gòn, the "liberation of the south," as the communist cadres arrogantly used to say, generated a new classification of people—the "April-30 Group." This title referred to the group of scoundrels who immediately jumped on the VC bandwagons on April 30, 1975, pretending to be loyal supporters or underground communist cadres embedded in the south during the war. They were barbarians as well. With their very narrow and shallow minds, they were doing everything they could to build up their fake loyal images to survive under the socialist regime and benefit themselves at the expense of the suffering of innocent people.

The men in civilian clothes, including the owl-like man standing guard near the interior door, were from the "April-30 Group." They were waiting for an opportunity to make my life miserable. I could tell from his evil look that the owl-like man would be unlikely to hesitate to slice my throat off with a bayonet just to show he was a genuine loyalist of the newly established socialist state.

"Weren't you an officer from the puppet regime?" the man in uniform suddenly asked. He quickly tossed the written papers on the table. "Didn't you fly during the war to kill the heroes of people?" He called himself and his comrades "heroes of people." And his question suddenly set off a loud alarm in my mind.

"No, comrade. I was a mechanic trained in the U.S. to repair damaged helicopters," I replied, lying consistently.

Nervously, I wondered why he asked those questions. He must have received some information or heard from someone about me being a military pilot during the war.

He might also have gotten his hands on some records from Tân Sơn Nhứt Air Base.

"Were you at Tân Sơn Nhứt Air Base on April 30 or the day before?"

Suspiciously, I sensed he might set up a deadly trap to catch me in a lie.

"No, comrade!"

I was telling the truth. However, my friends and I were not too far away from Tân Sơn Nhứt that day.

"I was at home at least a week prior to April 30." I flatly denied my presence at the base.

"When and how did you meet your wife?"

He suddenly changed the focus but continued asking pointed questions while reading from the papers he held.

That was a tricky question. If there were some underground communist cadres embedded in my wife's neighborhood during the war, they might have seen me. I used to wear the air force officer uniform with a blue flight cap embellished with silver piping. I used to borrow my elder brother's red Suzuki motorcycle to visit my wife-to-be. Luckily, that was a crucial part I wrote nothing about in my completed papers.

"She was my cousin's friend," I responded. Then I explained, "After the liberation, my cousin introduced her to me, and my father wanted me to get married before he left for the reform study."

I told him half of the story but shifted the date of the first meeting with my wife-to-be about six months into the future.

That meant, in my mind, if one of the underground communist cadres saw someone coming to visit Mai, that person could not have been me. Besides, I no longer had the red Suzuki motorcycle. I lost it at the U.S. Embassy on April 29, 1975, a day before VC took the Sài Gòn Capital. After the war, I always rode an old light blue bicycle. I thought my story made sense and was relatively consistent. If I still drove the old Suzuki, that evidence could have proven fatal. Losing my brother's motorcycle might have been one of the best things that had ever happened to me.

As time passed, the interrogation revolved around the suspicion that I might be a pilot and an air force officer from the "puppet government." However, my mind had already cemented the fake story of being an aircraft mechanic to memory, and I would not give up.

Finally, the man in uniform stood up, left with the scoundrels in arms, and disappeared into the front room after closing the interior door, again depriving me of adequate oxygen to breathe. I hoped they would leave the door open for air to circulate through the interrogation room. Around noon, the man in uniform suddenly walked in with my wallet in his hand. He threw it on the table. I had to catch it before it fell off the edge.

"We are going to let you go. Do not go anywhere!" the man said, with his index finger pointing at my face.

At first, I thought he was playing games with me, but then he sounded like threatening. "Stay home until we contact you again!" he said, warning me he would meet with someone from Tân Sơn Nhất[r] to verify what I had written.

He then turned around and walked out of the interrogation room. I stood up as quickly as I could and followed him through the interior door. None of the other guys who came to take me away from my wife's home were there. They were likely in one of the local cafes, drinking coffee while scouting people with fierce owl-like eyes.

After they had let me go, I returned to my mother-in-law's house. And it was the last time I appeared in daylight in her neighborhood.

My wife and her mother and aunt sat dismally in the front room. They didn't know how to get me out of the dangerous situation. It

---

[r] "Tân Sơn Nhất": Formerly Tân Sơn Nhứt Air Base.

seemed hopeless. I was told that earlier that morning, my mother-in-law talked with the district chairperson at his house, and he assured her I would receive fair treatment, whatever that might mean. He told her to go home, wait, and let the district security cadres do their jobs.

My wife's family couldn't believe they had released me, but they were still extremely worried. My wife hadn't slept since last night when they took me away. Her eyes were red and puffy. Our son was sleeping upstairs.

I quickly told them a few things about the interrogation and cautiously explained someone might have informed the district security office about my true military past. I didn't know who could have done that, but I neither had the time nor the desire to find out. There were more pressing matters in my mind.

As these events were occurring, my parents were completely unaware of the dilemma I had found myself in. My mother-in-law didn't tell them. She feared for my life and was nervous my parents might blame her. She asked my wife to tell me to hide somewhere before the district security cadres returned with more questions or worse intentions.

They had tried it twice on me—two interrogations!

"Third time's a charm!" my mother-in-law said.

The situation was grave, and it was too risky for me to stay. So, I agreed with my wife's mother and told them I would leave. Then I went upstairs to hug and kiss our son.

I didn't know when I might return, if at all. But I spoke with my wife, comforting her and promising to visit whenever I could to see them. My wife cried while the cruel reality invaded her mind. We hugged our son close, with hearts breaking, before she urged me to go away.

"Go!" she said with a raised voice, forcing me to leave. Tears streamed down her face. "You've got to go! You must run away from here. We will be fine!" she comforted me while holding our son closely in her arms. "You've got to live, too!" she said, implicitly reminding me not to throw my life away as I'd tried in the past. I bit my tongue and held my lips closed to curb the many emotions that all seemed to want to pour out at once. I kissed them all goodbye. Then I went downstairs, thanked her mother and aunt for caring for them in my absence, and quickly left on my old bicycle.

That day, I felt like someone had ripped the last piece of my broken heart out. I couldn't live peacefully with my wife and son. I was still alive but transformed into an outcast with a battered soul and a deplorable longing for a free world we caught a brief glimpse of before North Vietnam ripped it away.

The socialist state's claws were closing in, creating a ripple effect of fear that surged through innocent minds whose repressed desire was simply to live. They promoted their fictitious ideology, in which the means would justify the end.

This was not how I wanted to live my life. It was not the dream world I envisioned for my loved ones to embrace.

The day I left my mother-in-law's house on a bicycle to go into hiding was the day I determined to defy the impossible nature of achieving my dreams. The more freedom they took from the world I lived in, the less reluctant I was to risk my life to restore it—not only for me but also for my loved ones.

Somehow, I believed Death would strike my loved ones again, which made me fearful, except concerning my own life—I became someone who was no longer afraid to die for what he believed to be right in this dark world.

BOILING HOT WATERWAY

I returned to my parents' home in the afternoon the day they let me leave the district security office. My parents were not aware of the near-missed incarceration. I didn't want to tell them because it would only make matters worse. During that time, I had alternately stayed at my mother-in-law's and parents' houses for a few days, so no suspicions arose.

When I came home, Cậu Mợ sensed nothing unusual about my return. Quickly, I went upstairs to the small room on the flat roof. I had not slept for at least 20 hours, and my body could no longer tolerate the rising physical and mental distress. Immediately, I dropped my entire body onto the bed and fell into a deep sleep. During that slumber, my dream sparked a journey into the unknown!

In the evening, after a long sleep, I sat down in the dining room and told my parents and elder brother I would leave Sài Gòn to go to Bạc Liêu to seek a way for all of us to flee the country. Although the government changed the name of Sài Gòn to Hồ Chí Minh City, many people were still using its original name in their conversations. Bạc Liêu was a small province about 270 km southwest of Hồ Chí Minh City. It was one of the coastal provinces where people went to flee by boat. One of my friends, Tuấn, who lived there, had previously asked me to come and stay with his family.

Father couldn't believe what I had just told the family. My elder brother was extremely nervous about what I said, explaining how risky and deadly to escape from the communist state. He cited brutal stories from the Soviet forced labor camps, gulags, to purge the crazy thought of escaping by boat from my mind.

Mother said nothing, but her wariness was all over her face.

I shook it off, as their negative comments didn't bother me much. Their thoughts were entirely valid. They exposed the reality of the situation—but I knew the reality of staying behind could be far worse.

How can I possibly help my loved ones to escape while I'm in such dire financial circumstances?

I thought about it repeatedly but didn't know the answer. Do I fully understand what the consequences of this move could be and how risky it is? I pondered to myself.

"I will leave in the morning," I said, my voice firm. Then, I asked Mother to tell her nephew, my cousin who worked at the military hospital, that I would be off for a few weeks to recover from sickness. My students knew I was ill, so this would not come as a surprise. I repeatedly told my parents and elder brother not to mention to anyone where I would really be going. The security cadres, if they knew, would likely follow and try to capture me.

Escape Path

I WOKE EARLY the following morning, stood still at my deceased brother's altar, and said goodbye to him. With faith, I believed he would follow and protect me. I spoke aloud about what I was planning to do for the family and repeated my promise to care for the loved ones. Shortly after, I left my parents' house for the western region bus station, where people purchased tickets for travel to the Mekong Delta provinces. The station was a few kilometers west of Hồ Chí Minh City.

The sun was still sleeping when I walked out of the house. I didn't want to leave after sunrise for fear of accidentally running into any district security cadres or "April-30 Group" scoundrels. They used to stroll to the market or cafés in the early morning. It was risky, but I also had to leave early to get a bus ticket.

During that time, many people frequently traveled back and forth between provinces to trade. After waiting a few minutes at the major intersection near the children's hospital, I hopped onto a five-wheel tricycle, already crowded with passengers, and eventually arrived at the bus station.

Very dirty on rainy days, the vicinity of the bus station was a bustling area full of people walking every which way. Last night, the rain had turned the areas of bare ground into a slippery, muddy mess, making it easy for one to fall if not careful. I carried only a few sets of old clothes and miscellaneous personal items in a burgundy cloth bag with a shoulder strap.

With little money in my wallet, I could buy a bus ticket and eat for a few days. I also carried my paper badge from the military hospital where I worked, which was to expire in a few weeks. That was all I carried! Tuấn, single and living with his parents to take care of the family, had said I should not worry about finding a place to stay or food to eat.

It took me almost an entire day to go from Hồ Chí Minh City to Bạc Liêu by bus. I had to cross the Mekong River and the other waterways by ferry.

Along National Highway 1, there were several security checkpoints at major locations. All the buses going in both directions must stop at those key posts. At those checkpoints, bộ đội, regional security, and the "April-30 Group" scoundrels searched the bus passengers, opened containers, and freely confiscated what they deemed "illegal" items under their jungle or fake laws. They yelled at people to get out of the bus, granting them free rein to search every corner of the vehicle and every passenger's seat, including the poor, nervous traders.

That was the first time I went to the western region by bus. I didn't know what they were looking for. Of course, they might want to see if anyone hid any weapons or look for potential "reactionaries"—those who were against the communist government. But after a few trips back and forth, I eventually realized they primarily focused on the poor traders, mostly women, likely to extort bribes.

I later learned many things. Those crooks—sucking blood from poor people along that trading route—were at key points and equipped with weapons, including AK-47s. Many of them were nasty and got mad easily.

When they talked to passengers, their language was rough and disrespectful, without no need to hide it. Occasionally, the searches seemed to last forever, as though they deliberately wanted to find something. The passengers, of course, had to carry their identification papers at all times.

"HEY! Your bag!"

One of the security men climbed up the bus steps, shifted his beady, gunmetal-colored eyes in my direction, and zeroed in on my face. I was sitting next to the steps, therefore an obvious target, but it was also probably because I was the only man sitting in the first few rows on the bus—that and I was wearing a military khaki shirt, which I preferred because of its durability.

After a few trips, I realized why sitting toward the back of the bus seemed psychologically better for traders who wanted to hide small things from those money-thirsty rogues.

By the time those scoundrels reached the end, the hope was that they might have already filled their pockets with more than enough bribes and kickbacks, perhaps that they would be happier and less greedy. When those unabashedly money-hungry young men approached the end of the bus, they were already tired because of the extreme humidity and heat inside the bus under the shining sun.

Obviously, sitting far away from the door felt safer. Unfortunately, it was my first time traveling by bus to the western region, and I was unaware of many tricks the traders had already learned the hard way.

I still had to learn many things to survive those fierce checkpoints. But, for now, I had nothing to hide except my inner resentment, a "reactionary soul," and the determination to take my family away from hell on earth as quickly as I could.

"Here, comrade!" I coldly handled my cloth bag to an "April-30" guy with a crafty face.

He nastily pulled the bag toward himself, inserted his dirty hand inside, and began searching like a chicken digging holes to look for fat worms.

After finding nothing of value, his face twisted to become an even more grim scowl. "Where is your ID?" he asked in a discourteous manner.

Swallowing an intense feeling of disgust, I pulled out the paper from the military hospital and gave it to him. He glued his eyes onto it for a minute as though he wanted to pull out every word from the small, faded pass. I hoped he could read. Abruptly, he turned around, quickly jumped down the steps, and walked over to a man in uniform, a bộ đội, who was standing in front of the bus and enjoying a cigarette. Then they all looked down at the paper in their hands. I was a little nervous, but it was valid for at least a few more weeks.

Suddenly, both climbed on the bus steps.

"Greetings, comrade!" the guy in uniform said. He smiled and looked at me, calling me "comrade." Good sign! I thought. "Where are you going?" he asked without waiting for me to greet him back.

"I'm going to Bạc Liêu to visit a few friends," I replied.

"You should cover this paper with plastic to protect it from fading," he said, giving me a piece of friendly advice. "It is becoming difficult to read."

"Thank you, comrade!" I blurted out. "I will have a new badge in a few weeks, anyway." Hiding the icy feeling in my soul, I shot a slight smile at the "April-30" scoundrel when he returned my burgundy shoulder-strap bag.

"In the meantime, I will cover it with plastic," I tried to make small talk.

"If you need anything, just let us know, okay?" he said.

The man in uniform was unexpectedly nice. Then, he waved his hand for the "April-30" guy to move on to other passengers to suck their fresh blood.

The "April-30" guy couldn't read!

The man in uniform might be the head of the search group at that checkpoint. He recognized the red star emblem on the paper—the symbol that certified I was working for a military base in Hồ Chí Minh City.

The badge didn't list any specific details of what I was doing or my function except a small black-and-white photo of my face. Without a written job title, it created an air of mystery—my function was unknown. It induced a state of confusion, allowing the security staff at the checkpoint to assume that I could hold an important function at that base. For all they knew, I could be a security cadre or an intelligence agent of the Communist Party of Vietnam assigned to the base.

During that time, mental torment and lack of food had caused me to look very skinny, tattered, and pale as VC had when they had first intruded into Sài Gòn. As I was born in the north, I was adept at speaking with the accents of people who lived in Hà Nội, the Capital of the new regime in Vietnam.

Even if they suspected something, I knew it would be difficult to check the information on my paper.

They would have to detain me while contacting the military hospital where I worked to verify the authenticity of the pass. But there was no contact information on it. It just listed Hồ Chí Minh City as where the base was located. If they held me up and later found out that my paper was legitimate—and it was—it could have been a serious embarrassment for them.

That was the first time I went through a security checkpoint before boarding a big ferryboat to cross the Mekong River. Another major post was near Cần Thơ, where I went through without problems. The trip was an adventure, to be sure, but I would soon learn many helpful tricks of the trade to make coming and going much safer and easier.

In the late afternoon, I arrived at the local bus station in Bạc Liêu. It had rained earlier during the day, leaving the station's arrival area muddy and crowded with travelers and small street vendors offering all kinds of food.

People sat and ate on the ground beside the vendors' cooking pots. I was starving since I had eaten nothing all day. I had little money and was trying to save it since I still had to find a job and get paid. "We'll try to find something for you. We will get you work," Tuấn, my friend, told me once in Sài Gòn, assuring me it would be fine to come and stay with his family.

Bạc Liêu is a province in the western region with vast rice fields and fertile land; it is near the coastline of the South China Sea in the south and southeast.

Shortly after the war, the government combined Bạc Liêu and Cà Mau to become Minh Hải (MH) Province. A large population of the Chinese-Vietnamese people who lived there was very rich. In the region, waterways were major routes for daily commutes and making connections between Bạc Liêu and the small hamlets deep in the countryside, where there were no roads for ground vehicle transportation.

I heard rumors that many people fled Vietnam by boats registered with MH numbers. It was a good place for me to hide while trying to plot an escape for my family.

Plenty of three-wheel bicycle taxis were waiting in the bus station's arrival area. I took one to go to my friend's house, located not very far from there.

It was a typical large, old ranch house with a low-pitched roof. I met Tuấn's father a few times in Sài Gòn at my friend's apartment when he and I went to the same senior high school. His father was a very thoughtful and well-respected man in his hometown, and his mother was a tender and kind woman. My friend had four siblings; he was the third in his family. One of his married sisters lived with her family in Sài Gòn, and another one lived locally in Bạc Liêu. His older brother was an ex-Navy soldier in the former regime.

While I was staying at my friend's house, his brothers were not there but were living in the U.S. I didn't know how they left the country. Besides Tuấn's parents living at home, one of his close relatives on his mother's side, her niece, also lived there. While quiet, she handled much of the work around the house, including cooking.

Tuấn knew I might visit him someday, but he didn't know exactly when I would come. Luckily, he was home when I arrived at his house and was happy to see me. He was a year younger than I and very poetic, but also a street fighter.

During my senior year in high school, we almost engaged in street fighting with another group of students who bullied us. While in Sài Gòn, he lived alone in a little apartment deep inside a small blue-color section of Sài Gòn where there were several lumber companies and warehouses. When I left my family and quit going to school for a few weeks in 1971, after my older brother's death, I used to hang out with him there.

It was the first time I met Tuấn's mother and other relatives. All of them were very humble and kind—the typical people who lived in small towns or farming regions.

In the evening, I gratefully had dinner together with my friend's family. The food had low calories but was delicious. It was the first time I ate cooked rice with "Cá Kèo," a small fish abundantly caught in fishing nets or raised in Bạc Liêu, and boiled "Hẹ" or Nira grass, a derivative of onions normally used in soup.

While eating, we talked about the situation in Vietnam under the socialist regime and speculated about the future of our country.

During my stay there, I had many conversations with Tuấn's father. One night, he advised us to leave Vietnam.

"Build up your knowledge and skills in the western civilization," he said. "You cannot do anything for the country by staying here in this situation."

Tuấn's family was aware of who I was during the war, but they didn't seem overly concerned about my presence there. My friend, I thought, must have registered me at the local district security office. Although the local security cadres didn't know my past, I was always extremely cautious about what I said or did. Shortly after April 30, 1975, I heard they had executed quite a few people from South Vietnam in Bạc Liêu.

"This place may be worse than Hồ Chí Minh City!" I thought.

Over the next few days, Tuấn took me around town to meet his friends and showed me a few places in Bạc Liêu.

Đức was an army pharmacist in the previous regime. He went to the "re-education" camp for about two years, and then they let him go. He was still single and wanted to flee Vietnam.

Anh Minh was a tailor who had a small business downtown. He and his wife had two girls and a boy. They lived together with his parents. His father had diabetes and could only walk with a cane. The entire family was very kind and lived simply, although they seemed wealthy. They had a tailoring business. Anh Minh's family, except his parents, also wanted to flee Vietnam.

Anh Văn Ánh was a very thoughtful and knowledgeable scholar who knew Hán or scholar's script, similar to Chinese ideographs. It was the old Vietnamese writing, established under the rule of several Chinese dynasties prior to the Romanization of the Vietnamese writing system in the 17th century.

Interestingly, he favored Marxism as a philosophy. Hence, he sympathized with the newly established socialist government. However, he was a good man with a great love for Vietnam and its people. He knew who I was in the past, but he respected my principles and military background during the previous regime. Like many other new acquaintances, he eventually became one of my friends in Bạc Liêu.

I also met Anh Tín; he was "tài công"ˢ and had a family with a wife and three little kids.

And Tuấn, of course, was my close friend from high school before April 30, 1975. He was from Bạc Liêu, but before the war, he went to school in Sài Gòn. Because of his poor eyesight, the South Vietnam Air Force rejected him. He then attended the College of Literature for a few years. After the fall of Sài Gòn, he returned to Bạc Liêu to live with his parents. He didn't have a job but secretly worked with a few boat owners to organize escapes for other people. His parents didn't want to leave the motherland, so he stayed to care for his aging parents.

When I was staying at Tuấn's house, in the early mornings or evenings, we normally went downtown, which was not too far away from his house, to drink coffee and exchange small talk. We didn't discuss in public what I truly wanted to do while in Bạc Liêu, but when we were back at his house in the late evening, we would burn the midnight oil to discuss the means and options to flee Vietnam.

When I came to Bạc Liêu, the exodus by land and sea had secretly been going on for at least a year in several locations in Vietnam. Many people, traveling in small groups, crossed the border on foot to enter the Cambodian territories. From there, a bus or truck sent by the paid organizers would transport them to the nearest border of Thailand.

A few years later, my younger aunt, who lost her husband in the concentration camp, became a street trader. She had saved some money to pay for someone to arrange for her older sister and three young children to flee on foot via the Cambodian route. It was a very dangerous attempt, but because of the strong resentment against the Vietnam communists who killed her husband, she chose that deadly option over allowing her children to grow up in a socialist regime with a doomed future. My elder aunt was single, devoting her entire life to helping raise her younger sister's children. Their attempt to

---

ˢ "Tài công": Boat navigators, many of whom were also fishermen.

flee by land failed. It terrified all of them. Luckily, the elder aunt came back home alive with her nephews.

Boat people fled Vietnam via the coastlines along the South China Sea. Both means, land and sea, were equally deadly. Many boats they used were not seaworthy or too small to cross the ocean, sinking easily when they ran into heavy storms or waves. Many people drowned. The coastguard caught many boat people; sometimes, they shot them, I heard.

Pirates[80] were another deadly problem. They raped many innocent women and girls or killed them right in front of their families while on the high seas. Those bloodthirsty, soulless pirates had no pity and shed no tears for those victims, whether young girls, children, pregnant women, or the sick and elderly. It was horrific, but the Vietnamese people, particularly those from the south, were still trying to flee the country, running away from the Vietnam communists by any means[81].

Amazingly, some people living in the north also tried to flee the country by land via the Hong Kong route. Even people who had migrated from the north to the south after April 30, 1975, wanted to flee Vietnam[82]. When I was in Bạc Liêu, I knew a medical doctor originally from the north who was also seeking a way for his family to flee the country.

Clearly, the one-party communist policy—without true democracy and freedom and that favored suppression and retaliation, including the killing of former military officers and officials in the "re-education" camps—had caused deep resentment and boiling anger. The powerful bitterness stayed permanently ingrained in the inner souls of those who lived in the south. They cast their grievances in stone, even after years of "re-education." Year after year, celebrations from the socialist regime, proclaiming the "glorious victory of spring 1975… the gigantic movement of the people… and Communist Party,"[83] painfully re-opened the deadly wounds that didn't seem to heal, no matter how much time had passed.

Evidently, the Vietnam Communist Party was tone-deaf!

After a few weeks in Bạc Liêu, I felt comfortable and more secure in hiding there. The paper from the military hospital gave me a protected status. I could go around freely without watching my back carefully out of fear of being followed by the local security cadres.

During that time, I contemplated a plan for my loved one's escape by boat amidst those who didn't seem to believe or couldn't imagine what I was doing. I, myself, was uncertain whether a man in such dire financial circumstances and an outcast of the socialist society could pull it off. All I knew was that I had a dream and faith; they would remain present whether I had freedom. They were like water and air, giving me spiritual and physical strength in a languishing body. Superstitiously, I also sensed that the ill omen from the dark dreams was closing in on us, particularly my next younger brother. The warning from childhood was still vividly alive in my 24-year-old mind!

Everybody in my family, particularly my wife and Mother, desperately wanted me to leave Vietnam because they feared for my life if I stayed.

"I beg you!" Mother used to persuade me whenever she saw me at home. "You must leave Vietnam!" Sometimes, she sounded desperate while raising her voice, "Leave your wife and son here and save your own life! I will take care of them for you."

My mother-in-law didn't want me to stay, either. But nobody was aware that I no longer cared about my fate—just getting them out. All I wanted was to take my loved ones out of Vietnam and fulfill their dream and my unspoken promise to my older brother—even if I had to die while trying. I wished to give my loved ones a future in the dreamland of the U.S., where I once lived.

The sacred vow to protect my loved ones' future gave me absolute mental strength, as strong as steel. It led me to discover a greater purpose that shaped my perspective of how I should live the one life given to me.

During that time in Bạc Liêu, many Vietnamese people had already fled Vietnam using small wooden boats. Some had succeeded, but many others had drowned. Eventually, the Vietnam naval forces and coastguards discovered the trend and started operations to capture those who tried to escape. There were rumors of soldiers shooting and killing those escapees when their boats were spotted and chased in Vietnam waters.

There were also stories that the local government authority had staged fake escapes to trap and capture unlucky would-be boat people, even before they could board the boat. I heard they captured and sent many of these poor people to prisons.

There were also reports about scams conducted by scoundrels who took money from families who blindly trusted them, eventually learning that their crooked organizers had suddenly disappeared after taking many taels of gold from them.

Tuấn had a small "shrimp-tail" boat powered by a piston engine. It was about five meters long, with a small cabin space for sleeping. He sometimes used the boat to carry bags of rice or other stuff to sell to people who lived in hamlets or small towns along the rivers. One day, I went along with him. We carried water and food to last us a week, anticipating we might be on the rivers for a few days, traveling through the winding streams. We planned to go along the river parallel to National Highway 1, come down to Cà Mau—one of the major towns in Minh Hải Province besides Bạc Liêu—and then get on the Gành Hào River to reach the market. From there, we could see the river merged into the South China Sea, where it would be open to international waters. This location was probably where many boat people secretly gathered on a pre-determined date to board their boats to flee the country.

It was a very exciting trip for me as it was my first time traveling on a small boat to distant villages in the western regions. We made stops at various places during the day and docked at night along the river to rest and sleep.

One evening, while sitting on the edge of the boat drinking coffee, I couldn't stop thinking about the fate of my loved ones. As I sat, I took in the sight of the warm dim lights coming out from the thatched houses scattering along the dark river. The tranquility of the darkness and the soft, mysterious sound of flowing river water touched my heart. It penetrated deeply into my mind—giving me a strange feeling and offering a glimpse of what my loved ones and I might endure on the dangerous journey as we fled by boat on the high seas. I feared the dark forces that might twist our fate, but I was also faint-hearted about the diminishing freedom and dismal future my loved ones faced in Vietnam.

I prayed it would be well worth it if I needed to give my life away for freedom and a better future for all of them! Living in the socialist society so far, I knew I might not fulfill my dream without having to give something up—and that "something" might be my life or several of our lives.

I hoped it would be me instead of my loved ones!

Gành Hào River was a rich waterway full of fish to feed villagers along the river. The brown water contained good minerals and was used to irrigate thick green rice fields. One day, we stopped and docked the boat in a very rural area to sell rice to a family there.

It was around noontime. The owner, a middle-aged man, and his family were very nice and simple. After we completed our business, they offered us lunch.

We all sat on the bare ground inside his house to eat. They offered cooked rice and fermented fish taken out of a big brown ceramic jar. I was hungry and ate many of the high-protein tasty fish. While eating, I suddenly saw a few fat, milky-colored maggots crawling out slowly from the edge of the jar.

Immediately, I stopped eating and made a gentle gesture, using my elbow and eyes to show them to my friend. He didn't seem surprised but smiled, explaining that those fat maggots were tasty and nutritious. He then picked and ate one of them, a shiny, fat one, while I watched in disgust!

That was the day I got into trouble!

After we left the family who offered us the maggot-fish rice for lunch, I developed severe stomach pain and diarrhea. Throughout the night, I had almost constant liquid bowel movements. We didn't have any medication, so all I could do was lie flat on the rough floor near the edge of the boat for quick access to the river when I had bowel movements. Luckily, it was nighttime. There were fewer boats or people around.

The diarrhea slowed somewhat the following day, but I was too weak to move on. On the way back to the river along Route 1, I told Tuấn I wanted to return to Hồ Chí Minh City for a few days to visit my family and recover. It had been a few weeks since I left Sài Gòn. Eventually, we found a section of National Highway 1 where I could catch a bus to go back home.

I will never forget that embarrassing condition and horrible stomach pain—particularly the sight of my friend and the people in that village eating the milky fat maggots, alive!

Returning to My Hometown

I ARRIVED AT the Hồ Chí Minh western regional bus station in the evening, which was good, as I didn't intend to show up at my wife's home in daylight.

When I got to her house, I peeked into the front room through a door gap and softly whispered her name when I saw my wife inside. She was shocked upon hearing my voice but quickly and quietly opened the door for me to sneak into the front room.

I embraced and tightly squeezed my wife and son in my arms like I was about to lose them. Her mother and aunt came down from the second floor when I was about to come up to greet them. My wife's younger sisters were home, but her two younger brothers were not. One of her brothers was in training somewhere after joining the local security force upon advice from the district chairperson—a family friend. The other younger brother volunteered for the hard labor program in the "new economic zones" outside Hồ Chí Minh City.

My aunt-in-law said I was so pale and thin that I looked sick. Of course, I had just experienced severe diarrhea after eating raw fish and maggots—and drinking local water I was unaccustomed to—sending my body into that uncontrollable pain with frequent bowel movements.

Feeling pity for me, my wife's aunt gave me some leftover food.

Her family seemed to have accepted their present life. My wife worked as a salesclerk at the district fruit and vegetable store to earn money to feed our son.

Curiously, they asked what I was doing in Bạc Liêu. I told them I was still looking for something to do down there to earn money. They informed me that the district security cadres had not come by the house since I left.

They also told me that a family in the neighborhood might have previously turned me in. Their house was near the main road, intersected by the alley where my wife's family lived. They frequently saw me in a military flight suit, riding the red Suzuki motorcycle, when visiting my wife-to-be, Mai, before the fall of Sài Gòn. Their son was an army officer in the former regime and had been in the "re-education" camps since June 1975. Before I even knew Mai, his parents had wanted their son to marry her. Mai heard that but didn't like the idea. They had never dated or talked to each other before. Then, even unintentionally, I came into the fold and destroyed the hopes of Mai's neighbor to wed her.

Hearing the story, I didn't care who had turned me in. But I told my wife's family to be careful!

Even though we were all happy to see each other again, my wife, particularly her mother and aunt, still worried about the risk of me being captured again in their house.

"We cannot guess what they may do," my mother-in-law said. "It's too dangerous for you to stay here!"

I fully understood why my wife's mother didn't want me to stay long and told her I would leave soon. That evening, I played with my son for a few hours. I told my wife I would be at my parents' house and asked her to come by with our son. I left her home shortly before midnight to go to my parents' house.

Mother usually stayed up late to clean up and rearrange things after a long day in the front room, her convenience store. When I came home, she was still working. Father had already gone to sleep. Mother was surprised but happy to see me back and wanted to prepare something for me to eat.

I told her I had already eaten at my wife's home and wanted to talk to her before going to bed. So, we sat in the small dining room behind a tall wooden storage rack, nearly reaching the ceiling and extending about two-thirds of the room's width. We used it as a wall to separate the dining room and storefront, and the shelves were full of miscellaneous items. Sitting in the dim light, I softly told her the stories of the boat people who fled Vietnam successfully.

She was scared but seemed interested in hearing more and wondered how I could get enough money to pay for the escape. I told her I would find a way for the family to get out. At that, she insisted I must try to escape the country alone while I might have a chance. I knew she was afraid of having another dead son. I didn't argue or say anything to upset her before heading upstairs to the small room on the flat roof to sleep.

While I was back in Hồ Chí Minh City, I stayed at my parents' house for a few days. After work, my wife would come with our son to visit me. During that time, I always remained inside the house. My neighbors probably didn't even know I was home.

Dũng, my next younger brother, still worked as one of the security escorts for the government's vegetable distribution groups. He normally accompanied a delivery truck, which also often carried a lot of money. He enjoyed his job. Sometimes, his truck also distributed vegetables at my wife's district store.

The other younger brother, Tuân, might soon have to join the People's Army of Vietnam because of the draft. My parents were often worried about his future, but no one knew what to do or how to help. They didn't want him to serve in the communist army. There was a rumor going around that they normally ordered the young soldiers, who were children of the "puppet government," to carry the heavy ammunition containers for bộ đội or be at the forefront of the battle, to act as a cover for them. During that time, Vietnam was fighting against the Khmer Rouge forces in Cambodia[84].

Obviously, there was tremendous pressure on me to find a quick solution for Tuân, even though nobody had asked me to do anything. After all, no one thought I could help anyone, anyway. As an outcast in the socialist state, I was still a financially poor person.

The Boat Owner and Teacher

IN EARLY 1979, I frequently went back and forth between Bạc Liêu and Hồ Chí Minh City. Gradually, I became acquainted with some local security cadres and scoundrels from the "April-30 Group" along National Highway 1, which I had to go through to get to Bạc Liêu. They had become familiar with my suffering face. To them, I was just a person who had nothing of value to rob and carried little more than a few old articles of clothing and the fading paper from the military hospital.

While those money-hungers busily searched the bus and other passengers, I used to stand comfortably with the cadres in uniform, sharing cigarettes and small talk. I was a chain smoker. I always had plenty of cheap cigarettes to share with them. Many of those soldiers also smoked. They called me "comrade," so I did the same. We chit-chatted as though we were friends who knew each other very well.

In 1979, Vietnam engaged in a brief border war with China[85]— the "big brother" who used to supply weapons and ammunition to fight against the "U.S. Imperial." China sent its elite troops to capture some provinces in the northern part of Vietnam temporarily. It was a punitive action against the invasion of Hà Nội into Cambodia in 1978 and their mistreatment of the Chinese-Vietnamese people who lived in Vietnam during that time.

As reported later, the intrusion resulted in a huge number of soldiers and civilians killed. Both countries, who were previously brothers in arms, claimed victory! Subsequently, the Vietnam government sped up the "permitted departures" of the Chinese

Vietnamese living in their country. Hà Nội allowed them to leave Vietnam, mostly by sea.

Even though the government indirectly expelled them, they still had to pay the boat owners and local Vietnam officials with gold for protection. Depending on the location and whom the ethnic Chinese-Vietnamese people were dealing with, it might cost them at least five or seven taels of gold or more for a space on a boat, which still didn't guarantee their arrival or survival at an unknown destination. In 1979, a tael of gold might be equivalent to around 300 American dollars or more. So, if they paid, the local government, which was full of corrupted security cadres and crooks from the "April-30 Group," would protect their exit plan.

While protecting the Chinese-Vietnamese people who paid to leave Vietnam, the coastal local government continued to launch sea operations to capture those illegally escaping by boat. Many were Vietnamese men, women, and children from the former regime.

While staying in Bạc Liêu, Tuấn also took me to other places where they were building boats, supposedly for fishing. Secretly, it was for fleeing Vietnam.

Eventually, I met a few boat owners. However, no matter what, I still needed gold to pay. Realistically, I was still totally dead broke and depending on my close friend and his family, who had big hearts and were full of generosity. I was like a fish gasping for air on dry land, waiting to die.

Gracefully, they came into my life at the worst moment and took me to where I could survive, at least for the time being. They provided me with food and sanctuary, which kept me alive to figure out how my loved ones could flee Vietnam. While I was trying to avoid the tongs of the socialist society, amazingly, the beautiful hearts of people whom I called angels embraced me warmly. They truly existed in my life. And because of them, I could sustain my existence and continue to search for an escape path. Without those angel hands, the dream for my loved ones' future could have been short-lived—just an in-actionable possibility.

Feeling the weight of these human blessings, I put my life into the hands of angels to guide my path while plotting the risky journey—but I still had uncertainty.

How could a fugitive like me do anything for my loved ones? Other people might doubt it was possible, asking that same question. Or, perhaps, even laugh in my face, believing the idea to be impossible nonsense. At that point, I didn't care. No one could take away the burning desire I was nourishing with my mother. She had already dreamed about her children's lives in America. Except for Mother, nobody else believed in the dream. Father certainly didn't. To him, if I couldn't feed my son, how would I materialize this crazy dream with nothing but my poverty-stricken bare hands?

My wife's mother had no confidence that I could do anything to make money effectively, let alone seek freedom in what I saw as the promised land. Her aunt-in-law became frightened by the potentially deadly aspects of being on the high seas, hearing the rumors circulating about those who fled Vietnam by boat. Even my wife didn't fancy fleeing Vietnam; it seemed too much of a fictitious dream. They merely accepted the reality they were living and the fate it cast on them.

Desperately, they tried their best to make ends meet and raise our son in the newly established socialist society that praised "peace, freedom, and independence" daily. As the stubborn propaganda loudly preached, it clearly showed "an empty vessel makes the loudest sound." The inadequate mental grasp of democracy and propaganda sent an awakening shockwave, altering the future of millions of Vietnamese people in life-changing ways.

As the exodus of the boat people from Vietnam increasingly continued in Bạc Liêu, the scrutiny of the local security cadres also multiplied. They finally knew Tuấn's activities.

One day, the local security agents launched an operation, capturing both Tuấn and Anh Tín and putting them in jail. Anh Tín was a "tài công" who had a family with a wife and three little kids. Luckily, I was not there during the arrest, or it could have meant more trouble. As soon as I discovered they had arrested my friends, after discussing it with Tuấn's parents, I moved elsewhere to avoid further complications that could affect his family's safety and my plan.

During that time, my tailor friend, Anh Minh, frequently asked me to move in with his family. He lived downtown. To avoid suspicion and continue with my strategy, a few hours after they came and took my friend away, I packed up and went to Anh Minh's house without delay.

While I lived with Anh Minh, I wanted to teach his children how to speak and write in English. The family liked the idea, so I started giving them lessons a few nights per week in a room on the second floor. The room had a blackboard, and they used it as a place for the kids to study.

In Bạc Liêu, the exodus grew, partly because many rich Chinese-Vietnamese people lived there. They were fleeing Vietnam at a fast rate, leaving the country under the paid protection of the local government authority. The Vietnamese citizens, unfortunately, could not do the same and would go to prison for leaving illegally if caught. Besides paying the boat owners, they had to pay fees in gold to the local authorities. Once very poor, government officials and district security cadres suddenly became filthy rich.

With a permit from the socialist state, Chinese-Vietnamese families could leave the country by boat to enter international waters without being shot at or captured by Vietnamese navy forces or the coastguard. From there, they could travel anywhere. Many successfully landed in Malaysia or Indonesia, while others died on the stormy high seas.

While in Bạc Liêu, I worked part-time as an English teacher for one of the wealthy Chinese-Vietnamese families. They had three daughters and two sons, and I went to their house a few times weekly to give them English lessons.

The family owned a boat and was preparing to leave Vietnam in a few months. Mr. Thái Đức, the father of my students, was a Chinese-Vietnamese business owner. He had a few close relatives and partners working with him to handle the registration and pricing of those who wanted to leave the country. The boat, about 19 meters long, could carry approximately 200 people. He could easily make good money for his efforts.

One day, while he and I casually talked about the exodus, he mentioned I should also leave the country. I realized he could easily put me on his boat if I wanted, and it likely wouldn't cost me any gold. After all, they needed someone who could speak English fluently to accompany them in case they ran into foreigners on the high seas. When he brought it up, I told him I would not leave alone, that I was determined to remain in Vietnam until I could get my family out, and that I was poor and had no gold for even myself to leave.

Our conversations on the matter didn't go further, as he was a businessperson. I was a homeless person. What else would I expect?

So, I kept giving English lessons to Mr. Thái Đức's children to make enough money to live while I plotted and concealed my plan. During that time, his older son was busily coordinating the boat's preparation for departure in June 1979.

THE LASTING TRUTH

Fleeing Vietnam was a dream, not a reality, for my poor wife and her family. They didn't have strong enough stomachs to think about the prospect, nor could they afford it. It was simply beyond their reach, priorities, and risk tolerance. Without gold, there was no opportunity for anybody to talk with the boat owners.

My financial circumstances remained dire, and I could not even feed our son. The innocent 3-year-old boy frequently waited by the deteriorating door, hoping his grandmother or mother would come home with food. He was hungry all the time! Before North Vietnam took over the south, my wife's family was prosperous. After April 1975, they eventually became so poor that they saved every "sous" or penny they made to buy food for our son. So poor that they could only buy beef-noodle soup or Phở for him without meat because it was cheaper that way. While I was away from home and his grandma and mother worked during the day, my wife's aunt devoted her time to caring for our son.

My wife fully understood our situation, accepted her fate, and tried to raise our son the best she could without my financial support. She desperately wanted me to flee the country—even if it meant without her and our son together as a family.

When the district securities cadres detained me for interrogation during the previous arrests, it mentally tortured her more than enough. Continuously living in fear that they might arrest me again caused too much mental suffering for her to bear. Another interrogation would likely lead to my death or life in a gulag! In contrast to her acceptance of life with no future, there was not a single day I didn't think about taking them far away from Vietnam, my lost homeland, even if it might cost my life.

When the rumors of the Vietnamese exodus by boat had finally reached their boiling point, flooding Hồ Chí Minh City overwhelmingly, the possibility finally flowed into my parents' and elder brother's minds. They showed growing desire and hope amid proportional fears. My dream, once thought of as a crazy and desperate idea to take my loved ones, including my siblings, out of Vietnam, suddenly resonated in my family's conversations. During that tumultuous period in the socialist state, it became the only hope we all could rely on to survive.

Having overcome many doubts and fears about fleeing Vietnam by boat, Father also looked for a way to leave the country. One day, he asked me to help find him a place in Bạc Liêu to live temporarily while looking for an opportunity to escape. Knowing his intent, I helped him move to Bạc Liêu to stay with one of my friends, Anh Văn Ánh. When Father got there, he set up a bicycle repair business on the street, just like what he had in Hồ Chí Minh City, to disguise his intent from the eyes of the local security cadres.

Father was not the only one temporarily staying at Anh Văn Ánh's apartment. My second younger brother, Tuân, was also hiding there. The socialist state's army had drafted him into service. He stayed in the military briefly before deserting and hiding at home. Because of our parents' highly visible convenience store in such a busy section of Sài Gòn, they feared the repercussions of his desertion. Uncertain and afraid of what the government might do to the family if they discovered him there, they asked my younger aunt to hide Tuân in her house. She graciously accepted and helped for a while, but my brother couldn't stay there forever. The district security cadres might eventually find out, which would become a problem for Tuân and our aunt.

Because there was no one else to turn to, Mother asked me to help Tuân to save him from the jail time or severe punishment he would face if caught. "Please save Tuân for me… I'm begging you!" Mother desperately asked me. I couldn't say no! But there was no place to hide him in Hồ Chí Minh City, so I moved Tuân to Bạc Liêu to stay with Father in Anh Văn Ánh's apartment.

Anh Văn Ánh was a good man. Although he seemed favorable to the Marxism philosophy and the newly established socialist state, he did not turn in Father or my deserter brother, even knowing their intentions. Instead, he courageously dared to provide them with a sanctuary shelter. I will never forget what he did for them, with nothing to gain for himself except our eternal friendship and our genuine respect for each other. However, staying in his apartment and hiding in Bạc Liêu was only temporary. I knew I must find a permanent solution for them as soon as possible, or it could be disastrous.

After the victors released my elder brother from the "re-education" camp, he was no longer teaching. Instead, he became an attendant for a bus owned by his wife's family. The business seemed to be doing very well, and his bus served the western cities, including Bạc Liêu. By then, he realized my dream of fleeing by boat was not fictitious. When he and his in-laws began actually considering fleeing Vietnam, they asked me for help, so I told Tuấn and Anh Tín to visit Sài Gòn to meet them and discuss the possibilities. The meeting occurred before the capture of Tuấn and Anh Tín by the local government.

When my friends came to see my elder brother's in-laws, we sat together in the living room on the second floor of their house, right next to my parents' convenience store. But the discussion failed to lead to an agreement on the next steps because he and his wife didn't seem to trust my friends.

They didn't like how Anh Tín responded to some of their questions. My brother said he was too slow to reply when asked, but I knew it was just Anh Tín's personality. He always took his time to think things through carefully before offering an opinion. He was an overthinker, like my elder brother!

After the failed meeting, my elder brother and I rarely ran into each other. I continued to hide in Bạc Liêu to gather more information on how the local government authority was handling the departures of the ethnic Chinese-Vietnamese people. As soon as I was fully aware of every step of the government-supported exodus machine from Bạc Liêu, I could explore various strategies to raise enough gold to pay for my escape plan.

I knew my elder brother's in-laws could easily finance their way out of Vietnam. But not that simple! Who could they trust to handle the entire family's escape without compromising their safety and gold assets? Who could help them flee successfully without falling into local enforcement traps and potentially losing all of their gold in the process? Many knew crooks faked escape plots to scam people out of their savings. After that failed meeting, I remained confident they would eventually need my help. So, rather than following up with my elder brother about his in-laws' plans for the future, I patiently waited for them to start those talks.

Consistent with my expectations, one day, while in Bạc Liêu, my elder brother came looking for me. We eventually met at the local bus station one late afternoon. He took me to one of the street vendors at the arrival area to eat "Bánh Xèo," a shrimp-studded crepe rolled up in lettuce leaves and served with fresh herbs, which was dipped in fish sauce when eating. After dinner, we went to the top of his bus to talk. He asked me again to help his family and in-laws leave Vietnam. We didn't discuss the details, but I agreed to help and told him I would work on a plan. That night, we slept on top of the bus in the arrival area of the Bạc Liêu local bus station. He left early in the morning to return to Hồ Chí Minh City while I stayed in Bạc Liêu.

After he left, I went to see Mr. Thái Đức to discuss the fees and the amount of gold each passenger would have to pay to board his boat to leave Vietnam. His plan to depart Vietnam was still to occur in June 1979. I told him my family was planning to flee Vietnam and would need fake family register documents to get on his boat. He said his people would take care of the paperwork. Since I was his children's teacher, he would give me a discounted price: the amount of gold payable to him. But I still had to pay the fee for bribing the district security cadres. His price fell within a reasonable range for someone who hoped to get on a boat to flee Vietnam in Bạc Liêu. I trusted him since he was a very successful businessperson, and his entire family and relatives would leave the country on that same boat. I knew his plan was real, well-thought-out, and protected by the local security machine of the socialist state.

Although the armed district security cadres would protect the boat people and escort them to the open sea, there were still some risks we had to face. For example, the government permitted ethnic Chinese-Vietnamese families to leave but didn't allow Vietnamese citizens out of the country. In most cases, one could easily recognize the distinctively different facial characteristics between Chinese and Vietnamese people.

So, the security cadres in the boarding area might realize the differences if they checked the passengers carefully.

The other challenge was how to carry all the required gold—a significant quantity—from Hồ Chí Minh City to Bạc Liêu before departure without being discovered by the security cadres at checkpoints along National Highway 1. We would have to submit the agreed-upon amount of gold to Mr. Thái Đức well before the departure date. I had to figure out a way to address those issues quickly. But the most challenging task was convincing my elder brother's in-laws to loan us enough gold to pay for our family to go. They owned a transportation business and were wealthy. They might have enough gold for us to borrow so we all could flee the country, but whether they would do it was uncertain.

Of course, we had to have their trust. They must believe we would definitely pay them back once we reached the promised land and had jobs in America. I thought they would be agreeable, knowing that finding a job in the U.S. might be easier for me. They knew I had lived there for over a year prior to 1975 and could speak English. I still had a diploma from the U.S. military flight school. I could become a commercial pilot. Those skills, especially the ability to speak English, would be significant and beneficial once I returned to the U.S. I also suspected my elder brother's in-laws would feel more comfortable and safer if I accompanied them out of Vietnam.

Somehow, unexpectedly, I became a person of some worth and value, maybe not in the socialist society, but among those who yearned to seek freedom in the U.S. or other western countries. Suddenly, I became a helpful person to have in the family. I had become a floatation device for them to hold on to—the North Star that could provide the instructions to my loved ones that would set them free.

With the discovery of this value came some new thought processes; I devised a psychological strategy to negotiate with my elder brother's wife and in-laws.

I hoped to borrow as much gold as possible to enable my loved ones to leave for the promised land. With such a big family, I was confident all of us could work to pay back the borrowed gold easily once we had jobs. It worked out well for them, too. If they let us borrow their gold to pay for the boat ride across the South China Sea, they wouldn't have to carry their life savings on the boat—an enormous risk. If we were unlucky and ran into pirates in the Gulf of Thailand, their money would be gone forever.

My elder brother's wife wanted to flee Vietnam together with her husband, two small children, and blood relatives. She had a mother, two married older half-brothers, and an unmarried sister about a year younger than me. If all of them, including children and cousins, wanted to leave, there would be over 20 people. Of my family alone, there would be about ten, including my parents, five brothers, and three sisters. So, there was the potential for our group to include at least 30 people from both families. Then, my younger aunt also wished for her son to flee, and I planned to take at least the oldest son of my widowed aunt out of the country. If I could make it happen, I wanted him to have a future that would allow him to help his family later.

That was my original wish list, which I had carefully contemplated. Within a few weeks, I would discover the true complexity of the fight to keep as many of my loved ones on that virtual roster as possible. I wasn't sure whether I could raise enough gold for everyone. I couldn't include the elder aunt or my younger aunt's family in the plan. Neither could I include my wife, son, and me on the wish list, knowing it might be more than what my elder brother's in-laws might loan. Besides, with the growing internal conflict between the rich sister-in-law and me, and negative gossip contaminating my family's kinship, I sensed my wife and son would probably be nowhere on the boat manifest, regardless.

The relationship probably eroded right after I married Mai. After the war, when the wealthy sister-in-law's father passed away, my wife and I were not home and, therefore, unaware of his death. Around that time, Mai and I had a big argument about our financial situation. She took our son to visit and stay with her father's youngest sister, who was living in Đà Lạt, one of the beautiful cities in the Central Highlands region. When I learned where she had gone, I went there to ask her to come home.

Several days after the funeral of my elder brother's father-in-law, we returned home from Đà Lạt. When we learned the sad news, I asked him to take me to his wife's house next door to burn incense and pay my respects. Later, I heard gossip that showed the sister-in-law believed the visit was too little too late and a waste of time.

When my elder brother asked me to help his family flee, my wife and I had already overheard many personal criticisms from this sister-in-law concerning my poor family. But there was nothing we could do to stop the gossip. I was too preoccupied with the plan to help my loved ones escape, including those who spread such negativity. Mai could not say much because she was very poor and tried to stay as far away from my elder brother's wife as possible.

Facing constant antagonistic impetuosity, I accepted the rocky relationship as one of the dark forces I was fighting against to reach Mother's and my dream. Despite those black clouds, I figured if my elder brother's in-laws wanted me to help them flee the country, they should at least let us borrow enough gold for all my younger siblings to be on Mr. Thái Đức's boat. My wife, son, and I could stay behind if need be!

The Daring Plan

MAI AND HER family were completely in the dark and didn't know I was planning for my elder brother's family and in-laws to flee Vietnam. They never once thought about leaving Vietnam, instead focusing on their struggle to survive and well aware that they would never have enough gold to pay for the escape by boat.

Their meager savings were dwindling, which they only had from selling their previous house. None of them made good money because they didn't have stable jobs. The socialist state frequently induced young people, including my brothers-in-law, to volunteer to complete hard labor in the "new economic zones."

During that time, my wife still worked at the district fruit and vegetable distribution store as a sale associate with an embarrassingly low salary. The few bucks she made scarcely fed our 3-year-old son. I felt terribly sorry for Mai. Even after her father, an army major in the Republic of Vietnam Army under President Diệm in the 1960s, passed away because of health complications, her family remained financially sound.

After the war, the communist regime degraded them to the lowest level—even below the status of poor peasants, the group that the socialist society should have strongly supported.

After the first meeting with Mr. Thái Đức to discuss my big family plan to flee Vietnam, I returned to Hồ Chí Minh City several times to meet with my elder brother and his in-laws. In exchange for my help, I wanted to know how much I could borrow to determine how many people on the wish list I had in mind could escape.

The original offer from his wife and in-laws was only for enough gold that the two youngest siblings from my family could get out of the country. She also wanted to lend gold for me to leave—but not enough for my wife and little son.

The loan terms she was offering kept changing, causing great confusion. Frustratingly, Mother was not happy because of vague words and the amount of uncertainty.

One day, the rich daughter-in-law promised to lend gold for Mother's youngest son and daughter to travel if, when asked, they would babysit her 2-year-old child. Another day, she said she only had enough gold for one of them to go.

When Mother voiced concerns about the well-being and safety of her older sons under the communist regime, the rich daughter-in-law promised to lend gold for only one or two of her older sons and me to go. But the rest, including the youngest son and daughter, would have to stay behind in Vietnam because she said she didn't have enough gold.

Even my youngest siblings, only 11 and 12, knew about her vague and ever-changing promises. Full of emotion, they flexed their noses and told Mother, "I will still go!"

These frequent about-faces from the rich daughter-in-law deeply concerned Mother, causing her many unnecessary anxieties. In that situation, how could Mother hope to borrow enough gold to get all her children out of Vietnam? And if she couldn't, which ones might have to stay?

Mother knew the entire family might not leave the country. So, she wanted all her sons to flee, leaving the others behind. "Hùng, you must get all your brothers out first!" she told me. Mother didn't worry about her daughters as much. She said they could stay with her and were in no imminent danger. Whenever I went back to Sài Gòn and listened to what Mother repeatedly told me about her rich daughter-in-law's changing terms, it pressured me to find a solution for my siblings. It also irritated me because the constant stress of wondering who would take the journey, day in and day out, caused Mother to lose appetite and sleep. She was deeply concerned about the uncertain and dangerous future her sons could face if left behind.

Knowing Mother's unconditional and unconstrained love for her children, I felt great pity for her and became determined to achieve her dream, even at higher risk. Besides, because there might not be enough gold for all my loved ones to flee the country, I thought it would make sense for my own small family and me to stay in Vietnam and find another opportunity later. We didn't have gold, anyway! During that time, anything I said or suggested went to Mother or my elder brother, who would discuss it with his wife and in-laws. The rich sister-in-law preferred that I accompany her family but mentioned nothing about my wife and son. But I had already determined not to run away and abandon them in the dark world we lived in.

So, one day, to negotiate for more gold to fulfill my mother's dream of taking at least all her sons out of Vietnam, I explicitly explained I would take care of myself and my wife and son, and leave later. I didn't want to borrow their gold for me.

Then I suggested using the gold she wanted to lend me to pay for my siblings to go instead. I explained my strategy to my elder brother and his wife, telling them I knew a way to reduce the age of my loved ones and the nephews of my elder brother's wife on official papers to get a significant reduction in the amount of gold required to pay for spaces on the boat. I wanted to borrow enough to finance Mother's dream of getting all five younger brothers and the youngest sister out of the country.

My recommendation shocked everyone I shared it with. They thought the age-reduction tactic was too aggressive, and it worried them. Many heated discussions took place late in the evenings. My elder brother and his wife didn't believe I could trick the local communists and boat owner into significantly reducing the amount of gold required to pay for the trip.

While we were expressing our opinions, we frequently lost our tempers. The arguments sometimes became so loud that Mother had to stop us since the small dining room where we sat was only about six meters away from the main blue iron door.

Other times, to make it difficult for anyone outside to hear the back-and-forth yelling, Mother would create loud noises by rubbing and banging the cooking pans together as though cleaning them.

At one point, I was close to giving up on my entire plan to help get my siblings out of the country. But eventually, I overcame my frustration and pursued our mother's dream.

My elder brother and his wife understood what I proposed but were concerned, primarily because they didn't realize how much I knew about the boarding operations on the night of departure. They were unaware of what I had already learned while staying in Bạc Liêu, so they didn't believe my tactics would work!

Mother opposed my suggestion because I wanted to stay behind with my wife and son. In fact, Mother took an extra step to criticize and scold me for my stubborn behavior.

"Why do you want to die here?" she asked angrily.

Her concerns certainly didn't fall on deaf ears, but I was trying to test Mother's rich daughter-in-law and her family to see how desperate they were for my help to flee the country.

I wanted to determine whether they could afford to lend more gold. If they could, there was still a chance of helping my remaining siblings leave on the same boat.

Everybody seemed scared of my daring age-reduction plot. Each of us had a breaking point! I fully understood the situation. If the plan felt too risky, and I couldn't develop a safer solution, they might not want my help and could back out.

I feared I was close to the rich sister-in-law and her family's risk tolerance threshold. The age-reduction idea was probably at or near my elder brother's risk acceptance limit, as evidenced by our explosive arguments.

To make matters worse, besides the risky trick everybody seemed deeply opposed to, the personality conflict between the rich sister-in-law and me grew unstoppable. I closed my mouth and held my tongue, trying to avoid any family clashes that could compromise our mother's hopes and dreams.

I certainly didn't want to add more fuel to the fire. The antagonism could blow up and destroy all that I had planned to that point. However, I deliberately wanted it to appear as if I cared little about leaving and had little interest in my future.

It wasn't until a few weeks before the scheduled departure of Mr. Thái Đức's boat that my elder brother, his wife, and in-laws finally accepted my plan, which would save them a substantial amount of gold. They agreed to lend us enough gold to cover all my younger brothers and the youngest sister—six siblings from my family—just like Mother wanted.

To my great surprise, they also offered enough gold for me to accompany them and more to pay for my wife and son to be on the same boat. The news astonished me because I had never asked—let alone begged—anyone to borrow the gold for my wife and son. Apparently, they had finally realized I would not abandon my small family, leaving them behind. And if my elder brother's in-laws were leaving the country, they needed me with them.

But there was still a catch to the situation!

During that stressful period, I was aware of the rich sister-in-law's irritation with my family. Solely based on our poverty level, our lives and feelings didn't seem worthy of her attention or interest.

After a few months as a sales clerk, my wife's boss promoted her to fund manager for the district produce store. Upon learning this, the rich sister-in-law suggested Mai steal the easier-to-access money from her place of business to pay for a portion of the total amount my wife would need to cover her space on the boat. Since my son was only three years old, there was no charge by the boat owner or government for him to take the journey. Stealing would be a desperate, crazy, and naïve act. I cared too much about those from Mai's family and mine who would stay behind and felt we needed to eliminate any consequences that might dangerously fall onto them upon our departure.

No matter how much against the communists' brutal policies I was, I would never ask Mai to do such a thing. So, I completely ignored the rich sister-in-law's unreasonable insistence that my wife steal from the socialist government, which would have easily aroused their anger and led to dire repercussions.

Poor, yes—but I was not foolish.

My younger aunt wanted her oldest son to flee with my siblings during that time. She had some savings from her daily street trading. I planned to falsify and reduce my cousin's age to two years younger than he was so it would cost two instead of the five taels of gold set by the boat owner for his actual age. Knowing his true age, the rich sister-in-law still wanted to collect the entire amount. I rejected her greedy notion, foiling her desire to profit by reassuring my aunt that she only had to pay two taels of gold.

One day, one of my father's cousins, Cô[†] Thủy, somehow knew I was planning an escape by boat and wanted me to help her family flee. With her aggressive tendencies, the rich sister-in-law determined she would be the one to discuss the plan with Cô Thủy and her husband. Tired of dealing with her condescending personality, I let her handle the talk with Cô Thủy's family. Eventually, everything had to go through me. Then I would interfere as needed. Unusually, after meeting to discuss the fees, Cô Thủy and her husband didn't return to follow up with the plan's next steps to be on Mr. Thái Đức's boat. They must have had doubts about whatever the rich sister-in-law told them or perhaps demanded. Eventually, my father's cousin got another lead, and their entire family left Vietnam successfully.

[†] "Cô": Similar to "Aunt" on the father's side.

The rich sister-in-law seemed to think she ran the whole escape plan and that I was working for her. She wanted to take advantage of my wealth of knowledge and the age-reduction trick I'd developed. So, any interference or opposition to how she was doing things was enough to make her blood run warmer than normal. I knew one day I would pay dearly for those obstructions. But for now, she needed me to carry the plan forward for her family.

By then, I was told there was no more gold to borrow. So, our parents and two other sisters would have to stay behind. Of course, my aunts shared a similar dark fate. Based on my wish list, only the oldest son of my younger aunt would go as planned. His remaining siblings would have to stay behind.

Loose Ends That Changed Life's Journey
MOTHER ALWAYS BELIEVED I would eventually die or be sent to the concentration camp if I stayed behind.

Regardless, in my mind, I had already prepared to remain in Vietnam with my wife and son.

Of course, the offer to give us more gold for my small family to leave was good news. However, I truly had mixed feelings. At that point, I knew my elder brother's in-laws still had substantial gold. Normally, I wouldn't care about the size of someone else's assets. However, in this case, my job was to find as much gold as possible. Bound by the moral values that I felt I had to uphold, I knew I had to try as hard as I could to get the remaining loved ones from my family on a boat out of Vietnam.

Tormented by constant thoughts about my next steps, I tried not to instigate the rich sister-in-law, who seemed to be just waiting to burst. A few more interactions would bring us closer to the breaking point, and the departure date was rapidly approaching. It would then be too late!

I recognized it was my elder brother and Mother's love and influence during the last few weeks before the boat departure that sealed not only the destiny of my siblings but also myself, my wife, and my son's fate. That day—the day the rich sister-in-law and her family finally determined how much gold they wanted to lend us— I talked with Mother and my elder brother. When they saw my face, painted with a lack of optimism and deeply unenthusiastic, they frowned and criticized my stubborn reluctance to take the offer. In fact, I was just deep in thought, wondering why the rich sister-in-law would not use the gold to get the remaining loved ones of her husband, instead of me and my wife and son, out of the country.

I knew she didn't care more for my family than her husband's parents and younger sisters—but she needed me to be on that boat for several reasons. However, everyone knew I wouldn't leave my wife and son behind. Therefore, the only option was to lend me more gold so my wife and son could leave with me.

Knowing my stubborn behavior might have almost crossed the breaking point, I eventually agreed to the offer. That week, before returning to Bạc Liêu, I sat down to discuss a few important details with Mother and my elder brother.

First, I couldn't coordinate our group's transportation from Hồ Chí Minh City to Bạc Liêu since I would already be in Bạc Liêu to ensure we had safe places to stay for a few days before departure. While I would not be in Hồ Chí Minh City that day, my remaining sisters who were not on the list to go should travel down to Bạc Liêu with the group.

I knew that the night we were boarding would be very chaotic. Because of that, the district security cadres might not be in full control of the entire operation. If I was lucky, I could help them sneak onto the boat without being detected or bribe the government agents on the spot to let the additional siblings board. I wanted my unlisted sisters to come with the group to Bạc Liêu so that they could take advantage of any last-minute chance to leave Vietnam. They could always return home unharmed if I failed to get them on the boat.

Second, during that time, my elder brother's younger sister-in-law, Hoa, and three of her nephews had already left with an underground group to flee Vietnam. It was much more dangerous than the ethnic Chinese-Vietnamese departure program, which the government protected. If they failed and returned at the last minute, I would not swap and allow them to get on board in place of my siblings.

Third, it would cost two taels of gold to have someone fabricate the required documents, including personal papers with fake Chinese-Vietnamese names and the family registers. Since I could create falsified papers showing Chinese-Vietnamese names with reduced ages, Mr. Thái Đức's staff would only charge a tael to develop the family registers.

I told my elder brother I still wanted to charge two taels of gold. While we would only pay Mr. Thái Đức one, I wanted to give the other piece to Mother before our departure. One tael of gold was equivalent to about 300 American dollars or more. Mother could use it for whatever she might need to survive for at least six months, possibly longer, in Vietnam after we left. My elder brother agreed.

I clearly explained the instructions to Mother and my elder brother. Then I asked him to collect the agreed-upon amount of gold for me as I had to submit it to Mr. Thái Đức soon.

While still at my parents' home that week, I fabricated the documents for those on the list to leave, reducing the ages of my siblings, cousin, and elder brother's nephews-in-law using copies of their birth certificates. Having done this before, it wasn't new to me. I used to change the expiration date on the hospital pass from the base where I had worked to keep it current. By then, I had already quit teaching there for almost a year. However, I used the falsified paper to go through the checkpoints when traveling back and forth between Bạc Liêu and Hồ Chí Minh City.

A few days later, when I returned to Bạc Liêu, I went to Mr. Thái Đức's house in the evening and handed him the fabricated documents and the list of my people expected to be on his boat. He said he would determine the total amount of gold we had to pay. Since I already knew the price per person, based on the ages and how much he would need to pay the local security office, he and I only had to confirm the number of people and the total cost for my group.

After that, I spoke with some of his children to see how they were doing with their English practice. I didn't come to his house for the last few weeks to teach very often. They knew I was busy traveling back and forth between Bạc Liêu and Hồ Chí Minh City to prepare my family for the boat trip.

Mr. Thái Đức had beautiful children. They were kind and polite and treated me with high admiration. People in Vietnam used to treat teachers with the utmost respect—a tradition that we must preserve to sustain a morally sound society.

His children were glad to hear I would travel with them. Most people registering to leave on Mr. Thái Đức's boat were Chinese-Vietnamese folks. None of them spoke English. So, he and his family seemed happy to know I was planning to be on their boat.

After the meeting with him and his children, I left and went to Anh Minh's house, my tailor friend.

Anh Minh also had a wonderful family with three nice kids. Although they didn't know the details of my family's escape plan, they knew I was working with Mr. Thái Đức to help my relatives flee Vietnam.

They also wanted to get out of the country and likely had enough gold to afford the boat trip. However, they were not planning an escape during that time. I trusted Anh Minh and his family completely. That day, I told them I would leave with my family on Mr. Thái Đức's boat.

That didn't surprise them. I also mentioned I would need to carry a large amount of gold to Bạc Liêu the following week and that I needed a safe place to keep it. They agreed to keep the gold in a secured location until I could deliver it to Mr. Thái Đức.

The next morning, I went to see Đức, another friend of mine. He was a military pharmacist from the ex-regime. He was also working with someone to flee the country.

I told him I would leave Vietnam with my family soon, then asked him for an unexpected favor. I asked if he had any powerful poison I could bring on the boat trip.

He was shocked and curious to hear my explanation for the request. I told him the truth—that I was the mastermind of a large escape plan that involved a lot of gold from my elder brother's in-laws. If I failed and lost all the gold, I would kill myself. However, I also shared that I was confident that the escape plan would work.

Of course, I hoped I wouldn't need to use it! My plan shocked him, but he eventually agreed and told me he would give me something in a few days. About two days later, he came to Anh Minh's house, where I was staying, and gave me some white stuff in a small clear plastic bag.

"What is it?" I asked him softly.

"Cyanide!" he replied.

"Thanks!" I took the plastic bag and put it into my khaki shirt pocket, thinking that would at least be a quick way to die. Then we headed to the café in downtown Bạc Liêu to drink coffee.

A week earlier, while in Sài Gòn, during one of the rumbling arguments with my elder brother about the age reduction, I swore that if the plan failed and we lost the gold, I would kill myself.

Of course, everybody knew my death would solve nothing. But it was a way to let my elder brother and his in-laws know how serious I was about planning the escape strategy. I knew all departures took place at night under dim lights or, sometimes, only under the cover of moonlight.

Normally, the security guards and boat owners didn't even check the age of the boat people when they were boarding. It would also be difficult to know whether a young man's age was 17 if he falsely claimed 15 based on looks alone. Neither could anybody recognize the exact age of a girl who was truly 13 if listed as 11. One only needed to lower the age by one or two years to drop it below the established threshold, then the fee for boarding would be a few taels of gold less per person.

The trick saved my elder brother's in-laws a significant amount of gold and allowed me to cover six siblings instead of the two or three we could afford if we had to pay the full price based on their actual ages. If I hadn't dared to falsify their ages, I could only fulfill half of Mother's dream!

Of course, if I got cold feet, my aunt would have to pay five instead of two taels of gold for her oldest son to leave the country with us. I wasn't sure if she could afford that much!

That week, while staying in Bạc Liêu, I visited some other friends. I met with Tuấn's family. Tuấn and Anh Tín were both in a local prison during that time. I was told I might see them in one of the public areas where they normally completed punitive labor for their "committed crime"—helping people to flee Vietnam. His family told me to go to a place a few kilometers away from his home and provided a time frame.

I went to the area and sat quietly in one of the sidewalk cafés. Indeed, as expected, the prisoners eventually arrived, escorted by security guards equipped with AK-47 rifles. I could see both from a distance. They might also have seen me, as I was the only one sitting outside, across the narrow dirt road, drinking coffee. The prisoners were thin with dark skin from a life of hard labor under the sun. I felt extremely bad for Anh Tín. He went to prison, leaving his wife and children unsupported, and the dream for his family's future had evaporated and might not be recoverable.

I couldn't stay long since they only allowed them out on the punitive labor policy for a short duration. When they were about to leave, I quickly made a gesture to express my farewell and then left. It was the last time I saw them in Vietnam.

Years later, after finishing their prison terms, Tuấn told me that Anh Tín had successfully navigated his boat into international waters and fled Vietnam with his family. They eventually resettled in Australia. Subsequently, Anh Tín went back to the fishing business. Unfortunately, one day, his boat ran into a big storm and went down, taking him to the bottom of the ocean.

The next day, I went to a few places to arrange for my relatives' accommodations for the days and nights before they boarded the boat. My younger brother, who had deserted the communist army, was hiding in Anh Văn Ánh's living space in an elementary school in Bạc Liêu. He was gracious enough to help me hide my younger brother and Father in his tiny apartment.

When I saw him, I told my brother he would leave Vietnam soon—news that thrilled him since he had already run out of options and could not hide there forever.

I asked Tuân about Father. He said Father had gone back to Sài Gòn about a week ago. That was when I first knew Father might have fled the country. I was in Sài Gòn then but did not see him at home. Over a month ago, I returned home to collect my relatives' birth certificates and get some materials I needed to change their ages and names.

Father was also home.

One night, he wanted to talk with me in private. We went up to the open patio on the top of the house. At the corner near a pile of unused aluminum roof materials, Father softly told me, in a very low voice, that a Chinese family who owed him a favor for something in the past promised to give him a free space on their boat in the next few weeks to flee Vietnam. Father asked me not to tell anyone. I thought they let him go with them without paying because Father could also speak English. Under the previous regime, Father had gone to Fort Monmouth in the U.S. for military training in communication equipment.

Because Father was not completely certain that his friend's verbal promise would hold, or if he did not make it out with his friend and had to return, he wanted to have the option of going with the rest of us later.

Father only knew a little about my plan for the family to escape. And he didn't know whether I got enough gold for everyone in our family to leave. Upon hearing Father's plan to flee the country with his friend's family, I was happy and thought it would be good for him to follow us if needed, as an unlisted one. After all, I didn't have enough gold to help him; his rich daughter-in-law could. She knew my father would take the risk again to avoid the tongs of the communists. He did it once during the "land reform" in 1954. But, then again, she kept saying there was not enough gold for everybody, including Mother's remaining two daughters—although she seemed to get along very well with the younger one.

So, when Tuân said Father had gone home a week ago, I knew Father might be somewhere in the South China Sea. But I didn't tell him anything about our father's escape.

Shortly after that, I left. While walking back to Anh Minh's house, I quietly prayed for Father's safety with a heavy heart and mixed feelings regarding the uncertain future ahead.

A few days later, before I returned home, I went to Mr. Thái Đức's house to see how much gold I would have to collect for him. The first list I gave him had 14 people, including my elder brother's family and in-laws. The second list had ten people, including all five younger brothers of mine, the youngest sister, myself, my wife and son, and the oldest son of my widowed aunt. There were 24 people. Based on the submitted lists and the age of each person, I had already estimated the total amount of gold necessary. When he gave me his figure, it was the same amount I had calculated. I asked him to prepare for the registration and agreed to deliver all the gold by the following week.

The following day, I went back to Hồ Chí Minh City. While at home, I sat down with Mother, my elder brother, and his wife. I told them everything had gone as planned. Then, we discussed the amount of gold I had to carry to Bạc Liêu.

"Do we trust the boat owner?" they nervously wondered aloud. I was a little annoyed that this question only arose during the final stage of the planning, but I also understood the genuine concern given the proximity of the journey.

"How will you carry the gold?" the rich sister-in-law asked. "There will be a lot, and you must go through several checkpoints along the main western route."

They bombarded me with so many questions that it didn't allow my brain enough time to respond.

"I trust Mr. Thái Đức, and I can go through the checkpoints with gold!" I told them not to worry about any of those issues.

It was my mistake that I didn't explain clearly to my brother how I would transport the gold safely, causing mounting fears of getting caught to upset him.

"How will you do that?" he suddenly got angry and raised his voice. "TELL ME!"

I should have known to expect this. My brother easily became nervous at relying on unconventional, dangerous tactics. I fully understood his anxiety over the situation. I had carefully plotted out the entire plan, but I could not eliminate all the uncertainties and risks. We would have to go forward despite our inherent fears, trying to keep them under control. Nothing was 100 percent certain or risk-free in this world—let alone plotting a plan, taking 24 people with me to flee from a communist country.

There were a lot of dangers, but we just had to deal with them one at a time. If we didn't have the stomach to face these challenges, we might as well quit and stay home. We were planning to flee Vietnam by boat, not preparing for a cruise vacation.

I was exhausted!

My older sister had just injected me intravenously with another B12 dose to get me back on my feet. I had not seen my wife and son for weeks. I had been busting my butt to ensure I was not compromising the lives of 24 people.

Those responsibilities were heavy and monumental, and the awareness that this trip could be deadly was grave enough to break a man. I just wanted to be left alone to do my dirty and dangerous work instead of being bombarded with more questions. And I still wanted to live—but the cyanide in my pocket should have shown that I was very serious about my actions. I knew what I was up against and the consequences of failure!

I spat out anger like venom, trying to compete with my elder brother's voice, so loud that Mother had to rub cooking pans together to block the conversations from being heard outside.

Eventually, with Mother struggling to help, we became civilized again. I explained to him I would carry all the gold in my cloth bag and clothes pockets and walk past the security guards at checkpoints. That was truly my plan. I told him he could come with me if he wanted to help carry some of it. For 24 people, I had to carry about five to seven kilos. Abruptly, I ended the discussion. I was beyond tired and wanted to go to bed.

Crossing the Mekong River with Gold
THAT WEEK, I left with my elder brother to carry the gold from Hồ Chí Minh City to Bạc Liêu.

I wore a normal khaki shirt and carried a burgundy cloth bag full of gold pieces. My elder brother carried some as well. He was an attendant on the western bus owned by his in-laws, and I was the passenger. The bus attendants normally stood on the doorsteps of the bus while it was slowly coasting to the checkpoints. I wanted to sit near the bus door so that I could jump down quickly during that time. My brother was very nervous but paying complete attention. I knew what I was doing, so I was less edgy.

In June, the weather in the western provinces is normally warm with high humidity. I was sweating amid the noisy conversations between passengers and traders.

Most of them were also nervous because they were trading illegally and had to bribe the security staff at checkpoints. I held the heavy bag and placed it on my lap while sitting. I secured the small clear plastic bag my ex-pharmacist friend gave me last week in my left khaki shirt pocket.

At that moment, my body was worth a lot of money. I had never held that much gold in my hands before. Each piece looked beautifully shiny. A tael of gold was physically thin and light. It didn't occupy a large space. But the total amount of gold for 24 people was enough to make them heavy if held for a long time. I had to carry them for about eight hours in a very humid environment, all the way from Hồ Chí Minh City to Bạc Liêu.

Of course, I was edgy, too. For me, it wasn't mainly because of the checkpoints. It was because I held the future of 24 people in my hands, including my loved ones.

Mother could forgive me if I failed. But it was likely that nobody else, including myself, could do the same as Mother could.

The stakes were too high. The responsibility was so monumental that I could not handle another failure in my life if the plan didn't work. I knew I must fulfill my loved ones' dream—the dream they were powerless to achieve under the socialist state.

I wanted to see them smile with true happiness, particularly the little brothers and youngest sister. Father and Mother were too poor to give them a chance to live the life every parent wants for their children and loved ones.

Faith that a better life existed and that we could reach it empowered me to dare to attempt the harrowing escape.

Everyone knew if I failed, that would be it. This was their last chance! Twenty-four lives were in my hands, including my wife and 3-year-old son.

I hoped I never had to open my khaki shirt's left pocket. In it was another item among the gold I wanted to protect—the cyanide.

"HELLO, FELLOWS… HELLO, FELLOWS… CHECKPOINT… CHECKPOINT!"

One of the bus attendants yelled out, ready to jump down to see the security guards who were readily standing along the road in front of their posts with AK-47s. When the bus was about to stop, I stood up and jumped down onto the ground.

The burgundy cloth bag, with its long band strapped around my neck in a diagonal position, hung on the right side of my waist. I rushed toward the security cadres in uniform, scanning around to find a few familiar faces.

All I needed was just one! Suddenly, a crook from the "April-30 Group," approaching me from the opposite direction, gestured for me to go back toward the bus. I ignored his sign and continued walking. Luckily, I found one familiar face just in time.

"Salute, comrade!" I vigorously waved at the security cadre I recognized with my right hand while tapping slightly on the bleeder's shoulder with my left hand when he stopped before me.

"I am going to go over there to smoke with my comrade friend," I told the man while pointing my index finger toward one of the military men, sidestepped the scumbag, and kept walking forward. He still didn't move!

I sensed his eyes were tracing my back. For a moment, I thought I would need to walk faster before he stopped me again. Then, my savior came to the rescue!

"Salute, comrade!"

The man dressed in uniform recognized me and greeted me back. The bleeder certainly saw him and unmistakably heard his words before turning and rushing away toward the bus to rip other people off. Comfortably, I strolled to my "friend" with a big smile!

Standing beside him, I pulled out a pack of cigarettes, shook it a little, and smacked one out for him. Then I put another one in my mouth. He quickly pulled out a match and lit up mine first.

"What a nice guy!" I thought. I used to see him practically every time I traveled between Hồ Chí Minh City and Bạc Liêu.

He knew I was working for one of the military hospitals in Hồ Chí Minh City; therefore, there was no need to check my paper, which was still valid—thanks to my newly gained forging skills.

"Where are you going today, comrade?" he asked with a northern accent while blowing out a cloud of thick smoke.

"I am going to Bạc Liêu to meet with some of my medical comrades. How are you doing?" I replied, continuing the conversation with him while looking at the bus.

Some scoundrels were inside checking passengers' small bags while several other men were checking big boxes and containers on the roof. A few security guards were standing next to us, but they didn't pay any attention to our conversation.

So, I just kept exchanging a bit of chitchat with my "friend," who must have been a senior in the group. He didn't have to take part; once they got all the kickbacks and bribes, his people would share the collected money with him.

The gold pieces in my bag gradually exerted more pressure on my left shoulder. They all, mixed between layers of my old clothes and miscellaneous personal items, remained safe and unchecked in my cloth bag.

It took the security guards about 30 minutes to search through boxes and containers and check people's ID papers. They had become rather efficient with their stealing. The bleeders were fierce and money hungry. Finally, when they'd taken their fill, they yelled to the attendants to move on and started walking away from the bus toward where I was standing with a group of security cadres.

"Your comrades were fast!" I pretended to praise their performance and pulled out an unopened pack of cigarettes sitting on top of a stack of thin, shiny gold pieces in my cloth bag.

"Comrade, keep this one," I told him. "I will see you next time!"

He quickly took it and slightly tapped his other hand on my shoulder. "Comrade, have a wonderful trip!"

"Thanks, comrade!" I shook his hand and started walking toward the bus.

When I was about halfway, I ran into some bleeders who were walking back. I didn't know them. Quickly, I turned my body 180 degrees while slowly walking backward toward the bus, yelling a last message at the "comrade friend" with whom I had been talking.

"Oh, I forgot, comrade! If you need any medication, just let me know. I can get you some from my base!" I wanted to ensure those crooks didn't think they had forgotten to search my bag.

"See you next time!" I shouted, waving at my "friend."

"Thank you, comrade!" he yelled back at me while waving his hand in midair.

I finally felt safe and began boarding the bus full of irritable people who couldn't wait to leave the checkpoint. I saw my elder brother standing on the steps by the door at the back of the bus. He stood there, motionless and stunned! I was the last one to get on the bus. Those miserable traders seemed annoyed to see me taking my time, talking and laughing, with those security cadres. They might think I was one of them. So, nobody would say anything to me. Nobody dared to mess with me. Another type of person I knew I had to be careful of while traveling on the western bus was thieves. If they knew I carried valuable items, particularly gold, they wouldn't think twice about trying to rob me. I had to remain vigilant, acting cool and showing the unemotional, faithless face of a communist security cadre. It wasn't hard for me to do that, as 24 lives were still hanging in the balance over my sore shoulder!

That day, I traveled to Bạc Liêu with my older brother without incident. From there, I went directly to my tailor friend's house to give him all the gold to hide in his parents' safe. My friend's family was nervous to see that many gold pieces, especially knowing I carried them from Hồ Chí Minh City to Bạc Liêu!

After the successful journey, it restored my hopes that everything would go smoothly. I was exhausted but felt I had accomplished a critical goal. I took a cold shower, joined my friend's family for dinner, and went to bed early. Tomorrow, I had to turn the gold over to Mr. Thái Đức and, in the evening, go with one of his sons, Thái Hưng, to the docking area to hide them on his boat. I didn't know why they wanted to do it at night, but it was fine with me. I trusted his son. He and I had spent the night on his father's fishing boat. He was born and raised in this area, and many people knew him and his family well. I didn't have any significant concerns and felt it would be safe. That night, I had one of the best nights I'd had in recent memory.

The following day, I went to Mr. Thái Đức's house to tell him I had the gold for the escape. He told me to bring it to his house in the early evening around dinnertime. Then, his elder son would take me to the boat docking area by motorcycle.

The meeting was short, and I left his house only 15 minutes later, returning to Anh Minh's home and remaining there until it was time to go to Mr. Thái Đức's again.

In the late afternoon, Anh Minh's parents opened the safe and returned the gold I asked them to keep for me. With it safely tucked away in my burgundy cloth bag, I set off for Mr. Thái Đức's house to complete the next step.

In his family room, we sat down and verified the amount of gold I had handed him. He found the exact amount he and I had agreed on in the bag, and he was happy. He felt no need to confirm whether the gold pieces were real. As a business owner, he was familiar with them and could visually detect if they were fake.

His elder son was not at home yet, so I had to wait until after dinner to go with him. The house still looked as though nobody was leaving to go anywhere long-term. The furniture and household items remained unmoved. Family pictures still hung on the walls. Mr. Thái Đức seemed calm and healthy. He was tall and gave off the aura of a successful man, which made me more confident about the entire operation and the plan to flee Vietnam.

Finally, his son came home, but the sun had already gone down. After a quick meal, we mounted his motorcycle and set off, heading toward the shore. I was sitting aft on the saddle, right behind him and holding tightly around his belly. My bag—full of gold—sat firmly between his lower back and me.

Thái Hưng was very familiar with the roads of Bạc Liêu. He was born in the region and knew every corner of the local and surrounding areas like the back of his hand.

We passed open areas with wide rice paddy fields on both sides. There were a few other vehicles on the roads. We didn't talk. I didn't know what he was thinking, but I was praying nothing bad would happen to us at night in the middle of nowhere. His motorcycle seemed to run mostly fine, but occasionally, the engine made a noise that sounded like it was choking.

We rode for about an hour and eventually arrived at the docking area. I saw the riverside from a distance and noticed Mr. Thái Đức's most trusted people guarding the boat. Many of them were his relatives. They normally slept, ate, and worked there—never leaving the boat unprotected. We stepped onto a narrow wooden plank used as a bridge to get on the boat. It was flexible, moving up and down slightly with the weight of our bodies.

Once on the boat, I handed Mr. Thái Đức's son the gold bag. There was no need to count them again, so he took it quickly. A few men were sleeping on the top floor near the pilothouse. He asked me to wait where I was while he went to the lower level and disappeared beneath the top floor.

I looked around and saw several bags of rice stacked up around the room. I guessed they would hide gold in some of those sacks. Fifteen minutes later, he resurfaced on the top floor, returned the now-empty bag, and gestured that it was time to go.

We rode back to Bạc Liêu that night, and he dropped me off at my tailor friend's house. Anh Minh and his wife were still up. But their parents and the children had already gone to bed. They asked if everything went as planned. "All went fine," I said before sitting down with them to talk a little before bed.

The next morning, I went back to Hồ Chí Minh City, arriving home in the late afternoon.

Everyone seemed stressed, and I felt my blood pressure creeping up. I was still trying to think of any potential glitches or snags that could surface between that day and our planned departure. I asked my elder brother whether he had heard any news from his in-laws, who had already fled the country with an underground group. He said there was no news. I asked Mother if she had received the tael of gold from my elder brother, as I suggested earlier. Mother said she received it, and then I reminded her to tell my remaining sisters to accompany the group to Bạc Liêu, just in case we were fortunate enough to get them on board at the last minute.

Nobody mentioned anything about Father, but everybody must have known that he was no longer in Vietnam. We didn't want to talk about it. I had many things to worry about, but my mind reassured me that Father was already out of the county by then. I prayed he was alive and would come ashore somewhere safely.

On the following day, I talked with my brothers and sister, who were on the list to go. I told them to find small, tightly fitted clothes to wear on the night we were to board the boat. Those petite outfits might make them look smaller and younger since I had reduced their ages on paper to get lower fares.

They looked thrilled, knowing they were about to leave Vietnam, potentially for the U.S. I wasn't sure whether they acknowledged or completely understood the genuine danger involved in the boat trip and the escape, but they smiled and talked to each other excitedly.

I asked Mother to tell my widowed aunt to prepare her elder son for traveling on the high seas. He would also need to wear a tight outfit when boarding. I had reduced his age on paper so his mother could afford to send him, paying two rather than five gold taels.

My elder brother and his in-laws planned and coordinated the transportation for everyone from Hồ Chí Minh City to Bạc Liêu. They were leaving in two days. We divided the group into smaller ones so they could temporarily stay in several locations before heading down to the boarding area.

My wife and son and I would be at Anh Minh's house. On the day we were to board the boat, we would go together to the boarding area and wait until nightfall to gather around with the other Chinese-Vietnamese people waiting to be called to leave. Because we were not actually Chinese Vietnamese, I reminded everyone not to talk too much. We had to be extremely careful with the Vietnamese dialects. I would stand in front of my group and, when called, give a hand signal for my relatives to get on board.

Around 10:00 p.m. that night, I went to see my wife and son; it had been several weeks since the last visit.

Everyone was glad to see me but concerned, pointing out how skinny and unhealthy I looked. I talked a little before gesturing for my wife, her mother, and her aunt to come upstairs to talk.

They sensed something was wrong and seemed nervous about the discussion.

Once we were upstairs, under the dim ceiling light, I told them of my plan to take my wife and son to flee Vietnam. Further, I informed them we would leave for my parents' house in about 30 minutes. They would sleep there for two nights, and then, on their last morning in Sài Gòn, they would depart for Bạc Liêu. I told them not to bring anything except for a few articles of clothing.

I didn't talk long, just a few minutes, before stopping to hear their responses. By the end of my instructions, my mother- and aunt-in-law looked like they could have had a heart attack. They didn't fully believe what I had just said and wanted to be sure I was not crazy or delusional.

The news came as a shock to my wife's family.

"Now?" my aunt-in-law asked.

"Yes, now—as soon as she can gather some clothes," I replied.

"Is it safe… are you sure?" my mother-in-law asked nervously, unable to hide the worry from her face.

I didn't know how to answer her question. So, instead, I kept pushing my wife to prepare. "Pack some clothes, quick!" I told her.

Mai had been quietly listening to the conversation the entire time. She just stood there in shock without saying or asking anything. She was terrified and had no desire to leave her family immediately, with so little time for goodbyes.

Finally, the reality of the situation soaked into her mother's mind. "Let's pray at your father's altar before you go," she said.

So, we did! We said farewell and prayed for a safe trip with his protection. I headed downstairs while my wife prepared a few things for the trip. I had told her not to worry about bringing any food or money, but she had nothing much to bring, anyway!

A half-hour later, we finally said farewell to her family.

Mai's face was as white as a sheet. She tried not to cry, fearing the next-door neighbors might hear. Her mother and aunt were scared, not knowing what might happen next. They knew they would be in the dark for a long time regarding whether we had survived the journey or were already dead. But we all faced the same predicament—do it or don't! There was nothing in between to choose that could soften the mental agony.

Finally, we quietly tiptoed out the main door and walked toward my parents' house. It was the last time that my wife and I were with her family in Vietnam. Unknowingly, we would never see her beloved aunt ever again.

That night, we all slept in the small room above the second floor of my parents' home. The next morning, I woke up early. While my wife and son were still sleeping, I sneaked out of bed toward the open patio.

Several years ago, the space was completely flat but surrounded by brick walls that reached about chest level to prevent us from falling over the side. I was around 14 years old and used to come up here to play.

From the top of the two-story house, I could glimpse a large area of my neighborhood. It was a place forever ingrained in my memory, one where I flew my kites high in the sky while wondering how the colorful paper could float in midair, dancing in the wind. I made them using paper and plastic framed by light bamboo sticks.

After my older brother's death, I dreamed I was flying. I knew how vibrant my dream was back then and how painful and heartbreaking it became when I lost it all after the fall of Sài Gòn. Then, Mother's dream began forming in my subconscious, encouraging the continuation of my existence and restoring my will to survive. She loved her children beyond anything else and wanted us to depart from our lost motherland to start something new and full of opportunity. Her dream grew from her worst fears and the potential suffering awaiting the chosen ones, pre-destined to a horrible fate.

I used to think about the open patio of my parents' house as a haven for the juvenile mind of a boy full of dark dreams, a sanctuary to avoid the cruelty of the Vietnam War. Subsequently, Father had a contractor build a small room occupying the front half of the space, and he used it to raise chickens for business. He asked me to feed them and collect their eggs to sell. However, our chicken business didn't last forever. One day, he sold all of them and converted the space into a small bedroom.

The air that morning was fresh. It was still early, and the entire area was quiet and seemed peaceful. I looked around my neighborhood, unable to stop the poignant sentiment and sadness as I thought about leaving Sài Gòn forever.

For me, it was a one-way path. There was no turning back. I had already crossed the point of no return. From that day on, I had to accept my fate and faithfully place my loved ones' lives and mine in the hands of angels, but, hopefully, not in the hands of Death. I had done all I could and was ready to face the consequences.

I quickly freshened up and started packing. Like my wife and son, I had little to bring except a few old clothes. I also took the U.S. military flight diploma, a few pictures of me in uniform, and a thin old medical dictionary—which Dr. Truyền, one of the bộ đội physicians at the military hospital, had given me as a souvenir. I secured them all with plastic wrap to prevent potential damage from seawater and stuck them in my burgundy cloth bag.

The clear plastic bag containing cyanide was still in my shirt pocket. It was my one-way ticket if the cost of fulfilling the dream of my loved ones was too high to bear.

I desperately hoped I would not have to use it.

Nobody knew about my plan for suicide except myself and my ex-pharmacist friend.

I came back inside the room and gazed at my wife and son momentarily, watching them sleep, deep in their own natural calm that came with slumber. They both looked so innocent. I felt my heart clench painfully. I didn't have a crystal ball, nor did I wish for one for fear of seeing unwanted outcomes.

It was time for me to go. I gently shook my wife's shoulder to wake her up. Mai opened her innocent eyes, taking a moment to recognize where she was. I held her hands and waited for her to be completely awake before softly telling her I would wait for her and our son in Bạc Liêu. I told her not to go back to her house under any circumstances. She was extremely nervous—rightfully so, as things were happening so fast and unexpectedly in her mind.

She had never been away from her mother, brothers and sisters, and aunt for more than a few days.

She had no money, and, just like me, her worldly possessions comprised only a few clothes for her and our son. If I had just told her to go home, she would happily have returned to her family immediately, without question.

Unfortunately, I could not do that. Instead, I asked her to take our son on a very dangerous journey in which death was not an unrealistic expectation.

Even if we made it to international waters, where would we go from there? Amazingly, I did not know! I hoped to land ashore somewhere safely, of course, in a free country nearby.

Besides, all I knew was we were going to an unknown, unplanned destination. We only wanted to get out of Vietnam—the rest didn't matter. My emotions were running high, mentally torturing my mind with what we were about to face.

I tried not to think about it anymore, quickly kissed my wife and son goodbye, and stepped downstairs. My life was full of tragic partings of ways, but I still could never get used to saying goodbye to my loved ones. There were too many goodbyes in the dark world in which we were living.

I had already talked with Mother and the rest of my siblings a day earlier. I said farewell to Mother. Again, she softly cried and begged me to care for her young children. Clenching my lips to prevent myself from crying along with Mother, I reassured her of my promise to protect them. Then I left on foot for the bus stop, eventually hopping on a three-wheeled Lambro cab to travel the rest of the way to the western bus station.

That was the last day I was in Sài Gòn, the Pearl of the Far East, where I grew up amid the chilling casualties of war, solemnly pledging to protect my motherland and excruciatingly witnessing her demise—a fateful tribulation of my country.

It was one of my most unbearable, excruciating days, knowing that once I stepped out of the house, I might never see Mother and the remaining relatives again.

~

IN JUNE 1979, many strangers, mostly ethnic Chinese Vietnamese, flooded Bạc Liêu. They came from different places, including Hồ Chí Minh City. The local authority and residents knew why they were in town.

Those people desperately wanted to leave Vietnam. The government protected them under the permitted departure policy and agreements between the government and boat owners. But for the rest of us—people from the "puppet regime" as labeled by communists—we had to be very careful and on guard against local security cadres. They knew there would be many of us among the Chinese-Vietnamese groups trying to escape.

The day I expected my family and relatives to arrive began like any other day for me in Bạc Liêu: getting up around 5:00 a.m., drinking coffee with Anh Minh at the nearby café, eating delicious Chinese buns, and listening to rumors on a variety of diverse topics. The café was full of common people and smokers. I was deep in thought, more so than usual, and looked tense. Anh Minh sensed my concerns and addressed them as best he could.

"Don't worry, Dỹ… Anything I can help you with?"

The cascade of elements that came together to create our reality and future had already begun, and I was nothing more than the handler in the center of everything, standing firm while the dynamic events whirled, unstoppable.

Let fate step in and take over from now on, I thought. That was all I could do. I reassured myself with faith to kill the growing nervous feelings that worsened as the morning passed. Nothing could change or stop whatever may come—whatever the outcome. Fate had fixed the future. Tomorrow was already here today—too late to change the incoming fate of my loved ones, including my own. I felt as if I was holding the pieces of a puzzle in my hands, merely taking the small pieces to a bigger picture and placing them into the spaces where Heaven and Buddha have already decided they would go.

But, for each of us, the canvas of the future was being painted by what we have committed from the fragments of a lifetime that was swiftly passing by.

Nothing could change my faith! An absolute belief in what I pledge to fulfill. Lord Buddha knows what I'm doing, I thought. Or, perhaps Lord Buddha was giving me a lesson or test in both forms: *The Raft* parable[86] and *The Water Snake* simile[87].

The Raft is a story used to explain the spiritual principle in Buddhism that states one should not hold on to the raft for the sake of its highest good after having survived the fierce-flowing river. In my mind, our raft was not the boat we were about to board. Rather, it was the path we had already taken to get here and the journey we were about to endure to continue to the promised land. Both could become an opportunity to preach to the next-generation offspring of the rich goodness of human beings or, perhaps, the corroding perspectives that justify the human mind's dark side.

The Water Snake is another spiritual principle that speaks of the consequences of grasping a snake incorrectly by the tail!

In Buddhism, understanding spiritualism, which paves the way to ceasing misery, is monumental in seeking enlightenment. The principles behind *The Raft* and *The Water Snake* show the importance of properly understanding Dharma—Buddha's teachings—to eliminate suffering.

That day was the beginning of a one-way ticket to hell or the paradise of genuine freedom. The next journey was there to take. Still, I wondered, would it take me farther than the plastic bag in my khaki shirt, well within reach? Could either free me from suffering? The journey may become a poisonous snake, and I won't know if I am grasping it by the neck or tail until it is too late. I knew I would find out soon, though! I thought, give me the boat, and I will embrace the journey. Let it bite my hand, sending the venom to my battered heart. The snake or the journey could kill me, but I knew it would never destroy the faith that had already been rooted deeply in my heart.

If no one else ever understood what I was thinking, I sincerely hoped my wife and son would someday. I contended with my soul in defending my selfishness of freeing myself from suffering. Defying the odds, I reaffirmed my determination without hesitation. Anh Minh could not read my thoughts but knew I had sunk deeply into wariness. "Thanks, Anh Minh," I said. "You and your family have already helped so much! There is nothing else you can do."

On the day my family and relatives were coming, I had nothing much left to do except wait for them to arrive at the bus station in the afternoon. I was nervous about moving such a sizeable group from Hồ Chí Minh City to Bạc Liêu. Still, I was also confident in my elder brother and his in-laws' abilities to take care of the transportation component successfully and safely. They would use their own bus to move our group.

I still had no news about Father. I couldn't do anything at all about it. Father must have been far away on the high seas—or already landed on an island somewhere in the South China Sea. I prayed for his safe arrival at a peaceful destination, with his health intact and newfound freedom to rejuvenate his soul. We might reunite someday, somewhere, but at this moment, only our Creator from Heaven would know our future.

It was a stressful day because of the long wait and the unpredictability and uncertainty regarding what to expect. If they inadvertently left someone behind in Sài Gòn, it would be very difficult, if not impossible, for us to get that person to Bạc Liêu in time.

A little jittery and losing some patience, I told Anh Minh I would go to the bus station right after lunch to wait. I wanted to scrutinize the bus station area thoroughly to see if I could detect anything abnormal or suspicious. Anh Minh agreed. We walked back to his family-owned tailor shop, where I continued to wait nervously, immersing myself deeply in feelings of uncertainty and wariness.

~

A DANGEROUS PLACE! I thought. The bus station was where undercover agents would most likely scout for people like us. Don't make any mistakes, I told myself. One small, stupid, or thoughtless act could cause the entire plan to fail.

Open your eyes wide—watch out! I kept reinforcing my mind to stay vigilant with warnings. The bus station's dynamics, combined with its suspicious appearance, continued to push me closer to the thin edge of mental instability.

The smell of food escaping from the steaming pots of the street vendors dangled in midair amid unbearably sticky humidity. It took me from the deep thought I had faced non-stop since the early morning. People were running, walking, pushing, and talking in high-pitched voices. It was a confused setting but appeared relatively peaceful on the surface. Try not to be fooled by its look, though—I warned myself.

Who could look for us? My eyes constantly shifted around, eyeing people's faces with only the faintest hope of unveiling the hidden presence of local security cadres. I knew I had to act cool—like an agent. Choose someone who has a nasty face and look him in the eye. Right there, near the ticketing office; why is he just standing there doing nothing? Another one, leaning against the electric pole! I asked him for a lighter to fire up my cigarette. He doesn't smoke! Stupid, I thought. Smoking makes you think much better!

Eventually, I found a smoker. "Lighter?" I rudely asked. The poor guy timidly pulled out a match, avoiding looking at my nasty eyes—perfect acting! I was a natural, I thought.

Cigarette in my dry mouth, I slowly walked around, mentally intruding into the mind of anyone with a suspicious face with my stern eyes. I returned the same look even more provocatively if they looked at me nastily! With the military badge in my pocket, with no mention of job title or rank, I could become their worst nightmare if touched. Crazy thoughts emerged from my stubborn soul, committed to helping my family get out. It's amazing what people can think and do if cornered and desperate!

Swallowing more caffeine and filling my lungs with thick smoke, I skimmed the area for hours, wearing a lookalike face to the bộ đội soldiers who stormed Sài Gòn on April 30, 1975.

Black Hands!
FINALLY, IN THE late afternoon, the bus of my elder brother's in-laws arrived, carrying my family.

Most of them could not hide their nervous, suspicious faces. My wife and son were visibly shaking and looked ill. Mai's face relayed the secret that she would return to her mother immediately if given permission. Everyone on the list was there, as planned. However, somehow, my unlisted sisters were nowhere to be seen.

The satisfaction that they had successfully arrived quickly evaporated into the thin, stinky air and transformed into frustration, which changed the color of my face to an angry, reddish hue. The nastiness I had been feigning earlier became genuine. While in Hồ Chí Minh City, I asked Mother to let the remaining sisters go with the group even though they were not on the list—the first instruction. Yet, disappointedly, none of them had arrived with the others on the bus that afternoon. Nor did I hear any immediate explanations for why they were not there! Even if I had been told that my unlisted sisters didn't want to come, I wouldn't have believed it for a moment. Everyone in my family wanted to leave Vietnam, particularly my older sister. She hoped this would have been her opportunity, even without being on that precious list. Why didn't they come? Why weren't they allowed to go along with the group?

It started raising many questions in my mind. Primarily, I realized I had made a mistake by not taking them down here with me on my last trip from Hồ Chí Minh City to Bạc Liêu. But who could have guessed what would happen to them? I couldn't believe Mother or my elder brother would tell them not to go. It made no sense!

"Who blocked them?" I asked, unable to stop my deep, lingering disappointment from exploding into fiery anger. Someone must have used the power of money to satisfy the desire to act on the vendetta caused by personal conflicts. I worried about the future of my remaining sisters, to whom few paid any attention. However, when I tried to help with the limited means I had available, someone tried to sabotage it! When I instructed they should bring my unlisted sisters to Bạc Liêu, I expected it to be done as told. It was a part of the escape plan, which nobody should have altered without consulting me. I truly regretted not handling it myself when I had the opportunity—and there was not enough time to fix it.

My face no longer showed the initial nastiness. Instead, it shifted my features to express deep rage and frustration—an authentic, exasperated face!

I wanted to hold someone by the throat and dump all my anger into their corrosive soul, which was already overflowing with three of the most horrible traits—delusion, greed, and ill will!

I was fuming as my temper raged under the outward pressure. A headache began pounding! My eyes turned bitterly cruel, wanting to awaken the inner wickedness found deep within all humans to punish the malicious act!

But wait, I knew I needed to calm down. It wasn't the time for this type of chaos. I slowly swallowed my disappointment and exploding feelings, putting them out of my mind as best I could in the heat of the moment. You don't want to compromise the entire plan, I told myself. This is Buddha testing me on Dharma, I thought. This is a vicious snake, but don't fall into that trap. Let's move on! There was not enough time to fix the situation.

I knew I needed to save my energy and remain vigilant about the potential security threats surrounding the group during the next few days. Bạc Liêu was a dangerous and volatile place, and I needed my faculties to remain intact to keep everyone safe!

Beneath the surface, I was invisibly struggling to restrain myself and barely succeeding. I could have done much more to show my wrath—but what for? Sure, I wanted to expose who did it—but what then? It wouldn't have solved anything. I knew I needed to save energy for potentially bigger challenges along the road to an unknown land. Internally, I tore my mind apart, battling the conflicting emotions about how to satisfy my frustration.

I finally settled for a peaceful solution, set behind a burning rage mixed with boiling blood. At that moment, I painfully suspected our journey would not end peacefully and that there would be incidents to come, potentially with deadly consequences.

Now fully aware that the first instruction I gave completely went down the toilet hole, I became more cynical! It was the first collateral damage caused by the dark forces that fell upon my shoulders while walking along our treacherous path toward freedom.

Over a year later, in the letter my elder aunt sent me from Vietnam, she confirmed the truth. My mother's rich daughter-in-law had deliberately prevented my unlisted older sister from coming with the group to Bạc Liêu. It didn't surprise me one bit as I read my aunt's painful letter.

On the arrival day, I knew precisely why my unlisted sisters didn't come down to Bạc Liêu and who had stopped them. I held my anger beneath the surface, buried in my inner soul so that the other siblings could leave Vietnam in peace together, preventing a potentially broken kinship or the end of my elder brother's marriage.

A Lasting Decision—Once Upon a Time

WE DIVIDED THE group into several smaller ones to stay in different designated areas that week. I took my family to Anh Minh's house. My wife and son were glad to see me again—but extremely tired and hungry.

Anh Minh's family expected us to stay for a few days and graciously accommodated us, providing anything we might need. We had dinner together with them but went to bed early as my wife and son were exhausted. We slept, unaware that chaos and unexpected outcomes would surface over the next few days. I had already done my best to assemble many hard puzzle pieces to get where we were, but the hardest part was yet to come.

I hoped the remaining logistical bits, except the missing unlisted sisters, should still be in place at the end of this week. I was overly optimistic, unknowing that the situation would change drastically, forcing me to make the most excruciating, heart-breaking decision of my entire life.

Shortly after their arrival, our son got sick with a high fever. My wife and I were very nervous, knowing that if his condition persisted, I would have to change the plan.

Late in the afternoon, with no signs of improvement, Anh Minh's wife took Mai and our son to a local doctor to treat his fever and get him some medication.

Luckily, his health improved that evening, and the fever came down. My son had never traveled to any western provinces before, so it could have been a combination of fatigue and other environmental effects that caused his illness. Fortunately, he recovered significantly by the next day.

We were very grateful for Anh Minh's wife, who deeply cared for our son with her gracious heart. While I was grateful that one issue had remedied itself, another big bombshell soon exploded, threatening to send my loved ones' dreams into an unrecoverable tailspin. The vicious snake came again, forcefully luring me into its venomous trap, as my mind sensed another Dharma to challenge my life journey and inner soul. The rich sister-in-law's younger sister and her three nephews, who previously went with an underground group to flee Vietnam, unexpectedly returned and went straight to Bạc Liêu to look for us. Their escape plan had completely failed, and they had lost all the gold they had paid. Luckily, they survived and didn't get caught.

When they arrived, my elder brother's wife and in-laws asked me to put them on the same boat we were about to board. The biggest problem was that they were not on the list to get on Mr. Thái Đức's boat, meaning I would have to leave four of my loved ones behind and replace them with the rich sister-in-law's younger sister and her three nephews.

I was furious! "No way! I told you before!" I exploded, hissing as quietly as possible not to draw attention to the issue. My circumstances triggered the most debilitating headache I'd ever had, but I fought through it.

I had clearly warned them of this before I completed the plan. It was, in fact, my second instruction—if the unlisted relatives of my elder brother's wife came to Bạc Liêu at the last minute, they might not get on Mr. Thái Đức's boat. Nobody listened. Or, they knew it could happen but didn't know how to deal with it, so they ignored the potential issue. It was just the way it was.

If Mother had been in Bạc Liêu witnessing the event, this situation would have certainly infuriated her with what they asked her son to do. For a moment, I tried not to allow my mind to paint the painful image of the desperate and hopeless look on my younger brothers' and sisters' faces if left behind. They were so close to achieving their dream. It would be a deadly blow to my loved ones to lose it now.

"I will not let that happen!" I reassured myself. Removing my siblings, my wife, and my 3-year-old son to replace them with the rich sister-in-law's unlisted relatives was ridiculously unreasonable. Under extreme pressure from his in-laws and wife, my elder brother's mind and heart were also deeply confused and uncertain about how to proceed.

Of course, he couldn't ignore his in-laws' problem, but neither could he willingly remove our siblings. But he had no clue how to cope with the situation. I knew it also tore him apart; one side was his wife's relatives, and the other was his blood siblings, but it was his wife's family's gold we borrowed for our loved ones to go on Mr. Thái Đức's boat. Had I not been there, I'm still uncertain what my brother would have done, faced with the possibility of leaving his siblings behind. He might not have fought as I did! After all, his marriage depended on his wife and in-laws, while I didn't depend on them for anything at that point.

There was no formal written agreement between the two families, but neither was any law applicable during that volatile time. They could not simply take my siblings off the list and replace them with their unlisted relatives. They needed me to do it for them.

So, I intended to do everything in my power not to leave my loved ones behind. The rich sister-in-law's unlisted relatives could go to the boarding area and take their chances, and I would certainly try to help, if possible, in the last minutes before departure.

They could still count themselves lucky that someone told them to be in Bạc Liêu for the opportunity to board a boat, even if it was slim. My unlisted sisters, whom someone blocked from traveling with the group, didn't have such a chance. Nobody seemed to care about their fate at that moment—except me, who continued to wonder why the rich sister-in-law stopped my sisters from coming down to Bạc Liêu.

My mind continued to struggle internally to suppress my frustration and anger. I couldn't help but think that because it was his in-laws' mistake, my elder brother should suffer the consequences and stay behind, instead of our younger sibling, to enable an unlisted nephew or younger sister of his wife to go.

I contemplated this and several other rationales amid my now-explosive discontent over our circumstances. I knew I would forever remember those last agonizing days in Bạc Liêu! They forced me to make a tough decision that would certainly have a detrimental impact on the future of my loved ones, but there was no way I would remove and leave them behind. What could I possibly tell my younger brothers? Take the bus and go home? How could I tell Mother to forget about her dream? What would I tell my ill-fated brother? Sorry, but I have failed again and cannot protect our loved ones? I kept bombarding my head with rebellious thoughts and excruciatingly painful lines of questioning.

The next two days were extremely bewildering and mentally tortuous for my elder brother and me. I didn't have enough time to fix the problem, and there was a narrow window to fight for my loved ones' presence on that boat. I was alone, as always, fighting and fighting an uphill battle—and wandering around, lost, in my world of pain and suffering. No one could help me during that confusing, tumultuous time.

During those last few days in Bạc Liêu, and even many years into the future, no one could truly comprehend what I was going through or how my conscience would form the most important decision in my entire life.

No one who witnessed the event, except my wife and me, would even try to correct the false narratives of what had happened. And as our lives moved into the future, time would tell that what I had seen then was just the tip of the iceberg for how one could go to any length to follow the dark side of humanity.

I could have told my elder brother's in-laws I would not leave my loved ones behind and proceed as originally planned. I certainly could! Nobody could stop me at that point—our names were already on the list. However, it would be certain to tarnish my elder brother's relationship with them in the future. Would I be willing to do that, knowing my action could damage his marriage irreparably?

Thousands of thoughts went through my mind—every second, every minute, and every hour during the last few days in Bạc Liêu. In my bewildered inner soul, I continued to search for the right solution and gauge the consequences. Making the right decision was crucial to the future of my loved ones. The pressure was so astronomically high that it could have easily blown the top of my head right off. Depending on my potential action, it might tear family relationships apart, and resentments could flood hearts eternally.

Hiding behind my stern face, I harbored revolving rationales and thoughts of what I could do to soften the long-lasting effects. Suppressing my emotions from within, and with a serious expression, I told them I would take two of my siblings off the list and replace them with two unlisted relatives from their family. It was the only solution I offered, and I stood strong, camouflaging the pain inside my heart. It was the sole and final one! In my mind, it was a morally sound but unfair decision. It was a moral one because I made it while considering the preservation of my elder brother's marriage and his future relationship with his in-laws.

However, the decision was unfair because it broke the gentlemen's agreement and the terms of the original plan at the high cost of my loved ones' futures.

It was the most I could do for my elder brother's in-laws. I would not take all four of my loved ones off the list!

After several arguments and lengthy discussions, eventually, they agreed on a solution. They had little choice but to accept it because it was still a better deal for them than the alternatives; two of their unlisted relatives could get on the boat. For them, in the worst-case scenario, I could leave all four of their loved ones behind.

While we were deciding, the hard choices were far from over. Next, I had to determine who I would choose to stay behind from my family members.

Even if the rich sister-in-law wanted my wife to be removed from the list, she couldn't be because our 3-year-old son would have to be left behind, too—and I couldn't replace him with an adult. That option would compromise the entire plan. My elder brother's unlisted in-laws were clearly much older than 16. Hoa, the younger sister of my elder brother's wife, was around 23 years old. Therefore, taking my wife and 3-year-old son off the list was impossible without being detected by security, eventually.

The rich sister-in-law would certainly want me to be one of the two who would stay behind rather than her husband. If my thoughts were correct, I suddenly became someone no longer needed on Mr. Thái Đức's boat at the last minute. Fortunately, by then, I had absolute authority to decide who might stay or leave—and everyone knew it. Who would stop me in those last few days in Bạc Liêu if I became rebellious and didn't want to swap anybody? No one could do anything about it. So, I suggested that my elder brother should stay behind as one of two siblings. I needed to be present with the group to handle the entire escape.

That shocking recommendation rapidly turned the rich sister-in-law's reality into a horrifying nightmare!

I let the impact of my suggestion completely soak in. Then, about a day before our scheduled departure, I asked my elder brother and his wife to come with me to visit one of the boat owners who had a fishing boat. The man was also planning to flee the country with his family, and I wanted to see if I could trust the boat owner enough to put the future of my remaining loved ones and the rich sister-in-law's relatives in his hands.

My elder brother, his wife, and I went to his house. When we arrived, I introduced everyone to the boat owner and asked for a few details about his departure plan. He promised to help but offered no solid plan or time frame for when he would depart. From my experience, this was relatively normal since nobody would reveal the intricate details of their escape plans to anyone who was not within a close-knitted and trusted planning circle. I knew I wouldn't have, anyway. My brother would need to work closely with the boat owner to establish his trust.

That was how it went during our brief conversation. To make matters worse, during that time, Mr. Thái Đức's boat, supposedly, might be the last trip the government could protect under their policy to permit the ethnic Chinese-Vietnamese people to leave Vietnam. That would make things much more complicated—and dangerous—for anyone trying to escape!

After the meeting, we walked back toward downtown Bạc Liêu, where we were temporarily staying. It was the same dirt road I had walked on so many times in the past, but somehow it became entirely new that day, with a dusty haze hanging low along the winding path. It was as though I had never walked on it before. During that long slow walk, witnessing firsthand the fearful feelings and aggravating temper of the rich sister-in-law and hearing my elder brother's words, I suddenly felt a strange sensation—a deep and overwhelming sadness.

From the flood of bitter words mixed with wariness from them, I experienced the delusional perception that I had mistreated my elder brother by asking him to stay behind. Carefully considering my words and actions, I tried to determine what part of my recommendation might qualify as "ill-treatment of my elder brother."

If I were to stay behind or select one of my younger siblings instead of my elder brother to do so, would it still be "ill-treatment" toward one of us? I quietly tried to infer from their bitter emotions, which were beyond logic and common sense. While walking, I was deep in thought, trying to get control over the mental pain that was soaring within my soul.

Listening to their voice spouting worried and confusing words, I felt unbearable distress. The deep sadness within grew while my love and pity for my beloved blood brother grew exponentially. At that moment, my mind suddenly understood and came to terms with what needed to be done. I became calmer and more calculating, knowing exactly what had to be done to end my elder brother's suffering, which revolved around his inner conscience and the burning in his heart.

I knew I had to overcome my frustration and conflicting emotions and think beyond myself to something bigger. What's done was done, and it didn't matter anymore! As we spoke, the future had already snuck into the present irreversibly. Pieces of the puzzle of our future were falling into the places destined by fate.

I continued to assess the situation, realizing, suddenly, that I was born with a greater purpose—chosen to take the blow and shield my loved ones from misfortune during our journey to walk through the darkness that became our world to seek freedom. I knew I had to walk the entire length of the path fate had paved for me, regardless of the suffering it may bring.

At that point, I knew I had already decided. I felt calm and purposeful after refreshing my mother's dream, recommitting myself to achieving it, and returning to righteous principles. The value I seek in life is not always to get what I want to have or desire to win. It is for my actions to positively impact people and achieve the outcomes that bring my mind peace. Again, part of this is selfish. I told myself that it was about my conscience only. If I had left him behind, my elder brother's suffering would have naturally berated my soul for the rest of my life and, particularly, made my last day on Earth void of peace and contentment.

I couldn't do that! I yearned to build happiness for others so I could live and finally rest in peace. And achieving bright futures for my loved ones, including the elder brother's freedom and happiness with his family, guarantees my calm journey into eternity.

It's all about my soul, myself, and how I live in this unstable world. I am a selfish man, I told myself. I didn't know why I thought that way, though.

Why was I berating myself for selfishness? I thought, from a psychological standpoint, I was perhaps trying to give the dark side of humanity a petty victory so it would accept the big decision the good side was making.

I believed everything that happened in my life occurred because of a forthcoming intended purpose. My air force career was brief, but I was in the military for a reason. They trained me to act on orders and quickly make tough decisions in extreme and dangerous environments. They transformed me into a soldier who solemnly pledged to protect my country and people, even if it meant losing my own life. With the future and dreams of my loved ones being taken away, there was never a more critical time to fulfill that pledge. One was already too much of a loss!

I knew then that I could not ask another younger brother to face the possibility of death in Vietnam to save either my elder brother or me. It was he or I who must stay behind!

The rich sister-in-law's agonizing, mumbling voices that filled my mind spoke words that unpleasantly penetrated my ears from within as I walked down the dirt road. They followed me to the end of a long country path leading to the downtown outskirts of Bạc Liêu. By that time, while walking along the winding trail, I had realized that my elder brother could never make it in Vietnam if I left him behind.

He lacked that certain street-fighting knowledge that would allow him to survive and the motivation to inspire him to do daring things when necessary. He didn't have a strong enough stomach for risky ventures and was not like me, who could risk my unworthy life as an outcast in the socialist society.

I truly didn't think he would survive long amidst the money-hungry crooks running around everywhere—let alone while dealing with the mental and emotional distress of being separated from his wife and children.

Still deep in thought, I knew it was time for me to end the unbearable agony expressed to me. I needed to stop the incomprehensible grievance that seemed to criticize me every step of the way, questioning why I was "mistreating" my elder brother.

My mind had effectively coaxed my soul out of the deep sadness, leading it to a state of enlightenment, suppressing the inner mental pain and suffering. I knew I must decide and do whatever was necessary to help my family, despite any potential blemishes that may come from those actions. In my mind, nobody could judge me, except Heaven and Buddha, for the way I lived and fought in this world full of dark forces.

My decision was not without negative consequences. I will always remember the pain it put my wife through during one of her darkest, most trying times. I knew I would carry that weight while transitioning from Earth to the afterlife and into eternity.

For her, the boat journey was just the beginning of a long, excruciating ordeal. I knew that her pain would be severe, especially given the challenge of poverty, which had become a sin cast on her life. However, it came down to a moral decision—no matter how painful it was for my wife—that I had to make to prevent my elder brother from a very dark future.

Again, the military had trained me to protect others first and then myself. If I abandoned my elder brother behind, and something happened to him, that high cost was too much for me to bear. In the past, I couldn't do anything to protect my older brother, and I cried continuously for a long time, carrying the omen from my dark dreams into the future.

No matter what, I could not let another undesirable fate come to my elder brother because I loved him as much as I loved my deceased brother, whom I still missed dearly.

This time, I had the power to change how things would play out, and I had to take advantage of that before it was too late. I had to let him board the boat. I could not leave him behind.

I was deep in thought when my heart finally consented with my mind. Both head and heart agreed that I would take the chance to protect my loved ones instead of trying to save my own life. Suppressing the pain growing in my inner soul, I knew I had to make my decision known immediately, abandoning the idea of leaving my elder brother behind, alone, to face a miserable life.

"I will stay behind with one of my younger brothers!" I calmly said out loud, walking faster to get back to Anh Minh's house.

On the day we went searching desperately for the next boat for those loved ones who were to be left behind, rumors flew that Mr. Thái Đức's boat might be the last one allowed to leave Vietnam under the government's permitted departure policy. To me, it didn't matter. I had already consulted with my inner soul, which was in harmony with my decision.

My elder brother and his wife clearly heard every single word I had just stated. Neither said much in response. Both were quiet, as though my words didn't resonate. But I knew shortly thereafter they would start feeling the effects of what I had just said. Once it hit her what this meant, the rich sister-in-law stopped whining almost immediately. She was making every attempt to regain the stability of her mind, which had been in a state of turmoil ever since the shocking suggestion that her husband should stay behind. Her feelings quickly became at ease, like a peaceful summer breeze under the shade of the big old trees that lined the dirt country road.

I didn't feel significantly different. It was my fate, just as I had suspected from the very beginning while planning the family's escape. I could sense it all along! After all, the omen from the dark dreams might have been for me. Didn't I consent to my predicament and accept my dark future? I had, indeed. All I wanted was for my loved ones to get out of a country that was wiggling under the tongs of the communists.

I wanted the omen to remain with me for the rest of my life instead of with them. It was most acceptable for me to stay behind. I was ready for the dark forces, which were about to build up steam.

I had completely accepted my doomed future, recognizing that the dreams of my loved ones were bigger than my destiny. I will never forget my older brother's last words before he left Sài Gòn to fight for our motherland, "take care of the young siblings for me!"

The last day before my family's departure, I finally comprehended the seriousness of the responsibility my older brother empowered me in that little café in Sài Gòn in 1971 before he came back in a military coffin a few weeks later. I wanted to fulfill my unspoken promise to him without hesitation, no matter what consequences might fall upon me.

Ultimately, I finally reached the tough decision made only out of pure love and constrained self-interest, but not for gold or money. I loved my elder brother the same as my already deceased brother and the other siblings. There was no way I could separate him from his wife and children. It didn't matter for how long. Simply, I couldn't do it at all, period. I was afraid of the ever-lasting mental agony I would face throughout the rest of my life journey. I didn't want to live out my days with a deep sense of eternal repentance for my actions, especially should something happen to my elder brother because I left him behind.

But a judgment day would eventually come—for the cruelty I must have had to push my wife and son out onto the high seas without a husband and father. I knew I could not protect them during the horrible stormy days ahead.

They would be vulnerable as the hands of Death reached for them from every angle during their journey, and the cruelty of human complexity would fall upon two pitiful souls!

I may have ended the agonizing mental ordeal regarding my elder brother and his wife, but it opened a new world of pain for me. It began a long and challenging test of my wife's resiliency and an unfair fate for her and our young son.

So, I told my elder brother I would stay behind with Dũng, my next younger brother. Dũng previously had a job as one of the security attendants for the government produce distribution truck in Hồ Chí Minh City. If he stayed, he might take that job again since he was under no imminent threats from the socialist government. He had been the brother I was screaming for my parents and others to save from the fire behind our house when I was about 12 or 13. From a safety standpoint, he was the most suitable person to stay behind with me. His younger brother had deserted the army and would face a military court-martial and eventually go to prison if they caught him. The rest of my siblings were too young to leave behind, potentially compromising their entire future.

Knowing my widowed aunt desperately wanted her oldest son to leave Vietnam, I didn't want my cousin to stay behind with me. The elder son of the unwavering yellow freedom fighter—whose body still lies somewhere in the wilderness of the Hoàng Liên Sơn mountains—must live on to, hopefully, take care of his family left behind in Vietnam in the future. After reaching the promised land, I wanted him to tell the free world and his family's next generation about his father's heroic history and acts.

I returned to Anh Minh's house that evening and had dinner with his family. I talked a little while eating. Anh Minh's family might have sensed something strange but didn't ask. That night, my family went to bed early on the second floor. In the morning, we would go to the boarding area. It knew exactly how my wife would take the bad news. She would certainly try to remain behind with me, which I would not allow. I spent the entire night deep in thought, desperately trying to figure out how to force her to push aside the fear and take a leap of faith away from our lost motherland and toward a life of freedom.

Telling Dũng he would not be on Mr. Thái Đức's boat would also be difficult and unpleasant. He quietly took it in, showing no visible emotion, even though I knew he was both surprised and extremely sad. He didn't question, "Why me?" In fact, he didn't ask me anything at all. He just listened and nodded in agreement as though he had already known how his fate would unfold. I knew he didn't want any of his siblings to be left behind, either.

That certainly didn't make it easy for me to tell him, my dearest beloved brother. To even get the words out, I had to swallow my emotions. Regardless, it still tore my heart into pieces, seeing the hopeless expression from Dũng, whom I had always protected most, considering my prophetic feeling about his fate—even when I was only ten. Even the death of my older brother during the Vietnam War did not erase the omen from my dark dreams or the original fear I had always felt for Dũng.

Fire, as I had once tried to save him from, fortunately, didn't take him. I suspected that water still could. The omen, as I feared, might still follow my loved ones out to sea, looking for him. And he could be next if he was with the family, but without me, so I thought it would be better this way after all.

Maybe this was Heaven's will to set me up to save him this time. However, there was always the chance that he and I might be the next ones to face Death.

A Dark Time

DURING THOSE DARK times, my mother and aunts were aware of the rich daughter-in-law's behavior. They knew what she had done, but no one wanted to tell me out of fear and poverty-class syndrome, which continued to rise with mounting collateral damage.

A few years later, Mother and my elder aunt wrote to me in long letters, confirming her actions and state of mind. Of course, I had already known the rich sister-in-law's personality. Her fingerprints were all over the place as she defied the instructions I had explicitly given and explained before leaving Sài Gòn. Even during the last few days prior to departure, my gut instincts resonated in my mind precisely about who had prevented my unlisted sisters from coming to Bạc Liêu. I didn't bring it up then because I wanted to give my siblings, including my elder brother, the opportunity to leave Vietnam peacefully. Instead, I tried to bury my exploding frustration inside my head, keeping it to myself.

As I had instructed my elder brother, he gave Mother a tael of gold—the fee for creating falsified personal documents for registration—to survive for a few months. Appallingly, the rich sister-in-law took it back before she departed for Bạc Liêu. Incomprehensively, not only couldn't Mother keep a tael of gold to live off of, but she also had to give her small gold savings to the rich daughter-in-law in the last few days before the group left Sài Gòn.

My mother and aunts knew about all those acts. It seemed everyone knew except me during that time, of course! They didn't want to hurt my feelings. They wanted me to focus entirely on ensuring a successful departure.

Heart-Wrenching Departure

ON THE MORNING of June 16, 1979, we all went down to the riverside where Mr. Thái Đức's boat docked before departure.

Once we arrived at the designated location, we gathered around a large dirt area. Boarding would occur at night, and many people were waiting in groups. We stayed close together. As instructed, my younger brothers, the youngest sister, and my aunt's oldest son wore tightly fitted clothing that made them look smaller and younger.

Everyone was excited but still unable to hide their nervousness. I gazed at my loved ones, perhaps for the last time, with unbounded love, trying not to allow my thoughts to linger on the deadly journey they were about to embark upon. The price of freedom was high, and I'm not talking about gold. I refer, instead, to the collateral damage to family relationships and deep remorse for the rifts that were inherently created throughout the ordeal, even before reaching the turbulent and gusty South China Sea.

The price included the unwanted and unexpected testament of bounded love based on circumstances and conditions and the unmasking of the dark side of the human soul. I wanted to discover neither of these facets of humanity and while I could survive those collateral destructions, the prospect of losing my loved ones was too much for me to bear. Yet, we were still not even halfway through the escape! I still had the small plastic bag containing cyanide, the poisonous serpent's tail rattling in my mind, and my heart was on the verge of breaking down. I would find out soon what end of the venomous snake I was holding and how the repercussions of my choices would play out!

Fleeing Vietnam was a monumental task. It was just the beginning of a horrible journey for countless boat people, including my loved ones, who were trying to escape. In less than 12 hours, I was to send them off into a vast body of water, hoping for the best, as I faded into the darkness of the lost motherland, leaving them to deal with the unknown waiting on the high seas. Fate would decide whether I would live with the consequences of my decision, thankfully or mournfully, for the rest of my life.

Either way, my actions would stay with me eternally—and the fear that came with that knowledge was painfully real and striking!

The hardest conversation my wife and I had ever had occurred on the banks of a strange riverside that had already sent so many people to hell and others to the promised land.

My mind felt like a separate entity, completely outside my slowly degrading body and fully occupied by an extraordinarily powerful will to get my loved ones on the boat and leave as soon as possible. It helped me break the bad news quicker, as even a second of delay would multiply my excruciating agony. Faith guided my mind. I knew that the more I considered my wife's feelings, the darker the fate of all of my loved ones would become. Mai wouldn't want to leave with our 3-year-old son, potentially compromising the entire plan, but she had to—and without further delay, I needed to tell her what was about to happen.

I pulled my wife and our son away from our group, taking them to a corner of the fenced-in dirt area where there were fewer people around. Even though Mai knew nothing about my decision to stay behind, I could see in her eyes that she would have taken our son and returned to Sài Gòn without hesitation if told. I knew she feared the boat trip, even expecting my presence. Fortunately, our son was too young to realize any of the risks and was enjoying something that looked like sticky rice with his hands.

I was quick but to the point. I didn't have time to beat around the bush. "You must leave with our son," I began. "We have already crossed the point of no return." My wife listened quietly, saying nothing. Then I began my closing statements, which I knew would haunt her.

"There is a problem. I have to stay behind to save the entire plan. It's the only way!" I started.

"You and Huy must leave without me," I spit out every single word, knowing it would be like venom to her, then immediately reassured her I would find another way to escape as soon as possible. To her, it was horrifying news that triggered a test of her resiliency that she would never forget.

As expected, and in shock, Mai started crying and questioning my words with a tone of sheer desperation. "Why?! Why?! Why do you have to stay?" She took my hands and shook them while salty tears rolled down her cheeks. I quickly embraced her, gripping her hands tightly while trying to explain the swap that would allow the rich sister-in-law's unlisted relatives to leave.

"There is no other way. You and Huy have to leave!" I told her. "I will find you soon!" Not explaining how soon it might be or how I would do it, I reassured her.

My wife kept crying as the cruel reality soaked into her mind, painfully tearing her heart apart. As I watched her suffering, my heart sank. I tried to comfort her, to no avail.

"We are going to stay behind with you!" she said.

"No!" I raised my voice a notch as I explained to her that replacing our son with another adult would be impossible. Leaving his name on the family register without his presence would raise consequential suspicions. Security cadres might not recognize a slight difference in ages, but they would certainly count the total number of people on each family roster.

"You've got to go to save the entire plan," I explained to her.

My wife kept shaking her head and wiping the warm tears away with her bare hand. I didn't look at her face, instead focusing my eyes on our son. He was licking his fingers and trying to get the last piece of sticky rice. It broke my heart, sending tiny, shattered fragments deep into my subconscious.

"I pray that you and Mom can make the trip without me," I reflected. If I ended up staying in Vietnam forever, I was certain that, someday, his mother would tell him the story of our last precious moments together, no matter how painful it might be. I hoped he would remember me as his loving father and use the suffering we endured as motivation to live a meaningful life in the New World.

While my wife continued to weep, another thought came into my mind, which I had to contemplate for a moment. I knew she didn't want to leave, but I had to get her to accept that it was the best option. I knew that the words I was about to say would freak her out completely, but I thought they would get her on the boat.

"If you stayed, we would have to let our son go alone," I said, my face morphed into a pained expression. "I would ask my elder brother's wife to care for him."

"No!" she immediately exploded.

"Then you must go with our son. Just go!" I kept pushing her mind closer to the edge. It was unfair and heartless to torment my wife's mind that way, but I needed her to go for the good of everyone. There was no choice. They could stay and live the rest of their life in fear, without a future, or leave in search of the freedom to nourish their dreams in the promised land.

My wife knew our family didn't have any gold. That day might be the only window of opportunity for my loved ones, including my wife and son, to flee the country. Even though the ultimate price was high, and it wasn't a far-fetched or unrealistic expectation of potential harm to some or all who fled with the group, it would still be worth it for the chance to arrive at the ultimate destination. She knew I would not tolerate another failure.

The annihilation of the futures of 24 individuals—if it became a reality because of my actions—would leave me with an eternal torment that would destroy my will to live. There would be no more purpose for living; if that were the case, I wouldn't last long. She knew if the escape failed, I would not survive the deadly outcomes of my actions—but she didn't know how easy it would be for me. Unbeknownst to her, the small plastic bag containing cyanide remained untouched in my khaki shirt pocket.

I still don't remember whether my wife ever agreed to go. Permanently embedded in my mind, the only thing I can recall was how she kept crying, clinging to our son as he held onto her waist. I will remember it forever.

Huy didn't understand why his mother was crying at his young age. He fell asleep in his mother's trembling hands, unaware of the gravity of the situation surrounding him. There was nothing I could have said to make her feel better, so I took them back to the group to sit among others.

Over 200 men, women, and children were waiting for the boat. Most of them were Chinese-Vietnamese people. My group had 24 people listed on several Chinese-Vietnamese family register documents. I told my loved ones to keep a low profile and not to talk to anybody unless it was absolutely necessary.

While waiting for nightfall, we just sat there quietly, speculating about what might happen when it was time to get on the boat and afterward if everything went smoothly and everyone got on board. At that point, it didn't matter what we discussed, as we could do nothing about it.

We had already accepted the risk that would lead us to either live a life of freedom or die in vain on the high seas. It was too late to have cold feet—except for my wife, who had been thrown an unexpected curveball and was now painfully going through the motions of my plan but would have gladly stayed behind if told.

My elder brother's cousin-in-law didn't know the details of the deal between the two families and was likely unaware that I would stay behind. He smiled happily and said out loud that if he were me, with the knowledge I had gained, he would remain in Vietnam and keep planning similar escapes as a business venture to get rich. I didn't know how much he had actually paid in gold for his family to be on Mr. Thái Đức's boat, but I'm sure it was a hefty sum. I didn't entertain him by discussing that business idea further, as I was trying to hide the insufferable pain of forcing my wife and son to leave and face the dangerous high seas without my protection.

Eventually, the sun disappeared. Nervously, we waited. My loved ones had to get out of there as soon as they could, as I felt I had to get my wife and son on the boat before she frantically changed her mind. I knew that there was a high likelihood that undercover agents might be among us. They were quietly scouting to see if they could detect any undocumented people trying to take advantage of the chaos during boarding. If the communist agents discovered them, they might still allow those people to get on the boat for a bribe, or they could send them to jail and confiscate all their gold. Either way, it would yield a nice big bonus for those who had worked overtime that night for the socialist state.

Around 10:00 p.m., they asked us to move closer to the boarding location within walking distance. It was a large area of dirt and mud illuminated only by a scattered, dim light here and there. The boat previously docked some distance away from the shore, but they had moved it here. They had a wooden plank stretched to the dock to be used as a bridge for the boat people to get on board. The crew probably moved the boat from its docking location to the boarding area sometime that morning. The plank flexed up and down as the tidal waves moved in and out gently. It looked like we might have pleasant weather, but one could never be too sure. I prayed that no monster tidal waves would surge during the trip, risking the lives of my family members and other people onboard.

From the boarding location, the boat would slowly move south on the long, narrow river before eventually entering the open sea at the end of the waterway.

People stood in various groups all over the place. There were many security cadres armed with AK-47 rifles standing nearby. One held a stack of papers in one hand and a portable loudspeaker in the other. He stood on a wooden platform, a flickering light providing just enough of a glow to allow him to read and call out the names of the registered Chinese-Vietnamese people expected to board the boat. I stood in front of my group, ready to signal to my elder brother's family and his in-laws to walk over to the boat once called. My family would be next. I had committed the fake Chinese-Vietnamese names of the group members to memory and had notes to use as a backup in case I forgot any.

While the security cadre on the platform was still busy sorting something out with the boat owner, I walked over to my brothers, sister, cousin, wife, and son, ensuring they were all still there. They were all nervous but eager to get on board.

My deserter brother, in particular, must have felt an overwhelming sense of relief. He had been hiding impatiently at Anh Văn Ánh's apartment, desperately hoping to leave Vietnam to avoid a potential military court-martial. My youngest little brother and sister, born only a little over a year apart, clung to our other brothers' hands with worried eyes. I tried to hold back my tears as I gazed at them. They used to cuddle up next to Mother every night while falling asleep. In fact, that week was the very first time they had been away from Mother for so long. That night, it fell heavily upon my conscience, knowing that they would experience the most unbearable and formidable journey in their lifetime at around 11 and 12 without their parents. I only hoped it would be worth it.

I looked at Trường, my cousin, with eyes welling up with emotion, feeling sad for him. He must have felt a great deal of lingering emotional pain, leaving a broken-heart mother and five young siblings behind without knowing whether he might see them again. His mother had lost her will to live once already after the tragic loss of her husband. That night, her oldest son would enter Death's domain without knowing where fate might take him.

I prayed for Trường and wished him a bright future and a meaningful life journey. I hoped he would choose to bring love instead of retribution for the cruel acts committed by the atheists from our lost motherland. However, I also quietly prayed that he would never forget his family's horrific ordeal, similar to many other Vietnamese families who lost loved ones in the "re-education" camps erected throughout Vietnam after the war.

Their story had to be remembered and told.

With a forced smile, and desperate attempts to resist the tugging heartache, I kept my mouth shut, hiding the change of plans from the others. The younger siblings knew about Dũng's habit of disappearing and his tendency to wander around telling no one. So, they didn't suspect that Dũng had stayed in Bạc Liêu instead of following the rest of the group that night.

I gently stroked my siblings' heads and backs—quietly prayed while fiercely fighting against my inner thoughts, which felt tainted by the darkness of uncertainty and an understanding of human mortality regarding the dangerous journey. I prayed that Heaven and Buddha would lead them down a shining path, taking them to a safe place where the beauty of freedom would grace them. Then, I held my wife and son tightly to say farewell.

Mai's eyes no longer emitted any vibrant signs; they were full of sadness and fear. She didn't say a word because she knew I had already fixed her fate, because she felt so desperately lost from learning the truth of what had transpired right beneath her innocent eyes, because of the unbearable suffering that numbed the broken pieces of her heart, and because everything was completely beyond what she could wrap her head around. Neither her hands nor mind was strong enough to fight the dark forces that pushed her husband away. She remained completely in the dark regarding when she and our son would see me again in the future, if at all.

Would they even be alive at the end of the horrific journey that seemed to wait to engulf them both? I could keep my fears at bay, knowing she would do anything in her power to keep our son safe and alive during the treacherous journey without me.

"You've got to be strong!" I said, my voice trembling.

I promised her I would find them soon. But in reality, I had absolutely no idea when we might see each other again.

No one could know.

It was not a matter of personal strength. I had no time to cry or think about anything else in those moments. I knew I should not cry in front of them and must hide the overwhelming pain that flooded my heart. A single teardrop had the power to grow into a muddy pond, burying the future I envisioned for my family—tugging everyone down like quicksand.

Worse than that, I knew my tears were even more powerful than the plastic bag containing the cyanide, which remained in my shirt pocket, simply waiting for the signal from Death to be pulled out and used.

I was so desperate to get them onto the boat and to put an end to our suffering! I was fearful because I knew if I made one wrong move or escalated the explosive emotions by a few notches, my wife could easily decide to stay behind with me no matter what it meant for the others. The time for departure was very close! Within a few hours, as the darkness fell, they would be on the high seas heading toward the vast, open area where Heaven and Buddha alone had the power to take them wherever their fate may lie. So, I held my tongue, keeping my mouth shut to avoid any words creeping out with my powerful emotions. I walked toward my elder brother, who remained close to his wife and in-laws.

"Brother! Please take care of them," I quickly said, looking toward our brothers, sister, and cousin, both of us knowing it was his responsibility as an elder brother in the family.

"I also ask you to protect and take care of my wife and son for me," I forced the words out, hoping I could utter everything I wanted to say from my dry mouth. As I spoke, I fixed my gaze on my wife and son, who seemed like lost souls amidst the chaos of the disorderly boarding event being held under dim light.

My elder brother looked stressed and overwhelmed by the surrounding activity, but he told me he would. He knew nobody, including me, would ever want to be in my position. But he also understood that someone had to do it.

"If Mai and Huy need anything, please help them!" I spoke in a flat tone, emphasizing each word as it escaped my lips. My wife and son had few possessions to bring along on the journey, but I knew his wife and in-laws had been more prepared. They had antibiotic medicines, which could be very important on the perilous journey. That was all I could say to my elder brother as tears threatened to break my words down into muffled sobs. He told me not to worry while his wife looked on at us.

I thought if only all of us could have cheered up a little as she had. After all, it was only a few hours away. Then, all of them would be free! That might be why the rich sister-in-law suddenly tried to cheer everybody up.

"Yes, don't worry," his wife added. "Once we get settled in the U.S., I will make your wife marry an American man!" She spit the senseless, venomous joke toward my pale, half-dead face and giggled happily—exposing her ingratitude, dark attitude, and immature mind that did not think carefully before allowing herself to speak.

I believed she thought it was funny. Unfortunately, it had a different effect than intended and instantly killed my desire for humor. I turned my fever-flushed face toward her and looked directly into her eyes. I couldn't believe she would speak such an offensive thought aloud, even in jest, especially during that extraordinarily sad moment for my sorrow-filled family.

I was speechless, but her mindless joke fueled me with an enormous sense of disappointment for all I'd gone through for her family. She could see the rage in my eyes. The rich sister-in-law's words that night were like an iron arrow piercing through the bleeding heart of the person who had willingly stayed behind so her husband could be together with her and her family.

As illustrated by the obscene joke, her view of me clearly portrayed the idea that I had already become worthless to her. I had already laid out the plan and led the group, including her loved ones, to the departure area. There was nothing much for me to do now. I became the living dead once I stayed behind.

To be less dramatic, her cruel joke showed her confidence that I would not see my wife and son again. She knew the boat she was about to board might be the last to carry the Chinese-Vietnamese people out of Vietnam if the rumors spread had any truth. I saw her demeanor as a sign that she was overconfident, that from that moment on, she owned my wife's life and future because of the gold she had lent. To me, that was the implication behind her tasteless joke, the only one I could think of, anyway.

Obviously, she had a short-term memory that had allowed her to forget the agony in her own voice just a day earlier as she walked that winding dirt road, and I suggested her husband should be the one to remain behind. It horrified her about the potential separation from him, which I saw as a little humanity in her for a short time. However, knowing that her entire family would leave the country together, she returned to her former self, unreservedly laughing at my beloved family's separation—and making a mockery of the unbearable torment faced by someone who had just thrown her family a lifeboat. Not only had I given her family the opportunity for survival and freedom, but I had also enabled them to avoid the separation of husband and father from wife and children.

I will never forget that distasteful addition to my extraordinary suffering during the darkest time for my family. No pity for me, indeed! We were finally to be apart. It was as though the darkness within the soul of a losing mind had set it up all long—and the time had finally arrived.

In the last hour with my loved ones, waiting in a dimly lit area within sight of the gate to freedom, those disappointing thoughts flowed through my turbulent mind. Despite the growing bitterness within, I tried to bite my tongue so my beloved elder brother could leave Vietnam at peace with his family.

The rich sister-in-law should have been counting herself fortunate that I chose not to retaliate, for she remained unaware of what I could still have done if I chose, even at the last minute. It would have been easy for me to walk straight onto the boat with my wife and son and all of my brothers, sister, and cousin—leaving her unregistered relatives standing at the dock holding the bag.

Remember, we were still on the roster to board the boat, while four of her relatives were not. Fortunately for her, I wouldn't have done that based on my firm determination not to compromise my elder brother's family relationship and his future. But, from the unique personality and moral value she had shown, I knew my commitment to keep my elder brother's marriage intact might become completely useless in the future.

Despite the challenge to stay calm, I said nothing back in response to her cruelly poor joke. I didn't want to waste my precious time swapping insults. I had only a few minutes with my wife and son before our lengthy separation, possibly forever.

Regardless of the urge to hold them close and keep them with me as long as possible, I wanted them to board that boat immediately when they were called. I wanted them to be on their way, going far away from the lost motherland.

The waiting was agonizing—even a moment of waiting felt like forever during this painful, devastating time in my heart. Then, the crucial moment came! The security cadre read the names of people from the list he was holding to the noisy, enormous crowd. Sometimes, it got so loud that I couldn't hear the names clearly. Fortunately, just as I had expected and told my elder brother, they didn't check the age of each person.

About halfway through, luckily, I heard the fake Chinese-Vietnamese name of my elder brother, his wife and children, and the rest of his in-laws. They gathered their loved ones and, one by one, dashed toward the boat, carefully stepping on the flexible wooden plank and eventually disappearing inside Mr. Thái Đức's boat.

Then, the security cadre continued with my second group. "GO… GO!" I quickly signaled for my brothers and sister, cousin, and the rich sister-in-law's unregistered nephews to move one by one toward the boat plank. Holding back tears and overcoming the mental pain as best I could, I expressed a last whispered farewell and accepted the uncertainty of whether we would see each other again someday. I abruptly hugged my wife and son one last time, knowing it was time for them to go.

"I love you all!" I vowed to them.

Tightly, I held my wife and son in my trembling arms, saying nothing else as warm tears quietly flooded my eyes, tucked behind my wife's and our son's heads. I felt dead inside. My mind felt dead, as did my soul.

At that moment, only my tattered body remained, with pieces of my broken heart plummeting into an endless dark hole. Time appeared to have stopped, and I stood frozen in place, unaware of anything happening around me!

I saw only in shades of gray as darkness fell upon me. I watched as if from the outside looking in as people yelled out, miserable souls calling to each other, echoing as though they came from a distant world. Even the faces of my loved ones, showing fearful wariness, were fading away.

Within a fraction of a second, everything around me was clouded and confused. I had become delusional, and nothing felt real anymore. I surrendered to the horrific feelings that enveloped me in a pain that my brain absorbed and magnified as we walked past the last piece of dry land we would, possibly, see as a family together.

As her heart collapsed in her chest, like mine, our frightened son clung to her skinny waist, terrified by the chaos of that dark night. My wife embraced me, pulling me close with her remaining free hand, her eyes full of fearful tears. Her face showed no sign of any hope. I squeezed both in my arms one last time, knowing with no doubt that she would protect our son with her own life on their journey into the darkness through the stormy water of the South China Sea.

Finally, she released me and dashed toward the darkness without looking back. I had specifically told her not to.

While watching her take several shaking steps across the wooden plank to get on the boat and eventually disappear inside, I could no longer control or hide my suffering. I burst into tears and let them flow freely down my cheeks as my heart and soul collapsed completely. Life did not pity me! It gave me no breaks or favors. I was alone, with a broken mind and a cavernous void in my heart.

It was the last time I had any awareness of the surrounding commotion. I stood there quietly with warm tears incessantly running down my cheeks, feeling the odd sensation of deep and unbearable pain over the separation and a sense of satisfaction in carrying out the plan to its end successfully. At last, soon, my dearest loved ones would be out of Vietnam for good!

People were still pushing around me to get on board as the cadre read their names. The voice over the loudspeaker became annoying to me as it fiercely penetrated my eardrums. I didn't know what to do next and hadn't had time to consider this moment—the after. I just stood there, feeling drained.

The entire ordeal had come to a head and shattered my mind and heart, but my eyes remained glued to the boat.

It must have been more than an hour before the boarding area became less noisy. The men on the ground started pulling the wooden plank away from the boat, finally throwing it along the riverside. While the boat was waiting for a signal to depart, it moved up and down slightly, the bobbing perfectly synchronized with the rhythm of the small waves.

Finally, the security cadre gestured with his hand for it to depart. Mr. Thái Đức's boat moved forward and toward the middle of the river. Momentarily, another boat, with a few armed people on board, escorted it into the deep, hollow darkness.

It was a night I would never forget. They were gone!

I had finally put my loved ones on the path that might lead them toward freedom and the start of new, more promising lives. Still, my heart shattered into the tiniest fragments as I witnessed this once-in-a-lifetime event, their rough departure into the unknown in the middle of the night. I tried to control my feelings and avoid thinking of anything else, including the deadly aspects of the perilous high seas.

Extraordinarily as it might seem, I wasn't sure how to restrain my heart-wrenching emotions while hiding my now-dead soul that night. It was all too horrendous to bear, but I didn't expect anyone to fully comprehend what I had done, how I did it, and how I felt.

I was certainly aware of the potential consequences of my decisions and actions, both positive and negative.

The images of my loved ones quiveringly as they hurried toward Mr. Thái Đức's boat that night would stay with me for the rest of my life, like a congenital birthmark or mole that was present at birth and would never fade away. At that moment, I asked Heaven and Buddha how they could give me such a painful and monumental task without taking away my heart, which remained full of extraordinarily agonizing human feelings.

I had fulfilled my siblings' dreams of seeking a new future in the promised land. But I forced my wife to fight against her desire to stay with me, pushing her and our son into a dark passage on the stormy high seas with no protection from a husband and father. I also expected many challenges to be sent upon her from the Creator—to test her resilience, survivability, and absolute will and determination to protect our son at all costs—who placed them at various points along my wife's passage over the next few months. Whatever would happen was left to fate, but of course, I knew the consequence of my decisions and actions, as well as the sense of responsibility, were mine to bear and would follow me wherever I might go to complete my life's journey.

For the rich daughter-in-law in the family, similar tests would finally embolden the complex characteristics within—embedded in life and hidden deep inside her faulty soul—in which the truth wasn't fixed or eternal, but rather like a clod of clay, molded as desired, into an ugly shape, to cast doubt and incite tearing conflicts of kinship. It was all to satisfy the dark human side Heaven and Buddha planted to contrast the bright, shining souls starkly.

That night at the riverfront, I finally recognized that unless we were experiencing the Creator's tests, we might never discover the complexity of human personalities, which become brighter or darker as we move through life and its many tests.

Mr. Thái Đức's boat, registered as "MH-4112," finally carried my loved ones away, plunging into darkness at around 1:00 a.m. on June 17, 1979.

I prayed for everyone aboard and wished them well on their journey, hoping it would lead to freedom and a bright future. It was the last time I was with my siblings, wife, and son in Vietnam. I had fulfilled my mother's dream—and the implied promise to my brother—and, in doing so, erased the haunting feeling of having sinned by being unable to take them out of Vietnam during the last days of Sài Gòn. My mind no longer lingered on my internal struggles since losing my beloved motherland to the dark forces.

Angel or Messenger of Death

AFTER MR. THÁI Đức's boat had left that night, I didn't return to Bạc Liêu right away. My elder brother's unregistered sister- and nephew-in-law, who went with me to see their family off, and I found a barn nearby to stay. We slept on the ground and waited for the morning to go back. Dũng had stayed in Bạc Liêu and didn't want to see anyone off. I guessed he was sad about not being able to leave Vietnam. His only hope for escape was now gone, and I figured he might be in denial.

Before Anh Ba Long—my elder brother's half-brother-in-law—and his family left that night, he left behind a bag containing over 25 pieces of gold and asked me to take care of his son and younger half-sister, who were to stay behind with Dũng and me.

That amount of gold, he said, would be enough for all four of us to get on another boat to flee Vietnam if the opportunity arose. Grateful for his trust, I told him I would try to take his son and sister out of the country again if I could. Admittedly, I had just told him whatever he wanted to hear.

I wasn't sure what I could do in the future. My body ached from head to toe, and I had little energy left. I didn't even want to keep the bag full of shiny gold with me. So, I asked his younger half-sister to keep it without even looking into the bag.

I appreciated his genuine trust, even though it came too late. If I had all those gold taels during the planning phase several months ago, the entire family from both sides, including my sisters and me, could have been on the high seas at that very moment. But it was over! We just needed to move on, and I didn't hold any resentment toward him. Having experienced a few interactions with Anh Ba Long throughout the planning stages of the escape, I knew he was a good and caring man.

One early morning in Sài Gòn, he took me to see his elder half-brother to convince him and his family to join us as we fled Vietnam. He also hoped I might borrow additional gold for some or all of my remaining loved ones to make the journey. Even though his elder brother was considering leaving then, he decided not to go with us on the same boat. Subsequently, I heard he paid someone else to assist his oldest son in fleeing Vietnam. Tragically, the journey proved a deadly failure, and his elder brother lost everything—his son and the gold he had paid for the attempt. The circumstances were dire, and I felt terrible that I could not help him.

The following morning, my elder brother's remaining in-laws and I took a bus to return to Bạc Liêu. I told them I might return to Hồ Chí Minh City and then head to one of the rural mountainous areas to stay for a while.

I sensed my health had deteriorated over the last year because of the hardship and mental agony I suffered while preparing the whole escape plan while my wife and son were starving. I wasn't sure if I would ever be healthy enough to develop another plot to help the rest of them leave Vietnam.

Returning to my parents' house was not a good idea. By then, the local district security cadres may have been aware of the disappearance of 24 people in their controlled area. They would likely learn that I had masterminded the escape, therefore making a return to Mother's home like walking into the tiger's mouth.

My elder brother's younger sister-in-law and her nephew said very little but appeared confused. The night before, they had witnessed a very successful operation that got 24 people, including their loved ones and mine, out of Vietnam. Then, it was as if, suddenly; I didn't seem to care about leaving anymore. Her half-brother had left behind a bag of gold that I didn't even care to keep. I knew the contents of that gold bag were all my elder brother's remaining in-laws had left. If they failed and had to come back after a foiled escape plan again, even if they survived like the last time, it would be the final straw for them. So, I became the only outsider whom they could completely trust.

By the time we arrived in Bạc Liêu that morning, it was too late to take a bus to return to Hồ Chí Minh City. Instead, we had to stay there for one more day. My elder brother's in-laws returned to their previous rental place downtown while I spent the night at Anh Minh's house.

Anh Minh's family was happy to see me back. The day prior, before we went to the rendezvous area for my group to board the boat, I quietly explained to them, without my wife's presence, that I would stay behind. So, they were expecting me back. I told them that everything had unfolded as planned and without incident and that the boat was heading out to the high seas. Anh Minh's family was certainly glad to hear the news. They were good people, and happy to know my relatives had already left Vietnam.

After we finished discussing the events of the day before, I went inside to take a bath. I had been dirty, unshaven, and unwashed for at least 24 hours.

The bathroom was small and dark. An exterior wall came down and stopped right on top of an invisible line dividing the above-ground rectangular concrete pool into two halves. One-half of the pool was inside the bathroom with an open top; the other half was on the other side of the exterior wall to collect rainwater via a downspout. There was a plastic water scoop for bathing.

I had bathed in Anh Minh's bathroom with rainwater before, and there was nothing physically different this time, but it seemed like it was the coldest bath I had ever taken. Suddenly, I felt an intense shiver running down my spine. My body trembled, jolting me upright. Naturally, I folded both arms across my chest and leaned against the wall for a few seconds. Something had gone wrong, I thought. I quickly wrapped myself in a cloth towel and ran upstairs to look for a thick blanket to take the chill out of my body. Then I dropped onto the bed, cuddled under the blanket, and eventually passed out.

I didn't wake up until Anh Minh came upstairs and asked me to join his family for dinner. I must have slept nonstop for a few hours, but I still felt lousy. Regardless, I went down to the dining room to join Anh Minh. The food was good, yet I ate very little. I knew it could be my last meal with Anh Minh's family.

Our life in Vietnam was so uncertain and fragile. I felt wounded and somber but somehow content at successfully completing the escape plan as Heaven and Buddha had intended. I might never be back here again, but I felt fortunate to have friends who helped me greatly when I had nothing to offer. Those types of people were simple but extraordinarily honest human beings—the best part of living on Earth—and I will never forget them. These people were the living angels who protected my family during their most dangerous journey, and for that, I am eternally grateful.

Anh Minh's family probably knew I worried about my loved ones who had already left. So, they tried not to start any conversations about my family, particularly my wife and son. Trying not to think about it anymore, I finally filled up my stomach with food. After all, Anh Minh's wife was an excellent cook and truly a good daughter-in-law to the family.

After dinner, Anh Minh and I sat in front of his tailor shop, drinking coffee and getting some fresh air. Đức, the pharmacist friend who had provided me with the cyanide, coincidently came by and ended up joining us. Anh Minh's tailor shop was located downtown, on a busy street in Bạc Liêu. Though it was the evening, quite a few people walked back and forth in front of the store. While we sat there, a man suddenly appeared at a distance and began walking toward us. Under the dimmed light, his body was intermittently moving slowly around the corner of the street, dragging his crooked shadow with him.

I noticed him looking back behind him and around the area cautiously, as though he was checking to be sure no one was following him. Then, he approached closer and stood right in front of me. He was around 40, but I didn't recognize his face or know his name. Somehow, the stranger knew my name and face.

"Greetings, Thầy Dỹ!" he greeted me, suspiciously keeping his two hands in his jacket pockets.

"Greetings, Ông[u]!" I said in a serious tone.

The weather had not even had a hint of a cool breeze that night. It was warm and humid. Normally, people don't wear jackets around there. I looked up at him guardedly.

What does he want? The question ran through my mind, sending an icy shiver down and along my spine.

---

[u] "Ông" or "Mr.": Used to call an older or respected male.

He may be an undercover cadre! I have just sent 24 people illegally out to international waters to flee Vietnam. I'm a fugitive to the socialist regime carrying a military ID paper with an altered expiration date and other fake features. A counterfeit expert could easily discover the truth behind my amateur work. They had already interrogated me twice in my hometown.

At that moment, I believed that evening could be the beginning of my journey to the forced labor camps in the north. Honestly, I didn't care anymore since most of my loved ones had already escaped the government's claws.

My unhealthy body was likely to become worthless soon, and they could certainly have it without my resistance. This flow of turbulent thoughts ran through my rebellious mind until the man interrupted me.

"Thầy Dỹ, do you want to cross the border?"

The stranger intruded into my mind, bringing me out of my suspicions and back to reality. He didn't wait for me to ask anything. "Cross the border" was the phrase normally used to describe an illegal operation that involved leaving Vietnam by boat.

I looked at him skeptically, trying to recall who he was and how I might have run into him before, as he appeared to know who I was. The stranger kept talking to me and appeared not to care whether I wanted to ask anything.

"There is a boat departing tomorrow night if you want to leave Vietnam," he said.

"They have a planning meeting tonight, and I can take you there to talk with them. It's only a 15-minute walk from here."

After providing the information, he stopped speaking, waiting for my reaction. I continued to look deeply into his black eyes, hoping I could detect any bad intentions or dark thoughts in what he was trying to communicate.

"Do they go underground or half-official?" I asked. "Go underground" meant escaping by boat illegally, whereas "half-official" included those exits that the government program permitted ethnic

Chinese-Vietnamese people to leave Vietnam by boat with protection if they could pay.

"Half-official," he quickly clarified.

His firm response ignited a few working brain synapses, firing up a still-faint desire to survive. I couldn't say I wasn't intrigued.

"What time do they meet?"

"Around 9 o'clock tonight."

"Where?" I asked, and, for a few seconds, my mind sounded an alarm as he pulled one of his hands out from his pocket. I knew I should be cautious, but most of my loved ones had already escaped the government's grasping talons.

"This is the address where they are meeting tonight," he added, handing me a small piece of paper with a handwritten address.

"Goodbye, Thầy Dỹ. Hope to see you there!" he said, slightly bowing his head before dashing away and completely disappearing into the dark corner of the street where he had come from.

My friends had been sitting there the whole time but said nothing until he had left.

"Do you know him?" Anh Minh asked.

"No, I don't!" I replied, internally debating whether I should attend the meeting, which would take place in only about two hours.

"He may try to trick you so he can steal your gold!" he was concerned, casting a veil of doubt on what the man told me.

"Don't do it!"

"I need to meet with my brother's sister-in-law to see what she thinks," I said before standing up and gently patting Anh Minh on his shoulder. "Don't worry!" I added before saying goodbye to my friends and walking toward Hoa's place of lodging, which was only a few blocks away.

Of course, the rich sister-in-law's younger sister and her nephew would want to leave Vietnam if they heard about this new opportunity. The question, however, was whether I could trust the man who appeared out of nowhere like a ghost. Again, during that turbulent time, relying on my gut instincts became critical. When dealing with all kinds of people in Bạc Liêu, my experiences strengthened my ability to judge character and trust my feelings about people. It trained me to assess an event as it emerged and quickly decipher people's hidden intentions from their behavior, body language, and spoken words with a high probability of accuracy. I was often correct in my assessments using my gut instincts, particularly in extreme situations involving high risk.

I met my elder brother's in-laws at their rental place. I was quick to the point because I knew they would be extremely excited to hear about the new lead. As expected, they both wanted to take the chance to be on that boat. I told them I wanted to meet with the organizer first, and I suggested Hoa go with me to the meeting location while Sơn, her nephew, remained at his place.

Shortly after that, we left.

Quietly but quickly, we walked along dark streets to the address on the scrap of paper I got from the mystic man. The house where the meeting was taking place was only about 15 minutes from the lodge. Because of the urgency and brief window of time, I asked Hoa to bring the gold with her in case we needed it immediately.

Under normal circumstances, carrying a significant amount of gold pieces with us in the evening was dangerous and stupid. Unfortunately, I had no choice but to do so! We didn't have the luxury of plenty of time to go back and forth, especially when faced with conflicting feelings of fear and suspicion.

We finally found the place. It was a large ranch-style house at the corner of an area set away from the crowded business section near Anh Minh's tailor shop. I looked around cautiously to see if I could note any suspicious activities around the area before knocking on the wooden door.

About a minute later, a man with a nervous look opened the door and quickly asked with a strong southern accent, "Who are you looking for?"

At that moment, I felt more confident and less worried about our security. The edgy face of the man who opened the door for us showed it likely wasn't a trap set up by the local security group. That limited my concerns about whether the escape plan was real or faked to get ahold of those shining pieces of gold Hoa was holding. As the "half-official" operations dwindled, money-thirsty sharks were vigorously swimming around in circles, looking to make as much as they could through their schemes.

I pulled out the paper with the written address and gave it to the man, saying nothing.

"Who gave you this address?" he asked, shifting his body to move his shoulder forward, halfway outside the slightly open door as he looked tensely in both directions of the quiet, dark street.

"I don't know his name," I said. "He was about 40 years old and a little tall." I tried to describe the man to him—the man who had appeared as if he were a phantom!

"Get in!" he declared, a rapid shift in his behavior as he waved us inside. We entered the house and walked through an empty room to another door, which took us to another area of the house.

The man opened the unpainted door and gestured for us to walk inside behind him.

It was a large space with a veil of pale misty light flooding the entire area from a few neon tubes hung below the ceiling. There were many people in the room. Some were sitting on chairs behind a long wooden table along the wall opposite the door we had just walked through. Others were sitting on the ground, and the rest stood on both sides of the door.

I quickly scanned the crowd, suddenly noticing the man who had been a stranger until he had appeared before me at dusk in front of Anh Minh's shop. He was standing with other people along the wall on my right-hand side. Coincidently, he was also looking at the door to see who was coming. He recognized me and gave me a half-smile. I smiled back, waved at him, and tiptoed toward the crowd.

"Greetings, Thầy Dỹ!" he whispered while shaking my hand.

The man who had opened the door saw me talking with the ghostlike man and stopped following us. He turned around and walked away. He must have seen our handshake and realized that his people knew me. So, he let Hoa and I stand there talking with the man who had told me about the meeting.

The people sitting on the chairs behind the table were the organizing members of the group. Most of them were Vietnamese, not ethnic Chinese-Vietnamese people.

Some of them, no doubt from their looks and voices, were military men from former South Vietnam. They were discussing where they might head once they reached international waters. Some men had commanding voices and sounded like they had significant navigation knowledge and skill.

The meeting and discussions lasted for about an hour. Then, people started leaving, saying nothing as they approached the door. They were likely aware of the pre-determined departure hour and location ahead of time but tried not to mention it openly for security reasons, I guessed. A few men stayed back to chitchat.

Most of the people who had been sitting at the table also left, except one. I assumed he was probably the leader. We had been waiting along the wall patiently when the stranger who had informed me of the meeting tapped me on the shoulder and asked me to follow him to talk with the leader.

The person he took me to speak with had been an army officer from South Vietnam, I believed. I thought he might also recognize me as an ex-soldier, noting our strong and warm handshakes.

I asked a few questions about the boat and learned it was not as big as Mr. Thái Đức's boat but could carry about 100 people, probably more. From how he spoke, it sounded like he knew how to navigate the boat very well and planned to go straight to one of the Indonesian islands. It was a "half-official" plan. He probably had a few Chinese-Vietnamese people handling the fake paperwork and fees to get the government's protection. I told him I had four people who wanted to leave Vietnam.

"Five taels of gold each," the man said. "We are leaving here tomorrow and departing in the evening."

"What riverside?" I asked.

"We will take you and your people there tomorrow," he said. "So, you don't have to worry about getting lost!"

I could tell he had purposely given me a vague answer to avoid telling me precisely where the rendezvous location would be.

It might be the same place my family had left from the night before or another riverside somewhere. He was cautious, I thought, which was fine with me. I told him I would need to discuss it with my relatives.

Then, I asked the man and my elder brother's sister-in-law to accompany me to the corner of the room to discuss the whole thing in greater detail. He said if we agreed to go, he could stay with us to ensure everything went as planned. I asked how much he would want for his commission or fee.

"Two taels for all," he said.

Then he reassured us that his nephew, about 14 years old, would also go with us. The boy planned to leave on the boat with no relatives accompanying him. As I listened to the man's words, I felt an overwhelming sense of sympathy toward him.

I still didn't know how he knew me but started conjecturing a plausible motive that he somehow knew I used to teach Mr. Thái Đức's children English. If that was the case, he could have seen me as a reliable person to accompany the boy on such a dangerous trip and to remain with him at the refugee camp if we survived. He likely may have chosen me to act as the guardian of his nephew and wanted to help me escape on the same boat.

But he did not ask me to take care of his nephew! It was a brilliant idea, I thought.

So, I talked with Hoa in private. Based on my street-smart gut instincts, I told her they seemed trustworthy. It would be her second chance if she still wanted to leave Vietnam. In fact, it was actually her third chance.

She failed the first time and lost all the gold. Her second chance would have been to go on Mr. Thái Đức's boat, but I could not remove another one of my loved ones for her to go. This new lead could be the last opportunity for her to flee Vietnam. As expected, Hoa consented to take advantage of the opportunity and told me she wanted to leave together on the boat the next night.

After that, we returned to the leader and told him we agreed to take the trip, handing him all 20 taels of gold for our four people. Separately, in the room's corner, we also gave the ghostlike man two taels for his role in facilitating the connection.

Twenty-two taels of gold were equivalent to about 7,000 or 8,000 American dollars in 1979.

Again, as with the deal with Mr. Thái Đức, no contracts, documents, or records existed for the transaction. It was purely based upon a gentleman's agreement and luck.

If it turned out they had tricked us, that would be it! If we lost all the gold, our dream of freedom would also be gone. After the meeting, we left. Hoa went back to her rental place. I returned to Anh Minh's house to sleep.

Throughout that night, I stayed in bed, tossing and turning, with many lingering thoughts invading my mind. If my sisters had been in Bạc Liêu then, I could have negotiated to get them on the boat scheduled to leave the next day using the remaining gold. I still suspected the rich sister-in-law had stopped them from joining the group. It haunted me. I couldn't stop thinking about why she would do that. There was no way that I could go back to Hồ Chí Minh City in the morning and be back in Bạc Liêu with them by the evening of the same day. It wasn't possible. For the rest of my life, I would kick myself for not asking them to go with me when I left Hồ Chí Minh City for the last time.

Then, a vision of the ghostlike man entered my mind. Who is he? I kept asking myself. Why did he pick me instead of another? Perhaps someone much richer wanted to leave Vietnam? Doesn't he know I am dead broke? It would have been impossible for him to know that my elder brother's sister-in-law was holding a bag of gold! It was deeply puzzling. How did he find or know of me? Anh

Minh has lived in Bạc Liêu since birth, and the town is not that big. He knows many people there but has no clue who the man is or where he came from.

Could he be the messenger of Death? I superstitiously thought. Or, perhaps, a mystic or angel sent from Heaven?

What if this entire boat plan was really just a hoax? I had never met or even seen any of those men present at the meeting we attended. Could I trust them? Regardless, our future is now in their hands, I eventually conceded.

Over the course of the night, I continued to think about everything that had transpired at the meeting to uncover any suspicions or reasons not to go forward. If it was a trap set by the local security district, I had no choice but to give up the gold to save us from being captured. Finally, by the time the sun rose, I got tired and exhausted from looking for potential suspicions. Still, I could not find any reasons for not going.

What made me believe those strangers I had just met and knew nothing about? I wasn't sure, but we would discover whether my intuition was right or completely wrong in less than 24 hours. We would either be sailing on the high seas or waiting somewhere, holding the bag. Or, worse, we could prove to be the newest victims of a secret plot operated by the local security group.

By early that morning, around the time I became mentally and physically exhausted, Mr. Thái Đức's boat had already been traveling on the high seas for about two days. I knew that if I still had heard nothing during that time, they were likely somewhere in international waters. If something bad had happened, it would likely have come out via the rumor mills in Bạc Liêu. I closed my eyes, quietly prayed for everyone, and eventually fell asleep.

Farewell to the Motherland

THAT DAY, JUNE 18, 1979, I finally said goodbye to Anh Minh's family. It was a touching moment. My wife and I will forever be indebted to them for their genuine love and friendship.

Anh Minh's parents were so kind, and they treated me like a son in their family. His wife had a big heart and the bright face of an angel. We will certainly never forget her love and care. Their children were beautiful. I prayed they could leave Vietnam someday and have a good life and future. Before I left, I gave Anh Minh all my remaining money. The trip was a one-way ticket for me, regardless of how it worked out! So, I figured I wouldn't need it, and it would be of better use to his family.

I only carried my military flight diploma, an old French-English-Vietnamese medical dictionary, and a few photographs of me in uniform; all were inside a plastic bag.

I still had the cyanide in my shirt pocket, uncertain whether I might need it. I had nothing else with me except for a few old articles of clothing.

After gathering those few belongings, I left Anh Minh's house to meet with my relatives. Shortly after, the four of us walked to the house where we had attended the meeting the night before.

Hoa was a year younger than I was. Her nephew, Sơn, was one of the young kids I used to play with in my neighborhood. One day, we got into a fight. I knocked him down flat on his back, then pounded his chest with one of my feet. I was very skinny and around 12 years old. The force wasn't that brutal, but it was enough to get his dad mad at me.

His dad was Anh Ba Long, the rich sister-in-law's oldest half-brother whom I sent to international waters with his loved ones and mine two days ago. He was the one who gave us the small bag full of thin, shiny gold pieces during his last day in Vietnam. After paying for our trip, we would probably have a few taels left.

Dũng couldn't believe he had another opportunity to leave so soon, but he was very excited. His dream became vibrant again, and I could see the hope in his eyes. He smiled with his lips closed. I felt great having him with me. Somehow, I had always worried about him—ever since I was about ten years old. I couldn't put my finger on the reason, but throughout my life, something in my mind triggered me to worry about his safety. I often feared something might harm him when he wasn't with me. Of course, I worried about the safety of my siblings, but Dũng seemed different from us.

When we arrived at the house again that second night, I felt an enormous sense of relief, like someone had lifted a weight off my shoulders. The man, a phantom I credit with getting me onto that boat, and the boat leader stood together with a young boy. A few other people were standing by, but I didn't know any of them.

We greeted each other quickly. I guessed we were still waiting for a few more people.

Finally, after waiting about an hour, we boarded an old bus waiting outside. I intended to stay awake to see exactly where we were going, but after a few minutes, I fell asleep while the bus was slowly maneuvering through the narrow streets.

It must have finally turned onto the main road, heading toward the riverside. I didn't know how long we had been on the bus, but when it finally stopped, Dũng abruptly shook me by the shoulder.

"Anh Hùng, we are here! We are here!" he raised his voice excitedly. I opened my tired eyes and looked around in confusion.

"Where are we?" I asked, but nobody responded.

They were likely just as unaware of our precise location as I was. The leader had already jumped down from the bus to the ground below since he sat near the bus door.

The wide river and boarding area looked familiar, but it was not the same place Mr. Thái Đức's boat had docked a few nights ago.

We walked closer to the water and joined several other people already there when we arrived. Altogether, there were about 100 people, which was significantly less than what the previous boat carried. I could tell that there were more Vietnamese than Chinese-Vietnamese people present. I also noted quite a few armed people in civilian clothes walking around!

The man and his nephew stayed with us, as he said they would. When the curtain of night fell deeper upon us, we waited under the dimmed light for several hours.

I didn't know why they still had not allowed people to board the boat. I was extremely nervous and tired, but I kept my eyes open wide and remained alert. We had no choice but to wait. The sooner we got on board, the better, as far as I was concerned. I didn't enjoy sitting there while the security cadres walked around with their shifty, owl-like eyes.

For a while, I zoned out, drifting among different, confusing worlds, each full of dark shades and flickering images of my loved ones. Suddenly, I awoke amid noisy disturbances around me. I no longer saw the ghostlike man in my vicinity, but the boy was still sitting among us. I hoped he was really the man's nephew. That suspicion passed through my mind in a flash. The man seemed very honest, and I reassured myself I should not worry about it.

When we started boarding, it was close to the early morning. A loud screeching sound from the loudspeaker suddenly erupted as if from thin air. A distance away, near the docking boat, the armed security cadres had turned on a few portable lights and faced them toward the wooden plank as though they wanted to trace our last steps. People started moving towards the area and yelling for their loved ones, who had wandered somewhere nearby to stretch their legs or speak to those in other groups.

I figured my group might be near the end of the list, but I knew we must get ready. Many things could happen at the last minute. I told my elder brother's in-laws and Dũng to stay close to me. The man's nephew was to board first. I would be next. When they called my fake name, I would walk toward the boat. Then, each of them must follow one after another, no matter what name they might call after that. The organizers had given each of us a fake Chinese-Vietnamese name earlier. So, it would likely sound familiar when called. I looked around and grew somewhat uneasy. There seemed to be significantly fewer Chinese-Vietnamese people boarding that night than there had been on Mr. Thái Đức's boat. That made me a little nervous! The security cadres might detect that too many Vietnamese people from the ex-regime were fleeing.

We were nervously waiting for our turn, eyes and ears wide open. The call resonating from the loudspeaker was steady, but the wait seemed like forever. We were not too far from running out of patience. What if they had already called our name, and we missed it? The tension gradually elevated. I could feel my relatives' stress levels also running high. I tried to find the man who had told me about the opportunity again, but still couldn't see him.

"Where the hell did he go?" I became deeply concerned. He said he would stay with us until the last moment. I couldn't find him anywhere, and fewer people were still standing. My entire head throbbed while the number of people in the crowd waiting to board continued to decrease.

He might leave us holding the bag!

Suddenly, as my fear took over, someone signaled the ghostlike man's nephew standing before me to go. Shortly after that, I heard the familiar Chinese-Vietnamese name I got. Finally, I knew it was time. I dashed toward the boat while signaling my brother to follow. It was a little tricky stepping onto and across the wooden plank used as a bridge to get on board. The plank flexed up and down with the small waves. I felt slightly dizzy and tried to get on the boat as fast as possible. Near the end of the plank, I jumped down to the solid floor and walked straight to the lower level, following the boy and the other people in front of me.

On the crowded boat, people had little choice but to sit close next to each other. Some were already resting, with their palms overlapping behind and underneath their heads. I looked for a space, found one, and sat beside another person. I barely saw his face under the dim, pale light coming down from the deck. Then I lay on the floor and rested my head on my burgundy cloth bag while looking up the stairs.

I had not even rested for one minute when suddenly I jumped up as though someone had electrocuted me.

I was in shock and panic!

"Where are they?" I asked aloud to myself.

I began shouting their names but did not get any response from my elder brother's in-laws or Dũng. Terribly, I became frightened and felt as if I was having a heart attack. I stumbled around on the lower floor, searching for them. I kept yelling out their names, but no one responded. It was dark, and I could only see a blurred vision of people sitting and lying around. I had to get my face very close to those people to see if I could recognize anyone from my group. Then I suddenly heard a voice from the deck above.

"No more? Hold it... Let me untie the plank!"

Someone on the deck was shouting to the security cadres, and they were ready to remove the wooden plank that provided the only access to the boat.

I was in full panic by then and gave up searching on the lower floor. It was not bright enough for me to see much, and none of my relatives responded. I doubted they were down there. Instead, I wanted to get to the deck to see if they were still on the riverbank.

So, I ran up to the upper floor.

A brawny man standing near the last step tried to push me back down, asking with a strong southern accent, "Where are you going, brother?"

I quickly pushed his arms away and shouted into his face with my trembling voice, "My people! They're not on the boat yet!" Then I ran over to the man, trying to untie the rope holding the plank.

"My people aren't on the boat yet!" I yelled into his ear with all my might, desperately searching the shore area.

I could see little beyond a few unrecognized people still standing there, talking. At that moment, I considered jumping into the water and swimming to shore to locate them. I knew I could not leave Dũng behind. Neither could I abandon my elder brother's in-laws. The man who had attempted to block me from coming up still followed close behind me. He grasped my hand and tried to pull me back to the stairs.

"The boat is leaving!" he angrily shouted at me.

"Go down! Down! Down, down—now!"

Again, I pushed his hands away and kept looking toward the riverbank. Miraculously, I saw the ghostlike man standing near the armed men.

"Brother… BROTHER!" Desperately, I shouted out to him from the edge of the boat. I was no longer concerned that the armed security cadres standing next to him might recognize my pure Vietnamese accent and remove me from the boat. I had to find them all! Luckily, the man heard and recognized my screaming voice. He turned toward the boat, where I was about to jump, and saw me waving frantically.

"Look for my people! Please! They are not on board!" I screamed at him while struggling to push off the hands of the man, who was still naively trying to pull me back with all his strength, without a shred of mercy or understanding of my situation.

"My people are not up here!" I reiterated, repeatedly yelling at them in a horrifying, panic tone while waving madly at him. Realizing what was happening, fortunately, he turned his head to look around the area behind him. Eventually, my elder brother's in-laws and Dũng heard my shouting voice and emerged from a shady area. They desperately waved back at me just before the ghostlike man finally saw them. He quickly approached one of the armed men and said something to him. Immediately, the other man hastily shouted at the men who had just about finished placing the wooden plank on the riverbank.

"Hey! Put it back, comrade! Put it back!" he ordered the men repeatedly, gesturing for them to return the wooden plank to its previous position to allow access to the boat. After they had already repositioned the plank, the ghostlike man walked toward my relatives while signaling them to proceed. They rushed toward the bridge and waited for it to be secured to the boat.

By then, the muscular man was no longer trying to push me toward the stairs. Instead, together with the other crew on the deck, he was trying to catch the end of the wooden plank. Once they got hold of it, they placed it on the edge of the boat and tied it down firmly with a long, thick rope. He then signaled for my relatives to step on.

I froze for a second, staring at them.

All of them, one by one, walked carefully onto the bridge and across, finally arriving on the floor of the boat. I gestured for them to follow me to the lower level while turning around and searching for the man who had come to my rescue—my guardian angel! He was nowhere to be found to accept my signals of gratitude.

It was as if the man materialized out of thin air, helped me back onto my path, and disappeared into the darkness. It was the last time I saw him. I will never forget his shadow and how he talked to me at Anh Minh's house with his hands in his jacket pockets. Yesterday, he said he would only leave after we all got on the boat. He did as he had said, leaving right after that. I was eternally grateful to the man, no matter who he was.

Subsequently, I spent a great deal of time pondering his identity. Was he one of the senior undercover security cadres? How else could he order the other men to return the wooden plank and let my people get on board that easily? The armed cadres followed his order quickly without asking questions or feeling the need to check whether my relatives were on the roster.

Whoever he was, to me, he had become *deva*[88]—a Buddhist angel or spiritual being. After I had unexpectedly stayed behind against my fate, a *deva* steered me back to where I belonged so I could complete the intended journey of my life. It had to be true. I had finally uncovered a belief in angels and fully restored the beautiful hope and dream I was fighting for. I needed that faith to live on and survive without being overtaken by dark forces. In those last moments, my mind suddenly expanded spiritually to embrace faith, which truly formed and proved itself to be worthy of belief right in front of my eyes during that miraculous moment.

The ghostlike man was one of many who had become my saviors during the daring journey. These extraordinary people helped me fulfill the dreams of my loved ones.

Witnessing and observing such a genuine miracle, I absolutely believed that all I had done and continued to do came from the purposeful canvas Heaven had painted for my life, merely leaving out certain details for me to fill in.

I was only an instrument—a living body with a battered soul the Creator sent to a complicated world to overcome mountainous obstacles and dangerous challenges. A person must walk the journey of human life, one step at a time, despite it being full of mental and physical pain. It was a mystical passage that both Heaven and Buddha intended me to pass through to arrive at emptiness, a state of enlightenment.

So, I sought no redemption for what I had done beyond merely trying to complete the path the Creator had put me on and to act righteously despite contradictions from the complexity of human minds. How I had lived during my passage, unconditionally helping others with a wide-open heart, likely pleased the Creator tremendously. As Mother used to say, "You reap what you sow." And she was right. Indeed, on the early morning of June 19, 1979, a *deva* led me back to the path chosen for me—my undeniable fate.

"Go to the lower level! Go... Go... GO!"

The brawny man on the deck suddenly yanked me out of my deep emotions and the hypnotism of a lingering shock from the miraculous event that had just occurred before my eyes.

Not wanting to cause any other problems, I whisked downstairs to the lower cabin, where I eventually met my relatives. I quietly sat beside my elder brother's sister-in-law, saying nothing.

Everyone on board was silent. Nobody talked to anybody. The only audible sound was the popping and slapping noise from the pistol engine. I felt the boat move forward slowly. There was likely another boat accompanying us to the open sea before releasing our nervous souls to international waters.

As the boat steadily moved toward the river exit, streams of sunlight slowly sneaked down the stairs, providing a narrow path of light from the upper deck to the lower cabin. Most of the surrounding people were half asleep. I sat up and slowly tiptoed to the steps. I went up to the top stair, rested my elbows on the floor, and leaned forward to look around.

It was a spectacular, peaceful scene!

The waterway flowed smoothly under the half-awake morning sun, steadily carrying us along the beautiful riversides. The water was light brown, containing abundant fish resources for the villages near the river and providing plenty of water for irrigation. Sparkling on the water was the sunlight, dancing across the river.

The escort vessel was moving ahead of our boat to take us to international waters, preventing potential interference from the Vietnam Navy Coast Guard. A few armed men stood upon the lookout watchtower aboard the escort vessel.

I could see smoke rising from a few thatched huts along the riverbanks. The villagers were preparing breakfast for their families on clay stoves with fresh wood. We passed a few small trading boats going in both directions.

The scene was familiar! We might as well have been on the Gành Hào River, where I traveled a few months before with Tuấn to trade—that place where I memorably ate the raw fish soaked in a jar full of salt water with live, fat, milky maggots.

Or, we just as easily could have been floating down the Bạc Liêu River.

The river opened its mouth, allowing the boat to enter the vast blue waters. Emerging from the river, the boat swiftly entered the open sea. It was pure magic! The beautiful sun had risen halfway above the boundless watery horizon and was about 90 degrees to my left. We were finally in the South China Sea!

The boat could head for Malaysia, Indonesia, or wherever it could land ashore—anywhere except Vietnam. I looked back and saw trees and a strip of land along the shoreline, slowly withdrawing from our boat. My eyes suddenly felt heavy and warm. Tears ran down my cheeks as I glued my eyes to the shoreline until it became only a very light-shaded area with a thin contour.

The escort boat was no longer leading ours. Behind us, it had already become a small moving object in front of the long strip of land silhouetted in the distance. It was the greatest moment of my relentlessly precarious life!

Four years after the fall of Sài Gòn, that was the first time I could smell freedom again. I was about to be free.

No, I realized suddenly that I *was* free. The moment we entered international waters, I would become *totally* free! There was an invisible but distinct line of sensibility between liberty and suppression. The line was recognizably wide that we could not be senselessly standing on it without knowing where we were.

The sun continued to rise slowly from the direction of Côn Sơn—the largest island of the Côn Đảo Archipelago of Vietnam. It was used to hold prisoners during the Vietnam War.

After 1975, there were many stories from the Bạc Liêu rumor mills that the Vietnam Coast Guard vessels often captured the boat people and put them there. So, we might not be out of the woods yet. We were still within the Vietnam boundary waters and not too far away from Côn Sơn Island. It would take another hour before we would safely enter the international waters of Singapore, Malaysia, Brunei, and Indonesia.

I returned to the lower cabin and sat beside my elder brother's sister-in-law. I slowly moved to rest on my back, carefully avoiding disturbing her sleep. Her nephew was lying nearby. Someday, I might want to ask what had truly happened on their previous journey and who told her to come to Bạc Liêu.

But it didn't matter.

We were finally on the South China Sea, heading away from Vietnam as if running from a deadly plague. Dũng was also lying nearby. Through our success at boarding the boat, I had restored his hopes and dreams, but I could see a trace of the fresh wariness and deep preoccupation stemming from an awareness of the dangerous journey we were about to endure. I couldn't see the ghostlike man's nephew, but I knew he was sleeping somewhere in that area. He had boarded the boat before me, so he must have been around. I felt exhausted and fully drained of all my energy. That last incident almost gave me a heart attack. If I had left Hoa, Sơn, and Dũng behind, even because of a simple human mistake, I would never be at peace mentally for the rest of my life.

If we survived, I was still uncertain when or how we might reunite with our relatives who left on the first boat. The two boats had a similar plan—head to an unknown land far away from Vietnam. However, even if they had the same ultimate destination, they might still not navigate to that spot safely and successfully. The boats we were on were not seaworthy for long-duration journeys on the stormy high seas. They had exceeded the boat's carrying capacity, jamming people in like sardines in a can.

Besides, many captains or "tài công" didn't have enough experience on the high seas or reading nautical charts to navigate the journey effectively. As a result, few could foresee navigational hazards and determine how to maneuver around them.

Bad weather or monster waves could easily send us all to the bottom of the deep sea or, if we were lucky, push the boats into different, unknown directions. Even if we could survive, it would be a miracle if we could meet again at our destination. We all knew we might be unrealistically nourishing an American dream while fighting against too many odds. And it could prove deadly!

I started floating in and out of these and similar lingering, murky thoughts. My loved ones' faces flickered in my mind as distant memories. I had fulfilled the last wishes of my ill-fated brother and Mother's dream, finally returning their lost hopes and dreams to my siblings. I missed them so much! Not a moment passed when I didn't wonder if they had landed or were still drifting with my wife and son somewhere on the high seas.

Remorsefully, I felt terribly sorry for my wife and son. For the past few years, I could not be around them as a normal husband and father should have been. Intentionally, I kept my wife in the dark regarding what I was doing, simply for her protection and other security reasons. Faithfully, she raised our son without my help and without thinking much about her dark future.

Admirably, she weathered the family conflicts involving my sibling and the rich sister-in-law as best she could without dwelling on the minuscule issues that were biasedly magnified by the complexity of human minds. Innocently, we were unaware of the damage already inflicted and the hatred that remained dormant then but that would someday return discriminately to complicate the kinship beyond any reasonable understanding.

Of course, my wife had a similar dream somewhere deep down inside. For her, though, the cost of a dream like mine was too high. Even just imagining the price tag, including our son's life and mine if we were fatally unlucky, diminished the hope that accompanied the dream of freedom, causing her to bury it at the bottom of her subconsciousness.

Then, I came back and forced her to swallow a horrendous pain and face the riskiest journey of her entire life without me.

The anguish was unbearable, but it naturally fused our unwavering hearts together into one. We could be physically apart, but I knew our souls were together. She sensed I would have never abandoned them in Vietnam, leaving them behind. And she knew what she had to do in the end, so closing her eyes, she faithfully put our son's life and hers into the hands of Death and angels. She released any sense of control and allowed them to fight for the fate of her and our son. She did not do it for herself—but for our child and me! And I knew, before she even took the first step onto that fateful boat, that she would protect our son from any threats stemming from the complexity of humanity and dark forces with her own life. I knew she would pass the tests Heaven and Buddha had planted along her journey to freedom.

My mind must have played with my shattered heart, pulling its strings this way and that for over an hour while the boat, running at full speed, left our motherland behind—the land I had solemnly pledged to protect with my own life.

I knew we should soon reach international waters, or at least out of the jurisdiction of Vietnam's naval controls. Most people were sleeping, and a few threw up because of seasickness. My stomach was almost empty. I didn't vomit but felt completely exhausted with a pounding headache. The monotone, low bass-toned popping and slapping sound of the boat's piston engine added pain to my half-numb head.

The lower cabin became warm and humid. I sweat heavily, then turned cold, sending a shiver along my spine. The engine noise was aggravating. My head throbbed with each bang and crash, making it unbearably painful. I felt like I also might have had a fever. Around then, I passed out just as our boat, MH-0747, was speedily entering international waters. The journey to find my loved ones, including my wife and son—as I had promised on the dark riverbank—began while I was in a deep state of sleep, experiencing another delusional dimension while I floated around in the South China Sea.

And that was the last time I was in Vietnam—on that early morning on June 19, 1979, about two days after my loved ones had left on the first boat, MH-4112, which Dũng and I should have been on, together with them.

THE
ABYSS

I didn't know how long I had been unconscious. But when I awoke, it was dark. I could not even see my hands when they were right near my face.

For a few seconds, I thought I had died!

Then, that annoying, ear-penetrating sound from the running engine brought me back to life. My mouth was dry, and my abdomen hurt, with the pain coming and going. I didn't know what was causing the pain, but I figured it must be due to hunger. I didn't bring any dried food to eat. In fact, I had nothing edible at all!

The cabin had a very low ceiling and gave off a rotten-smelling stink! The awful smell came from the half-digested food of those who had thrown up on the floor and, sometimes, onto the person nearest them. I couldn't stand the smell for another second, thinking I needed to get to the upper deck for some fresh air and to look for something to eat. While trying to move, I could not even rise into an upright position to get to my feet. I was too weak and felt so dizzy that the area surrounding me seemed as if it was spinning. But I must get out of that cabin!

So, I rose onto my hands and knees and crawled slowly toward the stairs, where I saw some pale amber lights leaking down from above. People were lying everywhere on the floor. I struggled to maneuver over many of them on my path toward the steps. Some moved slightly as my knees accidentally hit them, while the rest lay still as the dead.

Given my method of transportation and the obstacles I had to bypass, it took me several minutes to get to the upper deck.

Thick darkness enveloped the top-level area, except for the flickering light escaping from the boat pilothouse, where I saw some people moving inside.

There was no moonlight beyond the blinking stars such a vast distance away. I kept crawling along the upper deck, again moving over or around a few sleeping bodies lying on the boat's surface. They must have done what I was trying to do—headed up to get some fresh air and avoid the horrid smell and unbearably sticky humidity in the lower cabin.

The upper deck floor was not too far from the top of the boat's side hull board. I crawled closer to the edge, sat down, and dropped one of my hands over it, hoping to catch some seawater to splash onto my face. Unfortunately, I couldn't reach the ocean's surface! I didn't have enough strength to raise my upper body and lean forward, even just a little more, to drop my hands far enough to get a scoop of the cool water. It was too far down, and the water looked dark and deadly. I was afraid if I leaned forward with both hands, I would fall overboard while the boat was steadily speeding up and over the ocean waves.

Nothing was moving around us in that deep dark space we were occupying—nothing except the lonely boat and the seawater tapping against its sides. There were two distinct sounds: the monotone popping and slapping noises from the boat's engine and the magical yet frightening sound of dark waves faintly crawling toward us. Beyond the people on the boat, there were no living things around us. It was just us—a bunch of half-dead bodies scattered on the deck and snugly squashed like sardines into the lower cabin. There were not even any seagulls since we had already traveled far offshore, having been on the high seas for several days. There was no horizon. It was merely a dark space with a vague, shady boundary that expanded horizontally and mixed with unbounded vertical emptiness, only confined by the flexible surface of the deep black ocean.

I felt lost in that dreadful dimension—dark, vast emptiness and dreadfully deep isolation from the rest of the world. The haunting space surrounded and touched me, causing a cold, shivering sensation and an overwhelming feeling of frightening uncertainty. It created a stream of conflicting emotions within my battered mind. On the one hand, it created a sense of sorrow and pain, which consumed my shattered heart and fueled my distraught inner soul. It burned as an infinite flame in an endlessly expanding space—undying and never-ending. On the other, it created a feeling of deep hollowness, like the dark sky I felt I was sinking into, where nothing mattered anymore. Nothing could alter or reshape the strange dimension I was experiencing, so there was no use in concerning myself over it.

Hatred and love became a perception my mind could no longer differentiate. The feelings became one and eventually diluted into the spiritual space of my near-death body. Gradually, my subconsciousness slipped into a delusional judgment day. Neither sad nor happy, I comprised nothing more than pieces of a lost soul with an unavoidable desire to surrender to the growing uncertainty and black emptiness of the South China Sea. At that moment, exhaustion took over again, and I slumped onto the upper deck like so many others around me and fell into a deep sleep.

At some point, as I was lying under the veil of darkness, lost in the shady little corner of my subconsciousness, I heard footsteps, which stopped at me. Then, a man's voice rang in my ears, but it sounded like it came from a distance. He lifted my head slightly to pour fresh water into my dry mouth. I hastily swallowed a gulp of the precious water, choked, and spit some out. The man tried a few more times, but I couldn't drink very much. He then rested my head back down carefully and walked away toward the pilothouse.

I didn't know how long I had been lying near the edge of the boat's side hull board. My brain had completely lost the ability to track time.

Then, another or, perhaps, the same person came and fed me something. It tasted like cooked rice mixed with warm water, and my abdomen pain returned—this time stronger.

Feeling uncomfortable, I twisted my head away to avoid any further feeding, which caused the warmed rice to spill onto my cheeks. I couldn't open my eyes but felt like the entire floor and my body were spinning uncontrollably! I didn't know how much I ate or drank from the food and water given by those who were probably boat crew members.

One day, I found myself back in the lower cabin area again. I didn't know how I had gotten back there, but I figured the crew must have brought me down under the deck to avoid sunburn and dehydration. Coincidently, every time I awoke, there was no daylight! While I was barely conscious, the painful reality and agony of not knowing whether my loved ones were still alive engulfed my consciousness and crushed my broken heart.

Unbearable thoughts of the excruciating suffering they were also going through at that moment lingered eternally in my mind. It was like being pushed through the gates of hell repeatedly while floating aimlessly on the South China Sea. Yet, I could do nothing about it. Like a limp noodle, I was lying partially on top of a strange, stinky half-dead body, just like mine.

I wasn't even aware that daylight must eventually come. My brain had already lost the ability to hope. I was gradually losing the flow of thoughts through my brain. My mind and body were slowly giving up their essential functions and the sensations that made human life worthwhile.

I had no control by then. I placed myself entirely in the hands of Death and angels who fought the battle of my lifetime, each seeking the fate they believed I deserved to have.

A Resort and Tow Rope

ONE DAY, WHILE drifting in and out of consciousness, something disturbed me, waking me up.

People were moving around. I saw Hoa, Sơn, Dũng, and the boy. They were also awake. They seemed ragged but appeared to be in significantly better condition than I was.

"Fellow citizens, look! Land! Land!" Breathlessly and continuously, someone shouted with great excitement from the upper deck.

"Everybody, get onto the deck of the boat! Quickly, quickly!" Another voice ordered us to move to the top surface of the boat, which I took as an excellent sign!

When the boat people saw a commercial ship passing by, they normally went up to the upper deck space to make it abundantly clear how grave and dangerous the situation they faced was aboard the overcrowded boat. The purpose was to arouse the humanitarian mercifulness of foreigners, hoping they might rescue the refugees, taking them to a safe place—on land. Those cheerful voices gave me the strength to reach the upper deck. When I arrived, I sat down immediately, resting against the pilothouse wall. From a distance, a strip of land quickly flashed before my eyes, then disappeared.

People stood in front of me, yelling excitedly, mostly blocking my view. Then, I heard the roaring sound of a boat engine I knew wasn't ours. I stood up and saw a patrol vessel splattering water in a wave from both sides of its nose, trying to get closer to us. Aboard, there were a few armed members of the coastguard in uniform. One of them made several gestures for us to follow them.

We were extremely exuberant! At last, we had reached our previously unknown destination. Well, I still didn't know where we were. My best guess was that we were likely somewhere in Malaysian waters.

The armed men on the patrol boat were naval coastguard members who wore identical uniforms and had dark skin.

It was a beautiful area with stunningly blue water. As our boat coasted closer to the land, I saw people on shore. There were quite a few tall palm trees behind the waterline. The area looked like a resort! One of the armed men on the patrol vessel instructed us to come closer and dock our boat in an isolated area, far away from the locals standing in small groups, curiously watching us.

Then, he gave hand signals showing we should get off the boat and follow them. So, I moved with the crowd, following closely behind my relatives.

When I first stepped on the firm ground and started walking, I felt the earth move under my shaky feet because I was experiencing motion sickness. I hoped we would stop somewhere soon.

The location we had landed was, in fact, a resort area. We walked by a large, grassy area where I saw a few westerners sitting and enjoying drinks in the distance. Farther away, I recognized a golf course with a beautiful, pristinely green fairway. The entire area was spectacularly clean and well-kept. Certainly, we were in one of the more civilized countries.

Knowing we had finally made it to shore kept me going. I dragged my feet, balancing my ragged body to keep up with the other boat people. I could tell I was walking like a drunk!

Sometime later, we arrived at a large area with a lot of tree shade. They asked us to stay together in that area and told everyone not to stray from it. I figured it was late afternoon by then. The sun was drifting farther away from its previous location, directly overhead. I lay down on the green grass and felt much better than walking or standing.

The other boat people sat down together with their loved ones. My elder brother's in-laws, Dũng, the man's nephew, and I all stayed close to each other. We were beyond exhausted at that point. Our eyes seemed to imply we only had half a soul remaining each and could speak volumes about all that we had gone through during the last several frightful days on the high seas. Moments later, I fell asleep again.

"Anh Hùng... Anh Hùng... Anh Hùng!" I suddenly heard my brother's voice calling out to me and thought, for certain, I was in a dream. I opened my heavy eyes and saw a colorful juice box being waved right in front of my face.

"They gave us something to drink," Dũng said, pushing it into my trembling hand.

I took the juice box, hastily sucking in the fresh liquid using a short plastic straw. I felt better after drinking the juice and looked around. All of us were quietly sitting on the grass, waiting, but none of us knew what we were waiting for. I hoped they would take us to a refugee camp soon.

We were already on their soil, and it was clear we were seeking political asylum. I could easily prove I was an outcast from the socialist state and a political refugee from Vietnam. I had kept my burgundy handbag close to my waist via a cloth band over my neck. Curiously, I unzipped it and looked inside to check the status of my belongings. Safely tucked inside, the flight certificate and other personal items covered in plastic were still in good shape.

That day, they confined our people in that beautiful area for several hours. Then, when the sun was about to disappear, the guards said they would take us elsewhere. We all figured we would go to a refugee camp. The location we had just landed ashore was a commercial area. They couldn't allow us to stay there too long.

Reluctantly, we all followed the order, walked back, and eventually re-boarded our boat. They observed us carefully to make sure no one stayed behind, either intentionally or accidentally. Then, they threw a long, thick line over to our boat and asked one of the crew to secure it to the prow. They said the rope would prevent us from getting lost on the high seas.

By the time we were all set to go, the sun had already gone below the distant horizon. The patrol vessel slowly towed our boat away from their land. In about 30 minutes, when we were far away from the resort area, the towboat sped up. Our boat's engine roared noisily, breaking the quietness of the ocean while struggling to keep up with the speed of the patrol vessel.

They kept towing our boat at their high speed, causing it to rock and tilt from side to side violently. I was afraid the rope might break under such extreme force. Our weather-beaten boat was no match for the coastguard vessel.

As our boat rocked fiercely, seawater washed over the upper deck and poured into the lower cabin. In a panic, people started crying, praying, and yelling loudly.

"Oh, Heaven… Lord Buddha… Jesus… please save us!"

Frightened and trembling voices roared through the crowded cabin while we—little more than stinky pieces of living meat violently shaking in a horrifying dark box—rolled and bounced uncontrollably from side to side, bumping into each other brutally.

The noise of our boat's piston engine acceleration sounded like the death cry of an innocent animal fiercely struggling to resist the pull of its captor. And the side-to-side shaking of the towed boat resembled a chained slave, piteously stumbling behind a rope, trying to catch up with a cruel owner. Every second that went by added more chaos and heightened the feelings of terror among those on board. I could imagine the sense of horror felt by the boat people who were aware of such terrifying scenarios well in advance but still risked their lives to escape the communists. Our wooden boat could easily have become a mass coffin, buried with us still alive beneath the cold, deep waters of the high seas.

Like the others, I was also extremely fearful, particularly for my relatives. Unfortunately, there was nothing I could do to help in that situation. I was just as deep into the potentially deadly fate!

For about an hour, they forced us to follow them. We sincerely hoped we were going to a refugee camp somewhere, ending our treacherous journey on the high seas. Terrifyingly, the towboat showed no sign of slowing down and kept sailing into the vast darkness. We no longer saw any land, but it was dark anyway. I became worried. We were not going along the seashore. In fact, we were traveling away from land at high speed in a straight line. They had not changed their trajectory since we departed from the resort area. After thinking it over, I realized our direction contradicted what they had previously said.

Then, suddenly, from the upper deck, someone was screaming and cursing in a state of panic into the empty darkness.

"They are cutting the rope!"

"MOTHERFUCKER! They cut the rope!"

Eventually, our boat slowed down while the coastguard vessel's roaring engine noise gradually blended into the tranquility of the dark ocean as it moved away from where we had accidentally landed. The only noticeable sound I could hear was the familiar popping and slapping noises coming from the running piston engine of our boat and the crew's furious cursing and conversations from the upper deck, which leaked down to the lower cabin area where we were still praying for our lives.

The Malaysian coastguard had towed our boat away from their land and mercilessly abandoned us in the middle of the night in unknown international waters. Our hope evaporated quickly—as fast as the towboat that almost sank us disappeared, leaving us stranded in the middle of nowhere! We had no choice but to continue our journey on the dangerous high seas, hoping to reach another unknown land. Unfortunately, nobody, including the crew, knew where that might be.

While experiencing those potentially deadly moments, I questioned how long I could keep my mind going. Thinking about my loved ones fighting for their lives under similarly horrendous conditions was excruciatingly nerve-racking.

Every time I was deep in thought, the suffering consumed my broken heart, piece by piece. I still held onto hope, but the dire situation gradually decimated it every day I was on the lost boat. The only thing that kept me alive as we carried on without enough food or water was faith. With only dismal thoughts and spiritual strength,

I continued to wander from the extremely harsh sunlight of the days and the frightful darkness of the nights in the vast, open ocean.

I couldn't tell how long we had been on the high seas at that point. I became confused, and I wasn't certain whether the island we ran into was reality or just an illusion or a dream in my subconscious. The only thing that seemed real anymore—likely because of its ever-presence—was the monotone popping and slapping noises from the boat's engine, which had been continuously cranking for several days.

Amazingly, during our journey, that annoying sound had become familiar and almost pleasant. Knowing the engine was still running was a blessing! If we ran out of fuel or the engine stopped working, we would have been drifting on the high seas without control. The strong currents could very well have pushed our boat back to the Vietnamese waters or to the Gulf of Thailand, where pirates had raped and killed countless boat people without mercy. Luckily, the crew went into the voyage expecting a long journey. The boat carried many metal containers full of fuel on board, and it would keep sailing until it reached the land of freedom.

Saved by the Mushy Ocean Floor

ANOTHER DAY, A similar disturbance suddenly woke me up. The crew saw land from a distance. Again, our hopes flew high amid the sticky humidity, blistering sunstroke, and heat exhaustion.

I dragged my feet to carry my stinky and skinny body to the upper deck to join the other boat people who had arrived before me. Looking around, I quickly noticed that we all looked extremely tattered. There was little room to move around, so some people stood on the pilothouse, screaming joyfully.

The boat became very noisy, with conversations and people yelling as they searched for their family members. While the battered boat rushed forward as though fighting for its last breath, it tilted from one side to the other, rocking everyone on the upper deck. Those who sat on the pilothouse fell violently, sending them plummeting onto other people below. I held onto the edge of the pilothouse structure to keep my body in place and protect my head from dizziness and spinning sensations.

I saw little, except for a few sketchy glimpses of shady mountain landscape far in the distance, which momentarily appeared when the boat's bow plunged deeper into the waters. When it rose again, all I could see was a vast, bright blue sky.

Suddenly, the boat vibrated erratically before the engine's pleasant popping and slapping sounds stopped.

Panic-stricken people started yelling, "The boat! The boat is going to sink! Jump! JUMP!"

That distressed scream from someone amplified the fright in all of our minds, wreaking havoc and sending the crowd into a downward spiral.

At first, a few people jumped into the water, but then another group followed. When a bigger group of men and women, several small children fearfully clinging onto their backs, threw themselves toward the ocean's surface, the chaos intensified quickly.

Children were hysterically crying while turning their dreadful eyes away from the sea. They were falling like sandbags being thrown into the deep ocean.

It didn't take long for the rest of the people on board to begin abruptly abandoning the boat, which was now handicapped by the inoperative engine. They were hopping into the water from all sides of the boat unevenly, which shook it from side to side, causing jolting movements that caused some to fall overboard when the boat tilted too heavily to their side.

The boat crews were no longer in control of anything.

"Jump! ANH HÙNG… JUMP!" Dũng yelled at me in horror as he tried to pull me up.

I attempted to force my exhausted body, as soft as a noodle, to rise. I had scarcely eaten for days! My stomach was as flat as a sheet of paper, causing my belt to drop well below my belly button on its tightest fitting.

I had neither the energy to jump nor swim.

"Go! Go! You go!" I shouted, pushing his hands away and telling him to jump first, "Dũng, you go! You go first… I'll follow!"

My words trembled through my shaking, dried-up lips as I tried, once again, to stand up. Dũng didn't know that I was too weak to spring overboard, so he dashed to the boat's edge and jumped over the side. I watched my beloved brother while a sad feeling overcame me, as I figured it might be my last time with him. I looked around but didn't see my elder brother's in-laws or the young boy who went with us. They must already be in the water, swimming for their lives. I sincerely hoped they would all make it to the shore alive!

The whole situation was utter chaos! Fear of being pushed back toward the high seas intensified as the boat appeared to drift outward with the withdrawing surface currents. The overwhelmingly popular opinion seemed to be that it was likely to sink soon with the dead engine, and no one wanted to stay on it any longer or move any further out to sea. I didn't think I could make it to the island, even if I could have jumped.

While I could see a strip of land between the distant mountains and the blue seawater, it seemed incomprehensibly far—completely out of my reach. The distant, mountainous terrain stretched from the left to the right side of our boat behind the hazy sky. I really wasn't sure how far the shore was from our boat. It could be quite misleading, and unfortunately, it very well might be too distant for me to make it. While on the high seas, the mountains and shorelines often appeared closer to our eyes than their actual distance.

For a moment, I conceded that I might have finally reached or be very close to the end of my life's journey. I had no regrets. I had fought against the odds and dark forces with all my heart and soul! At the least, I was glad I had tried everything I could for my loved ones. I would have done nothing differently, even if a doomed, tragic destiny awaited me at the end of the tunnel.

In my desperate, confused mind, I made an instant decision, leaned over the edge of the boat, leaped overboard with the last of my strength, and dropped myself into the ocean. My body splashed into the surface of the sea, submerging deeply into the vast cool seawater, which temporarily provided a sense of renewal and fresh energy. Despite the momentary invigoration, I was still too weak to hold my breath underwater and abruptly swallowed a large gulp of salt water.

Then, as my head emerged above the water level, I saw the strip of land and mountains dancing up and down from my line of sight. People were all around and ahead of me, each trying frantically to swim toward the seashore. I attempted to follow their path, swimming in their direction with my remaining strength. However, despite my best efforts, I felt I was still in the same spot I had started. Then, I even felt like I was swimming backward. The distance between those swimming ahead and me appeared to be expanding gradually. I tried to pull my body forward harder, harder, and still harder, fighting against the sea with all my energy. The more I swam, the less strength remained.

The sky, mountains, and shoreline mixed with the water line, flashing from side to side and up and down, blurring in the distance. I couldn't recognize anything clearly and had already used the remaining energy in my useless body. I tried to raise my head above the water to gasp for more air, but I couldn't. My head gradually dipped under the sea. I could see no one around me anymore.

Finally, I had lost my orientation toward the shore.

One moment I heard people's voices echoing indistinctly from a great distance, the sound waves traveling over the ocean's surface; the next felt like it had sucked me out of reality, and I was plummeting at light speed toward a scary emptiness. Then, seconds later, the surrounding sea became peacefully quiet. I could not move, even with clumsy movements, or make any further effort to survive. I spent all of my remaining energy just struggling for breaths.

There was no strength left to fight!

Within a flash, I went from feeling more helpless and frightened than I'd ever been to suddenly no longer fearing any physical harm.

My mind had reached a state of complete acceptance. I felt calmer, spiritually fulfilled, and internally satisfied with a single delusional thought flashing in my head—that I had deceived Death, fooling him into following me instead of my loved ones.

All the mental pain and suffering were about to be gone, and that would be true freedom. The omen from my dark dreams would die with me at the bottom of the sandy ocean. It gave me such a sense of relief, knowing I had done all I could with every fiber of my being and my heart for my family's future.

Then, my ever-conflicting consciousness fed my mind with unexplainable feelings, causing me to become completely confused. Floating up and down amid the cool ocean waters, I felt as though I wasn't about to die but that I was waiting to go somewhere, and it was just another journey I had to go through. I didn't feel like resisting the passage of time; there was no unwillingness to let it go. There was no terrifying shadow of Death or deep darkness to envelope me at the end of life. I didn't realize that I no longer felt any fear except the temptation to reach the destination of a new beginning quicker.

The sunlight above still pierced through the thick but clear layer of seawater as though it was laying out a path for me to follow. I eventually became submissive, my mind in a peaceful state void of all thoughts—empty. It allowed me to follow the thin film of light spreading below the ocean's surface. I could no longer resist the dominant feeling of temptation to be completely free from all matters and obligations. For a split second, I let my exhausted and skinny body follow that silky veil of sunlight as it cut through the surface of the water, dispersing into the vast area beneath.

My numb body floated momentarily while my confused mind was prepared to transition to another dimension. I struggled to keep my eyes open while seawater gradually engulfed my entire body. It felt like an eternity had passed as I sank toward the bottom of the ocean. I swallowed a few more gulps of seawater, then a few more, and still a few more. I had no choice but to push it into my flat stomach, which no longer had much feeling.

Then, suddenly, something jolted me out of that idle condition that my empty state of being had brought on.

It might be because my lungs were running out of air and naturally breathing in—sucking seawater into my nose, mouth, and windpipe. Or, perhaps, there were still a few functioning cells left in my nervous system that interfered, breaking the spell of that tranquil hibernating state of my mind.

Whatever it was, I became very confused for a few seconds and didn't trust the powerful sense of acceptance triggered by my half-dead mind. Instead, I felt the buoyant force of seawater nudging me upward. Then, when my body weight dragged me down far below again, I was stunned when I physically felt something underneath my feet. I floated back slightly, sank again, and bounced around amid the ocean currents. My body had to bounce up and down a few times before it finally struck me… I realized I was touching the mushy bottom of the ocean! My eyes flew wide open, and what little remained of my survival instincts jolted my numb limbs awake and quickly set them in motion.

I tried to spring free from the ocean floor, using my legs and bare feet that had somehow received a boost to their will to survive. The first jump didn't quite get my head above the water's surface, but the fingers of my hands breached it.

I felt a draft of air!

When I sank to the bottom again, I let my legs bend more and jumped up using all my remaining strength. I didn't know how long I was underwater, but I felt like I had just returned from a strange place. I could see the sky above my head and hear the indistinct noise from a distance on my right side again. Then my senses, which seemed to be slowly returning, naturally prompted me to turn toward the noise and keep jumping up and down.

Whenever my nose was above the water level, I gasped for air, took a deep breath, and held it as long as I could until my feet hit bottom. Then I quickly released the precious air before jumping up from the mushy ocean floor again.

I lost count of the number of times I had jumped up from the ground of the ocean. Graciously, it enabled me to breathe, drawing fresh air into my tight and heavy chest again. My head eventually emerged above the sea surface while my legs stood shakily on the bottom of the ocean.

At that point, I could see the shore and people in the distance. The ocean currents were still trying to push me outward, but I kept pushing my body forward against the heavy seawater mass while walking toward the shore and keeping my air-seeking nose above sea level. I stopped, walked, paused, and continued inching forward intermittently to regain my strength. Finally, my shoulders rose above the wavy surface of the blue sea. My full consciousness came back, restoring most of my senses. I hastily inhaled a heavy mass of air into both chambers of my deflated lungs, which were still flexing desperately in search of more air.

I was still alive. Barely!

So, I survived the most dangerous journey of my life and reached an unknown destination—a strange island. Later, I learned we had been on the high seas for about ten days.

I slowly walked ashore and set my bare feet on that unknown island on June 28, 1979.

AN UNKNOWN ISLAND

I walked slowly from where I had almost drowned, all the way to the shore. The sun gradually descended in the west, sending patches of pale, yellowish-colored light through the hanging clouds and onto the warm, white sand. I saw the dark green rainforest and mountainous areas stretching behind the shore at a distance.

On my left, a tall rocky hill stood separate from a long, precarious mountainous area. I didn't see any locals and wondered if we had, perhaps, come ashore on an uninhabited island. Then I walked to a dry sandy spot and sat down to rest. I felt so light and had no desire to walk any longer. I was already on the beach. There was no rush to go anywhere else. This place was much better than sitting in the boat's lower cabin, with people jammed in as tightly as sardines in a tin can, which made me sick! I felt a jolt of optimism and felt much better overall, probably because I was alive again.

I looked around to see if I could find my relatives. The boat people were lying everywhere, scattered along the stretch of shore.

Others were sitting together in small groups. I didn't see Dũng, Hoa, Sơn, or the nephew nearby, so I forced myself to stand up to extend my view along the shoreline.

My familiar burgundy handbag was still hanging on my hip, somehow, but now completely soaked. I walked along the outskirts of the forest, passing several groups of people who had already started looking for materials to build their temporary shelters or to cook before nightfall.

Eventually, I found my relatives. They were also looking for me. In their sopping-wet clothes, they looked like hell! Their eyes seemed like they had just come out of a theater after a horror movie. Their drawn faces looked dark and elongated, with slightly shallow sunken cheeks. I must have looked the same or worse, but we were all just happy to be alive at that point.

The ghostlike man's nephew also made it to the shore. As a farm boy who lived near the river, he was likely an excellent swimmer. My heart clenched tightly to see him in his current condition. He was too young to be away from his family and experiencing such a horrible journey so soon in his life. Certainly, he wouldn't be ever able to forget it. I didn't know if he knew anybody else from our boat, but I would make sure he knew he could stay close to us. That's what the man who led us to the opportunity—his uncle—had preferred, anyway. I still assumed he wanted me to become his nephew's guardian.

Dũng also seemed to be completely exhausted, but he appeared stronger than I was. I knew he was feeling good about coming ashore. Off that boat, at least he could dream about living in America now! My elder brother's in-laws also looked more confident than they had when I was with them in Bạc Liêu. They had firmly believed they would have to stay behind for good—after their family had left without them.

Unbelievably, they were alive on a beautiful island far from Vietnam. They had finally achieved what they had unsuccessfully attempted several times before. I felt deeply fortunate that I had helped them achieve the wildest dream of their life. I couldn't wait for the day when they would see their loved ones again for the first time after the shocking journey. Thinking about that moment, I was happy to enjoy the short but powerful feeling of complacency that touched my emotional mind.

All of us came ashore with empty hands. Luckily, the tidal waves washed the boat closer to the island. Even better, it became stuck in a shallow water area.

The boat crews swam out and eventually carried back several bags of rice, dried food, other useful supplies, and some cooking hardware from the boat. They made several trips back and forth until the sun had almost set, then the men waited for the next morning to return to get more supplies.

The skies quickly darkened as the sun dipped down below the far horizon. We had nothing to eat, so we just sat on the beach near the rainforest, far away from the water—but not too far. We didn't want to stay too close to the forest, either. It was like a dark blob to us, and we didn't know what might lurk there. Neither did we want to stay too close to the ocean, another dark area with the rhythmic sounds of small waves crawling ashore, triggering a naturally uncomfortable feeling after having struggled on the high seas for days.

It was an unbelievable time in all of our lives. We were completely out of Vietnam. My mind continued to adjust to the new reality and what I saw before my very eyes.

I was so starving at that point that I felt like I couldn't even hold anything in my hands. The muscles in my limbs were as weak as noodles. All I could do was lie flat on the salty sand, half-sleeping. My stomach was still growling nonstop, and I dreamed of having a steamy bowl of Phở to calm my appetite. Suddenly, several men carrying long burning torches made from dead tree limbs and pieces of cloth rushed toward the darkness and away from where we were staying. In my faint sleep, I overheard them talking while passing by, showing they were looking for a very young girl. Her parents could not find her after they had jumped off the boat.

Unable to keep my eyes open for another moment, I drifted into the deepest part of my sleep on that beach and under a vast open sky full of tiny stars blinking from the deep space far above.

Inhabitants

WHEN I AWOKE, the sun still partially hid below the horizon. My relatives were still sleeping. Some other boat people were wide awake and trying to make a small fire to cook on. I sat up and walked toward the shoreline. The ocean looked beautiful, a massive surface area of calm, light blue waters near the land that became darker far away in the direction we had come from after leaving the boat.

Motivated by curiosity, I tried to identify where I had almost drowned the day before. I felt much better after a peaceful sleep on the beach. On my right, the rocky hill stood monumental guard—massive in its closer proximity.

While I was admiring nature's extraordinary architecture and contours, out of the corner of my eye, I saw something move suddenly near the bottom of the hill. I quickly traced the movement and became ecstatic. They were monkeys! From the tall hill, with its scattered trees and sizeable rocks, several monkeys were running and jumping here and there. My eyes quietly zoomed in and continued to track their presence with astonishment. I had seen wild monkeys only on a couple of occasions in my life. It was incredible! Well, at least I had just discovered that we were not alone.

Feeling fresh and recharged with the dawning of a brand-new day, I moved away from the shoreline, walking toward a group sitting nearby. They were boiling something in an old metal container. A middle-aged couple greeted me while I slowly approached. "Greetings, brother... sister!" I greeted them back while looking at the girl and boy. They were sleeping close to each other on the sand—reminding me of my youngest sister and brother, whose fate was still unknown in the vast area of the South China Sea.

"Your children?"

"Yes," the mother answered with proud eyes.

"They are beautiful!" I honestly praised them. They were skinny and looked so innocent.

"What happened to the lost girl?" I curiously asked them about the search last night. "Did they find her?"

"Yes, fortunately, they did," the husband quickly answered in a friendly tone while his wife stirred something that looked like rice in the hot, smoking container.

Last night, the search team came back about an hour after I had fallen asleep. I was so pleased they had found her! According to the people on the search team, they had discovered her a few kilometers away from where we came ashore.

She was sitting there alone, naked, on top of a big rock facing outward to the dark ocean. She was around 12 years old and had spoken clearly before. After finding her, they took her back to the group, and she had said nothing since—not one word.

Superstitiously, they said that ghosts had captured and lured her there. Logically, I assumed the strong current carried her away after she had jumped into the ocean with her parents. It's possible that she was so scared that she had lost her mind from the enormous shock that would accompany this series of events.

However, I could not find any logical explanations for why the poor young girl's clothes were gone completely. Her parents didn't believe someone had raped her. I doubted anyone on our boat would do such an awful thing. We were busy fighting for our lives, and there was little room for stray thoughts. We had almost died. Frankly, I wasn't sure if the lost girl would ever recover to a mentally normal level again.

Two weeks later, she still could not talk or speak. It was such a tragedy and a high price to pay. I felt sorry for her and the family, but I could have done nothing to help.

"Brother! How long were we floating on the high seas?" I asked the husband for the details of our journey.

"I think around ten days," he said. "There was an old man who died when our boat was still afloat," he gave more detail. "We never learned how he died, but the family threw his body overboard because they couldn't keep him on the boat very long."

"So sad!" his wife chimed in with a lower, softer tone. "A young girl broke one of her legs when coming ashore as well."

"Yes, unfortunately, many of us faced challenges. I almost drowned!" I told them about my near-death experience.

"I was too weak to swim!"

After hearing my story, they felt great pity for me. The wife poured the hot soup into smaller cans and offered me one. With great gratitude, I took the can containing steaming cooked rice soup with a piece of salty dried fish about the size of my pinky finger. I slowly ate and drank, all without a spoon. My stomach was still as flat as a piece of paper. I could have eaten all the soup inside the hot container, which rested on big rocks that formed a triangle around the burning tree limbs, and still be hungry. Thinking about their small children who had eaten nothing yet, I thanked them for the soup, showed them where I was staying, and then walked away.

When I returned to where I had slept with my relatives the night before, they were already awake. After a good sleep, everyone looked dramatically better, seemed more energetic, and eager to build a temporary shelter. After living in a tight, overcrowded cabin on the high seas for several days, it was the best sleep we had experienced in a while. We felt safe to be on the ground, but all of us were starving! We knew we needed to ask around to see if anyone had rice and dried food to spare. The crew might have some extra cooking hardware and dried food from the boat.

So, we divided the tasks we knew we needed to accomplish between ourselves. Some of us went into the forest to gather dead tree limbs, palm fronds, and vines to make a shelter. We returned with several thick, solid branches, some of which were quite long, and palm leaves of many sizes. We continued to make trips into the forest to get more building materials as needed. Not wanting to go deeper inside the jungle for fear of running into a deadly wild animal, we stayed on the outskirts.

Making a small shelter was simple. We scouted out a suitable location, moving a little farther away from the shore to seek solid ground to hold the structure's supports in the ground firmly. We built several A-frames by tying two long, thick tree limbs with a vine at the intersection point, where they crossed each other near the end. Then we put a longer and thicker branch, which was almost straight, on top of the first frame above the intersection point, where two tree branches formed a "V" figure. The longer branch rested firmly inside the "V" section. We tied them together with another vine and then raised the first A-frame with the attached horizontal branch. Next, we tied the long branch's unattached end onto the "V" shape section of another A-frame.

Next, we dug fairly deep holes that matched the distance between A-frame's legs. We placed the entire shelter structure so that the ends of A-frame legs lined up and fell into the holes. Then we dug a few more holes for other A-frames to be installed between the first and last. We kept installing additional A-frames until we had finally completed the entire shelter structure. Then, we secured as many A-frame legs as possible to heavy rocks to keep them from being blown away under high winds.

While it wasn't perfect or particularly sturdy, it was durable enough to protect us under calm weather. However, if there were powerful wind gusts, it could certainly blow away. Under the circumstances, we did our best with what we had—no building tools, only raw materials, and working on almost-empty stomachs! Finally, we used long, large palm leaves to build the roof.

Voila! We had completed the first survival shelter on an uninhabited island.

Well, that was not true!

Just around the time we finished building our shelter, we heard several people yelling from a distance. We stood up, looked around, and saw people running toward the forest. My eyes curiously followed them, then suddenly froze as a look of surprise flashed onto my face. From the outskirts of the forest, several people who weren't from our boat were walking toward the shore where we were staying. Some were men wearing colorful shorts but no shirts, while others wore striped sarongs around their hips to the ankles. Their skin was dark brown. A few of them carried long wooden spears. Several women wore multicolor-patterned sarongs wrapped around their torsos down to the ankles. Upon seeing them, I became concerned and began looking for the rest of my relatives. They were still somewhere searching for food and supplies so we could cook. I worried the appearance of these people might not be a good sign. Those people certainly lived here, and we were invading their land.

What if they were cannibals? I considered.

My mind strayed wildly to this and other topics—an imagination influenced by reading too many adventure stories during my teenage years. A shiver ran down my spine, aching from too much sitting, followed by bending too many times to build the shelter. I walked toward a crowd of boat people talking with the island residents. Both sides made hand gestures as if they were communicating using sign language. As I got closer, I took another glimpse of the local people, taking in their appearances. They looked mean, particularly the ones with long spears. They spoke in angry tones as if something displeased them. Nobody could understand what anyone from the opposing group was saying, and even my English language skills were completely worthless in the situation!

One man from the island made a gesture. In a moment of epiphany, I thought I understood what he was trying to communicate. He pointed one of his fingers toward one of the boat people and repeatedly poked at his mouth while saying something. I realized either of two things might happen—either he was asking if we wanted to eat or showing we would be good for them to eat. What he was actually saying was still anyone's best guess!

The other boat people must have agreed with me, as they seemed to agree with my first translation of their gestures. In response, some of our people did the same thing—poking their mouths with fingers and nodding their heads. Then, without saying a word of goodbye, the villagers abruptly walked back into the forest. I worried our people might have unknowingly made them angry if they thought our group was trying to mock them.

So, unable to help the situation, I returned to my shelter with a heightened level of guardedness.

When I arrived at our shelter, my relatives were there with some rice and a metal container to cook. I told them what I saw and expressed my sincere hope that they would not try to kick us off of their island. With nothing more to do about it, in the meantime, we just rested next to the shelter, thinking about what had just happened and waiting to share the rice that was cooking.

About an hour later, another commotion from the same direction the residents had come from caught my attention. I saw a few groups of boat people running toward the forest as more and more villagers from the island appeared on the outskirts of the rainforest. Many carried stacks of bananas, coconuts, and bags with something inside. They were bringing food for us! Such a thoughtful and humane act shocked and moved me. Some women were carrying their small children on their hips, walking toward us in a friendly manner. Some spearmen also carried something, but what it was exactly, I could not recognize from a distance.

Over the next several days, the island residents frequently visited and gave us food. They were very kind and honest people. We didn't understand each other, but little by little, we learned to use our hands and fingers to express our thoughts. It worked out well. I wasn't sure if they knew we were all fleeing from Vietnam. All I knew was they felt pity for us and understood we had nowhere else to go. Based on their warm hospitality, it seemed as if it would be fine for us to stay on the island for as long as we needed. We didn't do any harm.

First Contact

UNDER SOME LIGHT wind and rain, our shelter held up well for several days. One night, there was heavy rain. Some of the palm fronds detached and flew away. We were all left lying on the wet sand, and throughout the night became soaked from the rain. I realized then that if we were to remain here for weeks or even months, we must build a better shelter.

During that time, we survived partly because of charity from other boat people who had brought some dried food and rice for their journey. From time to time, the island residents also gave us food to eat. My health seemed to improve even though I wasn't eating enough. I didn't care. As long as I didn't have to sit in that sardine-jammed lower cabin of the boat, I would be fine.

We felt isolated from civilization. There was no news coming in or out. We saw no ships or boats pass. In my free time, sometimes, I just sat under a tree on the outskirts of the forest, near the rocky hill, and watched the monkey families playing.

I often looked for a quiet place to lie down and let my mind stray to wherever my imagination took me—often with a desperate hope of reuniting with my loved ones who had left on Mr. Thái Đức's boat. I knew we had to communicate with the rest of the world and let them know we were here! But, for the life of me, I couldn't figure out how. How could we make contact? I thought about sending a message in a bottle but didn't have one. Nor did I have a pen or paper. Suddenly, I remembered the flight certificate and quickly opened my bag to check its condition.

"Oh, no!" I said to myself aloud. It was all crumpled and torn. Seawater had already eaten a small section away near the top left corner. There were a few small missing pieces along the edge of the certificate on the right side. The thin, shiny gold foil seal had faded away. Luckily, most of the words and black typescript on the paper were still readable. I carefully unfolded the rest of the damaged diploma and refolded it neatly before putting it back inside a thin plastic wrap. I always carried it with another set of clothes in my cloth bag. And a part of me was still hoping I might fly again someday. The medical dictionary and pictures I carried were also wet and damaged by the elements.

One day, a small boat with a "shrimp-tail" engine noisily broke the silence and tranquility of the beach. It appeared from the area behind the rocky hill.

We ran toward it and saw a man dressed in a sarong and a colorfully patterned shirt. A weird hat, which looked like a round cookie container made of dark fabric, sat on his head. He smiled widely, steering the small wooden boat with his right hand behind his back.

Some of us surrounded the boat to talk to him. He spoke broken English. He pointed his dark bony index finger toward the high seas.

"Vietnam?"

We all nodded our heads. Then he moved his finger and pointed it in the other direction, toward somewhere that also must have been accessible only via the high seas.

"Camp!" the man declared, tapping his hand on one of the boat people standing next to him and then pointing in the same direction once more. "Go camp!"

I thought I understood him. There might be a refugee camp out there somewhere! Then he opened one of his multicolor bags and pulled out a few fabulous watches. They all looked brand-new and fancy. I wondered why he would give us watches when we needed food more than those fancy things. It was a short-lived thought. The man raised both of his hands. Then he opened his palms and closed certain fingers on one, showing us how much a fancy watch would cost. They were not for free, as I had naively thought!

Of course, none of the boat people bought anything from him. I tried to talk to him about the camp he had mentioned. Unfortunately, he didn't have enough English vocabulary to describe anything that would be meaningful. Unable to sell any watches, he disappointedly roared his small boat away without wearing that big smile he previously had across his face.

After he left, I was optimistic. If he knew we were here, others might soon discover our existence on the beautiful, isolated island. My hopefulness turned out to be correct!

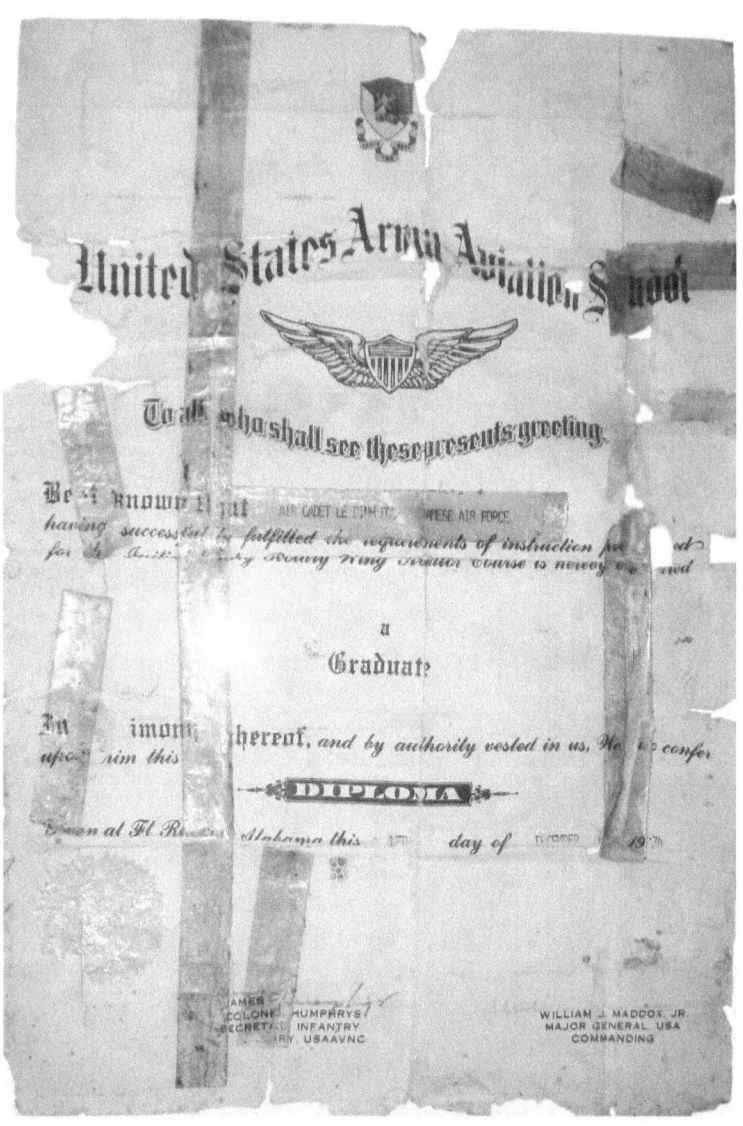

I also took the U.S. military flight diploma... and a thin old medical dictionary—which Dr. Truyền, one of the bộ đội physicians at the military hospital, had given me as a souvenir. I secured them all with plastic wrap to prevent potential damage from seawater...

**The damaged flight diploma.
(06/1979, Unknown Island, Indonesia)**

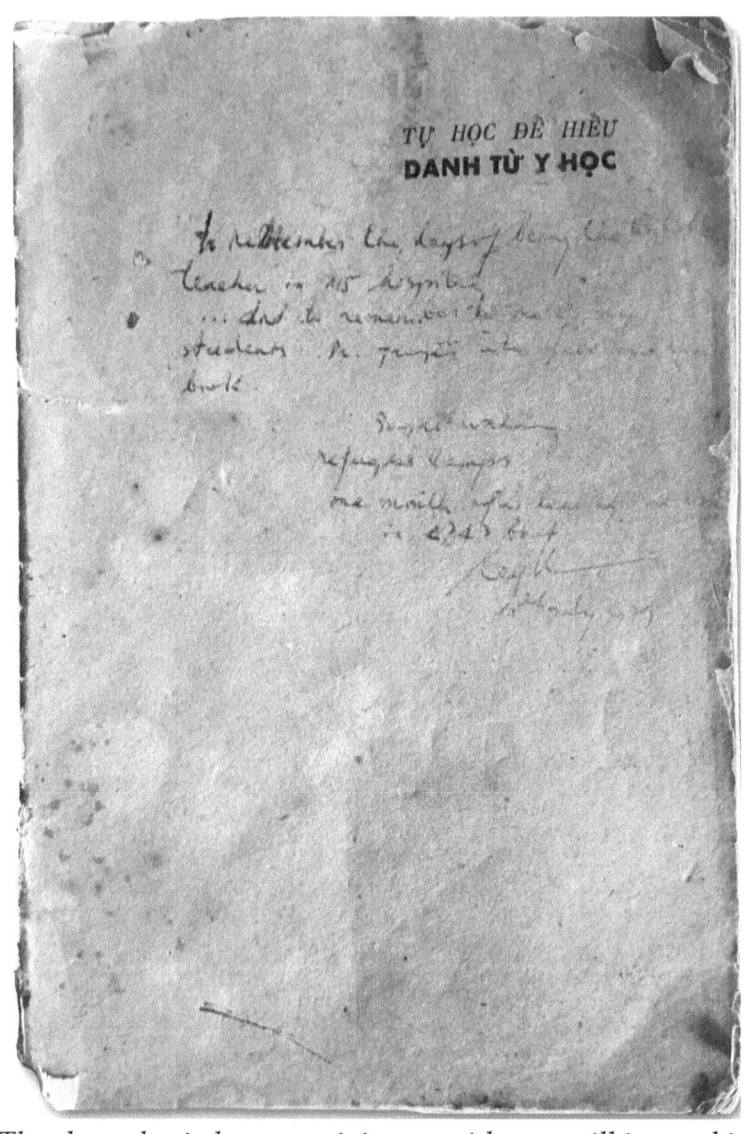

The clear plastic bag containing cyanide was still in my shirt pocket. It was my one-way ticket if the cost of fulfilling the dream of my loved ones was too high to bear. I desperately hoped I would not have to use it. Nobody knew about my plan for suicide except myself and my ex-pharmacist friend.

My old French-English-Vietnamese medical dictionary.
(06/1979, Unknown Island, Indonesia)

The next day, a bigger boat came with some people on board. They looked like they were from cities, dressing in proper pants and shirts. They spoke improved but still broken English. I was afraid they were there to sell something again, but I was wrong. Instead, they came to see how many of us there were and indicated they would return with a bigger boat to take us to another island. They didn't stay long on the island, but from our brief conversations with them, we learned we were on one of the Indonesian islands in the South China Sea.

I was a little paranoid, given the previous towing incident in Malaysia. However, my wariness quickly evaporated as I knew our boat had nearly sunk in the shallow waters. If they were to put us back on that same boat and tow it to the high seas, it would certainly sink—and we would surely die. I didn't think they would be that inhumane. Just like the Indonesian island people, they might look unfriendly, but they were, in fact, kind human beings.

GOD'S WILL

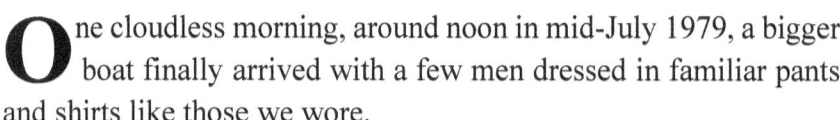

One cloudless morning, around noon in mid-July 1979, a bigger boat finally arrived with a few men dressed in familiar pants and shirts like those we wore.

Some of them spoke English. They told us they would take everyone to a refugee camp in Indonesia.

They asked us to collect our belongings and get ready to leave the island on their boat and told us they would wait until we could gather everyone in one spot before boarding. Upon hearing the news, some of us went to look for other people who may have been wandering somewhere in the forest.

Suddenly, a group of local villagers emerged from the forest and hastily ran toward us. We tried to explain that the newcomers would move us to another island, but we didn't know whether they understood what we were telling them. Some joined the movers, speaking to them as best they could in gestures as the rescuers waited patiently for us on the beach.

At that point, our local Indonesian friends realized those men would move us off their island. They didn't seem happy about our departure. Amazingly, a few villagers even cried, tears running down their dark brown, bony cheeks. Their beautiful hearts and generous hospitality deeply moved me. I held their hands and said something to the effect that we were grateful for their protection and care. I was sure they could guess what I was trying to say, even though they didn't speak English. Some of them didn't seem to want to release my hands! They kept moving them up and down while saying something, which I also understood as genuine farewells. I didn't want to linger with my deepening emotion any longer and gently withdrew my hands.

I will never forget their warm hearts and how they stepped in during our time of need. Their beautiful souls touched mine deeply.

My group had very little to carry with us. It was a quick task for us to prepare and get on board. Nobody had an exact count of how many people were on our boat, but the movers weren't in a hurry. They patiently waited for us to make sure we had everyone. They didn't want to leave any of us behind on the island. So, as one of the first groups to be prepared, we had to wait for a while before the boat would depart.

Eventually, it was time to leave. Many of us sat on the boat's upper deck, enjoying the fresh air. I felt great as I thought about the possibility of seeing my loved ones again. By the time we left, it was likely around 3:00 p.m. The sun was setting slowly toward the west. I paid attention to our direction. Our boat was not heading in the same direction as the sun, nor was it moving in the exact opposite direction. Instead, our course deviated slightly to the left of the sun's path, so I figured we must be heading southwest. If that was, in fact, the case, and we were somewhere in the South China Sea on one of the Indonesian islands, then as they said, we were truly heading inland toward Indonesia. That was a good sign for us!

After getting out of Vietnam and into the high seas, most crews tried not to stray into the Gulf of Thailand or Malaysian waters. We had heard many horror stories about deadly attacks from armed Malaysian and Thai pirates. They knew some of us would carry gold, jewels, or U.S. dollars. Once on board, they raped women and young girls, beat up anyone necessary to get anything they deemed precious, and killed many, including children, in cold blood.

The Malaysian government appeared to be quite harsh in dealing with the Vietnamese boat people crisis. As we had learned firsthand, they would tow the refugee boats back to the high seas if we sailed into their waters. As a result, many boat people died by drowning after their boats took damage while being towed back to international waters. The coastguard members that had violently towed our boat, I believed, were from Malaysia. Fortunately, we survived. Indeed, we were very lucky!

I looked around the upper deck area. Everyone seemed significantly less worried than before. Some wore clean clothes previously washed and dried while we had been on the island we had just left. My relatives and the nephew looked much better than before.

Dũng became visibly more energetic and talkative. He still smiled innocently, despite everything he had been through. I loved his beautiful smile because it showed a peaceful mind without hidden hatred. He was very outspoken and protective of his younger brothers and sisters. One time, when I was staying at my parent's home after the war, he violently snapped at me because he misunderstood something I had said to mean that I didn't care about our younger siblings. I also lost my temper and was mad at him for disrespecting me. We almost engaged in a fistfight that day, but our mother stopped us before we went to blows.

Dũng's feelings toward me had changed tremendously. He finally realized what I had done and stood for all this time. He understood the reason I picked him to stay behind with me. Based on his common sense and principles, he did his best to protect the younger ones from any harms. That was why he had never criticized my decision to keep him behind, even though the repercussions effectively destroyed his biggest dream. He said nothing when I told him—not even a single self-centered opinion, hoping to make me change my plan. He wanted to protect his siblings just as much as I did. And with that, he joined me in the quest to ensure the siblings' bright futures while forfeiting our own.

He did what any good soldier would have done and followed the order, especially during the most pressing critical moments. Righteously, he acted even when his life and future were at stake. He also knew and accepted that I did what I had to do by staying behind, even while pushing my wife and son out into the stormy high seas without a husband and father.

All this so that our siblings could leave without further complications. It was actions, not merely words, that allowed one to prove themselves—and the need for action often arose when facing serious challenges and in times of need.

I knew then that Dũng was a trusted companion whom I could rely on in the future for a long-lasting kinship. Sincerely, I believe he significantly contributed to our effort to secure the siblings' successful departure. The more I thought about it, the more I dearly loved him. Dũng understood and valued the bond of brotherhood, even while we were desperately struggling to survive such a dangerous situation during the darkest time of our lives.

Trying to kill time while on the Indonesian boat going to the refugee camp, I wandered deep in thought under a beautiful sunny sky. In the past, everything that had already happened in my life seemed to have some links to the future.

An unknown, mystical force connected events, as points in time, joined in some unknown way to pave an unfinished path for my life's journey.

I believed I was born into my family with a purpose. For that reason, I came to lead the fight against the dark forces, including the convolution of human minds cultivated from the most dangerous journey of our lives. Under the guidance of angels, every wrong turn I had made helped me comprehend and divinely embrace the right choice at each critical intersection of my passage. Faith didn't simply rise from my tattered mind, but from all the falls along the way. It developed from the solitary struggles and, especially, external challenges, all of which confronted my conscience during my long walk on the unfinished path.

During that tumultuous time, my loved ones, especially the younger siblings, admirably looked up to me as the only hope of reaching the New World.

We were all joined, sharing one mind and one voice, and helping them achieve their dream was the most precious time of my life's journey in a darkening, growing world. Mother had placed her children's fate into the chosen son's hands, pledging to shave her hair and eat no meat for months upon the news of our safe arrival in the free world. Without hesitation, my aunt put her oldest son's life in my hands with full confidence in my commitment to achieving freedom for him.

My wife, who previously knew nothing about my plan, fought against my shocking decision to stay behind without her and our child. However, she quickly accepted it, knowing I would only do what was right and finally put our son's life and hers into the hands of Death and angels. As she hurried onto the boat amidst the darkness of the riverbank, headed toward the South China Sea without me, she didn't look back—just as I told her. She knew I intended to shield her from seeing my pitiful dead soul collapsing on the bank of the dark river, broken.

How did an outcast in a socialist society, the poorest son who could not even support himself, lead our family's first and second exodus away from the motherland we dearly loved?

Faith!

It was—and had always been—a relentless spiritual companion that drew me into continuous tests of my absolute belief. I made all the risky decisions through deep faith, then let Death and angels decide our ultimate fates. Of course, distractions and dark forces were present all along the way, designed to break my soul and compel me to fall to my knees. I was not Moses, but I thought of those distractions as actions of fiery serpents[v], trying to break my belief and tatter my soul as I took on the daunting quest for freedom.

While I was deep in thought, the boat had been traveling for well over an hour. I was on the upper deck, enjoying the boat ride on the beautiful waters of the South China Sea and watching as the big orange sun crept toward the far horizon. I let my mind wander, pondering freely until a dark strip of land gradually became more visible from a distance.

As the boat drew closer, we saw beautiful mountainous areas with rainforests on both sides. It took the boat a while, sailing around several smaller islands and low mountains and changing direction slightly a few times before finally arriving at a long wooden pier that extended about 12 meters from land into the deep water.

It was a fairly large island with a continuous strip of low mountain range surrounding us. Upon arrival, the Indonesian movers asked us to disembark the boat and follow them along a wide dirt road. We did as they said, trailing them, saying little, but our minds were unavoidably thinking about what would happen next.

The path took us to a large area where we could see a few simple structures, including huts with roofs made from palm fronds. From a distance, I could also see a few silver-colored aluminum roofs, likely those of the military-style barracks, spaced neatly apart and located alongside the hills. There were quite a few of them in the surrounding area.

We were told to find any place we could that would be suitable to sleep for a night. In the morning, they would process the paperwork to admit us to the Galang Vietnamese Refugee Camp[89]. While listening to their instructions, I wondered what it would be like to stay on the island and when we might see our loved ones again.

Sleeping on the bare ground certainly wouldn't be a problem for us. We had slept on the sand under an open sky for a few weeks

---

[v] Fiery Serpents: The King James Version, Number 21:8, "And the LORD said unto Moses… that every one that is bitten… shall live."

already, plus about ten days during our hardship on the high seas. Mother Nature trained us well during that time to survive the harsh conditions. So, we did as they said.

Following their orders, we found a dry place to sleep and remained close to each other. It was a rough night as we slept on much harder ground than we were used to. It was a far cry from the wonderfully soft sand on the other island. My back ached, but I didn't want to complain as it was nothing compared to what we had gone through on the high seas.

~

I AWOKE VERY early in the morning but was still lying on the ground, looking up at the dark sky and hoping that my loved ones from Mr. Thái Đức's boat were in the camp somewhere.

Their boat had left Vietnam about two days before we departed. I was optimistic in thinking they must have landed ashore and had been at the Galang Camp for a while. They probably had to wait for the camp officials to complete our paperwork before coming to look for us.

After hypothesizing about my loved ones' whereabouts and reassuring myself of the joyful reunion, I finally stood up and walked around the camp to see what I could find.

I discovered a long creek with clear running water coming down from the higher ground on the mountain. Quickly, I washed my face with the cold water to eliminate any lingering, worrisome thoughts. I saw a thick rainforest from a distance when the boat approached the island. However, upon arriving, I noticed they had felled many trees, leaving a large space that was probably meant to house temporary shelters for the boat people.

As I was walking along the slope toward another area, I saw a beaten-up barracks covered with an aluminum roof; it looked like it was being used as an office for the camp. There were several other barracks in better shape along the slope going up to a higher area, where I noticed a white statue of the Virgin Mary. Seeing her on this tall monument sitting against the natural dark skies gave me such a blessed feeling.

After everything we had been through, I felt the symbolism of the power of *faith*—a sign I would want to see at that moment.

I walked around the camp for about an hour until the sun rose from the far horizon. Then, I came upon an area near what looked like the Indonesian military or security post. Standing outside were a few armed men dressed in dark green uniforms. Afraid I might cause trouble, having wandered too far out of the allowed range within the camp, I turned back and walked toward where I had stayed the night before.

By the time I returned to the group, the sun had completely risen above the horizon. I could see the entire area more clearly in the light of day.

We were on top of a hill, among many others, which spanned a large area. Looking back toward the vicinity I had walked through in the early morning, there were several rows of aluminum-roofed barracks along the side and at the bottom of the hills in the distance.

My relatives had awakened and were wondering where I had gone. I told them a little about the camp and what I had seen during my walk and reassured them we were all safe on the island.

A short time later, a few Indonesian officials from the security and camp office came to tally the number of people who had arrived on the boat. Eventually, they took our mug shots for the camp's admissions paperwork. They asked us to hold a small blackboard at chest level to display our name, birthday, and boat number, written in white letters using chalk.

That day, after our admission to the refugee camp, I talked with a few officials in search of those I hoped had arrived on Mr. Thái Đức's boat, MH-4112. Unfortunately, there was no record of that boat arriving at the camp, and nobody knew anything about it. Hearing that, I became emotional, and my face turned pale while they spoke to me. I thought they had to be wrong, repeatedly asking them to recheck their records. Again, they could not find any trace of MH-4112. The news came as a massive blow!

My loved ones should have been at the Galang Camp!

I desperately walked around the area searching for them, even knowing that the officials didn't have any record of Mr. Thái Đức's boat. I saw a small kid sitting on the ground outside of a barracks and, for a moment, thought he must be my son. Unfortunately, it was a dream, and he was not.

That day, the horrible stories of sinking boats and pirates' deadly attacks flashed back into my puzzled and tattered mind. Again, my hope had gradually diluted into a powerful and scorching sorrow. I walked up and down and crossed many small hills to other barracks to look for my loved ones.

Of course, I didn't find any of them on the island.

By then, I had already known that would be the case, but somehow, I couldn't stop myself from wandering around looking for them. After a few hours of searching in vain, the relentless heat and humidity soaked my shirt, worsening my sense of feeling.

My head hurt! It pounded as if I was carrying a heavy hot rock in a section of my brain. My heart clenched tightly, causing an ache in my chest while my mind was frantically going numb. I hoped they might still be alive somewhere, perhaps on one of the isolated islands in the South China Sea.

Dreadful thoughts about a potentially dark fate for my loved ones cruelly tortured my heart, making me feel sick. I stopped along the hill, bent over, placed my trembling hands on my shaking bony knees, and threw up yellow fluid from my empty stomach.

Feeling like I was in trouble, I moved to the side of the dirt road and sat there awhile to rest. I wasn't sure how I could live without knowing if my loved ones were still alive.

The mounting wariness was killing me—the emotional roller coaster of ups and downs. I became frightened, thinking that Death might have already ended my loved ones' struggle for freedom and survival! I was dying inside as though a terminal cancer was eating up every cell of my body at the speed of light. Then, I suddenly remembered the cyanide I had brought with me.

The plastic bag had disappeared!

I had only brought two shirts, which I had washed many times since arriving on the first Indonesian island. I had completely forgotten about the plastic bag until my mind crawled back to the dark side of sorrow, fear, and uncertainty.

My Ill-Fated Student

WHEN WE ARRIVED at the Galang Vietnamese Refugee Camp, the area was still primitive and remote. The camp was in Pulau Galang, a part of the Riau Archipelago of Indonesia. A lot of excavation and building were still taking place to complete the camp. Officials from the United Nations High Commissioner for Refugees or UNHCR were there to coordinate and assist in the resettlement of fleeing people like us.

They didn't assign our group to any barracks for a few weeks. Other boat people who arrived before us had already fully occupied them. The authority was extending the area and building more barracks, anticipating a dramatic increase in the number of refugees would occur. So, we used our hut construction experience to build a better temporary shelter in the camp. We borrowed some tools from the people on the island. There were plenty of trees not too far away from where we stayed. Together, we built a simple one-room house measuring around 36 square meters with an inclined thatched roof. The front wall frame had an opening, serving as a main entrance but without a door panel. We also built a long wooden flatbed, which was big enough for a few people. It took us a few days to complete the entire building project.

The authorities at the camp gave us rice, cooking oil, and salt. Some local merchants would come into the camp to sell food and other supplies to whoever could afford it. Many street vendors and small shops were popping up all over the place, many run by other boat people who had arrived a few months ago.

When Anh Ba Long gave me and Hoa a bag of gold to care for his son and younger sister, I let her hold on to it. She still had a few pieces of gold left, I believed, even after paying for our trip. She even had some U.S. currency! So, with that gold and money, she bought food when needed and cooked for the entire group. Eventually, we met Hà and Trung, two young siblings who were about Dũng's age. They had fled Vietnam alone with no relatives. They stayed with us in the house we had built.

Shortly after we arrived at the Galang Vietnamese Refugee Camp, I wrote a letter to Father Piet Hoedemaekers upon referral from a few boat people. During that time, Father Hoedemaekers was staying in Tanjung Pinang, Unggat, which belonged to Bintan Island. Using a speedboat, one could reach that island in less than two hours from the refugee camp. In the letter, I asked him to help locate MH-4112, the boat my loved ones had been on.

On August 3, 1979, I received Father Hoedemaekers' letter. In his letter, he wrote he could only find a boat with a registration number of "4122MH," not "MH-4112." He also suggested that I contact UNHCR because they covered a larger area and may be of help.

I followed his suggestion and eventually wrote another letter to UNHCR asking for their help to locate Mr. Thái Đức's boat. Then, I waited for their response while talking to newcomers to see if they had heard or knew anything about MH-4112. While my feelings remained mixed, I still had not lost hope completely.

In August, the Galang Vietnamese Refugee Camp authority moved the people from our boat and others to several barracks where space became available. Each shelter could accommodate up to about 100 boat people. They assigned our small group to Barracks 9 in Zone 1, near a big dark gray tent where UNHCR and other delegations came to interview us to determine the best location for resettlement in other countries. Zone 1 was the first one built for the initial flow of incoming refugees.

In our early days at the refugee camp in Indonesia, a few countries came to interview us. One day, the Canadian delegation arrived. Unless we had relatives in the U.S. and wanted to wait for the American delegation, many of us wanted to settle in another country as soon as possible. So, when the Canadian team came in August 1979, we all registered for Canada except Tấm, the ghostlike man's nephew, as he had some relatives in the U.S. and wanted to go there to be with them.

On September 1, the Indonesian government moved about 400 boat people from Pulau Laut Island to our camp. I did not know where that island was, but after talking to some newcomers, I discovered it was north of the Indonesian Riau Islands. It probably took the movers a whole day to transport them from Pulau Laut Island to the Galang Vietnamese Refugee Camp. Unexpectedly, I ran into Hân, one of the ex-military pilots I knew from Nha Trang Air Force Training Center.

After a few warm conversations and catching up, I asked him about MH-4112. Miraculously, he recognized the boat number! A few days ago, he saw a big white ship identified as Ile de Lumiere[90]. There were many medical volunteers and physicians in what was essentially a "floating hospital," patrolling the high seas to help the boat people. When the physicians came to Pulau Laut Island, they carried the dead body of a girl who came from MH-4112. They wanted to bury the girl there on the island. After hearing the bad news, an unbearably sad feeling engulfed my mind while my heart surged with piercing pain. I kept asking for more information, but that was all Hân knew. He suggested I talk to someone who had arrived there with him—the Vietnamese medical doctor who had received the girl's dead body from the Ile de Lumiere ship.

It took us a while to search for the physician among the 400 boat people who had just arrived at the refugee camp that afternoon. Fortunately, we finally found him in the evening. He confirmed the girl's body was from MH-4112. Unfortunately, he didn't know where that boat had been or was currently.

From the remnants of the collected information my confused mind was trying to digest, I gathered that MH-4112 might not even be near any land. Why didn't they bury her there if it had already come ashore? The Ile de Lumiere ship must have run into MH-4112 somewhere. When Westerners saw the refugees on the high seas, they normally didn't rescue them unless their boats were sinking. Probably, the people on Mr. Thái Đức's boat didn't want to throw her body overboard, so they asked the Ile de Lumiere physicians to take her body away and bury it in the ground.

The news from Pulau Launt Island came as proof of the existence of MH-4112, but the knowledge I had gleaned consumed the rest of my broken heart. The boat that carried the Vietnamese refugees, including my loved ones, might still be on the South China Sea if it was still afloat.

I didn't want to show Hân or the Vietnamese physician my deadened face. I thanked them for the information and abruptly walked back to my barracks up one of the larger hills in the distance. As I was told, the dead girl was one of Mr. Thái Đức's children. I didn't know which one had died, but he had three daughters, and I had taught English to all of them when I was in Bạc Liêu. The death of one of my students destroyed my already-tattered soul even more.

What about the fate of other people on the boat?

I had to know! I wanted to cry! The overwhelming emotions and uncertainty regarding my family hurt so much that I wished I could go to the Galang pier, jump into the water, and end the unbearable torment. My confused mind triggered my heart to clench fiercely but also caused a sharp pain in my abdomen as I dragged my feet back to my shelter.

On September 2, 1979, I wrote another letter to Father Hoedemaekers telling him what I had discovered about MH-4112. My faith remained, but my hope dwindled to almost none.

The 81st Day After Separation

DURING THE WEEK of September 3, 1979, after receiving conflicting news of MH-4112's whereabouts, the only thing that kept my shred of hope alive was faith. The more I searched, the less I knew about that boat. Nobody could tell me where it was! During the day, I walked around talking to the newcomers to see if anyone had even a minuscule piece of information or a clue about the boat's whereabouts. At night, in bed, I prayed for a miracle, trying unsuccessfully to suppress the fear of my imagined tragic outcomes.

Then, one day, Father Hoedemaekers replied to my second letter, delivering promising news about the fate of the boat people from MH-4112. In his letter, dated September 9, Father Hoedemaekers wrote the boat was still in Sedanau. While the second letter gave my hope a much-needed boost, I couldn't help but wonder whether he mixed up the boat identification.

~

WHEN WE MOVED to Barracks 9, they assigned us a space. It was a corner "lot" next to one of the two main entrances. Each opening was in the middle of the external walls.

Inside the shelter were four long rows of flat wooden structures raised above the ground to be used by the refugees for everything, including sleeping and eating. We cooked on the ground near the structure we referred to as the bed. Our young friends, Hà and Trung, had a space on the opposite side, to our right.

Depending on how many members were in a family, they provided a certain amount of space on one of those flat wooden structures. They confined our living quarters to that small area. There, in Barracks 9, we met a very kind family. The couple had a little boy around my son's age and a younger sister around my wife's age. The husband and wife were both ex-pharmacists, but the husband, Anh Trọng, was also a former military officer. He and I frequently drank coffee together at the café outside Barracks 9. His younger sister, Cô Liên, was a medical doctor. They knew I was looking for my loved ones from the MH-4112 boat.

While I struggled to calm the relentless, never-ending stream of thoughts running through my mind after the newcomers didn't have any new clues about my loved ones' whereabouts, faith remained my only confidante. It sparked when the darkness was trying to take over my battered mind, and there was still a sliver of hope in me that someday Mr. Thái Đức's people, including my loved ones, might show up.

Just outside of Barracks 9, there was a small café where I hung around drinking coffee and talking to the owners, who were also from my boat. Most of the time, I drank coffee with a promise to pay later. They were officers from the former South Vietnam regime, so we had a special bond with each other.

The small café was a simple external extension on one end of Barracks 9, with a narrow roof installed. The shop had a few handmade tables and chairs for customers to sit down and enjoy their beverages. Many boat people working as camp representatives at the office nearby also came regularly to drink coffee and talk. I knew most of them and frequently asked when the next boat might arrive from the other islands. Again and again, they promised they would let me know as soon as they found MH-4112 or when it could come to the Galang camp.

One early afternoon in late September, I had just finished my last gulp of coffee with Anh Trọng and the café owners and began walking toward the camp office.

During that time, the moving of boat people from various Indonesian island archipelagos intensified. I wanted to check on what boat might arrive next and from where.

"Do you have any news on MH-4112 yet?" a person out for a stroll asked while passing me. He was one of the boat people from Barracks 9, where I was staying.

"No, not yet!" I quickly replied in a depressed tone, then kept walking down the road.

Suddenly, a man emerged from the office and started running toward me after seeing me in the distance. He shouted my name loudly while maneuvering to avoid knocking into other people on the path.

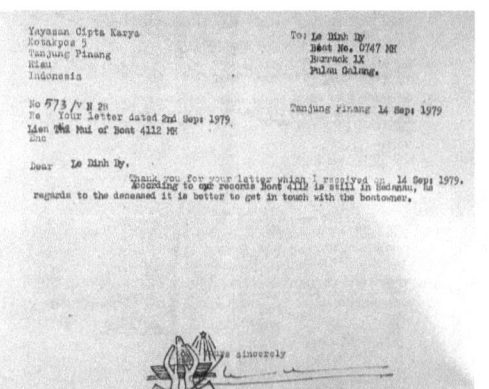

Father Piet Hoedemaekers' letters responding to my requests for assistance in search for loved ones.

In search for loved ones.
(1979, Galang Vietnamese Refugee Camp, Indonesia)

I received Father Hoedemaekers' letter... he wrote he could only find a boat with a registration number of "4122MH," not "MH-4112."

Camp architecture map.

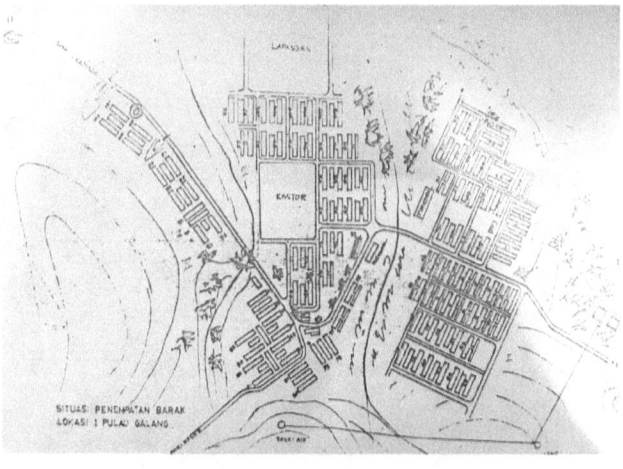

Galang Vietnamese Refuge Camp. (1979-1980)

Newly built temple.

"DỸ... DỸ!"

He knew my name and pronounced it correctly. He was certainly one of my friends.

"What!?" I yelled back, rushing toward him.

He almost stumbled onto the ground as he took the last few steps toward me. Then he bent forward in front of me, his hands supporting his upper body on both knees. He was trying to catch his breath while raising his head to look at me.

"MH-4112... It arrives this afternoon!" he shouted out. I suddenly felt like someone was pouring an entire bucket of cold water over my steamy head. My heart pumped faster. I felt like several thuds were so hard that my heart was trying to get out of my chest.

"Are you sure?! When?" I shuddered at his skinny shoulders in disbelief.

"MH-4112... left Sedanau Island... this morning!" said my friend between his slowly returning breaths.

In shock, I repeated the name of the island, "Sedanau! Isn't that the name of the island Father Hoedemaekers mentioned in his second letter?"

Over the prior few weeks, I had tried to familiarize myself with the Indonesian islands on the South China Sea. Sedanau Island was on the west side of the Riau Islands, northeast of the Galang Vietnamese Refugee Camp. Pulau Laut was not too far from the north, where they buried one of Mr. Thái Đức's daughters.

I hastily thanked my friend and ran toward Barracks 9 to look for my relatives to tell them the good news. If the MH-4112 boat people had already left that morning, they would arrive at the camp soon! I figured we should go to the pier to wait for them now.

I was running while talking to myself about my plan. It took me about half an hour to find my elder brother's sister-in-law, her nephew, and Dũng. Together, we rushed to the main pier, where the newcomers would normally disembark from the moving boat. We were all thrilled! It seemed like we had been looking for them for such a long time, and each day that passed was a day of lost hope.

We sped toward the pier on the same dirt road we had followed since our arrival, but it felt much longer this time.

Finally, we all arrived at the pier. The boat had not reached it yet, so we looked for a place to sit and wait for their arrival.

Naturally, that afternoon became a beautiful day. I felt jubilant for the first time in many years. Faint hope transformed into realistic anticipation. Dũng and my elder brother's in-laws must have been feeling the same. After all, it was splendid news for everyone. For months, we all had been waiting in vain for a miracle about to become a reality.

Suddenly, I became much calmer but extremely alert, with my eyes focused nonstop on the vast blue ocean. We waited impatiently, but not directly on the pier as we wanted to leave room for the newcomers to get off their boat. Instead, we nervously strolled around in an open area on solid ground.

Finally, a big boat arrived, much like the one we took to get here in July. The upper deck was full of refugees. It slowly maneuvered to the pier and docked. People started hopping from the boat to the pier quickly.

There were so many people, and I couldn't recognize anyone from such a distance. A few groups of the boat people had already passed us, looking at us curiously. I didn't know any of them.

"There they are!" Dũng's voice blasted into my eardrum. He kept pounding on it with his ecstatic shouts of excitement.

"See them? Do you see them!? There!"

He pointed his finger toward a group of people passing through the midway of the pier. Suddenly, my elder brother's in-laws ran in that direction. A few other people on the pier also started running toward them.

One of them emerged from the group to walk ahead of the others. A middle-aged man with a familiar round face and sturdy body rushed toward them. He had a big smile, but his eyes were full of tears. He was the father of my elder brother's nephew-in-law, the boy who left with me. I used to call him Anh Ba Long. They hugged, cried, and screamed at each other, unwilling and unable to hide their outbursts of extreme emotion and happiness. I had never seen Anh Ba Long so thrilled before. Then he saw me as I was walking closer to join them.

"They are here! They are here!"

Upon seeing me, Anh Ba Long shouted toward another group of people just stepping on the pier behind him.

"HÙNG IS HERE!" he called out, using my nickname, then released his son and rushed toward me. When he bumped against my body, he gripped it tightly like a reticulated python trying to coil around its prey and squeeze it tightly so it wouldn't get away.

"You saved my son!" he shouted. His voice penetrated my ear. He kept screaming while his warm tears ran down his cheeks. He held me so close that the short black hairs from his beard almost punctured the thin skin of my neck. His hands tightened around my lower body, lifting it up and down ecstatically, like a child playing with a big toy. His wife stood nearby, smiling happily.

For a moment, I said nothing because I could hardly breathe. I just smiled. The event overwhelmed me and also left me speechless. Then Anh Ba Long suddenly released my aching body and yelled my nickname again while looking toward the pier. Finally, free of his squeeze, I tried to catch a quick breath!

"HÙNG IS HERE!" he shouted again. His face glowed with extraordinary happiness. "Where is Mai!?" he screamed ecstatically, looking for my wife. Then, a woman dressed in a pair of female pants and an old short-sleeve shirt with a gray flower pattern descended from the pier. She hurriedly ran toward us with a child sagging on her waist while crying.

The running woman was Mai, my wife! The boy, dressed in a small blue T-shirt and shorts, was Huy, our 3-year-old son! I dashed toward her and embraced them both with my trembling arms. She cried, cried, and cried some more—just as she had the night I forced her and our son to leave while I stayed behind. The only difference was that she was not trying to suppress her crying this time. There, at the Galang pier, I hugged her and our son tightly while tears of joy filled my eyes and ran down my bony cheeks.

"I have you all now," I whispered into her ear while our son played with my long hair. He didn't know why we were all shedding tears, but he followed suit, rubbing his eyes with his hands and crying with the rest of us.

"I told you... I told you I would find you!"

While trying to comfort our son and my wife, my tears continued to run down and roll over my lips quietly. The night I had to bite my tongue to push her and our son onto the MH-4112 boat, I must restrain my tears for fear she might refuse to board.

Now, nothing could curb my overwhelming emotions as they surged through me at that extraordinary moment of reunification. I let our tears run down, and I cried quietly while the rich sister-in-law was quickly passing by.

Anh Ba Long's wife kindly helped comfort my wife, asking her to forget the ill-treatment Mai and our son had received while staying on the other islands.

It was all my fault. I was not there to protect my wife and our son. Coldly, I had pushed them onto the stormy high waves of the deep ocean toward unknown islands without a husband and father. I had done it to protect my siblings, the family, and the relatives of the rich sister-in-law. I will never forget those moments on that dirt road when I numbly realized that I had to break up my family for the sake of others.

It was all about fate, and only the Creator could materialize the end effects of our actions. My loved ones were finally safe in my arms. All along, Heaven and Buddha hadn't abandoned our pitiful souls, but we even had angels to guide us along our treacherous path. Grand moments during our journey through the dark world and the spectacular scene that transpired that day as we reunited served as additional proof of the existence of angels.

My younger brothers, sister, and cousin stepped onto the firm ground one by one, rushing toward me. They all looked unhealthy but alive! Their skin had turned a shade of dark brown. Their smiles were freely radiant. We hugged each other as though we would never let each other go. It was an absolutely blessed moment that would never fade away! It would stay forever in my heart, mind, and even my eternal afterlife. I would never let it go. It was invaluable and utterly priceless.

Throughout my life's journey, few experiences could even come close to being more astounding than that miraculous reunion at the Galang Vietnamese Refugee Camp pier that day. The genuine transition of that instant engraved a permanent acceptance of hope onto the inner consciousness of those with good hearts and unscrupulous minds, a precise point in time that we all could not deny marked a shift in our lives. It might become an untold story. But nobody could erase or distort that passage of life without burning their soul and conscience to nourish the dark side of humanity.

In late September 1979, I finally ended my unbearable suffering and fulfilled my unspoken promises to Mother and my ill-fated brother. At long last, my loved ones whom I had sent on a deadly journey into the darkness of the South China Sea came back one by one—physically unharmed—and landed in my arms once again. Also, those I took with me on a deadly journey on the high seas on the morning of June 19, 1979, arrived safely at the same location under my protection.

We were all finally in a free country!

That day, in the Galang Vietnamese Refugee Camp, I felt complete and could absorb the genuinely pure happiness, a blessing from Heaven and Buddha, and an extremely generous gift from Heaven. It fully convinced my mind that there had been a reason a piteous man like me was a chosen one to lead my family's exodus into the South China Sea in search of freedom.

I still remember what Mother often told me in the past. I was born in the north but grew up in the south while North Vietnam consistently tried to invade the free land of the yellow people. When I was a few months old, living in Vĩnh Yên, a small town of Vĩnh

Phúc Province in the north, my hair naturally grew into three thick, clearly noticeable patches in peach-like shapes: one on each side of my head right above the ears and the third one near the forehead. Mother used to say I had a good, righteous past life and the physical features of the ministering monk—a round head with three peach-like hair patches.

"You are the son of Lord Buddha," Mother said.

Dark forces had thrown me into a pack of wolves. With my sacred faith as my only persistent invisible companion, I saw the hands of angels at every deadly fall or stumble I encountered. They showed me things I would not otherwise have seen and guided me from uncertainties into an absolute belief that I was on the right path. I led my loved ones on a narrow, deadly path while, unknowingly, the angels' invisible shining light firmly guided me in the right direction. Truly, my hope faded from time to time because of my tormented mind, but faith always reignited that last minuscule hope that remained. Saved by miracles from the persistent faith, my deep conscience had never thought of glorious redemption but only wanted peace of mind and a righteous submissive soul upon the monk's last day.

As for my family, we had been in hell on earth for the last 81 days as a test of our spiritual endurance and belief. However, my family's reunification, as time would prove, only increased the hatred and sped up the personal attacks and defamations from the rich sister-in-law with an intent to create conflict and sow the seeds of distrust among our family members. But at that moment, I no longer cared what she could or couldn't do in the future. I had already rightfully fulfilled my moral obligations. No one could ever condemn how I lived during that passage through hell on earth. And nothing could ever deviate my soul from retaining and following righteous principles for the rest of my life and beyond, particularly in the promised land.

Humans are capable of many things, including twisting the truth of the story of one's past. However, we might only change our future through righteous actions and corrective redemption, with genuine faith and an untainted soul.

The passage through hell on earth, while fighting against the dark forces, had given me a rational purpose—the goal of achieving a dream once thought impossible and delusional by so many. Many torments we unwaveringly experienced during our deadly journey lived with us for the rest of our lives but would ease our last breath on Earth. The dangerous path we took would remind us and the next generations of where we came from, how we got here, and the price and collateral damage we had to pay to be free again.

A FATEFUL DISEASE

They merged my wife and son into my registration as family and put us in Barracks 9 together. My brothers, youngest sister, and cousin stayed in one barracks about a little over a kilometer away.

The living conditions at the Galang Vietnamese Refugee Camp were poor, with potentially serious diseases easily spreading throughout the camp. We wanted to get out of there to reestablish our lives in another country as soon as possible.

Before our family reunification, the U.S. team had not yet come. However, the Canadian delegation had already interviewed and accepted me, Dũng, and my elder brother's in-laws, who had come with me. When my elder brother and his in-laws arrived, they wanted to resettle in Australia. If they preferred that, I told them we would split, and my family would go to Canada. My younger brothers, sister, and cousin agreed with my decision. Eventually, my elder brother's family and in-laws changed their minds and applied for Canada instead of Australia.

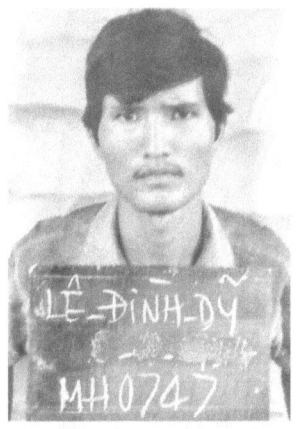

The night I had to bite my tongue to push her and our son onto the MH-4112 boat, I must restrain my tears for fear she might refuse to board. Now, nothing could curb my overwhelming emotions as they surged through me at that extraordinary moment of reunification.

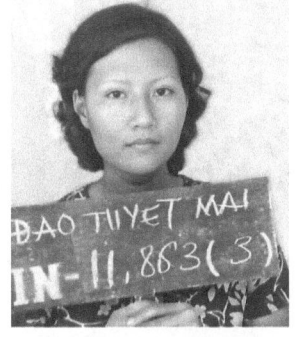

"Mugshots."

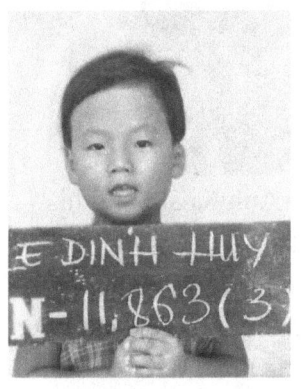

**Family reunification.
(09/1979, Galang Vietnamese
Refugee Camp, Indonesia)**
Baracks 9 where my small family stayed. (*Gaylord Barr*)

Our love to Anh Khâm and his family is always warm in our hearts. Credits are given to him for taking many precious pictures shown in this book.

**We made it!
(1979-1980, Galang Vietnamese Refugee Camp, Indonesia)**

One day in September 1979, the U.S. delegation finally came to interview the boat people. Since Canada had already accepted Dũng and me, they suggested the rest of my family join us and resettle there. The Americans promised to contact the Canadian team to combine my wife, son, and me into one file and add the younger brothers, sister, and cousins to Dũng's file. Unfortunately, that didn't happen fast enough.

On September 26, 1979, Galang Vietnamese Refugee Camp officials received a list of 240 boat people to be transported to Tanjung Pinang, Unggat, to complete resettling in Canada. The list included Dũng and me, but not my wife, son, or the rest of our siblings and cousin. That evening, they were ready to transfer us to Tanjung Pinang and had a big boat waiting at the pier. I refused to go and asked Dũng to go ahead while I stayed behind to adjust my family's status with the Canadian delegation and to take care of the rest of my loved ones. Taking my advice, Dũng left that evening with the other people on the Canadian list.

A few weeks after Dũng left, the Canadian delegation returned to interview more boat people. My wife and son and relatives were among them. They also interviewed my elder brother's family and his in-laws. We were all finally accepted by Canada. Two weeks later, we took the required medical examinations, including a chest X-ray, as part of the routine visa application process. After completing the medical examinations, all we had to do was wait for the results before transitioning to Tanjung Pinang. From there, they would transport the refugees who had received acceptable medical results to Singapore to board flights to Canada.

Although the world eventually learned about the Galang Vietnamese Refugee Camp, the condition of the camp remained unhealthy to live in, even temporarily. In the meantime, the exodus of people trying to run away from Vietnam intensified. An overcrowded population of boat people paired with increasingly unsanitary conditions had generated serious threats of potential disease outbreaks. The fetid public restrooms were extremely filthy and certainly capable of contaminating the surrounding environment. During that time, the Red Cross and UNHCR had not fully established their operations on the island. About 7,000 boat people were staying in the camp, and more were about to come.

To cope with the increasing influx of boat people, the Indonesian authority was expanding the area into several zones to build more military-style barracks.

Each barracks in the refugee camp had about 100 people living in it, including a selected leader. When we first moved into Barracks 9, our leader was Mr. Khải Quang, a Chinese-Vietnamese man. I used to call him Abiểu—a sturdy man with a round and shiny belly who always smiled with a generous and intelligent grin. He was a chain smoker and loved the Indonesian dark brown Djarum cigarettes. He spoke English fluently. Abiểu and I talked and joked all the time and became good friends.

While we were staying at the refugee camp, they gave us a standard daily food ration which was distributed to the barracks leaders, who would then divide the food among residents irrespective of their age. Each person would receive a package of about 400 grams of rice, 30 grams of cooking oil, and 20 grams of sugar. They also gave us powdered milk and cans of sardines. We didn't have any meat to eat.

Eventually, tap water would become one of the most luxurious facets of the camp—available only to international delegations and staff members—but in the beginning, we didn't have it. We had to bathe or wash our clothes in the river. Eventually, I found an abandoned tall metal container and placed it outside near the exterior wooden wall of our space to save water for daily use. We would carry large buckets of water from the river to our barracks.

We also collected rainwater for bathing, washing clothes, cooking, and drinking. Unfortunately, unwanted sky worms often infested the water. People don't always believe me when I say that those light brown or purple fat worms didn't come from the ground but appeared to have fallen from the sky with the rain—but I don't see how that's not the case. Their existence inside the tall metal container, always right after the rain, puzzled me.

How did they get inside?

The first time we mixed the worm-infested rainwater with powdered milk and drank it, our bellies made loud rumbling sounds. Shortly after, the members of my family had to go to the smelly public "restrooms" non-stop throughout the day. My wife also felt nauseous and dizzy. She couldn't stand it and stopped drinking milk entirely, but my son and I continued.

Eventually, we got used to the rainwater milk. Our frequent bowel movements stopped, which, unfortunately, helped bacteria to stay inside our bodies much longer. We knew if we kept drinking it, there was a high likelihood that we would develop intestinal diseases or parasites. Unfortunately, we had no other choice during that time. My son needed milk to grow. We also needed to supplement our food-deficient bodies with as many vitamins as possible, including B12, which was present in milk.

I had no money or gold to buy additional food or other essentials to meet our daily needs. After the war, I was completely broke. Since then, nothing changed except the freedom I finally regained for my loved ones and myself. Still, I didn't regret not trying to make money while planning my family's escape while in Bạc Liêu.

Feeling pity over my consistent level of extreme poverty, a few days after the MH-4112 boat people had arrived, Anh Ba Long, the rich sister-in-law's half-brother, gave me three taels of gold. It was also because he wanted to reward me for successfully helping his son and the rest of his family out of Vietnam.

In 1979, three shiny pieces of gold were equivalent to about 1,000 American dollars, more than enough for me to feed my family for many months while staying at the camp. However, as I had stated from the beginning, I didn't plan to make money while trying to get them out of Vietnam. So, of course, I didn't want to accept the gold he offered. However, he kept insisting that I take them. So, as a compromise, I told him to keep the gold but asked that he subtract that amount from the total sum my younger brothers and sister had borrowed to pay for their boat trip to flee Vietnam.

He agreed! I liked Anh Ba Long. He was a straightforward, good, caring, and thoughtful person. Of course, this meant that I still had no money. But it didn't matter to me. I was happy knowing I had already gained something priceless—freedom for my loved ones. In the meantime, my family had to hang in there just long enough to survive before resettling to another country. That's why we had to take the first opportunity offered to us, allowing us to leave the camp as soon as possible... and Canada was that first offer!

While at the camp, Anh Trọng, my barracks' next-space neighbor, referred me for a part-time job helping the local builder load and unload logs from the forest area near the pier to get them to various sites within the camp to be used in construction. The pay was not much, but sometimes, I could use it to buy a few grams of meat to sustain our strength.

At first, Anh Trọng and I worked together as a two-person team. Eventually, we added another team member, Anh Trung Chỉnh, a military physician from former South Vietnam. Besides being a medical doctor, Anh Trung Chỉnh was a famous singer during the Vietnam War. So, the three of us frequently hang off the back of a big truck going to and from the pier and various locations throughout the camp. Sometimes, Anh Trung Chỉnh also drove the truck.

On November 26, 1979, shortly before Anh Trung Chỉnh left for the U.S., he wrote a song and recorded it in my dark brown notebook, which I used to scribe my thoughts so that I could trace back the details of the events that occurred during our deadly journey.

By December 1979, Dũng, my younger brother, was still in Tanjung Pinang, Unggat, waiting to go to Canada. At the processing center there, the food rations for each person were much better, adequate even. They gave him rice, canned food, and small bags of instant noodles. My wife and I were happy he was doing well and would leave for Canada soon. He would be the first of us to arrive in the New World! In late 1979, the Canadian government sped up the transportation of the boat people they had already interviewed and accepted from the Galang Vietnamese Refugee Camp to Canada via Tanjung Pinang and Singapore.

We were all eager to depart but still awaiting the medical examination results. We were also worried because we could wind up traveling to Canada in the winter when it would be freezing. Living in the warm climate of Vietnam, my wife and I had only a few old articles of clothing, and they certainly weren't warm enough for a Canadian winter! They were scarcely appropriate for Vietnam's rainy season.

The Disease That Changed the Future

WHILE IN TANJUNG Pinang, Dũng frequently wrote me letters to provide updates on the status of our family's resettlement in Canada; particularly, I received one on December 3, 1979.

In that letter, he gave us the good news that all my younger brothers, sister, and cousin's medical results were normal. They would leave for Canada in January 1980, depending on flight availability. However, his letter also came with bad news. Sadly, our medical examination results were not good. Based on the chest X-rays, they diagnosed both my wife and me with tuberculosis.

Dũng urged me to seek treatment for my family and advised me not to work very hard—advice I could not follow because I needed money to feed my little son. He encouraged us to eat more nutritious food, which we didn't have because my idealistic mind told me not to take gold from Anh Ba Long to use it for my family's survival. He advised us to get plenty of sleep, which we also struggled to do because of our constant worries about what to feed our son tomorrow, the next day, and so on. We also lost sleep over concerns regarding how much longer we could survive, given the camp's unhealthy conditions.

A few days before I received Dũng's letter, Anh Trọng's family, our barracks' next-space neighbor, was also in Tanjung Pinang waiting to go to Singapore to resettle in the U.S. Anh Trọng was a pharmacist and military officer from the former South Vietnam regime. The U.S. delegation accepted his family quickly.

One day, while in Tanjung Pinang, Dr. Liên, Anh Trọng's younger sister, ran into Dũng and was told about our medical condition. She wrote me a letter instructing me and my wife to see Dr. Long, who was staying in Barracks 147, for help. She wanted us to get another X-ray and to receive immediate treatment while we waited for the Canadian physicians to arrive to follow up regarding our medical condition. Cô Liên also prescribed INH, Ethambutol, and Streptomycin for my wife and me. She didn't have any required medication for treating tuberculosis except Ethambutol. So, she sent us those pills and asked us to take them immediately. We were very grateful for her care. Angels were always on my shoulder, shining a light on my path and softening every fall I endured. The more I fell, the less it deterred me from rising and fighting again.

Although I was sad that we could not leave for Canada, we were still happy for our relatives who would depart in January 1980. Four of Anh Ba Long's children would leave for Canada on January 17, 1980, while he, his wife, and the remaining children were not. So, I helped him write a letter to the Canadian delegation in Singapore to plead his case and inquire about his immigration status.

By the end of January 1980, all my relatives, including my elder brother's family and his in-laws, had already left the refugee camp and departed for Canada. Before his family left, he quickly pushed a few U.S. dollar bills into my hand and said farewell.

Subsequently, they all arrived in Edmonton during the cold winter month of January 1980. Tấm, the ghostlike man's nephew had also left the Galang Vietnamese Refugee Camp to join his relatives in the U.S.

By fate, and because of the disease, I remained behind with my wife and 4-year-old son. We were both sick with a potentially infectious and deadly disease, if not properly treated. The hardship and mental agonies had finally taken their toll on me. The bacteria roaming in my weak body probably traveled to my innocent wife's healthy lungs from mine. According to the Canadian medical examination report, miraculously, our son was fine. But we constantly worried he might be next!

The road to freedom was still littered with many challenges, taking a toll on all of us. We had to prepare to stay for what might be a long haul at the Galang Vietnamese Refugee Camp. We couldn't even consider leaving until they could get rid of the disease from our bodies. But I knew we would eventually pass over every hurdle and survive.

My faith and determination remained strong, and I believed our angels would continue illuminating the right path for us—the one that would allow us to complete our remaining journey.

Beautiful Souls and Hearts

IN THE SUMMER of 1979, when we first arrived at the Galang Vietnamese Refugee Camp, the Indonesian authority had already established a temporary hospital while a new one was being built. The old clinic didn't have an in-patient facility. The new hospital would have around 40 beds. Physicians, pharmacists, and nurses normally ran the daily outpatient clinic; many were refugees.

One day, the hospital asked my family to come to the clinic for tuberculosis assessment and treatment. Subsequently, Dr. Long carefully examined each of us.

We underwent several sputum smear tests to evaluate the severity of our sickness and contagion. Fortunately, all our sputum smear test results seemed normal, and we were not contagious. We could not transmit the disease to another person.

Our chest X-ray films, however, had some anomalies. Huy's lungs and health were fine, which was good news. Although the medical reports devastated my wife and me, we accepted the results with enormous relief. We were happy about our son's good health.

That day and over the next several months, Dr. Long prescribed and provided us with four-week supplies of medication. His medical staff and he monitored our health progress closely and provided us with regularly scheduled chest X-ray procedures to assess the effectiveness of the treatment.

Taking the tuberculosis medication on a frequently empty stomach was a significant challenge for both of us. We tried to save our limited income, whatever I made from the part-time job, to buy meat or other nutritious food for the little one—our precious 4-year-old son. So, I kept drinking the worm-infested-rainwater milk and, many times, Mai and I continued to eat the tasteless white rice stew without meat or vegetables.

All my brothers, sister, and cousin had been doing well in Canada since they left the camp. They sent me letters asking how we were doing and expressing their hope that we would join them soon.

Dũng frequently wrote me long letters and had already contacted a few Canadian authorities, trying to resolve our health and immigration issues. But, according to their immigration policy, I knew it would be challenging. Canada, especially, didn't allow any refugees with diagnosed tuberculosis to enter their country until the disease was completely gone.

I knew it would be a long fight, which I could endure. However, I expected it would be difficult for my wife to recover quickly with such an inadequate healthcare environment and the shortage of essential nutrition. Unfortunately, what could I do? We could go nowhere. Fleeing again wasn't an option, and if it had been... to where? I knew I should prepare for a long stay on the island and focus on our survival.

One day, my wife and I received another letter from Dũng. Along with the letter, he sent us some money, in cash! Subsequently, he kept increasing the cash amounts as he could save more. We had never asked or wanted him to send us any money. The thoughtful mind, beautiful heart, and soul of a younger brother, who frequently thought about the unlucky and sick older brother's poor family, engraved his love into our hearts. We will never forget it! And we were happy for Dũng and the rest of our loved ones, knowing they were finally safe and excitedly shaping their futures in the New World.

A FATEFUL DISEASE | 311

My married elder brother was the oldest to settle in Canada. I was the next older brother with a wife and son. But we were still in the refugee camp. Dũng was my next single younger brother, who was in Canada then.

So, traditionally, he oversaw the younger brothers, sister, and cousin's welfare. From the many letters he sent me from Tanjung Pinang, where he had been waiting for resettlement, and Edmonton, where he lived in Canada, I could feel his deep love for the family, particularly the younger siblings. I saved all the letters Dũng had sent as precious treasures. They had become rare, invaluable memories from this world. Someday, I wanted to share my deep feelings of love and those letters with my children and others from the next generation as they perfectly depicted what a true, thoughtful mind, beautiful heart and soul, and bond of eternal brotherhood would look like, particularly during a time of extraordinary need.

And, to this day, Dũng's letters, with the misaligned lines of words and sentences, still make me cry whenever I get the urge to read them to feel the sense of still having him with us.

~

AFTER ALL MY relatives left the refugee camp for Canada in January 1980, I finally accepted the reality that fate intended for my small family to stay at the camp much longer than expected.

Nobody seemed able to tell us when they could complete the treatment. Every few months, we had to go to the newly built hospital for chest X-rays and sputum smear tests to ensure we weren't contagious. We did not know whether we could go to Canada, or anywhere, in the future—ever.

In November 1979, I volunteered to work for UNHCR as an interpreter. While being treated for tuberculosis throughout 1980, I wanted to devote more time to supporting the Indonesia Red Cross, UNHCR, and the U.S. Joint Voluntary Agency (JVA) efforts to process refugee applications for resettlement under the U.S. Refugee

Program. Dr. Iwan Jusuf was the Indonesia Red Cross representative, with his office in the new hospital. The UNHCR Resettlement Officer was Ms. Marion Tijsseling, based in Jakarta, Indonesia.

In 1980, the U.S. JVA delegation frequently visited the camp to interview the boat people. Other countries, including Australia, also came but less often. My duty was to help prepare the refugee application paperwork, translation, and interpretation during the interviews. The job was unpaid, but it allowed me to help people in a more direct way.

Mr. George Cosgrove was the U.S. Refugee Program Coordinator. His office was at the U.S. Embassy in Singapore. For the next several months, while working with the Indonesia Red Cross, UNHCR, and U.S. JVA delegation teams, I became appreciative of the hard work and caring personalities of many representatives: Marion Tijsseling, a quiet but very kind lady; Don Jarrett, a young gentleman who talked slowly and without smiling, but had a tender heart; Michael Knowles, a kind man with an amiable smile who could speak Vietnamese fluently, with knowledgeable-looking eyes behind his thick eyeglasses; Art, another gentleman—with a black beard and famous dark T-shirt—whom I only remembered by first name, was quiet but tough on ensuring information was accurate; and Helene, a skinny lady who was also very kind and humorous. I forgot her last name as well.

After Anh Trọng's family, my next-space neighbor in Barracks 9, had left for the U.S., another family moved in next to us. When they arrived, we became good friends quickly. They were waiting to go to Australia and had a 12-year-old daughter and an older son. They were also extremely kind people and frequently went to pray at the recently built church, which was not too far away, set back on the hill where the Virgin Mary statue stood on a tall brick and cement monument. Our neighbors were certainly not rich, but the couple had some money to buy food. They often saw us eating the cooked white rice stew without meat. Knowing we were dead broke, the wife, Chị Cúc, often asked her 12-year-old daughter, Ngó, to share cookies and some food with our 4-year-old son, who was always hungry.

One day, Chị Cúc took my wife to the Catholic church on the hill, and she talked with the priest about our situation. Miraculously, the priest gave my wife several thousand Indonesian rupiahs, enough to feed our family for a few weeks! We saved the money and only used it to buy food for our little son.

Soon after, I received another letter from Dũng, in which he mentioned our father. For the last several months, since our father disappeared without a trace, I had heard nothing from or about him. Dũng wrote our father had also successfully fled Vietnam and was living in York, Pennsylvania, in the U.S.

Hearing the good news, I was pleased. We had thought we might never see him again!

Subsequently, Father wrote me a letter asking about our situation. I wrote several letters back, but I was unsure whether he was receiving them all. In one letter, I told him my family was waiting to go to Canada but didn't know when because of our medical conditions. He received that letter and replied that he was unhappy about our decision to go to Canada instead of the U.S. I began considering this viewpoint, but I took no action to change our status.

When we first arrived at the Galang Vietnamese Refugee Camp, the boat people, with support from the Indonesian local government, established the camp committee and administrative staff to oversee the refugee population and address civil matters. The camp leader was Dr. Mai, one of the boat people. He was a very likable person with black-framed eyeglasses and a well-trimmed mustache. He spoke English fluently. The deputy camp leader was Mr. Kiệt. I knew little about him. The camp committee then voted to appoint Abiểu, my barracks leader, as Chief of the Resettlement Section and me as Assistant Chief.

They also appointed Abiểu as Head of the U.S. JVA delegation's interpreter team. His job, without pay, was to oversee a staff of several volunteers, including interpreters and administrative personnel, who supported the resettlement activities conducted by the U.S. JVA delegation. During that time, I also worked for the group. We had an excellent team of about 12 volunteers. We normally spent most of the day at the Resettlement Processing Center near Barracks 9, working on days when the interviews took place.

In July 1980, when Abiêu was about to depart for the U.S., they re-assigned me to Acting Chief for the Resettlement Section. They also appointed another man as Head of the U.S. JVA delegation's interpreter team.

I heard he came to the camp from a refugee camp in Singapore. He spoke English fluently and seemed to know a lot about U.S. football. He often hung around with another gentleman who came from Singapore with him. They normally dressed in beautiful colorful shirts, a drastic improvement over my faded, wrinkled shirt.

However, within a single week, I was told that the U.S. JVA delegation wanted to remove the new Head and appoint another. According to the local gossip, the new Head had a tainted history of corruption. I paid little attention to gossip, so I didn't know what was happening. A few days later, the U.S. JVA delegation and the camp committee appointed me to that position. With that, I unexpectedly became the Head of the U.S. JVA delegation's interpreter team. I assumed my record was clean and accepted the position with little thought.

After they appointed me to the position, I realized several issues that accompanied the job. For example, some rich boat people asked if I could help get their files processed more quickly. Others suggested I change their personal information slightly to avoid a potential rejection for resettlement in their first choice country, particularly the U.S. I firmly believed the U.S. delegation was aware of the issues, which was why Mr. Art was very tough during interviews, hoping to detect false personal information.

Some boat people were worried about Mr. Art's strict style and were afraid to be interviewed by him. Unfortunately, they didn't know he was truly a good man and very gentle. I realized why they had placed me in the Head role, as the issues that could lead to corruption wouldn't be a problem for me. I didn't even want three taels of gold, the equivalent of about 1,000 American dollars, from Anh Ba Long—even while my family members were starving! Certainly, I wouldn't be taking bribes from those pitiful refugees who sought to come out ahead at the expense of others.

So, I was fair in the position. I didn't do what the wealthy boat people asked of me if it reeked of corruption, unfairness, or went against our policies. I asked my wife to be careful of those who came and asked for me and not to accept anything from anybody, particularly money. When people came to ask me for help in translating Vietnamese documents, writing letters of inquiry, or addressing other legitimate issues, I helped them but accepted no fees.

So, they often tried to find other ways to compensate me for my help. When we were still sleeping in the early morning, they would come to our barracks, tiptoe inside the area, and leave a bag of fruit next to our feet on our assigned wooden platform. When we awoke, we would discover the unattended fruit bag. Since nobody knew who had put it there, we had no choice but to keep it.

For almost an entire year in 1980, over a year after we fled Vietnam in June 1979, we survived on the kindness and charity of friends and people who knew us. I continued to drink powdered milk mixed with worm-infested rainwater to regain my strength. As a result, my health seemed to improve significantly. I suddenly no longer felt sick, and the improvement enabled me to work harder to help the refugees resettle in other countries.

Although we had never asked, occasionally, Dũng still sent us some cash folded inside his letters, with encouraging words for us to hang on to survive. We spent his money carefully, knowing it came from his beautiful heart and resulted from his hard work in the New World.

Several months after beginning the treatment program for tuberculosis, I sent a few letters to the Canadian delegation to inquire about my family's resettlement status and request them to assess our health conditions. They didn't respond to any of my inquiries. Unfortunately, there was nothing more I could do to help my small family's situation.

During that time, after having already accepted a significant number of refugees and transported them to Canada, they rarely returned. Most of the time, our resettlement team was working for the U.S. JVA delegation, as they frequently came to interview people.

For several months, we helped the U.S. delegation team process many Indochinese refugees for resettlement in the United States. The U.S. JVA delegation members were truly happy with our support and progress. One day, during a break, Ms. Helene from the U.S. JVA delegation and I sat next to a wooden table used for interviews. She curiously asked me about my family's resettlement situation. Mr. Art and Knowles were also standing around us, chitchatting. I explained to her about our ongoing medical treatment for tuberculosis and that we were still waiting for Canada to accept us under the circumstances.

"How long has it been since you left Vietnam?" Ms. Helene curiously asked.

"Over a year," I told her with a straight face, void of frustration because I had already accepted my fate.

"Over a year!?" she exclaimed in a shocked, doubtful voice.

"Yes, over a year. Twelve months and a few days, to be exact," I confirmed.

Ms. Helene couldn't believe what she had just heard. She looked at Mr. Art, who was leaning one of his hands against the support column of the Resettlement Processing Centre, listening to our conversation.

"We must get him and his family out of here!" she said with determination.

Mr. Art dropped his hand from the column, scratched his black beard, and walked over to our wooden table. He sat down next to Ms. Helen, who was on the opposite side of the table from where I was sitting.

"Do you want to go to the U.S.?" Mr. Art asked. He didn't wait for me to respond before adding, "We can get you and your family out of here."

In all honesty, by that time, I had become comfortable living in the refugee camp. The Indochinese Red Cross, UNHCR, and local authorities did an outstanding job of improving the camp conditions. Of course, it was far from a perfect place to live, but I felt attached to my life at the camp.

In my free time, I would wander deep into the forest, listening to birds chirping. Other times, I took my wife and son or went with friends to the beach. I had many pleasant companions at the camp, many still waiting for resettlement.

All of them treated us well! One of them, Anh Khâm, a wealthy Chinese Vietnamese from Mr. Thái Đức's boat waiting to go to Australia, hung out with me almost every day. He normally carried a camera and often took pictures while we were working.

One day, he asked us to go up to the church, where he took a picture of me, my wife, and our son together under the Virgin Mary statue. Anh Khâm had a very honest smile and a bright face that my wife and I would never forget. He had never asked me to do anything for his family, yet he still came to my barracks every day to drag me to the café. Of course, he would pay for the coffee all the time.

So, at some point, the prospect of staying on the island as long as possible made me feel more relaxed. I didn't have to worry about anything except finding enough food for my family. As time passed, the Indonesian and international charity organizations even started providing adequate food supplies for us to survive. It felt like being kept here for long-term treatment might also be fine.

After leaving the camp for a few months, Anh Trọng, my previous next-space neighbor in Barracks 9, sent me a letter from the U.S. He strongly advised us to enjoy our stay on the island for as long as we could. Interestingly, he complained about the hectic and stressful life he and his family were experiencing in the U.S., which caused our concern over the prospect of building our future in the

New World. I felt our lives would change dramatically—and forever—once we left the beautiful and peaceful Galang island.

Even though I wasn't sure when Canada would consider our medical treatment program complete, I knew we would have to leave Indonesia someday. But when? Canada had left us behind at the camp, taking many others before, during, and after. They might have already forgotten about their refugee patients who didn't have medical clearance. And nobody had told us if or when we might resettle in another country, either.

So, I told Mr. Art that we would want to go to the U.S. if possible. I also told them my father was living in York, Pennsylvania. I explained about my family's current immigration status with the Canadian resettlement program, but Mr. Knowles chimed in and stated they would take care of that issue.

Before the fall of Sài Gòn, I served in the Republic of Vietnam Air Force, and they sent me to the U.S. for flight training to become one of the military pilots for the south. I fled from a communist country by boat.

Those factors alone provided excellent grounds to establish eligibility for political asylum. That same day, the U.S. JVA delegation quickly created my family's file and left the island after completing the interviews with another group of boat people scheduled for their regular visits.

Returning to my barracks in the evening, I told my wife about my conversation with my American friends. We tried not to get our hopes up, believing the process may still take quite a while. We remained deeply concerned with our health condition and several lingering issues; therefore, we still assumed a long stay at the refugee camp. We couldn't have been more wrong!

About a week later, the U.S. JVA delegation returned and informed me they had scheduled our family for the interview. Subsequently, they determined we were all eligible for political asylum. Then, they arranged and administrated the required processes, including our swearing-in before the U.S. immigration official.

And, to this day, Dũng's letters, with the misaligned lines of words and sentences, still make me cry whenever I get the urge to read them to feel the sense of still having him with us.

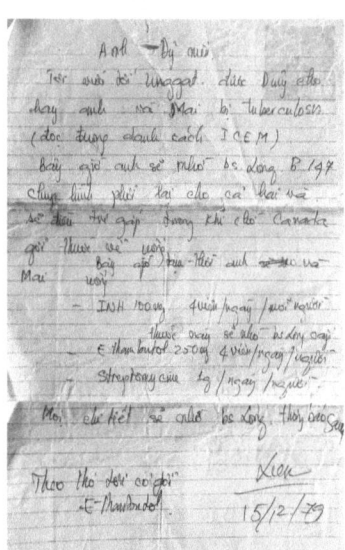

Letter from Dr. Liên.

My beloved brothers, youngest sister, and cousin. Dũng in the white shirt. (1980, Edmonton, Canada)

Don Jarrett, Tâm Đan, and I were interviewing the Vietnamese boat people.

(1979-1980, Galang Vietnamese Refugee Camp, Indonesia)

Galang Resettlement Processing Center. (*Gaylord Barr*)

A typical working day at the Galang camp. (1979-1980, Galang Vietnamese Refugee Camp, Indonesia)

My volunteer identification card from the Galang Camp Security Office.

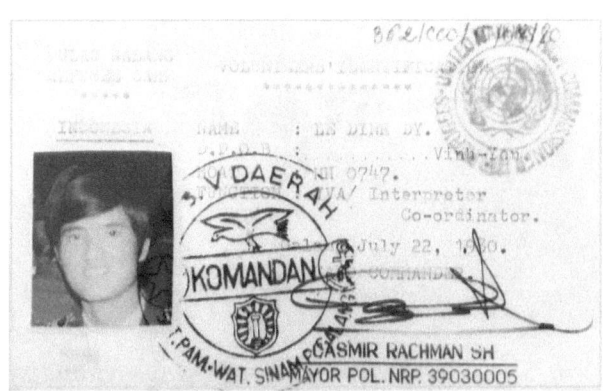

In the meeting.

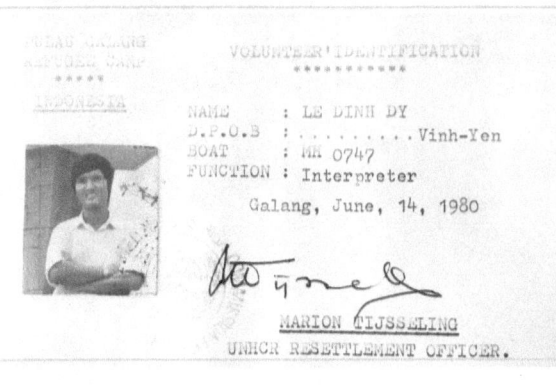

My ID card from UNHCR.

"Do you want to go to the U.S.?" Mr. Art asked. He didn't wait for me to respond before adding, "We can get you and your family out of here."

Canada had left us behind at the camp, taking many others before, during, and after. They might have already forgotten about their refugee patients who didn't have medical clearance.

**A disease that changed our future.
(1979-1980, Galang Vietnamese Refugee Camp, Indonesia)**
Our family was later accepted to resettle in the U.S.

A few days later, they requested the American Red Cross at the new hospital to examine my family's health and perform the required tests.

Soon after, the physicians at the hospital completed the medical procedures, including blood tests and chest X-rays. During the next two days, they gave us the sputum smear tests.

Then, there was nothing left to do but wait nervously for our health reports to come back while praying that the medications we had been taking had worked.

Finally, on August 15, 1980, the hospital notified us of the results. My son's health was still in perfect condition. Mai's medical examination report and mine were normal except for the chest X-rays. Our sputum smear tests showed "negative."

With that, they classified us as having Class B inactive tuberculosis. However, both reports also included a few critical notes: "No treatment received in Indonesia. To be followed up in the U.S.A." Despite the language in the report, the hospital still provided us with a supply of medications every four weeks. We continued to take the prescribed pills, and I still swallowed them with the worm-infested-rainwater milk.

After we had received the medical reports showing mixed results and confusing notes, a few days later, the U.S. JVA delegation came to interview more refugees. That day, their boat came in a little later in the afternoon than usual. They had interviewed no one yet and wanted to wait until the following morning.

Shortly after their arrival, Ms. Helene sent word to me. I went to the Resettlement Processing Center to meet them.

When I saw them, my American friends were leisurely sitting on both sides of a long, rectangular wooden table, and all looked pleasant. But I paid little attention, as I knew they always looked like that doing their jobs. They were happy to help the refugees.

"Hello, guys!"

I greeted them with a smile while walking up the slope to the interviewing area. There were no people around except the U.S.

JVA delegation members. They waited for me to sit down comfortably on a long bench. Then Ms. Helene slowly unfolded a rolled paper she was holding in her hand.

"Your family will leave the camp next month!" she said without reading what she was holding her hand. She didn't even give me a moment to react to what I had just heard before she spoke again. "Your family will stay in Singapore for a few days before the chartered flight to the U.S. arrives." As she said these words, her eyes shined even brighter than usual. Then, she gave me a firm date, stating, "You are leaving this camp on September 17."

I tried so hard to bite my lip because I didn't want to burst out crying right there in front of everyone. Despite my best attempts at holding back the tears, they suddenly filled my eyes, salty and warm. I tried to find the words to show gratitude for what my American friends had done for my family and me. My mind, however, had become cloudy with extreme emotion—not only because we were finally on the list to go to the U.S. but in the discovery of the amazingly thoughtful, kind, and caring hearts that existed and the way these individuals helped the boat people. I would have expected no one to do what they had for people they barely knew.

At that point, we had already given up our dream of going to the promised land. It was dead until they came and resurrected it. To them, it might have just been a simple humanitarian act, but for my family, they restored the hopes, dreams, and desires we once believed in so strongly—to get out of Vietnam and start over in the land that was considered, once upon a time, an abstract fantasy.

From my first conversation with the U.S. JVA delegation about our situation, it took them approximately one month to complete the security and background checks, perform our swearing-in, conduct all medical examinations, and make the reservations for us to travel to Singapore, then on to the U.S. As the Head of the U.S. JVA delegation's interpreter team, I knew what it took to handle each aspect of resettlement. I also knew that our American friends had done far more than what they had to, and in the most effective ways possible, to take us out of the refugee camp and send us to the U.S., rather than leaving us there waiting for Canada for what could have been a very long time. I was certain the U.S. delegation had also consulted with Canadian immigration officials to remove our family from the list of people who didn't have medical clearance and were still living in the Galang Vietnamese Refugee Camp.

We had passed another test of our faith.

The angels, once again, as ordinary human beings, brought us back onto the path that fate had already fixed for us. We were finally going to the promised land, just as we had always dreamed!

THE PROMISED LAND

We left the Galang Vietnamese Refugee Camp—where we had stayed for more than a year—on September 17, 1980. Strangely, I felt I was moving far away from my hometown rather than leaving a temporary shelter for fleeing refugees.

The Indonesian people, particularly those working on the island, were great. We made many good friends at the camp.

Ms. Janz, for example, was the Indonesian representative for UNHCR. She was a very nice young lady with a soft voice. Through her beautiful, shining eyes, I could see her kindness and genuine love for those suffering. She cared about all of us and tried to help in any way she could.

The hard work of the staff of the Red Cross and UNHCR was amazing and truly admirable. Most of them were volunteers, and all those I had met had big hearts and could feel our pain as if it was their own. Growing up during the brutal war in Vietnam, then experiencing the genuine graciousness of the Indonesian people allowed me a clearer view of the depth, diversity, and complexities of human behavior. Despite this knowledge, I could never fully comprehend the autonomous rise of the dark side in the human mind.

My wife and I felt bad for many of our friends who remained behind, but we knew they, too, would leave someday. Some were to resettle in Australia, Sweden, or other countries. I wasn't sure if we could see each other again in the future, which was difficult. My son had also lost many friends of his age. He was almost five years old and doing better than when they were on the high seas and when their boat first arrived on the island.

My wife felt a great sense of relief and had a restored optimism about the future. Unfortunately, the nightmares of her awful experience, particularly on the Indonesian islands while she was with the rich sister-in-law, remained. She had frequent flashbacks to those times. Fortunately, those close encounters with human nature and our brief separation had the opposite effect. They permanently cemented our two suffering souls into one. During the last hour before I pushed my small family onto Mr. Thái Đức's boat against my wife's will, the pieces of our broken hearts had already intertwined and became one, naturally indivisible. We both realized we had to walk forward along our paths—separate but united—in solidarity to fend off the dark forces. And we completely entrusted each other to go through the passage Heaven and Buddha arranged.

~

THE DAY BEFORE we left the refugee camp, Ms. Tijsseling, the UNHCR Resettlement Officer from Jakarta, came and gave me an excellent referral letter and praised me for all that I had done to help UNHCR and the refugees. The Indonesia Red Cross and Office of the Administrative and Security Command on the island gave me a beautiful Certificate of Merit for "meritorious services in connection with the maintenance of the Pulau Galang Vietnamese Refugee Camp." Ms. Udo Janz, UNHCR representative; Dr. Iwan Jusuf,

Head of the Indonesian Red Cross Hospital; and Colonel Cashmir Rachman, Camp Commander, signed the certificate.

With wet eyes, we said farewell to our beloved friends and the island we called home for over a year.

While we sat on the big boat with the other refugees fortunate enough to be heading to Singapore with us, we tried to capture and imprint an image of the place in our hearts and minds for the last time. Our hearts clenched tightly when the boat finally departed as a rush of somber feelings came simultaneously. Indonesia would remain in our tattered but warm hearts eternally.

Our American friends didn't go to the Galang Vietnamese Refugee Camp that day because there was no interview scheduled for that week. So, my wife and I didn't say goodbye and express our sincere appreciation and acknowledgment that they had gone above and beyond with what they had done for our small family. In our hearts, however, we would remember eternally and keep those remembrances with our other most beautiful memories.

At least there was one thing I could do to show them my appreciation. When they were at the camp last, they had asked me to do one favor for them. It involved caring for a minor Vietnamese boy who would be in transit with us. He had no relatives in the refugee camp and was traveling alone to Singapore for the flight to the U.S. He would be on the same plane with us to San Francisco, California. From there, he would take a connecting flight to Texas while my family would fly to Pennsylvania. I agreed and asked the boy to stay close to us as long as possible.

U.S. Joint Voluntary Agency in Singapore

WE TRAVELED TO Singapore on a boat with many other happy refugees who were on their way to resettle in other countries. Some were off to Europe, including France, Germany, and Sweden. Others headed to Canada and the United States.

The smooth boat ride took us to one of the Singapore harbors, where the authority would pick us up by bus to go to the refugee transit camp. Sometimes, the boat people had to stay there for a week before departing. They kept them in a confined and guarded area of the camp.

We had never been to Singapore before. As our boat slowly approached the harbor, our eyes opened wide, trying to get our first views of the city from a distance. People were excitedly talking and laughing wildly. Finally, they moored the boat to the dock and asked us to get off. We followed the flow of people moving away from the harbor, walking towards the parking lot where several buses were waiting for us.

Suddenly, someone shouted my name.

"Z... Z!"

It was a pronunciation of my Vietnamese first name. Only people who knew me would know how to pronounce it correctly. Well, not quite; he still couldn't pronounce the accent "~" sitting on top of the "y" letter. I turned away from the beautiful harbor scene on the right to search for the man whose voice originated from my left side. Suddenly, my jaw dropped!

In the distance, I saw Mr. Art and Mr. Knowles of the U.S. JVA delegation. They were waving at us. I abruptly dragged my wife and son with me as I hastily walked toward them.

"Hi, there!" I greeted each with a big smile and a firm handshake. My wife and I thought we would never see them again. They gave us big hugs and smiles.

"Welcome to Singapore!" they both declared, almost at the same time.

After we had exchanged a few brief pleasantries, Mr. Knowles passed me an unsealed envelope and asked me to look inside. I quickly opened it and pulled out a piece of paper. In my hands, I held an official letter from the Embassy of the United States of America dated September 12, 1980, five days before I left the Galang Vietnamese Refugee Camp. I read the letter, my eyes gradually becoming heavy and tense. The United States Embassy in Singapore had given me a great deal of credit for aiding the U.S. JVA delegation in processing many Vietnamese refugees for resettlement in America. In that invaluable letter, they praised my "faithful service" to the U.S. Refugee Program and the Vietnamese boat people. It was a breathtaking acknowledgment given by the United States.

I felt good knowing that my volunteer work and time had helped my countrymen, women, and children who were just like us—willing to die to seek freedom.

Regretfully, I couldn't give the U.S. Embassy letter and their awarded credit to the Galang Resettlement Processing team, who had worked very hard to help the Vietnamese refugees in their efforts to resettle elsewhere.

Ms. Helen was somewhere on another official duty and unable to see us that day, but I knew her beautiful heart also blended into the wording of the letter I received. Mr. Art and Mr. Knowles continued to surprise me with their kind hearts and thoughtful minds. They followed us to the Singapore refugee transit camp.

Upon arrival, they went to the office and met with the camp officials. I wasn't there; hence, I didn't know what they had discussed. Shortly after our American friends left, an official came and asked us to meet with him and others. I didn't know what they wanted, but I agreed, and my family went to see them in their office. They looked at all of us as if they wanted to learn more about who we were. Then, they told us that our family and the minor boy would stay in a private room in a barracks-style building in the camp.

It baffled me, but I couldn't get any words out to question them. Subsequently, we followed them to the building not too far from the public shelters where other Vietnamese refugees were staying temporarily. They had been specifically told to stay in the public space arranged for them. A young lady approached me angrily, asking why I received different, seemingly preferential, treatment. She demanded an answer.

I told her I didn't know and had just followed the order. I then invited her to bring her family over to stay with us—no need for quarrels! But she didn't come.

At the refugee transit camp, they also provided us with food rations while we awaited our departure. However, when we checked into our apartment, we had not received our food yet. Around 4 p.m., Mr. Art and Mr. Knowles stopped by the camp again and asked us to go with them for a car ride. They drove us through the chaotic Singapore traffic, finally arriving at a tall building downtown. After they had parked the car, we got out and walked toward the entrance of the International Plaza Building on Anson Road. Together, we took the elevator to the 25th floor and eventually entered Suite 2514. It was an enormous suite used as an office where the U.S. JVA delegation was working on the U.S. Refugee Program.

From there, we walked into another sizeable room. Tall shelves full of files in hanging folders stood against the walls. There were so many files that I could not even count.

"These are the files of the Vietnamese refugees you and your team have processed for us," Mr. Knowles said in an appreciative voice. He continued while looking directly at me, "Thank you for the work you have done for us!" He gently tapped on my shoulder as an additional gesture of thanks.

The volume of the Vietnamese refugee files and how they could track and follow each case amazed my wife and me. We were speechless the entire time.

After the tour of the U.S. Refugee Program Office, they took all of us to a local restaurant to eat. It was the first delicious and nutritious meal we had eaten since the fall of Sài Gòn in 1975. Then, after dinner, they drove us to a shopping mall to walk around and do some window shopping. Seeing the luxurious items neatly displayed throughout the mall, my wife's eyes opened wide in shock. She had never seen a big modern mall like this before. Then, my eyes locked on my son, who was flatly pressing his nose to the glass window of a children's store displaying beautiful, colorful toys. I knew he wanted them, but we didn't have any money.

That night, Mr. Art and Mr. Knowles dropped us off at the Singapore refugee transit camp. We finally said goodbye and hugged each other warmly. I felt somber, knowing we might not see each other again. They were good human beings who had big hearts filled with kindness. I also missed Ms. Helene, Mr. Jarrett, and the other U.S. officials I had worked with at the Galang Vietnamese Refugee Camp. I knew then that I would never forget their friendship and graciousness.

Less than two days later, my family and the accompanying boy departed Singapore for the U.S. Since then, I haven't seen or been able to contact my JVA friends again. I tried to contact Mr. Knowles a few years later, but the post office returned my letter.

An Unforgettable Reverend

AFTER A LONG flight from Singapore, on September 21, 1980, our flight landed in San Francisco, California. It was the first time I had returned to the U.S. and put my feet on the promised land since flight school. My beloved wife and son were finally safe and under my protection. No one could ever take our freedom away again.

Shortly after landing, they transported us to Hamilton Air Force Base Refugee Transit Center for processing and to wait for our connecting flights. They assigned every family to a private room in military-style barracks and gave us food rations during our stay.

On September 23, they drove us back to the San Francisco International Airport. We said farewell to the boy who had traveled with us as he was to board a connecting flight to Texas to reunite with his relatives while we were heading to Pennsylvania, where my father lived. Subsequently, my family boarded United Airlines Flight 126 to Harrisburg, Pennsylvania. From there, we would continue to York, where we would rebuild our lives.

We all felt exhausted but excited at the anticipation of the new days ahead. For the last several days, we had tried to eat as much as possible to recover our strength to sustain us over the long flights. My son loved the American food and ate everything we had at our mealtimes. We were excited to see Father, whom we hadn't seen for over a year and missed dearly. Upon arrival, we hoped to see him and our American sponsor at the Harrisburg airport terminal. In less than a few hours, my son would see his grandfather again. We didn't have any pictures of Mr. Wendell H. Sweitzer, our sponsor, and we wondered what he might look like. Regardless of his appearance, we believed he would be very kind. He was a reverend.

It was also a long flight from San Francisco to Harrisburg but not nearly as bad as the flight from Singapore to the U.S. From above, Harrisburg looked beautiful at night with various colors and lights blinking and sparkling like diamonds.

After landing, we followed the other passengers as they walked toward the exit. A few other refugees were on our flight, and I noticed that some of them had already met up with their sponsors and relatives in the baggage area. While we were still looking for Father and our sponsor, a tall gentleman in a short-sleeve gray shirt and a pair of long, dark pants approached us.

"Are you Mr. Die Lee?" he asked.

Although my name has only four letters, "Dỹ Lê," few people can pronounce it correctly at the first meeting.

"Yes," I responded. Immediately, I thought he must be our sponsor. And he was.

"Wendell Sweitzer, your sponsor," he introduced himself and greeted us. "Nice meeting you!" Mr. Sweitzer said as he shook our hands, including my son's little fingers.

He was very kind to us, communicating with simple conversation and big smiles. It was only our first meeting, and we already liked him a lot. He told us that, unfortunately, our father would not be there to welcome us. Father was working the second shift and could not take off to come to the airport. That evening, Mr. Sweitzer drove us to my father's apartment on Poplar Street in York.

The weather was dry, and the temperature was not that cold, but it was enough to make my wife and son shiver. Mr. Sweitzer had come prepared and brought a few thick jackets for us. While he drove his car along Interstate Highway 83, my wife was silent in the back seat, gazing outside through the car window. Our son eventually fell asleep on his mother's lap. In the front passenger seat, I spoke with our sponsor about the long trip over from Singapore.

Our trying and dangerous journey had finally ended!

We had survived the many challenges that threatened our authentic beliefs and endured endless suffering and mistreatment from all walks of life.

The treacherous path—from our lost motherland, over the high seas, and 14 months sheltering on various Indonesian islands—had allowed us to feel the preciousness of true love but also left behind the poignant feeling which lingered endlessly in our souls.

We could close the horrendous chapter of our story, that perilous journey, and begin the next phase as we lived as refugees and exiles in our adopted motherland. However, no matter how frequently I played cat and mouse with Death, in my inner soul, I would continue to awaken bewilderingly to the dark dreams of the past. The crying voice of that frightened 10-year-old boy still occasionally groaned from the darkness of the night. Some things aren't so easily forgotten.

THE  FAREWELL

With the interpretation and translation team and friends. They were exceptionally good and kind. I would dearly love to see them again.

Pictures taken by Anh Khâm.
(1979-1980, Galang Vietnamese Refugee Camp, Indonesia)

Galang Refugee Camp Office. (*Gaylord Barr*)

With friends at the Recreation Center. I was standing next to Anh Khâm who wore a hat.

Before we left for the U.S., Anh Khâm took our picture.

With our friends from Barracks 9.

Anh Khâm, our dearest friend.

Besides being a medical doctor, Anh Trung Chinh was a famous singer during the Vietnam War... shortly before Anh Trung Chinh left for the U.S., he wrote a song and recorded it in my dark brown notebook, which I used to scribe my thoughts so that I could trace back the details of the events that occurred during our deadly journey.

**My notebook.
(1979-1980, Galang Vietnamese Refugee Camp, Indonesia)**

EMBASSY OF THE
UNITED STATES OF AMERICA

Refugee Program
Singapore

September 12, 1980

TO WHOM IT MAY CONCERN

In the way of reference and recommendation this is to certify that Mr. Le Dinh Di served as the head of the U.S. Delegation's interpreter team while he was awaiting resettlement in Galang Refugee Camp, Pulau Galang, Indonesia.

For the several months that Mr. Di headed the team we were able to process a large number of Indochinese refugees for re-settlement in the United States. Credit must be given to Mr. Di as his organizing, interpreting and helpfulness in general were a great aid to us. His dedication and diligence was evident by the long hours he readily devoted to the job. He has said that his position afforded him the opportunity to help his people and he certainly has done so.

Thus I heartily recommend Mr. Di on the basis of his organizational skills, leadership qualities and faithful service to the U.S. Refugee Program.

Sincerely yours,

George T. Cosgrove
Coordinator

U.S. Refugee Program   3016 International Plaza   Singapore 0207

Regretfully, I couldn't give the U.S. Embassy letter and their awarded credit to the Galang Resettlement Processing team, who had worked very hard to help the Vietnamese refugees in their efforts to resettle elsewhere.

Reflection of our team's hard work.
(1979-1980, Galang Vietnamese Refugee Camp, Indonesia)

UNITED NATIONS
HIGH COMMISSIONER
FOR REFUGEES
Office for Indonesia

NATIONS UNIES
HAUT COMMISSARIAT
POUR LES RÉFUGIÉS
Délégation pour l'Indonésie

Telephones: 321183, 321247, 321439, 322079
Telegrams: HICROMREF Jakarta
Telex: 44042 IA

Wisma Kosgoro Building 11th floor
53 Jalan M.H Thamrin
P.O. Box 4806
Jakarta, Indonesia

Galang, 16 September, 1980

TO WHOM IT MAY CONCERN

This is to certify that Mr. LE DINH DY, born on at VINH YEN, Vietnam, during his stay at Galang Refugee Camp, Indonesia, worked for the American delegation from November 1979, to May 1980 as an interpreter, and from May to September 1980 as the team handler for the Joint Voluntary Agencies.

In this capacity, Mr. DY has worked hard and consistently, thereby greatly helping his fellow refugees and the UNHCR resettlement program for Indonesia.

I recommend him without hesitation for any undertaking that he may wish to pursue in his resettlement country

MARION TIJSSELING
ER RESETTLEMENT OFFICER

Recognition letters from UNHCR, Camp Security Office, and Indonesian Red Cross. (09/1980, Galang Vietnamese Refugee Camp, Indonesia)

REBUILDING OUR FAMILY

Our apartment (behind kids) on West Poplar St., York, Pennsylvania (PA).

Our new lives in the promised land. (1980, York, PA)

With Ms. Revela Bozman, our beloved landlord, at our neighbor's house. We love her dearly.

Our apartment backyard.

Winter at the Pennsylvania State University (PSU). (1983, State College, PA)

Visiting friends in New Jersey.

Mai in the kitchen of our apartment (a week before our baby's arrival). During that time, she worked for Danskin (women's and children's clothing manufacturer) while I was in college. In the summer, I worked as a gas attendant at a local Exxon gas station in York.

People from the Shrewsbury Church of the Brethren gave us what we needed for our newly born child.

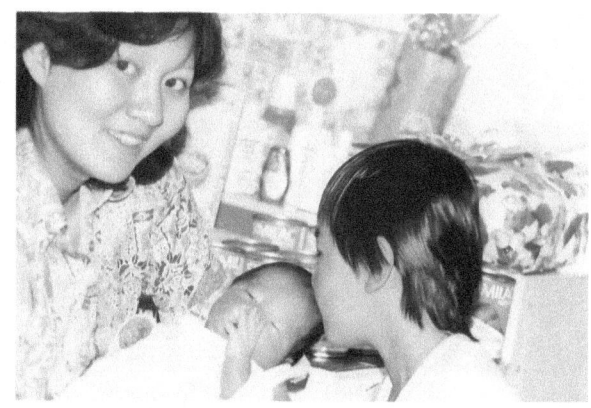

Pictures taken at York Hospital and at home in our apartment in York, PA.

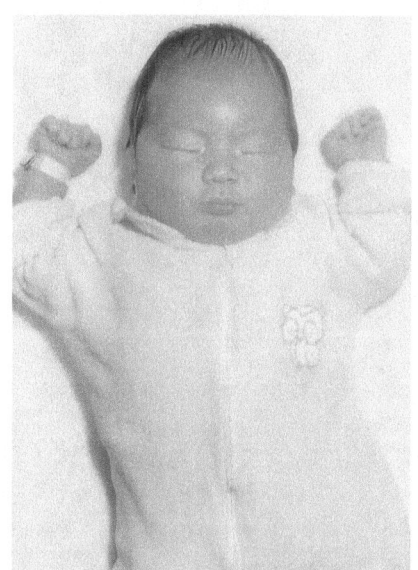

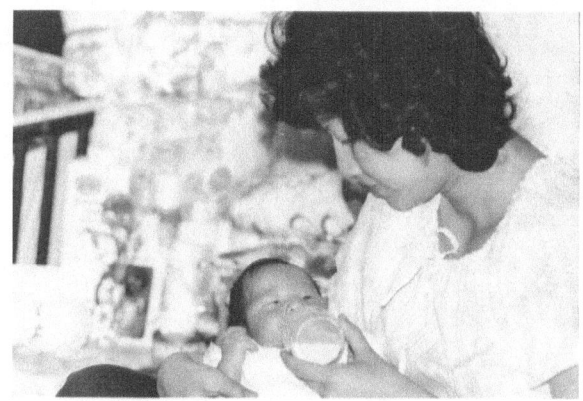

Still financially broke, but angels filled our lives with loves from many American friends. (1982, York, PA)

Mr. and Mrs. Wendell, Conchita H. Sweitzer, and people from the Shrewsbury Church of the Brethren wholeheartedly helped us get back on our feet.

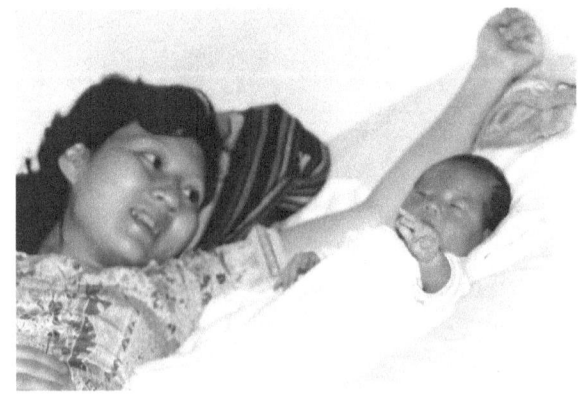

Mr. Sweitzer, Huy, and Mai with Hoàng. (1982, York, PA)

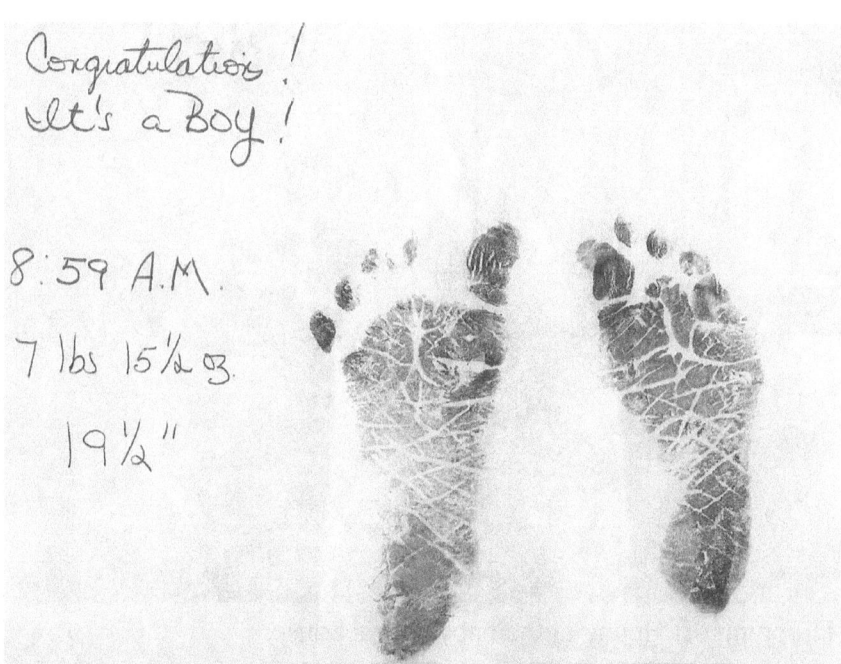

Hoàng's footprints. He is the first U.S. citizen in our family.

Few days after birth.

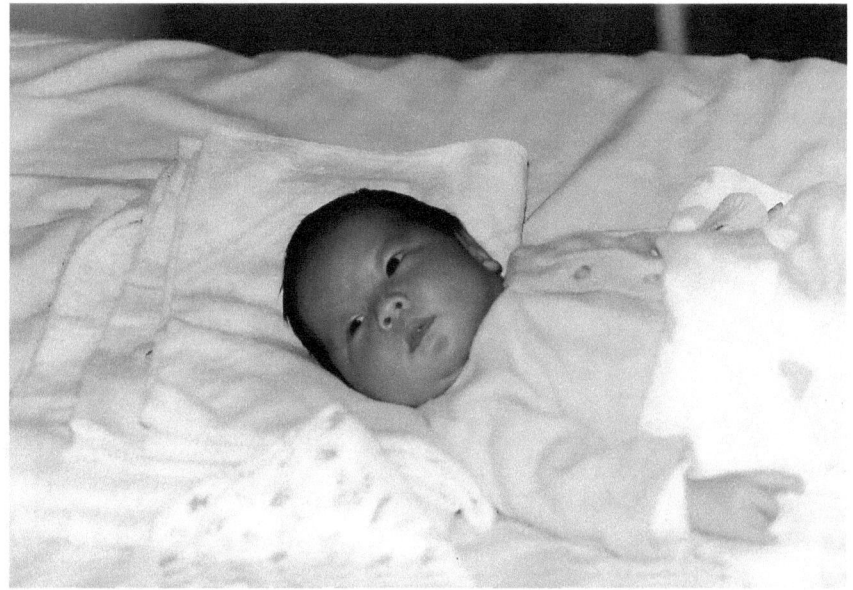

Dropping off Hoàng at the babysitter's house.

Inside the babysitter's house.

Ms. Revela Bozman was single and had no relatives. She treated us as her loved ones. We still miss her dearly. (Hoàng's first birthday, 1983)

Huy was decorating a cake for Hoàng's 4th birthday.

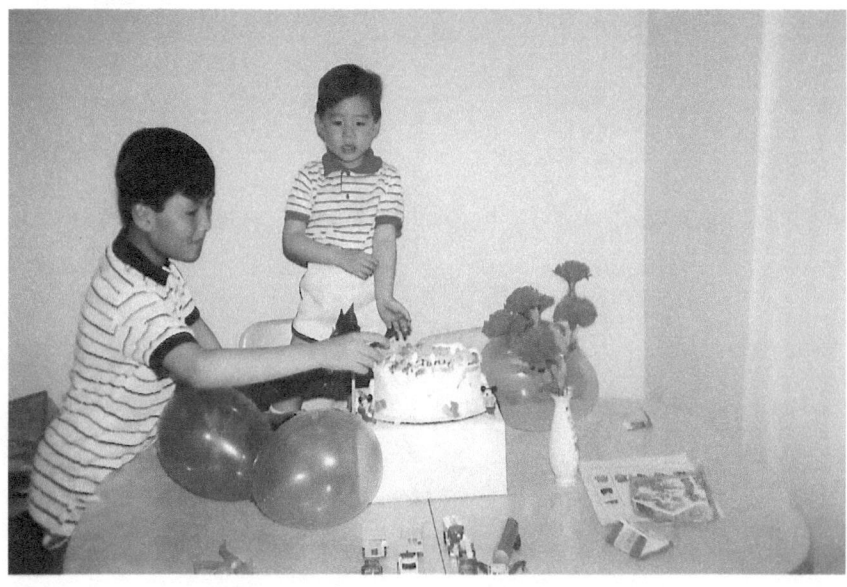

Hoàng's 4th birthday.

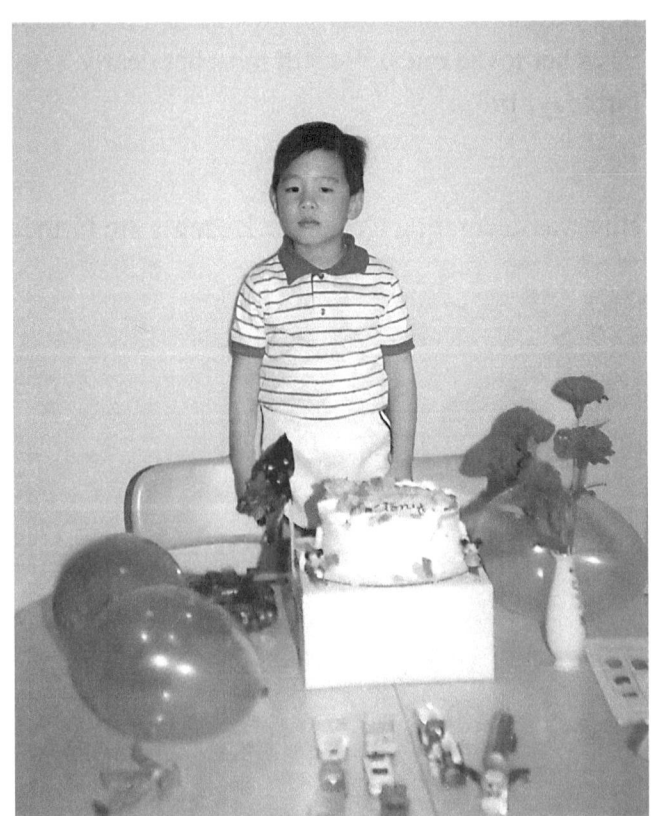

Traveling to Niagara Falls with my father and youngest sister.

Huy and Hoàng before going to the wedding.

Huy and Hoàng. (2018, PA)

THE DREAM
WORLD

Mother and son (Huy).

Hoàng was riding a horse in South America during his vacation.

Hoàng was standing on the upper floor of the aircraft carrier USS Abraham Lincoln (CVN-72), as it lay just off the San Diego coast of California (CA). He took a picture of President George W. Bush after he landed and declared "Mission Accomplish!" While in the senior year of high school, Hoàng got an internship from the U.S. Navy.

(05/01/2003, USS Abraham Lincoln, San Diego, CA)

**Huy's graduation from Temple University.
(05/2000, Philadelphia, PA)**

Hoàng's graduation from Drexel University.
(09/2006, Philadelphia, PA)

San Jose.

Carmel-by-the-Sea, Monterey.

**Vacation.
(Summer 2007, CA)**

With Mai. (05/2014, Ottawa, Canada)

Thanh is my charming cousin who introduced Mai into my life when I returned to Vietnam from the U.S. in 1974, bridging our hearts and minds together. Thanks to fate and my wonderful cousin, we married within five months. Thanh is an angel who has helped build our family into what we have today.

With Thanh. (05/2014, Montreal, Canada)

**Mai and Thanh.
(05/2014, Ottawa and Montreal, Canada)**

At our sponsor's home. During the visit, we normally went out for lunch, visited Wendell's resting place, and then came back to her house to chitchat before heading home. Mr. Wendell H. Sweitzer passed away in 2012.

Visiting our beloved sponsor. (2018, Glen Rock, PA)

With Lola and Teddy Bear. (Christmas 2012, Bel Air, Maryland (MD))

On our son's wedding day.
(08/2016, Phoenixville, PA)

PUBLISHER'S WORDS

After resettling in Pennsylvania, the author spent over a decade working closely with the U.S. Immigration and Naturalization Service to get his remaining 19 relatives out of Vietnam. His last family member from Vietnam arrived in America in 2010.

Unfortunately, his next younger brother—the one whom the author had fiercely tried most of his life to protect from the omen that haunted the 10-year-old boy's dark dreams—passed away suddenly in Norfolk, Virginia.

In the author's new book, *Lived Once–Inside the Mind of a Crying Boy*, to be published in the future, he wrote: *The beloved brother—whom I had consistently sought to protect for more than half of my life, beyond anyone's understanding, in order to change his dark fate, but failed—was the ill-fated one in the dreams of a 10-year-old boy... After he passed, my remaining life became completely hollow, and my feeling of purpose in life ceased to exist... I will always remember the failure, which was to allow him to depart from my protective arms forever.*

In the spring of 1980, after arriving in America, the author went to a U.S. Army recruiter and expressed his willingness to join the military as a pilot, but they rejected him.

Eventually, the author went to college, graduated, and then became an aerospace engineer and scientist—serving the U.S. government, including the Federal Aviation Administration, Navy, Army, and Texas Tech University for the past 37 years.

With Father on my graduation day.

With Ms. Revela Bozman. In the evening, she used to teach and play with Huy late into the night while my wife was taking care of our second son upstairs.

**The turning point.
(05/1985, Penn State, State College, PA)**

**With my family at the Nittany Lion statue.
(05/1985, Penn State, State College, PA)**

With Ms. Revela Bozman.
(05/1985, Penn State, State College, PA)

Earned my bachelor's degree in Mechanical Engineering from the Pennsylvania State University. (05/1985, State College, PA)

Earned my master's degree in Engineering Science from the Pennsylvania State University. (12/1992, State College, PA)

We are indebted to Mr. and Mrs. Wendell, Conchita H. Sweitzer, and many other good people from the Shrewsbury Church of the Brethren for providing tremendous support during the early years of our lives in York, Pennsylvania.

With Mr. and Mrs. Wendell and Conchita H. Sweitzer at our home. Unfortunately, he passed away in 2012.

Precious time together.
(2010, Bel Air, MD)

In 2016, when the author retired as Division Chief of the U.S. Army Research Laboratory, President Barack Obama sent him an official letter praising and thanking him for many years of service to the Nation and for his contributions to help defend the American people.

Congress also gave the author an American flag. On July 26, 2016, they flew the flag, with his name, over the Capitol building to recognize the contribution of the Vietnamese-American scientist.

Receiving a recognition letter from President Barack Obama. (2016, Aberdeen Proving Ground (APG))

THE WHITE HOUSE
WASHINGTON

December 16, 2016

Mr. Dy Dinh Le
Bel Air, Maryland

Dear Dy Dinh:

    I am pleased to join your family, friends, and colleagues in congratulating you on your many years of service to our Nation.

    Your hard work and dedication at the Department of the Army over the years have helped defend the American people and protect our way of life. Public service is an honorable calling, and it is my privilege to join in celebrating your career.

    Thank you for your service. I wish you happiness and good health in the years ahead.

Sincerely,

President Barack Obama's recognition letter and Author's picture displayed on base. (2016, APG)

Receiving the American flag from Congress.
(2016, APG-Bel Air, MD)

... the accompanying flag was flown over the United States Capitol on July 26, 2016... in recognition of Dy Le.
(Stephen T. Ayers, Architect of the Capitol)

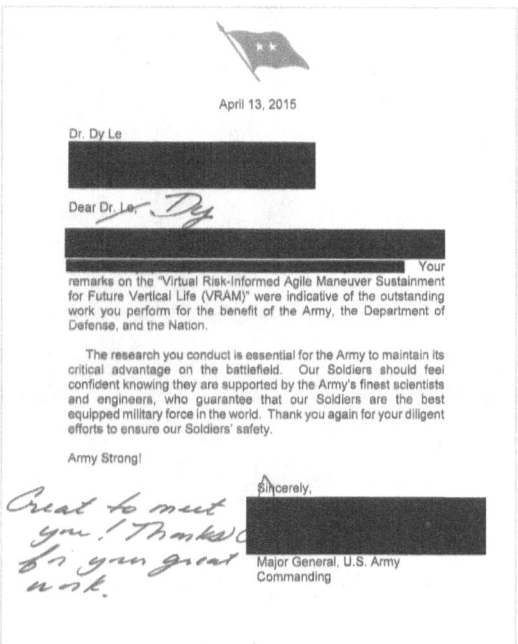

U.S. Army Commanding Officer's letters of appreciation. (2016, APG)

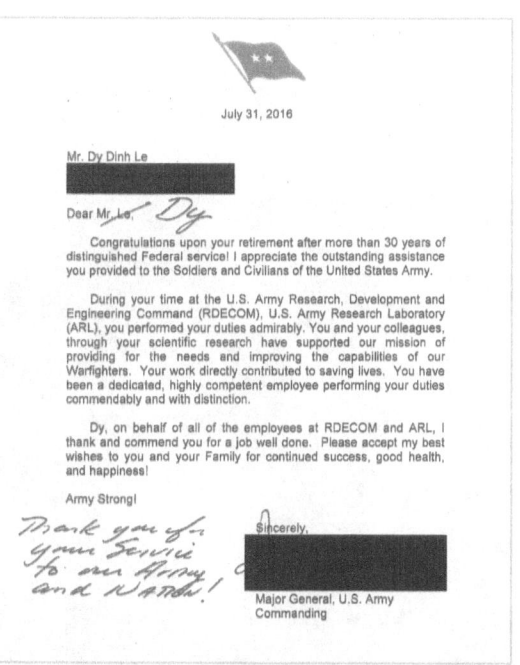

**Presenting the VRAMS technology concept at AUSA
and ABC 2 - In FOCUS interview.
(2014, AL - 2016, APG)**

YouTube: https://www.youtube.com/watch?v=DHuw35ZkWNE

Meeting with Drexel University's 10th president on signing the research collaboration agreement. (2016, U.S. Army Research Laboratory, APG)

Delivering keynote speeches.
(2018, Hangzhou, Qingdao, and Xiamen University, China)

"Handpicked" by ARL Director to prepare for a larger leadership role within the Army, taking a six-month assignment as Assistant Technical Director to the U.S. Army Test and Evaluation Command (ATEC), an Army command having 10,000 employees and $2B annual budget.

I wasn't born here. But this is where my loved ones and I live...

Graduation from the leadership skills training within the ATEC Command Group (Commanding General, Maj. Gen. Genaro J. Dellarocco). (09/2012, ATEC, APG)

... where our future generations will be born...

... I will certainly protect our country at any price.
Dy Dinh Le, Division Chief, U.S. Army Research Laboratory

Farewell speech at the U.S Army Research Laboratory (ARL)
and Certificate of Appreciation from
the Department of the Army.
(2016, ARL, APG)

DEPARTMENT OF THE ARMY

CERTIFICATE OF APPRECIATION

TO

Dy Dinh Le

ON THE OCCASION OF YOUR RETIREMENT, I WISH TO EXTEND TO YOU MY PERSONAL THANKS AND THE APPRECIATION OF THE UNITED STATES ARMY FOR THE MANY YEARS OF SERVICE WHICH YOU HAVE GIVEN TO OUR COUNTRY. I SHARE YOUR PRIDE IN THE CONTRIBUTIONS YOU HAVE MADE TO THE ARMY AND I TRUST THAT YOU WILL MAINTAIN AN ACTIVE INTEREST IN THE ARMY AND ITS OBJECTIVES DURING YOUR RETIREMENT. YOU TAKE WITH YOU MY BEST WISHES AND THOSE OF YOUR FELLOW EMPLOYEES FOR HAPPINESS AND SUCCESS IN THE YEARS THAT LIE AHEAD.

MY LIFE'S ANGELS

Many angels, unbelievably, came into my life in many shapes and forms, both spiritual and living. Throughout my journey, they have acted as extraordinary elements, inspiring a persistent faith in my heart, giving rise to an uncompromising will to seek happiness for my loved ones, and cementing my commitment to achieving Mother's dream in my soul.

Around every corner of the unpaved path full of vicious interferences, angels extended their hands to lift me up when I was down, guiding me back to the predetermined path that I sometimes deviated from because of human complexities. Those angels defied the laws of nature and humanity, and in doing so, they offered many unexpected chances to get back on my feet to complete the most dangerous journey of my lifetime.

Father had told me to cloak my past military background to avoid retribution after the war. And I did. Without his advice, my fate could have been different!

Mother didn't pass third grade but had a heart like Mother Teresa's, pouring out unequivocally never-ending love for all of us. She vigorously dreamed, not for herself, but for the 11 children under her wing, that they would depart from the dark world where she was living to seek freedom. She did so, even knowing she might never see them again. Mother always had a forward-thinking mindset, which inspired my determination to walk forward through fear, allowing her dream to materialize in its full splendor.

My aunts—Cô Môn and Cô Mi—took care of me as their own son during the early years of my tattered youth. They comforted me when, at around ten years old, I experienced many nights full of dark dreams that warned me of the end of life for someone in my family. They wiped my tears and calmed my fears as best they could during these difficult moments.

My elder brother saved me from my suicide attempt on April 29, 1975. He was an angel whom Heaven and Buddha sent with an intended purpose! Without him, the future of our loved ones could have been different and nothing like those we have today.

Brother Giới gave his life in Pleiku to defend South Vietnam. I believe he had spiritually followed along with my every step during my life's journey to help me fulfill his last words and my unspoken promise to "… take care of the young siblings…" for him.

My older sister took me to the Chợ Rẫy's emergency room while the funeral of my older brother was taking place. She injected B12 to give me strength when I became exhausted from the toll of the back-and-forth trips between Bạc Liêu and Sài Gòn as I looked for a way out of the dark world for the family.

Brother Dũng had a beautiful heart shrouded by a chemically imbalanced mind. He mended my tattered heart and provided me with living evidence and justification for the righteousness of my actions and steadfast determination to materialize Mother's wish. With only a few dollars to his own name, he frequently sent money to keep my small family alive while we were at the refugee camp. His letters gave us hope, and we knew there was a deep and true love from a solid heart with a mind thought insane. For the rest of my life, I will always remember my failure to protect him in the end, allowing him to separate from my protective arms forever.

My wife fiercely protected our 3-year-old son on her own during her dangerous journey. She has been with me during so many tough times—and for so many decades—without ever losing faith. She is a good person and a special angel. Despite considerable hardships and extremely unpleasant environments, she always amazes me with her resilience. It is difficult for anyone to endure constant bullying from all walks of life and fight back against humanity's inherent dark side, but she continues to do so. By intentionally turning a blind eye to her adverse surroundings, she has discovered the most powerful weapon for defying the destructive effects of evilness.

Thanh is my charming cousin who introduced Mai into my life when I returned to Vietnam from the U.S. in 1974, bridging our hearts and minds together. Thanks to fate and my wonderful cousin, we married within five months. Thanh is an angel who has helped build our family into what we have today.

Cường was my flight-training classmate. Without his heartbreaking visit to my sickbed, I might not have strongly stood on my feet to seek the righteous path for my loved ones. He lifted me up from the bottom of my tattered soul and gently pushed me into the winding, unpaved path to fight against the dark forces. Although Cường is now in a different dimension, the afterlife, he will always remain in the hearts of my wife and me.

The physicians, nurses, base commander, other friends, and my cousin who worked at the 115th Military Hospital in Sài Gòn—their openness and civilized treatment gave me a reason to continue to believe in the inherent goodness of humanity, even in the deadly world in which we lived. Graciously, I thank them all for giving me a green pasture in the dark region of the barren, rocky land.

My friends from Bạc Liêu Province, particularly Anh Văn Ánh, Tuấn, and Anh Minh's family, treated me as one of their loved ones, contradicting the proverb, "a drop of loved ones' blood is thicker than a pond of strange water." I will also never forget Anh Minh's family, including his parents and wife, who had taken our son to a local physician to save him from complications from high fever during our last few days before fleeing Vietnam. I still remember the meals we shared, simple but full of kindness and love, when Anh Minh and Tuấn's family fed me while I was hiding in Bạc Liêu, seeking a way for my family to leave the country. And Anh Văn Ánh was a hero for sheltering my father and younger brother, who was facing a potential court-martial if he got caught by the Vietnamese communists. Without the shelter and love of these friends and their families, it would be unlikely that we would have experienced daylight in the promised land.

The Indonesian government, UNHCR, Red Cross, and other international delegations were pivotal in helping my family resettle in another country and soothing the pain of heartbroken refugees. I offer special thanks and great appreciation to my U.S. JVA friends. I don't know where we would be now without their big hearts and determination to resettle my family as quickly as possible in the U.S. after they learned about our situation at the refugee camp. They will forever be amongst the angels who restored our dream and put us back on the predetermined path toward freedom, ending the endless waiting in vain for Canada to grant us asylum.

The local Indonesians allowed us to seek refuge on their islands and have always been in our hearts. We will never forget their genuine generosity, hospitality, and true love.

My American friends enabled us to rebuild our lives successfully. The boat people, like us, would never have succeeded without the pure love, friendship, and guidance of so many people in the promised land, the United States of America. We are indebted to Mr. and Mrs. Wendell, Conchita H. Sweitzer, and many other good people from the Shrewsbury Church of the Brethren for providing tremendous support during the early years of our lives in York, Pennsylvania. We will also never forget Ms. Revela Bozman, our beloved landlord, who used to teach Huy and play with him in the evenings while my wife was busy caring for our youngest son. These are the veritable angels from our adopted motherland, which we now call home.

Invisible angels are not to be forgotten. They brightened my path, guided me through many painful and treacherous corners of life, and protected my loved ones. One of those blessed moments was the night I departed, which I described in a forthcoming book entitled *Lived Once–Inside the Mind of a Crying Boy*.

When ordered, I thought my elder brother's in-laws and Dũng would follow me. I didn't know what had happened. But, mysteriously, something appeared to pull him back into the world we were fleeing—preventing him from getting on board. In my superstitious mind, I thought his life was hanging by a slender thread. Standing near the edge of the departing boat, my heart pounded as my soul released the trembling screams that pierced through the night. I was about to jump into the water to look for my beloved younger brother, believing the omen was returning in full force. At that moment, Dũng was missing, having disappeared into the darkness of the riverbank, where so many lives had fled to the promised land or fallen into the bloody hands of Death. Years later, when asked what happened, Dũng only said that a thick fog suddenly came, blocking his way to the boat. He couldn't hear me calling or see me, even though I was not too far ahead, giving signs for him and the others to follow. The area surrounding him seemed frozen, as though a strange force had instantly stopped everything, including the passing of time. Then, during that hollow time, which felt like forever, he suddenly heard voices, as if from Heaven, that guided him back to the boat.

The ghostlike man was also an angel sent to live on Earth as a simple human being. He arrived suddenly during the night when my inner soul had completely broken. Miraculously, he opened a path and gave me a last chance to lead my last younger brother and elder brother's in-laws, who remained in Bạc Liêu, to the promised land. That night, I felt an invisible force from an angel who had defeated

Death's shadow as it had tried to pull Brother Dũng into the darkness of the riverbank.

~

ALL OF MY spiritual guardians and angelic members of the humans illustrated the congenital goodness of people so that I might learn to become a good person.

During that painful, horrific journey of the past, I learned many lessons. I had successfully achieved what I was determined to do because I believed in Mother's dream completely and didn't dwell on my own interests. Instead of seeking personal contentment or concerning myself with who would get the reward at the end of the journey, I sought my loved ones' happiness as the highest priority.

According to Sir Harry S. Truman, "It is amazing what you can accomplish if you do not care who gets the credit."

THE AUTHOR: DY DINH LE

Dy Dinh Le wrote his first book, *Beyond the Fear of Death*, in the spring of 2017. A well-known writer in Vietnam also translated it into a Vietnamese script entitled *Vòn Bóng Tử Thần*.

During the Vietnam War, he was a pilot of the Republic of Vietnam trained in the United States. After the war, in 1979, he escaped by boat to look for 24 relatives, including his wife and 3-year-old son, whom he sent out to the high seas on another fishing boat two days earlier to seek freedom.

After coming ashore on an island, eventually, the local authority took him and the other boat people to the Galang Refugee Camp in Indonesia. In September 1979, at the pier of the Galang camp, he finally reunited with his loved ones while welcoming a new group of refugees arriving at the camp from other small islands in Indonesia.

During his over-a-year stay at the camp, he volunteered to work for various international organizations, including the Red Cross, United Nations High Commissioner for Refugees, and U.S. Joint Voluntary Agency.

In 1980, he and his family finally resettled in York, Pennsylvania, where he rebuilt his life of freedom.

He is a graduate of the Pennsylvania State University and has served—as an aerospace engineer and scientist—the U.S. government, including the U.S. Navy; FAA; Army; and public university, for 37 years. He has frequently delivered keynote speeches and given technical talks at conferences and universities in the U.S. and abroad. In his professional capacity, he has voluntarily served the Science and Mathematics Academy, mentoring high school students. He also funded and supported the FIRST Robotics Competition Activities and became the president of the Asia Pacific American Coalition of New Jersey from January 2004 to December 2007.

Currently, he lives in the U.S. and is the Director of the Institute for Materials, Manufacturing, and Sustainment at Texas Tech University.

He and his wife—separated only once for 81 days during their treacherous journey through the South China Sea to seek freedom—have been married for over 48 years.

They have two children and daughters-in-law, five grandkids, and Lola and Teddy Bear.

Author's wife and Teddy Bear. (2014, Bel Air, MD)

Author and Teddy Bear. (2014, Bel Air, MD)

THE EXECUTED SOLDIER'S SON: CHRISTOPHER LE

Christopher Le was born and raised in Sài Gòn, Vietnam. After the war, in 1979, at 14, he escaped the communist tribulation by boat and eventually arrived at the Galang Refugee Camp in Indonesia. In 1980, he resettled in Canada.

He is a graduate of Saskatoon University, Canada, with two degrees in sociology and psychology. In 1985, he migrated to the U.S., where he worked and graduated with a Bachelor of Arts in Music in 1992.

Christopher Le worked closely with the American and Vietnamese music communities in the U.S. and abroad. He is a member of the National Academy of Recording Arts & Sciences, with voting rights and opportunities to take part in the Grammy Awards. He has frequently supported, organized, and taken part in radio and TV programs, music topic discussions, and magazines abroad (i.e., *Thúy Nga Paris by Night*, *Vietnam Television*, *Hải Âu radio*, *Tay Phải*, *Sài Gòn Nhỏ*, *Văn*, *Diễm*, *Trẻ*, and *Văn Nghệ Magazine*).

Christopher Le has taken part in many charity events, including one to support hungry children in Africa, which was organized by the Southern California Charity Association and held at the Costa Mesa Convention Center. The activities included reporting on *Bringing Vietnamese Music to America* and an interview with the *Los Angeles Times*.

The first sheet of *Isn't That Really Sad? (Hỏi Thế Có Buồn Không?)* lyrics, which he composed in 1979 while at the Galang Refugee Camp, and was subsequently introduced by BBC in 1980, marked the second year of his father's execution in one of North Vietnam's concentration camps in the Hoàng Liên Sơn mountain area. Since then, he has produced a music album entitled *Raining on Clustering of Tangling Hair* (*Mưa Trên Vùng Tóc Rối*) and over 70 songs, which have been warmly received by Vietnamese communities in the U.S. and abroad.

REFERENCES

HELL ON EARTH
1. Communist Bloc, page 1: https://www.encyclopedia.com/history/encyclopedias-almanacs-transcripts-and-maps/communist-bloc
2. People's Army of Vietnam (PAVN), 2: https://www.globalsecurity.org/military/world/vietnam/army.htm
3. Republic of Vietnam (RVN), 2: http://republicofvietnam.org
4. Demilitarized Zone at the 17th parallel, 2: https://military.wikia.org/wiki/Vietnamese_Demilitarized_Zone
5. Việt Cộng, 2: https://www.thoughtco.com/the-viet-cong-the-vietnam-war-195432
6. National Liberation Front (NLF), 2: https://www.history.com/this-day-in-history/national-liberation-front-formed
7. Provisional Revolutionary Government (PRG), 2: https://en.wikipedia.org/wiki/Provisional_Revolutionary_Government_of_the_Republic_of_South_Vietnam
8. The bright-yellow flags with three horizontal red stripes spaced evenly at the center, 3: http://republicofvietnam.org
9. VC flags, 3: https://www.crwflags.com/fotw/flags/vn-vcong.html
10. a nontotalitarian country, which many North Vietnamese people, 3: Verbal conversations between Author and anonymous communist cadres

11. Paris Peace Accords, 3: https://www.nsa.gov/News-Features/Declassified-Documents/Vietnam-Paris-Peace-Talks/
12. "unabashedly delighted… art of negotiation," 4: https://time.com/4061794/nobel-peace-prize-winner-history/
13. destroyed 58,220 American lives, 4: https://www.archives.gov/research/military/vietnam-war/casualty-statistics
14. caused over three million deaths, 4: https://www.sparknotes.com/history/american/vietnamwar/section10/
15. to send hundreds of thousands of innocent men, women, children, and unborn human beings into the abyss of the South China Sea to die, 5: https://www.unhcr.org/3ebf9bad0.pdf
16. deadly effect would also result in the execution of over 100,000, 5: https://military.wikia.org/wiki/Vietnam_War_casualties
17. "Re-education" Camps, 5: http://self.gutenberg.org/articles/Re-education_camp#cite_note-dart-2 http://vietfacts.com/VF_RECamp/hidden-horrors-of-vietnams-re%5b1%5d.htm
18. "50 children of King Lạc Long Quân," 7: https://www.britannica.com/place/Vietnam/Sports-and-recreation#ref509928 https://scroll.in/article/830807/why-the-vietnamese-are-called-the-children-of-the-dragon-and-grandchildren-of-the-fairy
19. The "land reform" campaign, 7: http://www.geocities.ws/xoathantuong/dn_caicachrd.htm
20. Việt Minh, 7: https://alphahistory.com/vietnamwar/viet-minh/
21. During the famine in the north that killed millions of Vietnamese people, 7: https://japanesevietnam.weebly.com/vietnamese-famine-of-1945.html
22. Điện Biên Phủ, 8: https://www.britannica.com/event/Battle-of-Dien-Bien-Phu
23. Geneva Accords, 8: "Hiệp Định Geneva 1954": https://www.mtholyoke.edu/acad/intrel/pentagon/pent12.htm
24. Hồ Chí Minh, 8: https://www.britannica.com/biography/Ho-Chi-Minh
25. Emperor Bảo Đại, 8: https://www.britannica.com/biography/Bao-Dai
26. Marxist ideology, 8: https://www.britannica.com/topic/Marxism
27. Premier Ngô Đình Diệm, 8: https://en.wikipedia.org/wiki/Ngo_Dinh_Diem
28. hundreds of thousands of people in the north were openly executed, 9: https://www.rfa.org/english/news/vietnam_landreform-20060608.html
29. *We Want to Live*, 9: https://www.youtube.com/watch?v=E9aSONE_rnw
30. "Operation Passage to Freedom," 9: https://www.historynet.com/vietnam-book-review-operation-passage-freedom.htm
31. Hiền Lương Bridge, 9: https://anhxua.net/album/cau-hien-luong_170.html
32. Berlin Wall, 9: https://www.history.com/topics/cold-war/berlin-wall
33. President Nguyễn Văn Thiệu, 11: https://www.encyclopedia.com/people/history/southeast-asia-history-biographies/nguyen-van-thieu
34. Tết Offensive, 11: https://www.britannica.com/topic/Tet-Offensive

REFERENCES | 405

35. the Pearl of the Far East, 13: https://holylandvietnamstudies.com/blog/introduction-to-Sài Gòn-the-pearl-of-the-far-east/
36. A daughter of the Deputy Mayor of Huế recalled, 17: https://en.wikipedia.org/wiki/Massacre_at_Huế
    https://vva.vietnam.ttu.edu/repositories/2/digital_objects/143700
37. "who were Catholics, were our special enemy... the enemy of the Vietnam Communist Party," 17: https://en.wikipedia.org/wiki/Massacre_at_Huế
38. "U.S. and South Vietnam's puppet government" and those who were reactionary with "bad attitude" toward "revolution," 17: https://en.wikipedia.org/wiki/Massacre_at_Huế
39. when VC buried alive several thousand innocent civilian people, including many juveniles, 19:
    https://vva.vietnam.ttu.edu/repositories/2/digital_objects/143700
40. he stealthily blended in with the locals and killed an entire family, including a wife, six young children, and the 80-year-old mother, 19: https://sites.google.com/site/dlsnvn/viet-su/tuong-nguyen-ngoc-loan/tuong-nguyen-ngoc-loan-xu-ban-viet-cong-1968
    https://rarehistoricalphotos.com/Sài Gòn-execution-1968/
41. the Geneva Convention laws did not apply; he was a "francs-tireurs," an "illegal soldier," 20: https://sites.google.com/site/dlsnvn/viet-su/tuong-nguyen-ngoc-loan/tuong-nguyen-ngoc-loan-xu-ban-viet-cong-1968
    https://rarehistoricalphotos.com/Sài Gòn-execution-1968/
42. the U.S. news networks discouraged the will of the Vietnamese people with negative comments that South Vietnam and, particularly, the U.S. would not win the war, 20: https://www.theatlantic.com/politics/archive/2018/01/how-the-tet-offensive-undermined-american-faith-in-government/550010/
43. She straddled the VC's anti-aircraft gun—which had killed and was being used to kill American airmen—while praising and applauding North Vietnam's bloody policies, 20: https://patriotpost.us/pages/80
44. The Mỹ Lai massacre in March 1968—a devastatingly shocking episode and nightmare that killed over 500 innocent South Vietnamese people, 20: https://www.history.com/topics/vietnam-war/my-lai-massacre-1
45. after the Mỹ Lai massacre, the U.S. government brought those extremely crooked soldiers who gave the order or pulled the trigger to kill innocent Vietnamese people from that doomed village to court to face trials, 21: https://www.history.com/topics/vietnam-war/my-lai-massacre-1
46. Võ Nguyên Giáp, 21: http://totallyhistory.com/vo-nguyen-giap/
47. Giáp was ready and willing to sacrifice untold numbers of soldiers, 21: https://apps.dtic.mil/dtic/tr/fulltext/u2/a324505.pdf
48. discovered the dead body of a North Vietnam tank commander with his leg, near the ankle, chained with the "quarter-inch-thick chain links" to an internal solid structure of his tank, 22: https://danquoc.blogspot.com/2012/07/bo-oi-ho-bi-xich-chan-vo-sung-may-viet.html

49. Hồ wrote to the North Vietnamese people, 22: http://yenbai.gov.vn/hoc-tap-lam-theo-loi-bac/noidung/tintuc/Pages/chi-tiet-tin-tuc.aspx?ItemID=5&l=CuocdoihoatdongcuaC
50. in1968, Giáp lost over 40,000 North Vietnam soldiers, 23: https://www.theatlantic.com/politics/archive/2018/01/how-the-tet-offensive-undermined-american-faith-in-government/550010/
51. No matter whether Hồ died because of the heart attack, 24: https://www.theSài Gònpost.uk/2020/05/ho-chi-minh-co-sinh-co-tu-nhung-thuc-su.html
52. Flows of weapons and ammunitions, 24: https://alphahistory.com/vietnamwar/chinese-and-soviet-involvement/ https://dongsongcu.wordpress.com/2017/05/31/vien-tro-quan-su-cho-viet-nam-trong-chien-tranh/
53. Henry Kissinger, 25: https://www.history.com/topics/cold-war/henry-kissinger
54. Washington reached out and shook China's red hands, 25: https://adst.org/2013/02/nixon-goes-to-china/
55. to conduct secret meetings, 26: https://www.historyplace.com/unitedstates/vietnam/index-1969.html
56. The accords would also force Thiệu, the President of South Vietnam, to resign before the general election for a new leader to govern the south, 26: https://history.army.mil/html/books/090/90-26/index.html
57. Over 200,000 North Vietnamese regular units, 27: https://www.historyplace.com/unitedstates/vietnam/index-1969.html
58. Beijing contributed about 70-86 percent of the entire weaponry arsenals given to North Vietnam by the Communist Bloc, 27: https://en.wikipedia.org/wiki/China_in_the_Vietnam_War https://dongsongcu.wordpress.com/2017/05/31/vien-tro-quan-su-cho-viet-nam-trong-chien-tranh/
59. "paper tiger," 27: https://en.wikipedia.org/wiki/Paper_tiger
60. Nixon said, "… instead of teaching someone else to do a job, we like to do it ourselves. And this trait has been carried over into our foreign policy," 27: https://millercenter.org/the-presidency/educational-resources/vietnamization

THE LAST WORDS

61. *Nobody has the right to judge me. History will judge you as the red invader, or me, as the "puppet soldier." I fought for the freedom of my people. I have served my country, and I am not guilty. If you want to kill me, kill me. Do not blindfold me…*, page 38: https://vi.wikipedia.org/wiki/Hồ_Ng%E1%BB%8Dc_Cẩn_(đại_tá)#cite_note-9, https://en.wikipedia.org/wiki/Army_of_the_Republic_of_Vietnam#Generals, https://www.youtube.com/watch?v=pYI7aH0XMkQ, https://www.youtube.com/watch?v=GTwc8epBgU0

REFERENCES | 407

A FATEFUL TRIBULATION

62. The "Red Fiery Summer," page 50:
https://apps.dtic.mil/dtic/tr/fulltext/u2/a324505.pdf:
https://www.vietmessenger.com/books/?title=mua%20he%20do%20lua
63. the Gross Domestic Product of South Vietnam increased quickly and was twice that of North Vietnam's economy, 51: https://en.wikipedia.org/wiki/Economy_of_the_Republic_of_Vietnam
64. After the coup d'état—with the U.S. government and CIA support implicitly confirmed by the Pentagon many years later, 51:
https://en.wikipedia.org/wiki/Human_rights_violations_by_the_CIA
https://books.google.com/books?id=0Q3MDwAAQBAJ&pg=PA201&lpg=PA201&dq=Diệm+refused+U.S.+troops+in+Sài+Gòn&source=bl&ots=h0gbzNR7Of&sig=ACfU3U2ervXGSL0mzX97pIeaqat-vRTxofg&hl=en&sa=X&ved=2ahUKEwjixd_i_PvoAhVylnIEHUPrAbsQ6AEwAnoECAoQAQ#v=onepage&q=Diệm%20refused%20U.S.%20troops%20in%20Sài%20Gòn&f=false
65. "Horrible Highway," 52:
https://www.facebook.com/quansuvietnam2510/posts/1645890105655131/
https://www.bbc.com/vietnamese/vietnam-43911897
66. The military forces of North Vietnam, including 14 divisions and 26 battalions, together with modernized artillery and weapons, mostly supplied by the Soviet Union and China, 52:
https://apps.dtic.mil/dtic/tr/fulltext/u2/a324505.pdf:
67. the U.S. 196th battalion, idly waiting to be sent home, 53:
https://apps.dtic.mil/dtic/tr/fulltext/u2/a324505.pdf:
68. The mass-attack tactics and willingness to sacrifice three or even six bộ đội or North Vietnamese soldiers to kill one South Vietnamese freedom fighter, 54, Ref. pages 16, 25:
https://apps.dtic.mil/dtic/tr/fulltext/u2/a324505.pdf:
69. The Nixon Vietnamization policy and program, 58: https://www.history.com/topics/vietnam-war/vietnamization
70. In the meantime, the reduction of the U.S. military strength continued to accelerate, 58: https://historynewsnetwork.org/article/31400
71. "go where no one can find the fallen body," 59:
https://www.nhaccuatui.com/bai-hat/khong-quan-viet-nam-hanh-khuc-va.V2uZ4IVbrygN.html
72. (VOA) station, 64: https://www.voanews.com
73. "Domino" effect, 81, https://www.history.com/this-day-in-history/eisenhower-gives-famous-domino-theory-speech

THE RED SOCIETY

74. "three-day reform study," page 86: https://en.wikipedia.org/wiki/Re-education_camp_(Vietnam)
75. enough for a "short period" because it would only last about "ten days," 86: https://en.wikipedia.org/wiki/Re-education_camp_(Vietnam)

REFERENCES

76. "new economic zone," 93: http://countrystudies.us/vietnam/40.htm, https://trithucvn.net/van-hoa/ky-uc-vun-cua-mot-dua-tre-trong-vung-kinh-te-moi.html
77. But the world warned there might be hundreds of thousands of people whom the communists had executed or killed in the Soviet-style gulags, 104: https://miliary.wikia.org/wiki/Vietnam_War_casualties#cite_note-Desbarats-69, http://countrystudies.us/vietnam/40.htm
78. almost forced Hà Nội to surrender, 122: https://www.bbc.com/news/magazine-20719382
79. *One Day in the Life of Ivan Denisovich*, 123: https://en.wikipedia.org/wiki/One_Day_in_the_Life_of_Ivan_Denisovich

BOILING HOT GATEWAY

80. Pirates, page 139: https://www.washingtonpost.com/archive/politics/1980/09/02/pirates-plaguing-vietnamese-refugees/ad8d9a2e-d502-4a98-bd45-e742e7781347/
81. running away from the Vietnam communists by any means, 139: https://www.youtube.com/watch?v=xPYjVyBUJ10
https://www.bbc.com/vietnamese/forum/2013/05/130501_chay_tron_hoa_binh,
https://www.nguoi-viet.com/dien-dan/2-thang-nam-ngay-nguoi-viet-ty-nan-cong-san/
82. Even people who had migrated from the north to the south after April 30, 1975, wanted to flee Vietnam, 139: Author conversations with people from the north after 1975.
83. "glorious victory of spring 1975… the gigantic movement of the people… and Communist Party," 139: http://special.vietnamplus.vn/dai_Thang_mua_Xuan
84. During that time, Vietnam was fighting against the Khmer Rouge forces in Cambodia, 146: http://dcvonline.net/2019/01/15/cach-day-40-nam-cong-san-viet-nam-da-danh-bai-che-do-khmer-do-diet-chung-tai-campuchia-trong-mot-cuoc-chien-chop-nhoang/
85. In 1979, Vietnam engaged in a brief border war with China, 146: https://nationalinterest.org/blog/buzz/1979-china-and-vietnam-went-war-and-changed-history-forever-46017

THE LASTING TRUTH

86. *The Raft* parable, page 186: https://www.learnreligions.com/the-buddhas-raft-parable-450054
87. *The Water Snake* simile, 186: http://www.suttas.com/mn-22-alagaddupama-sutta-the-simile-of-the-snake.html
88. *deva*, 239: https://www.britannica.com/topic/deva-religious-being

GOD'S WILL

89. the Galang Vietnamese Refugee Camp, page 281: https://galangcamp.blogspot.com/2011/11/trai-ti-nan-galang-1-1980-1981.html
90. Ile de Lumiere, 287: https://reuters.screenocean.com/record/922621

INDEX

A

a man suddenly appeared at a distance stranger, ghostlike man, cross the border, underground, half-official, undercover cadre, fugitive, socialist regime, thầy Dỹ, stranger, half-official, 224
a small boat with a "shrimp-tail" engine noisily broke the beach's tranquility, 141, 272
Abiểu, 304, 313, 314
absolute authority, 196
Acting Chief for the Resettlement Section, 314
Administrative and Security Command, 327
administrative personnel, 86, 87, 313
Admas, 19
After a long flight from Singapore, on September 21, 1980, our flight landed in San Francisco Reverend, San Francisco, California, Harrisburg, York, Hamilton Air Force Base, minor boy, American sponsor, American food, Grandfather, Die Lee, Dỹ Lê, Sweitzer, Wendell H. Sweitzer, Poplar Street, Highway 83, horrendous chapter, 332
afterlife, 297, 393
age-reduction idea, 161
age-reduction tactic, 160
 age-reduction tactic, age-reduction strategy, 160–164
age-reduction tactic was so aggressive risk acceptance, exploding arguments, risk tolerance threshold, age-reduction idea, 160-164
air cadets, 57, 58, 62
Air Force
 Republic of Vietnam, South Vietnam, xiii, xiv, xxix, xxxiii, 2, 8, 11, 20, 51, 56, 57, 58, 109, 158, 318, 392, 397
aircraft mechanic, 87, 120, 121, 126

INDEX | | 411

aircraft technician, 121
aircraft's engine, 59
AK-47, 1, 38, 85, 94, 95, 109, 115, 116, 117, 118, 119, 122, 124, 132, 169, 174, 211
Alabama
   Fort Rucker, 58
allies
   Washington, 6, 54, 81
aluminum roof, 170, 281, 282
amateur work, 225
America, 2, 263, 329, 402
American actress, 20
American delegation, 287
American dream, 243
American friends, 318, 323, 324, 328, 330, 394
American ground forces, 53
American politicians, 5
amphibious ships, 10
an empty vessel makes the loudest sound
   socialist society, 148
An Lộc, 22, 52
An Lộc battle, 22
angels, xi, xxii, xxiii, 147, 148, 183, 224, 239, 244, 250, 279, 280, 296, 298, 308, 309, 328, 325, 391, 394, 395
Anh Ba Long, 221, 233, 286, 294, 295, 296, 305, 306, 307, 308, 315
Anh Trung Chinh, 306
Anh Giới, 40, 42, 60, 61, 83
Anh Khâm, 317
Anh Minh
   Tailor, 137, 149, 167, 168, 171, 177, 178, 179, 180, 185, 187, 191, 192, 201, 203, 222, 223, 224, 225, 226, 227, 228, 231, 232, 233, 239, 393, 394
Anh Văn Ánh
   Hán, Chinese ideographs, 137, 152, 153, 170, 211, 393, 394
Anh Tín
   tài công, 138, 148, 153, 154, 169
Anh Trọng, 289, 290, 306, 307, 308, 312, 317
annoying sound, 255
Another voice ordered us to move to the top surface, 250
Anson Road, 331
antibiotic medicines, 214
anti-war movement, 20, 23, 57
April 29, 1975
   fall of Sài Gòn, xv, 37, 38, 81, 84, 125, 392
April 30, 1975, xvi, 1, 3, 7, 85, 96, 124, 137, 138, 139, 189, 408
   Black Wednesday, 1
April-30 group, 2, 124, 131, 146, 147, 174
armed people, 56, 219, 234
Army captain
   Father, uncle Long, 39, 87
army major, 158
Army Rangers, 15, 87
Around 10:00 p.m. that night, I went to see my wife and son
   heart attack, next-door neighbors might hear it, last time that my wife and I were with her family, never see her beloved aunt ever again, 210
art of negotiation, 4, 404
artillery shells, xv, 53, 55, 56
Assistant Chief, 313
atheists, xxii, 61, 212
attack-while-negotiating, 25
aunt Thủy
   Cô Thủy, 163
aunt-in-law, 143, 148, 181
Australia, 169, 300, 312, 317, 327
autorotation landing, 61
awful experience, 327
awful smell, 246

B

B12
   older sister, 172, 305
B-40 bazookas, 1, 85
babysit, 159
Bạc Liêu, xxi, 129, 130, 131, 133, 135, 136, 137, 138, 139, 140, 141, 142, 146, 147, 148, 149, 151, 153, 154, 155, 161, 165, 167, 168, 169, 170, 173, 175, 177, 178, 179, 180, 181, 183, 185, 187, 190, 191, 192, 193, 194, 195, 196, 197, 198, 200, 205, 212, 220, 222, 224, 227, 231, 232, 241, 242, 263, 288, 305, 392, 393, 394, 395
Baccalaureate Part-I examination, 50, 55, 56

INDEX

bacteria, 305, 308
bad news, 41, 204, 206, 287, 307
bag of fruit, 315
bags of rice, 141, 179, 264
Ban Mê Thuột, 10, 62
Bảo Đại, 8, 404
barn, 220
barracks, iv, 63, 64, 79, 281, 282, 283, 284, 285, 286, 288, 289, 290, 293, 300, 304, 306, 307, 308, 312, 313, 314, 315, 317, 318, 330, 332
barracks leader, 304, 313
basic military training, 57, 61
beautiful heart, 112, 147, 277, 310, 311, 315, 330, 392
beef-noodle soup, 151
begrudged soldiers, 80
Beijing, 25, 26, 27
belief, 186, 239, 280, 281, 293, 298, 334
beloved younger brother, 395
Bến Đá, 55
Bến Hải River, 52
Berlin Wall, 9, 404
big brother China
    Red China, Communist China, Soviet Union, 53
big toy, 295
Bình Trị Thiên sandals, 2
Bintan Island, 286
bird,
    iron bird, birds chirping, 58, 59, 60, 317
birds chirping, 317
bitter words, 198
Black April, 3, 4, 5, 6, 97
black beard, 312, 316
black shadows, 11, 13, 14, 15, 16, 18, 24, 37, 79, 81, 115, 116, 117
black sheep, xi, 12, 40
Black Wednesday, 1
black-and-white television, 17
bled from the pain, 38
bleeder, 175, 176
bleeding heart, 42, 215
blood siblings, 193
blood-thirsty assassin
    shooting general, good guys, Admas, Geneva Convention, 19
bloody vendetta policy
    reform study, North Vietnam, 98
blue flight cap, 125
blue T-shirt
    dark T-shirt, 295, 312
bộ đội
    Việt Cộng, xvii, 1, 6, 10, 21, 24, 25, 54, 55, 56, 62, 95, 107, 109, 110, 112, 114, 121, 124, 131, 133, 146, 183, 407
bộ đội medical doctors, 114
bộ đội physicians, 107, 112, 183
boat owners, 138, 147, 149, 151, 168, 185, 197
boat people, 139, 141, 145, 148, 155, 168, 206, 211, 242, 250, 251, 253, 255, 262, 265, 269, 270, 271, 272, 278, 282, 285, 286, 287, 289, 290, 293, 294, 303, 304, 305, 307, 312, 313, 314, 315, 318, 324, 330, 394, 397
Boat people fled Vietnam via the coastlines, 139
brainwashed, 6, 21, 50, 51
breaking point, 161, 164, 165
brick wall
    SURRENDER, wanted to die with Sài Gòn, dark shower room, Forgive me, banging my head, xvii, 41, 83
taking him to the bottom of the ocean
    Anh Tín, fishing business, 169
Broken heart, xxii, xxiii, 98, 103, 105, 106, 112, 128, 217, 249, 254, 288, 327
Broken kinships, xxiii, 191
buckets, 293, 304
Buddha, 41, 186, 190, 200, 213, 219, 220, 223, 240, 244, 253, 296, 297, 298, 327, 392, 408
Buddhism, 186
Buddhist angel, 239
budget cuts, 57, 58
building materials, 267
burgundy cloth bag
    burgundy handbag, 131, 173, 174, 178, 183, 236
burgundy handbag, 252, 263
burning torches, 264
bus attendants, 173, 174
bus station, 131, 135, 143, 154, 155, 184, 187, 188
businessperson, 150, 155
bus company, 86
butterfly, 59, 60, 61

INDEX || 413

C

C-130 Hercules, 61, 80
Cà Mau, 135, 141
California, xxvi, 328, 332, 402
Cam Ranh, 53, 63
Cambodia
    Cambodian, 138, 146, 408
Cambodian, 138
Canada, xxiv, 58, 286, 300, 303, 306, 307, 308, 310, 311, 313, 316, 318, 325, 328, 394, 401
Canadian delegation, 286, 300, 303, 308, 315
Canadian government, 306
Canadian medical examination, 309
cancellation list, 57
canned food, 14, 306
cannibals, 269
canvas, 186, 240
captured, 19, 123, 141, 144, 149, 232, 242, 266
Catholic Church
    Enemy of the Vietnam Communist Party, 313
cat hides its wastes
    Horrible Highway, red fiery summer, 55
Central Highlands, 10, 40, 62, 63, 157
Central Vietnam, 13, 16
Certificate of Merit, 327
chain smoker, 146, 304
Đức
    army pharmacist, 137, 167, 224
Chào Thầy, 110
chaos, xvi, 63, 82, 84, 190, 192, 210, 218, 253, 256, 257
checkpoints, 10, 131, 133, 155, 166, 171, 172, 173, 174
chemically imbalanced mind, 392
chest X-Ray, 303, 307, 309, 310, 311, 323
Chị Cúc, 312, 313
chicken business, 182
Chief of the Resettlement Section, 313
Children's Hospital, 12, 131
Chinese dynasties, 137
Chinese ideographs, xiv, 137
Chinese-Vietnamese business owner, 149

Chinese-Vietnamese people, 135, 146, 147, 149, 154, 180, 209, 211, 215, 226, 229, 234, 235
Chinese-Vietnamese people who paid to leave Vietnam
    Chinese-Vietnamese people, boat people, 147
CIA
    coup d'état, 51, 407
civilized countries, 251
Class B inactive tuberculosis, 323
clod of clay, xxvi, 220
Cô Liên, 289
Cô Thủy, 163
Coast Guard, 241, 242
coastguards, 139, 141, 149, 250, 251, 253, 254, 278
coffin, 42, 64, 84, 117, 202, 253
coins
    xu, 51
cold war, 25
collateral damage, 191, 204, 206, 299
collect their eggs, 182
College of Literature
    Tuấn, 138
Colonel,
    commanding officer, 110, 111, 328
Colonel Cashmir Rachman, 328
colorful shirts, 314
commanding officer, 59, 108, 109, 110, 114
commercial pilot, 156
Communist Bloc, 1, 2, 6, 8, 13, 23, 25, 27, 53, 54, 57, 81, 85, 403, 406
Communist China, 24
communist government, 2, 132
Communist Party, 13, 17, 23, 134, 139, 405, 408
communist security agents, xiii
comrade, 57, 61, 79, 96, 115, 116, 118, 121, 124, 125, 133, 146, 175, 176, 238
comrades in arms, 57, 61, 79
Cô Liên, 289, 308
Cô Môn and Cô Mi, 392
Côn Đảo Archipelago, 242
Côn Sơn, 242
concrete pool, 223
conflicting emotions, 191, 198, 248
congenital birthmark, 219
Conchita H. Sweitzer, 394
contractor, 182

cooked rice, 93, 136, 142, 249, 267
cooking pans, 161, 172
corruption, 314, 315
counterfeit expert, 225
counterintelligence activities, 87
coup d'état
    President Ngô Đình Diệm, 51, 407
court-martial, 203, 211
Creator, 187, 219, 220, 240, 296
credits, iv, 234, 229, 330, 396
Christopher Le, iii, xii, xxvi, xxviii, 401, 402
crossed the border on foot, 139–140
cruel acts, 212
crystal ball, xxi, 183
Cường
    Gray-Hat Class, 113, 118, 393
cyanide
    Đức, 168, 172, 174, 183, 206, 209, 213, 224, 233, 285

D

Đà Lạt, 157
Đà Nẵng, 53
Dangerous tactics, 172
Dark attitude, 214
dark brown notebook, 306
dark dreams, xiv, xvii, xx, xxv, xxvi, xxviii, 11, 12, 14, 39, 42, 49, 81, 123, 140, 182, 201, 202, 204, 259, 334, 369, 392
dark fate, xiv, 49, 58, 86, 164, 284, 369
dark forces, xxvi, 56, 142, 158, 191, 200, 202, 213, 220, 239, 244, 257, 279, 280, 298, 299, 327, 393
dark future, 202, 244
Dark Negotiation
    Foreign diplomacy, Henry Kissinger, Dr. Henry Kissinger, 24-28
dark shades, 235
dark side, 199, 206, 285, 297, 327, 393
dark space, 3, 247, 248
dark time, xi, 18, 106, 204
dark T-shirt, 312
dark world, xxiv, 18, 128, 160, 184, 296, 392
dead body, 22, 122, 249, 287, 405
dead engine, 257
deadly consequence, xv, 117
deadly disease, 308

death certificate
    uncle Long, execution, Hoàng Liên Sơn, 98, 104
December 1974, xiii, 58, 61
dedicate this book, vi
deep hollowness, 248
delivery truck, 145
delusion, 192
delusional paradise
    North Vietnam, Hà Nội, 54
Demilitarized Zone, 2, 4, 52, 403
demise, 57, 58, 62, 81, 184
Democratic Republic of Vietnam
    North Vietnam, 8
Department of Education
    Mai, 87, 88
desert-like region
    Quảng Trị, Horrible Highway, 55
Desertion, 153
desperately wanted me to leave Vietnam, 140
deva, 239, 240
Dharma, 186, 190, 192
Diệm presidency
    South Vietnam, 51
Điện Biên Phủ, 8, 404
dirt road, 169, 197, 199, 215, 281, 284, 294, 296
district chairperson, 127, 143
district security cadres, 94, 95, 96, 98, 107, 114, 127, 131, 144, 149, 153, 155, 165, 222
Djarum cigarettes, 304
DMZ
    Demilitarized Zone, 53
Don Jarrett, 312
Don Oberdorfer, 17
đồng, 51
Đông Hà, 55, 56
doomsday, 3
downspout, 223
Dr. Henry Kissinger
    Nobel Foundation, 4
Dr. Henry Kissinger was "unabashedly delighted"
    Nobel Foundation, 4
Dr. Iwan Jusuf, 312, 327
Dr. Long, 308, 309
Dr. Mai, 313
Dr. Liên, 308
Dr. Truyền, 183
drawn faces, 263

dreadful dimension, 248
dried food, 246, 264, 268, 271
Đức
    Cyanide, 137, 167, 224,
Dũng, vi, xx, xxii, xxiii, 12, 49, 84, 145, 203, 204, 212, 220, 221, 233, 234, 235, 237, 238, 242, 243, 245, 250, 251, 252, 256, 257, 263, 278, 279, 286, 293, 294, 300, 303, 306, 307, 308, 310, 311, 313, 315, 392, 395, 396
Dũng's letter, 307
dusty black pajamas
    Việt Cộng, 2
Dy Dinh Le, xiv, 397

E

early release
    elder brother, 88
East Sea, 7
economy
    North Vietnam, 51, 407,
Edmonton, 308, 311
elder aunt, xv, xx, xxiv, 42, 83, 139, 157, 191
elder brother, xxiii, 40, 81, 83, 84, 86, 87, 88, 94, 97, 125, 130, 152, 153, 154, 155, 156, 157, 158, 159, 160, 161, 162, 164, 165, 166, 168, 171, 172, 173, 176, 179, 180, 187, 189, 190, 191, 193, 194, 195, 196, 197, 198, 199, 200, 201, 202, 203, 205, 208, 210, 211, 214, 216, 217, 220, 221, 222, 227, 230, 231, 235, 237, 238, 240, 242, 251, 257, 263, 293, 294, 300, 303, 308, 311, 392, 395
Embassy of the United States of America, 329
Emperor, 8, 404
end-justifies-the-means, 23
endless dark hole, 217
English language, 57, 111, 269
Enemy of the Vietnam Communist Party, 17, 405
escaping animal
    Hà Nội, 25
escort vessel, 241
eternal brotherhood, 311
Ethambutol, 308
evil Americans, 6, 22
evil landlords

Land Reform, xv, 8, 9, 104
exact amount, 178
Execution
    uncle Long, 5, 7, 9, 14, 16, 104, 402, 404
Executed colonel, 38
exodus, 5, 10, 11, 18, 138, 148, 149, 150, 152, 154, 280, 297, 303
Exodus soundtrack, 18
expanding space, 248
ex-pharmacists, 289
exploding, 83, 190, 205
evil landlord, xv, 8, 9, 104

F

fairy tale
    Nobel Foundation, 3
faith, 174, 185, 187, 204, 206, 239, 279, 288, 290, 298, 299, 309, 391
faithful service, 330
faithless communists
    North Vietnam, Việt cộng, VC, Hà Nội, 52
faithless face, 177
fake news, 5, 23
faked laws, 131
fall of Sài Gòn, x, 5, 81, 84, 107, 124, 138, 144, 182, 242, 318, 331
false sense, 114
fat maggots, 142, 143
fat worms, 133, 304
fatal agreement
    Paris Peace Accords, 5
fate, xviii, xix, xxi, xxiii, xxv, 1, 7, 42, 58, 116, 120, 141, 148, 183, 185, 186, 194, 198, 201, 203, 204, 206, 207, 212, 213, 244, 250, 265, 280, 284, 288, 289, 311, 325, 391, 393
Father, xviii, xx, xxi, xxiii, xxiv, 7, 8, 9, 11, 15, 17, 39, 41, 81, 87, 97, 103, 104, 105, 106, 107, 116, 117, 120, 125, 130, 135, 136, 137, 145, 148, 149, 152, 153, 157, 158, 163, 170, 171, 174, 177, 181, 182, 187, 203, 208, 215, 219, 243, 279, 286, 288, 289, 293, 294, 296, 313, 332, 333, 391, 394, 402
Father came home, 106
Father Hoedemaekers, 286, 288, 289, 293
father's escape, 171

few dollars, 392
fingerprints, 205
first beautiful son
    Huy, 97
First exodus from North to South Vietnam
    Operation Passage to Freedom, 10, 11
first instruction, 189, 191
first major invasion
    Tết, 20, 21, 24
Fishing business, 169
five-wheel tricycle, 131
flag-draped casket
    Giới, 42
flat roof, 82, 129, 145
flee the country, 129, 139, 141, 152, 156, 158, 160, 161, 170, 197, 209
flickering images, 235
flight diploma, 59, 85, 183, 233
flight maneuvers, 58
flight suit, 38, 39, 81, 83, 144
flight training,
    Lackland Air Force Base, Fort Rucker, Fort Rucker Aviation Training Center, xiii, 57, 58, 59, 61, 62, 103, 113, 318
flight-training classmate, 393
flip-flops, 2
floating hospital, 287
food ration, 304, 306, 331, 332
Food Ration
    powdered milk, sardines, tap water, luxurious items, rainwater milk, 304
food shortage, 94, 112
football, 314
foreign aggressor
    U.S. Empire, 52
foreign doctrine
    Marxism noodles, 52
forgive, 83, 174
forging skills, 175
former military officer, 104, 123, 139, 289
formidable journey, 212
Fort Rucker
    Fort Rucker Aviation Training Center, 57, 58, 59, 61, 103, 113, 121
Fort Rucker Aviation Training Center, 57

France
    Paris Peace Accords, 8, 25, 328
free country, 184, 297
free world, 1, 2, 21, 81, 123, 128, 203, 280
freedom, vii, x, xxvi, xxvi, xxvii, xxxiii, 3, 4, 5, 6, 7, 9, 10, 20, 22, 26, 38, 53, 54, 55, 56, 57, 62, 81, 86, 105, 123, 128, 139, 140, 142, 148, 156, 187, 191, 198, 199, 203, 204, 206, 209, 210, 212, 215, 216, 219, 220, 231, 242, 243, 255, 259, 280, 281, 284, 297, 305, 306, 309, 330, 332, 392, 394, 397, 398, 404, 406, 407
frightening, 98, 247, 248
fugitive, 148, 225
Fuller, 53

G

Galang Camp
    Galang Vietnamese Refugee Camp, 282, 284, 290, 397-398
Galang pier, 288, 296
Galang Resettlement Processing team, 330
Galang Vietnamese Refugee Camp, xxii, xxiii, xxiv, xxv, 281, 285, 286, 287, 293, 297, 300, 303, 307, 308, 309, 313, 325, 326, 327, 328, 329, 332, 409
Gành Hào, 141, 142, 241
gave me three taels of gold
    poverty, Anh Ba Long, thoughtful person, 305
generous gift, 297
Geneva Accords, 8, 9, 404
Geneva Agreements, 52, 54
Geneva Convention laws, 19, 20, 405
genuine miracle, 240
George Cosgrove, 312
ghostlike man, 228, 231, 235, 236, 238, 239, 242, 263, 287, 308, 395
ghosts, 20, 27, 266
Giáp, 21, 22, 23, 24, 25, 54, 56, 405
Giáp lost over 40,000 North Vietnamese soldiers, 23, 406
Giới, 40, 41, 42, 60, 61, 83, 392
give him a free space, 170
glorious victory of spring, xxxiii, 122, 139, 408

INDEX || 417

Go underground, 228
God, xi, 276, 408
gold pieces, 173, 176, 177, 178, 227, 233
golden time
   President Ngô Đình Diệm, 51
golf course, 251
good friends, 312, 326
good guys, 19
Goodness, xxvi, 186, 393, 396
gossip, 97, 157, 158, 314
Grand moments, 296
gray flower pattern, 295
Gray-Hat Class, 113
green fairway, 251
Gross Domestic Product, 51, 406
growing internal conflict between the rich sister-in-law and me
   rich sister-in-law, gossip, kinship, 157
guardian, 230, 239, 263, 396
guerrillas
   Việt Cộng, 2, 21
gulags, xvii, xviii, 5, 104, 105, 130, 407
gut instinct, 205, 226, 227

H

Hà Nội, 5, 6, 10, 11, 18, 20, 21, 22, 23, 24, 25, 26, 27, 40, 50, 51, 52, 53, 54, 55, 56, 57, 62, 98, 104, 105, 109, 122, 123, 134, 146, 147, 408
Hà Nội chained soldiers to heavy machine guns
   An Lộc battleground, quarter-inch-thick chain links, 21
Hải Dương, 10
Hải Lăng, 55
Hải Phòng, 10
half-brother, 56, 156, 221, 222, 223, 233, 305
half-dead bodies, 248
half-dead body, 249
Half-dead face, 214
half-digested food, 246
half-official, 225, 226, 228, 229
hamlets, 135, 141
Hán, xiv, 137
Hà, 286, 289
Hân, 287, 288
hands of Death, viii, xviii, 42, 49, 183, 203, 244, 250, 280, 395

hanging folders, 332
hardest conversation, 206
haven, 52, 62, 112, 182
He told me to bring it to his house in the early evening around dinnertime gold pieces, exact amount, trusted people, wooden plank, pilothouse, bags of rice, 177
Head of the U.S. JVA delegation, 313, 314, 324
healthy lungs, 309
heart attack, 24, 181, 237, 243, 406
heartbreaking visit, 393
Heaven, xxvii, 41, 186, 187, 200, 204, 212, 213, 219, 220, 223, 232, 240, 244, 253, 296, 297, 327, 392, 395
Heaven and Buddha, 186, 200, 212, 213, 219, 220, 223, 240, 244, 296, 297, 327, 392
Helene, 312, 316, 323, 324, 332
hell on earth, x, xxi, xxvi, 13, 54, 133, 298, 299
Henry Kissinger
   Nobel Foundation, 4, 5, 25, 406
he tried to commit suicide, xvii
Hiền Lương, 9, 52, 404
high crimes, 107
high fever
   Huy, 192, 394
high school classmate, 86
highest priority, 400
Hồ Chí Minh, xviii, xx, 8, 22, 24, 52, 86, 87, 93, 95, 107, 109, 112, 114, 121, 129, 130, 131, 134, 137, 143, 145, 146, 152, 153, 155, 159, 165, 167, 171, 173, 175, 177, 179, 180, 185, 187, 189, 203, 222, 231, 404, 406
Ho Chi Minh Trail, 24
Hoa, 165, 196, 226, 227, 228, 229, 230, 231, 233, 243, 250, 263, 286
Hoàng Liên Sơn mountains, vii, xviii, 98, 103, 104, 117, 203, 402
hoax, 232
Holcomb, 53
holding the bag, 232, 235
Horrible Highway
   red fiery summer, 52, 55, 105, 407
How many Vietnamese people ran away from north Vietnam in 1954? 800,000 Vietnamese, Operation Passage to freedom, First Exodus

from North to South Vietnam, xxxiii, 10, 51, 52
How will you carry the gold?
  unconventional tactics, plotting a plan for 24 people, cooking pans, seven kilos, 171
Huế, xxxiii, 11, 13, 16, 17, 19, 21, 52, 53, 55, 105, 405
human beings, 5, 16, 18, 186, 223, 275, 325, 332, 404
human complexities, 203
humanity, viii, xxiii, 5, 7, 16, 199, 206, 215, 244, 297, 391, 393
Hùng, xiv, xv, xvi, xvii, xviii, xix, xx, xxi, xxii, xxiii, xxiv, xxv, xxvi, 40, 41, 159, 234, 252, 257, 295
Huy, xxiii, 207, 209, 214, 295, 309, 395

I

I arrived at the Hồ Chí Minh western regional bus station in the evening, 143
I asked Tuân about Father
  open patio, verbal promise, give him a free space, father's escape, 170
I had become a floatation device for them to hold on to—the North star
  North Star, 156
I didn't know how long I had been lying near the edge
  annoying sound, awful smell, upper deck, pilothouse, no moon, half-digested food, lower cabin, dark space, seawater, half-dead bodies, sardines, seagulls, dreadful dimension, vast emptiness, conflicting emotions, infinite flame, expanding space, deep hollowness, spiritual space, near-death body, judgment day, 249
I finally said goodbye to Anh Minh's, 232
I suggested using the gold she wanted to lend me to pay for my siblings, 160
I went inside to take a bath
  concrete pool, downspout, shiver, Anh Minh, 223
I would kill myself, 168
idealistic mind, 307

Ile de Lumiere physicians, 288
Ile de Lumiere ship, 287, 288
ill treatment of my elder brother, 198
ill-fated, 11, 12, 83, 123, 194, 243, 285, 297, 369
immature minds, xix
immigration status, 308, 318
Impact of the budget cuts
  budget cuts, cancellation list, 57, 58
in cash, 310
In November 1979, I volunteered to work for UNHCR
  Red Cross, UNHCR, U.S. Joint Voluntary Agency, JVA, U.S. Refugee Program, U.S. JVA delegation, 311
Indonesia
  Indonesia Red Cross, 311, 312, 318, 327, 328
Indonesian Red Cross, xxiii, 328
Indonesian island people, 275
Indonesian islands, xxviii, 229, 275, 277, 293, 327, 334
Indonesian Riau Islands, 287
Indonesian rupiahs, 313
infinite flame, 248
INH, 308
inner soul, xvi, xix, xx, xxviii, 38, 40, 105, 139, 191, 192, 195, 201, 248, 334, 395
innocent people, xxiii, 6, 13, 16, 18, 19, 20, 25, 53, 54, 55, 56, 105, 124
inoperative engine, 256
in-patient facility, 309
instant noodles, 306
internal conflict, 157
International Plaza Building, 331
international water, 141, 149, 169, 184, 225, 229, 232, 233, 240, 241, 242, 245, 254, 278
interpreter team, 313, 314, 324
invaluable memories, 311
iron arrow, 215
iron bird, 59, 60
island residents, 269, 270, 271
It is amazing what you can accomplish if you do not care who gets the credit, 396
Ivan Denisovich, 123, 408

INDEX || 419

J

Jakarta, 312, 327
January 17, 1980, 308
January 1975, 61
Janz, 326, 327
Jasmine, 121
Johns Hopkins University, 17
jubilant, 294
judgment day, 202, 248
juice box, 252
July 13, 1977
    shot to death, uncle Long, 98
June 16, 1979, xviii, xix, 205
June 18, 1979, 232
June 19, 1979, 240, 245, 297
junior pilots, 63
JVA, 311, 312, 313, 314, 316, 323, 324, 329, 331, 332, 394

K

khaki shirt, 95, 132, 168, 173, 174, 186, 209
Khe Đá Mài, 17
Khe Gió, 53
kickbacks, 132, 176
Kiệt, xix, 313
killed in action
    Giới, 59
killing path
    Horrible Highway, 55
kinship, xxiii, 157, 191, 220, 244, 279
Kissinger, 4, 5, 25, 26, 27, 406
kite, 41, 182
Knowles, 312, 315, 318, 329, 330, 331, 332
Kontum, 52, 62

L

Lackland Air Force Base, 57
land reform
    evil landlord, x, 7, 8, 11, 105, 171, 404
Lao, 24
Laotian borders, 24
last breath
    Giới, xvi, 3, 6, 42, 255, 299
last day, 3, 6, 53, 54, 59, 184, 199, 202, 220, 233, 298
last days of April 1972, 54
Last Flight
    Fort Rucker Aviation Training Center, butterfly, 59, 60, 61
last minute, 166, 179, 193, 194, 196, 216, 235
last time, xix, 42, 80, 116, 117, 126, 169, 182, 205, 217, 218, 220, 222, 231, 239, 245, 257, 328
last time I saw them in Vietnam, 169
last time that my wife and I were with her family, 182
late September 1979, 297
laws of nature, 391
Lê Đình Dỹ,
    Dy Dinh Le, xiii-xiv
Lê Đức Thọ, 3, 5, 26
Lê refused the Nobel Peace Prize
    Nobel Foundation, 4
left with my elder brother to carry gold from Hồ Chí Minh City to Bạc Liêu
    khaki shirt, burgundy cloth bag, plastic bag, tael of gold, gold pieces, forging skill, cyanide, bus attendant, April-30 group, bleeder, scumbag, kickbacks, thieves, miserable traders, faithless face, Thái Đức, Thái Hưng, 173
legitimate country, 81
Lenin
    Soviet Union, 61
Liberate, xxxiii, 6, 51, 52, 53, 122
life journey, xxviii, 192, 202, 212,
life's journey, v, x, 1, 164, 220, 257, 279, 280, 297, 392
Lifeboat, 215
lifetime, 212
local people, 269
local prison
    Tuấn, Anh Tín, 169
long haul, 309
long journey, xxi, 9, 255
looking for someone to teach English, 107
Lord Buddha was giving me a lesson or test
    Raft parable, Water Snake simile, Water Snake simile, Buddhism, Dharma, Buddha, 186
lower cabin, xx, xxi, 240, 242, 245, 247, 248, 249, 253, 254, 262, 271
lower fares

age-reduction idea, age-reduction tactic, 180
lower floor, 237
Lunar New Year's Eve
  Lunar New Year, 13
luxurious items, 331

M

M-16 assault rifle, 63, 64
M-16 rifle, 64, 79
Mai, xx, xxii, 86, 87, 95, 97, 144, 157, 158, 162, 163, 181, 183, 192, 207, 214, 296, 310, 393
Mai's neighbor turned me in, 144
Mai's eyes no longer emitted any vibrant signs
  congenital birthmark, faith, fate, formidable journey, God, lifetime, June 16, 1979, last time, platform, portable waterway, stack of papers, wooden loudspeaker, 212
Major General
  William J. Maddox, Jr., 59, 62
Making a small shelter was not that difficult
  shelter, building materials, palm leaves, 268
Malaysian water, 250, 277
Mao Tse Tung
  Red China, Communist China, 61
Marion Tijsseling, 312
Marxism noodle soup, 24
Marxist ideology, 4, 8, 404
mass attacks
  Việt Cộng, 54
mass graves, 16, 17, 18, 105
mass-attack tactics
  mass attacks, 54, 407
massive airlift
  fall of Sài Gòn, 37, 81
mastermind, xx, 21, 26, 168
May 14, 1975
  wedding ceremony, high school classmate, 86
mayor's daughter, 17
medical condition, 308, 313
medical dictionary, 111, 183, 233, 271
medical doctor, 108, 114, 139, 287, 289
Mekong Delta, 131
Mekong River, x, 131, 135, 173

mental suffering, xviii, 152
metal container, 255, 265, 270, 304, 305
MH
  Minh Hải, Cà Mau, 135, 220, 245, 283, 284, 286, 287, 288, 289, 290, 293, 296, 305
Michael Knowles, 312
mid-July 1979
  villagers, Galang Vietnamese Refugee Camp, 276
Military Hospital
  chào Thầy, part-time job, 41, 107, 108, 111, 112, 113, 114, 130, 131, 133, 134, 140, 146, 175, 183, 393
military memoir, v
military men, 175, 229
military nurse, 107
military order, 59, 62
military pharmacist, 167
military pilots, xiii, 58, 87, 96, 120, 125, 287, 318
military regions, 23, 27, 51
mindless joke, 215
Minh Hải, 135, 141
ministering monk, 298
minor boy, 330
minor Vietnamese boy, 328
minuscule hope, 298
miracle, xxii, xxiii, 79, 240, 243, 289, 294, 298
miraculous moment, 239
misaligned lines of words, 311
miserable life, 201
miserable traders, 177
Mợ, xv, 18, 19, 40, 129
modern mall, 331
money-thirsty sharks, 228
monk, 298
Monkey New Year
  Tết, Tết Offensive, 56
monkey year
  Tết Offensive, 50
monkeys, 265
money-thirsty sharks, 228
moral values, 8, 164
Mother always believed I would eventually die
  breaking point, 164
Mother Teresa, 392

INDEX | | 421

Mother was not happy because of vague words
    flip-flops, babysit, rich sister-in-law, rich daughter-in-law, 159
Mother-in-law, 95, 96, 97, 113, 114, 115, 120, 126, 127, 128, 129, 140, 144, 181
motherland, xi, xiv, xvii, xix, 53, 54, 56, 58, 59, 61, 62, 138, 182, 184, 202, 204, 206, 212, 216, 220, 232, 244, 280, 334, 395
Mr. Art, 314, 316, 317, 318, 329, 330, 331
Mr. Thái Đức, 149, 150, 155, 158, 159, 162, 163, 166, 167, 171, 172, 177, 178, 179, 193, 196, 197, 201, 205, 210, 217, 219, 220, 229, 230, 231, 232, 234, 235, 271, 282, 283, 284, 286, 288, 290, 293, 317, 327
Mr. Thái Đức's daughters, 293
Mr. Wendell, 333
mug shots, 283
murderer, 19, 20
muscular man, 238
mushy bottom, 260
my elder brother came looking for me 154
my family, xviii, xxvii, xxviii, xxxiii, 8, 10, 12, 61, 82, 88, 93, 94, 96, 97, 104, 110, 112, 114, 117, 133, 135, 136, 140, 143, 150, 152, 155, 157, 159, 162, 164, 165, 167, 185, 187, 189, 191, 196, 200, 202, 203, 211, 213, 216, 224, 230, 259, 279, 288, 296, 297, 298, 300, 303, 305, 306, 307, 309, 315, 316, 317, 318, 323, 324, 328, 310, 332, 392, 394
medical examination results were not good
    bad news, chest X-ray, nutritious food, Dũng's letter, Dr. Liên, Dr. Long, Cô Liên, healthy lungs, Canadian medical examination, faith, 307
Mỹ Lai massacre
    silver plate, 20, 21, 405

N

narrow alley, 95, 107, 114, 117
National Highway 53, 55, 56, 131, 141, 143, 146, 155
National Liberation Front, 2, 110, 403
navigator wing, 57, 59, 60, 62
Navy-blue uniform, 59, 60
Near-death body, 248
never see her beloved aunt ever again, 182
new economic zone, 93, 96, 143, 158, 407
New World, 203, 208, 280, 306, 310, 315, 318
New Year's Eve, 13
newcomers, 276, 286, 287, 289, 293, 294
next-door girlfriend, 86
next-door neighbors might hear, 181
next-space neighbor, 306, 307, 312, 317
Ngó, 312
Ngô Đình Diệm, 8, 11, 51, 404
Nha Trang, x, 61, 62, 63, 64, 80, 287
Nha Trang Air Force Training Center, 61, 62, 287
Nha Trang military defense, 64
nightmares, 11, 12, 37, 39, 56, 103, 327
nightmares of her awful experience forgive, 327
Nixon
    President Richard Nixon, ix, 4, 25, 26, 27, 58, 406, 407
no moonlight, 247
Nobel Foundation
    Nobel Peace Prize, 3
non-commissioned officers, 86
North Star, 25, 156
North Vietnam, xiv, xv, xxxiii, 1, 2, 3, 4, 5, 6, 7, 9, 10, 11, 15, 16, 17, 18, 19, 20, 21, 22, 23, 24, 25, 26, 27, 38, 40, 50, 51, 52, 53, 54, 55, 56, 62, 63, 64, 80, 81, 105, 106, 107, 110, 128, 297, 402, 403, 405, 406, 407
North Vietnam fought for more, 4
North Vietnam's atrocities in Huế
    Tết Offensive, 16-18
North Vietnamese soldiers
    Việt Cộng, VC, 6, 16, 17, 23, 38, 50, 53, 54, 55, 62, 85, 407
North Vietnamese troops
    Việt Cộng, VC, 53, 63
November 1973, 57
Nutritious food, 307

O

Obscene joke, 215
official letter, 330, 377
older sister, 40, 49, 138, 172, 189, 191, 392
omen
  dark dreams, 12, 39, 42, 60, 93, 98, 103, 140, 201, 202, 204, 259, 369, 395
One Vietnam, 4
one-way path, 183
one-way ticket, 183, 186, 233
open patio, 41, 170, 182
open sea, xxi, 155, 211, 240, 241
Operation Passage to Freedom, 9, 404
original fear, 204
outcast
  Hùng, Việt Hùng, xxvi, 98, 122, 128, 140, 146, 200, 252, 280
overthinker, 154

P

pack of wolves, 298
painful letter, 191
palm leaves, 267, 268
palm trees, 251
Paris Peace Accords, 3, 4, 5, 7, 26, 38, 404
part-time job, 114, 306, 310
passage of life, 297
patriotic revolution, 52
patrol boat, 251
Paul Vogle, 17
pay dearly for those obstructions
  rich sister-in-law, rich daughter-in-law, 164
peace negotiation, 25
peach-like shapes, 298
Pearl of the Far East
  Sài Gòn, 13, 51, 81, 121, 184, 405
penicillin injections
  scar, X-Ray, 113
Pennsylvania, xxviii, 313, 318, 328, 332, 368, 394, 398
Pentagon, 51, 404
People's Army of Vietnam
  North Vietnam, 2, 145, 403
permitted departures
  Chinese-Vietnamese people, 146, 185, 201

personal gift
  medical dictionary, Military Hospital, 111
petite outfits, 180
Phạm Ngũ Lão, xviii
pharmaceutical laboratories
  Military Hospital, 112
Phở, 51, 103, 151, 264
Phủ Cam
  Phủ Cam Cathedral, 17
Phủ Cam Cathedral, 17
piasters
  Đồng, 51
pier, 281, 293, 294, 295, 297, 306, 397
Piet Hoedemaekers
  Father Hoedemaekers, 286
pilothouse, 179, 247, 249, 250, 255, 256
pistol engine, 141, 240, 245, 253, 254
piteous man, 297
plastic bag, 168, 173, 183, 186, 206, 209, 213, 233, 285
Platoon, 54
pleasant companions, 317
Please save Tuân for me
  Tuân, court-martial, desertion, 153
Pleiku, 10, 62, 392
plotting a plan, taking 24 people, 172
poignant sentiment, 183
poison, 167
political asylum, 252, 318
poor peasants, xv, 158
Poplar Street, 333
popping and slapping, 240, 245, 247, 254, 255, 256
portable loudspeaker, 211
post office, 332
poverty, xix, 88, 148, 162, 200, 204, 305
poverty-class syndrome, 204
powdered milk, 304, 305, 315
precious moment, 208
President Ngô Đình Diệm, 11, 51
President Nguyễn Văn Thiệu, 11, 404
President Nixon recognized Kissinger
  art of negotiation, 4
President Richard Nixon, 25
President Thiệu
  President Nguyễn Văn Thiệu, Republic of Vietnam, South Vietnam, 62
priceless—freedom, 306

priest, 313
private room, 330, 332
promised land, xi, 148, 156, 186, 203, 206, 209, 219, 298, 324, 325, 332, 333, 394, 395
Provisional Revolutionary Government, 2, 403
prow, 252
psychic feeling, 49
psychic power
    psychic feeling, psychic sense, psychic warning, 93
psychic sense, 12
psychic warning, 12
PT-76 tanks, 53
Pulau Galang, 285, 327
Pulau Laut Island, 287
punitive action, 146
puppet government
    puppet soldiers, puppet South Vietnamese Government, puppet regime, 17, 22, 23, 52, 108, 118, 124, 126, 145, 405
puppet regime, 111, 124, 185
puppet soldiers, 38, 86
puppet South Vietnamese Government, 22
pure love, 202
puzzle, 186, 192, 198

Q

Quảng Trị
    Horrible Highway, Red Fiery Summer, xxxiii, 52, 53, 54, 55, 56, 62, 105
Quang Trung Training Center, 87
quarter-inch-thick chain links, 22, 405
Quy Nhơn, 42, 53

R

Raft parable, 186, 408
rainwater, 223, 304, 305, 310, 315, 323
rainwater milk, 305, 310, 323
raise chicken, 182
ranch-style house, 227
raw fish, 143, 241
Red China, 6, 10, 27
Red Cross, xxiii, 304, 311, 312, 317, 323, 326, 327, 328, 394, 398

Red Fiery Summer, 25, 27, 50, 54, 55, 56, 62, 105, 407
red forces, 7, 52
red iron curtain, 50, 52
Red Soil Junior High School
    elder brother, 87
redemption, 240, 298, 299
re-education, xvi, 5, 17, 88, 94, 95, 98, 105, 106, 120, 137, 139, 140, 144
re-education program, 17
reform study, 86, 87, 95, 98, 104, 105, 120, 125, 407
refugee camp, iv, xxiii, xxiv, xxv, 105, 230, 252, 253, 272, 276, 279. 281, 283, 285, 286, 287, 293, 297, 300, 303, 304, 307, 308, 309, 311, 313, 314, 317, 318, 325, 326, 328, 329, 332, 392, 394, 397, 401, 402, 409
refugee transit camp, 328, 329, 330, 331
Releva Bozman, 394
remaining relatives, 185,
remaining sisters, 165, 179, 189, 190
re-opened the deadly wounds, 139
Republic of Vietnam
    South Vietnam, xiii, xxix, xxxiii, 2, 3, 8, 10, 11, 20, 51, 56, 57, 58, 97, 109, 158, 159, 318, 392, 397, 403
Resettlement Processing Center, iv, 314, 323
resort, xi, 250, 251, 253, 254
reticulated python, 295
reunification, 4, 296, 298
revolution, 52, 88
Riau Archipelago, xxiii, 285
rich daughter-in-law, 159, 160, 161, 170, 191, 204, 205, 220
rich sister-in-law, 157, 160, 162, 163, 164, 165, 171, 192, 193, 194, 196, 197, 201, 205, 207, 214, 215, 216, 217, 226, 231, 233, 244, 296, 298, 305, 327
rich sister-in-law suggested Mai steal the easier-to-access money
    rich sister-in-law, rich daughter-in-law, 162
rich sister-in-law determined she would be the one to discuss the plan
    aunt Thủy, Cô Thủy, younger aunt also wanted her oldest son to flee, 163–164

righteous past life, 298
righteous principles, xiv, 199, 298
risk acceptance limit, 162
risk tolerance threshold, 161
riverbank, 238, 241, 245, 280, 395, 396
riverside, 178, 205, 206, 219, 230, 234, 241
rocky hill, 262, 265, 271, 272
rolled paper, 324
Romanization, 137
rope, xi, 16, 237, 239, 250, 252, 253, 254
RVN
    Republic of Vietnam, South Vietnam, 2, 4, 13, 19, 22, 55, 56, 403

S

Sài Gòn, x, xiii, xv, xvi, xvii, xviii, 1, 2, 3, 5, 6, 7, 11, 13, 15, 19, 21, 26, 27, 37, 38, 40, 41, 51, 53, 57, 61, 79, 80, 81, 82, 84, 85, 86, 87, 95, 96, 103, 104, 107, 112, 121, 122, 123, 124, 125, 129, 134, 135, 136, 138, 143, 144, 153, 160, 168, 170, 181, 182, 183, 184, 187, 189, 202, 205, 207, 220, 221, 242, 318, 331, 392, 393, 401, 402, 405, 406
salesclerk
    Mai, 144
San Francisco, 328, 332, 333
Sardines, 243, 248, 262, 304
Sarge, 53
sawhorses, 84
scams, 141
scar
    fall of Sài Gòn, X-Ray, 104, 113, 114
scary emptiness, 258
scientist, xxiv, 370, 378, 398
scorching sorrow, 284
scumbag, 175
S-curve figure, 2
scythe
    Dead, xv, xxiii, 49, 98
Seagulls, 248
search team, 266,
seashore, 254, 258
seasickness, 245
seawater, 183, 247, 253, 257, 258, 259, 260, 261, 271

second instruction, 193
second letter, 289
security checkpoints, 131
Sedanau, xxii, 289, 293
self-serving, 5, 18, 19, 20, 23, 38
senior undercover security cadres, 239
Separation of husband, 215
seven kilos, 173
several people suddenly came and violently banged on the rotten door, 114
several people yelling from a distance striped sarongs, wooden spears, cannibals, island residents, sign languages, local people, villagers, spearmen, 268
She hurried
    Mai, Sedenau Island, Pulau Laut, 4112 boat people, pier, miracle, Anh Ba Long, gray flower pattern, blue T-shirt, Galang pier, 4112 boat, precious moment, spiritual endurance, 280, 295
shelter, 153, 263, 267, 268, 269, 270, 271, 282, 285, 286, 288, 289, 326, 330, 334, 394
shining souls, 220
shiver, 14, 223, 224, 245, 269, 333
shopping mall, 331
shot to death
    uncle Long, 98
Shrewsbury Church of the Brethren, 394
shrimp-tail, 141, 272
sign languages, 269
silver plate, 20
Singapore, xi, xxiii, 242, 303, 307, 308, 312, 314, 324, 328, 329, 330, 331, 332, 333, 334
Singapore harbors, 328
Sir Harry S. Truman, 396
Sister-in-law, xxi, 157, 158, 160, 161, 162, 163, 164, 165, 171, 192, 193, 194, 196, 197, 199, 201, 205, 207, 214, 215, 216, 217, 222, 226, 230, 231, 233, 240, 242, 244, 293, 296, 298, 305, 327
sky worms, 304
sleep crying, 11
small bedroom, 183
small café, 60, 290

INDEX || 425

small family, 160, 162, 164, 311, 327, 328
small room, 129, 145, 182
small gold saving
   rich daughter-in-law, 205
smashed-open head, 17
snake, 186, 187, 190, 192, 206, 408
socialist government, 86, 88, 97, 124, 136, 138, 139, 163, 203
socialist regime, 87, 88, 97, 124, 136, 138, 139, 225
socialist society, 86, 88, 93, 107, 118, 140, 142, 147, 148, 156, 158, 200, 280
Socialist state, 112, 124, 128, 146, 149, 152, 153, 155, 158, 174, 210, 252
song of Death, 14, 17, 83
Sơn, 227, 233, 243, 250, 263
South China Sea, xxiii, 5, 7, 135, 139, 141, 156, 171, 187, 206, 218, 241, 242, 245, 248, 249, 265, 275, 277, 280, 281, 284, 288, 293, 297, 398, 404
South Vietnam, xiii, 1, 2, 3, 4, 5, 6, 7, 10, 11, 13, 14, 15, 17, 18, 19, 20, 21, 22, 23, 24, 25, 26, 27, 37, 38, 39, 40, 50, 51, 52, 53, 54, 55, 56, 57, 58, 60, 62, 63, 64, 79, 80, 81, 82, 86, 87, 96, 103, 105, 106, 107, 114, 117, 120, 121, 122, 137, 138, 229, 290, 306, 308, 404, 405, 406, 407
South Vietnamese Army, 11, 40, 53, 87
South Vietnamese citizens, 5, 51
South Vietnamese freedom fighters
   Republic of Vietnam, South Vietnam, Sài Gòn, 53, 55, 56
South Vietnamese general
   Admas, 19
South Vietnamese soldiers
   Republic of Vietnam, 4, 5, 6, 7, 15, 16, 53, 63, 79, 81, 107
South Vietnamese troops, 54, 62
Southeast Asia, 1, 25, 26, 27, 57, 62, 81
Soviet Union, 6, 10, 24, 25, 52, 54, 106, 123, 407
spearmen, 270
special angel, 393
Special Forces, 15
Special People's Court, 7, 9
spectacular scene, 296
Speechless, 3, 82, 215, 295, 331

spiritual being, 239
spiritual endurance, 298
spiritual space, 248
sputum smear tests, 309, 311, 323
S-shaped Vietnam
   Vietnam, xix, 50
Stack of papers, 211
stale noodles, 23
Stalin
   Soviet Union, 61
sterile saltwater, 113, 114
sticky rice, 207, 208
storefront, 82, 145
strange island, 261
stranger, xxv, 104, 185, 224, 225, 228, 229, 232
Strategic Tactical Region I, 53, 54
street vendors, 135, 154, 188
Streptomycin, 308
striped sarongs, 269
strong accents, 108
subconsciousness, xxv, 109, 123, 244, 248
submitted lists, 171
suicide attempt, 392
suicidal fireflies
   Việt Cộng, 54
Suite 2514, 331
Surprise Raid, x, 106
SURRENDER
   he tried to commit suicide, xiv, xvii, 6, 37, 38, 104, 122, 217, 248, 408
survive for at least six months, 166
Suzuki motorcycle, 84, 125, 144
swap, 166, 196, 207
swearing-in, 318
swore that if the plan failed... I would kill myself, 168

T

T-54 tanks, 1, 53, 85,
tael of gold, 147, 166, 173, 179, 205
tài công, 138, 148, 243
tailor
   Anh Minh, 137, 149, 167, 177, 179, 187, 224, 227
tap water, 304
tasteless joke, 215
Tuân, 145, 146, 152, 153, 170, 171

Tân Sơn Nhứt, 57, 58, 61, 79, 80, 81, 125
Tân Sơn Nhứt Air Base
    Tân Sơn Nhứt, 57, 80, 81, 125
Tanjung Pinang, 286, 303, 306, 307, 308, 311
Tap water, 304
Telling Dũng he would not be on Mr. Thái Đức's boat
    Dũng, original fear, omen, 204
Television, 17, 20, 79, 402
temporary hospital, 309
termination cancer, 284
tender heart, 312
Tết Offensive, xi, 11, 12, 13, 14, 15, 16, 20, 21, 22, 23, 24, 25, 37, 39, 50, 96, 105, 115, 122, 404
Texas, 328, 332, 370
Thạch Hãn River, 53, 55
Thailand, 138, 156, 255, 277
Thái Đức, 149, 150, 155, 158, 159, 162, 163, 166, 167, 171, 172, 177, 178, 179, 193, 196, 197, 201, 204, 205, 210, 217, 219, 220, 229, 230, 231, 232, 234, 235, 271, 282, 283, 284, 286, 288, 290, 293, 317, 327
Thái Hưng, 177, 178
That night, we all slept in the small room above the second floor, 182
thatched huts, 241
Thầy Dỹ, 224, 225, 226
The communists had taken our land by forces, 123
I asked if he had any powerful poison
    poison, cyanide, plastic bag, swore that if the plan failed… I would kill myself, 167
There were 24 people, 171
they had discovered her a few kilometers
    search team, ghosts, young girl, 266
They had already forgotten the bombing campaigns from Washington, 122
they threw a long, thick line over to our boat
    towed boat, prow, rope, 252
thieves, 177
"Third time's a charm!", 127
thoughtful mind, 310, 311, 330
thoughtful person, 306
three daughters, 149, 288

Three instructions to Mother and elder brother
    unlisted sisters, swap, survive for at least 6 months, 166, 205
three peach-like hair patches, 298
three-day reform study
    non-commissioned officers, administrative personnel, 86, 87, 95, 407
ticket seller, 94
tight outfit, 180
tightly fitted clothes, 180
TIME Magazine, 4
took it back
    rich daughter-in-law, 205
towboat, 253, 254
treacherous journey, xxviii, 213, 253, 398
treacherous path, 191, 296, 334
tribulation, x, xvi, xxii, 1, 50, 184, 401, 407
true love, 334, 393, 394
Trường
    Cô Mi and Cô Mi, Christopher Le, 212,
Trường Sơn, 52
trusted people, 178
Tuân, 145, 146, 152, 153, 170, 171
Tuấn, 130, 131, 135, 136, 137, 138, 141, 143, 147, 148, 149, 153, 169, 241, 393, 394
tuberculosis, xxiv, 307, 308, 309, 310, 311, 315, 316, 323
two ways for the Vietnamese people to eat noodle soup
    Marxism noodle soup, 23
two-tongs
    Hồ Chí Minh, socialist society, 22

U

U.S. air power, 53
U.S. airmen, 58
U.S. budget cuts
    cancellation list, Vietnamization policy, 58
U.S. Congress, 57
U.S. delegation, 303, 308, 314, 316, 325
U.S. Embassy, xv, xvi, 38, 84, 125, 312, 330
U.S. Empire, 52

INDEX || 427

U.S. foreign policy, 26, 27
U.S. Imperial, 146
U.S. Joint Voluntary Agency, xi, 311, 328, 398
U.S. JVA delegation, 312, 313, 314, 316, 318, 323, 324, 329, 330, 331
U.S. JVA friends, 394
U.S. Marines helicopters, 38
U.S. National Security Advisor Henry Kissinger, 25
U.S. Naval Forces, 63
U.S. news networks, 20, 28, 55, 57, 405
U.S. Refugee Program, 311, 312, 330, 331
ugly shape, xxvi
unattended fruit bag, 315
uncle Long, 15, 87, 123
undercover agents, 188, 210
undercover cadre, 225
underground group, 165, 179, 192
unequivocally never-ending love, 392
Unggat, 286, 303, 306
UNHCR, 285, 286, 304, 311, 312, 317, 326, 327, 394, 404
uninhabited island, 262, 268
unique personality, 216
United States Embassy, 329
unknown island, xi, 261, 296
unlisted relatives, 193, 194, 196, 207
unlisted sisters, 165, 189, 190, 191, 192, 194, 205
unlisted sisters were nowhere to be seen
  unlisted sisters, first instruction, remaining sisters, older sister, vicious snake, collateral damage, painful letter, broken kinships, 189-191
unplanned destination, 184
unrealistic expectation, 184, 209
unscrupulous minds, 297
unspoken promise, 140, 202, 297, 392,
untold story, 297
unwanted outcome, 183
upper deck, 240, 246, 247, 248, 250, 253, 254, 255, 277, 278, 281, 294

V

vast emptiness, 248
VC, 2, 3, 7, 11, 13, 14, 15, 16, 17, 18, 19, 20, 21, 24, 39, 63, 79, 88, 122, 125, 126, 134, 189, 403, 405

VC's temple, 19
Venomous joke
  mindless joke, obscene joke, tasteless joke, 214
verbal promise, 170
vicious snake, 190, 192
victors
  Việt Cộng, VC, North Vietnam, vi, xvi, xvii, xviii, 2, 5, 37, 38, 81, 86, 87, 88, 98, 104, 105, 106, 117, 122, 153
victory for peace and prosperity, 122
Việt Cộng, 2, 403
VC flags, 3
Việt Hùng means
  Việt Hùng, xiv
Việt Minh, xiv, xv, 7, 8, 9, 11, 404
Vietnam, v, xv, xvii, xx, xxiv, xxviii, xxix, xxxiii, 1, 2, 3, 4, 5, 6, 7, 8, 10, 13, 15, 17, 18, 19, 20, 21, 22, 23, 24, 25, 26, 27, 28, 38, 39, 40, 50, 51, 52, 53, 54, 55, 56, 57, 58, 59, 61, 62, 63, 80, 81, 82, 84, 86, 87, 88, 93, 103, 104, 109, 110, 114, 121, 128, 134, 135, 136, 138, 139, 140, 141, 145, 146, 147, 148, 149, 150, 151, 152, 155, 156, 158, 159, 160, 163, 164, 166, 167, 169, 170, 172, 178, 182, 191, 199, 200, 201, 203, 204, 205, 206, 208, 210, 211, 212, 215, 216, 218, 220, 221, 223, 225, 226, 233, 241, 242, 277, 282, 286, 290, 297, 303, 306, 308, 313, 315, 318, 324, 368, 393, 397, 402, 403, 405, 406, 407, 408
Vietnam War, v, xxviii, 4, 20, 21, 23, 26, 27, 28, 58, 80, 110, 182, 204, 242, 306, 397
Vietnamese air cadets
  Republic of Vietnam, South Vietnam, 57, 58, 60
Vietnamese citizens, xiv, 5, 51, 149, 155
Vietnamese collaborators, 37, 81
Vietnamese dialects, 180
Vietnamese people didn't fully understand what it meant, 5
Vietnamese general shot a blood thirsty VC assassin
  Admas, Việt Cộng, VC, 19-20
Vietnamese medical doctor who received the girl's dead body, 400

boat people, Mr. Thái Đức's daughters, three daughters, Hân, dead body, Father Hoedemaekers, 287
Vietnamese refugees, xxii, 105, 288, 330, 331
Vietnamization policy, 58, 407
villagers, xxii, 142, 241, 270, 270, 276, 277
Vĩnh Phúc, 297-298
Vĩnh Yên, xv, 7, 9, 10, 107, 297
Virgin Mary, 283, 312, 317
visual inspection, 59, 60
Võ Nguyên Giáp
    Giáp, 21, 22, 405
Voice of America, 64
Vũng Tàu, 10

W

war repercussions
    re-education camp, 86
Washington, 4, 5, 6, 21, 23, 24, 25, 26, 28, 37, 53, 57, 81, 122, 406, 408
waste of time
    rich sister-in-law, 157
watches, 272
Water Snake simile, 186, 408
waterway, x, 129, 131, 135, 142, 211, 241
We planned to go along the river parallel to National Highway 1, 141
We traveled to Singapore on a boat 328-332
wedding ceremony, 86
Wendell, 333, 394
western provinces, 53, 86, 173, 192
western region,130-131, 132, 133, 135, 141
When my elder brother asked me to help his family, 157
"Why do you want to die here…," 161
wickedness, 190
widowed aunt

uncle Long, Trường, 157, 171, 180, 203
William J. Maddox, Jr., 59, 62
winding path, 117, 197
winding trail, 200
winter day, 12
withdrawal, 26, 27, 58
wooden flatbed
    dark dreams, 39, 83, 285
wooden plank, 179, 210, 217, 218, 235, 236, 237, 238, 239
wooden spears, 269
would-be boat people, 141
writhing bodies, 17

X

X-ray, 113, 303, 307, 308, 309, 310, 311, 323
xu, 51

Y

yellow flags, 3, 42, 403
York, 313, 318, 332, 333, 394, 398
young girls, 139, 264, 266, 267, 278
younger aunt to hide Tuân in her house
    Tuân, court-martial, desertion, 153
younger half-sisters, 9, 221
younger sister, xxiv, 8, 15, 97, 138, 143, 165, 192, 193, 194, 196, 222, 226, 286, 289
younger sister and her nephew would want to leave Vietnam, 226-232
Your family will leave the camp next month!
    Helene, rolled paper, American friends, angels, human beings, 324

Z

Z, 329
Zone 1, 286

PLATGEVITY
Bridging Asian – American Cultures & Sciences

www.ingramcontent.com/pod-product-compliance
Lightning Source LLC
Chambersburg PA
CBHW022006300426
44117CB00005B/58